I'M NOT THE

ETERNAL LIGHT

do not count on me

to shine

OR THE SHADOW

IN THE FLASH-

LIGHT

SPENDING A LIFETIME

TO HIDE

I'M NOT   I'M NOT

I'm Not

I'm Not

I'm not a trail   home

Leading you out to a cliff

you cannot

take a leap of faith of me

I'M NOT   I'M NOT

I'M NOT

SI

Aspen Art Museum

Pacific

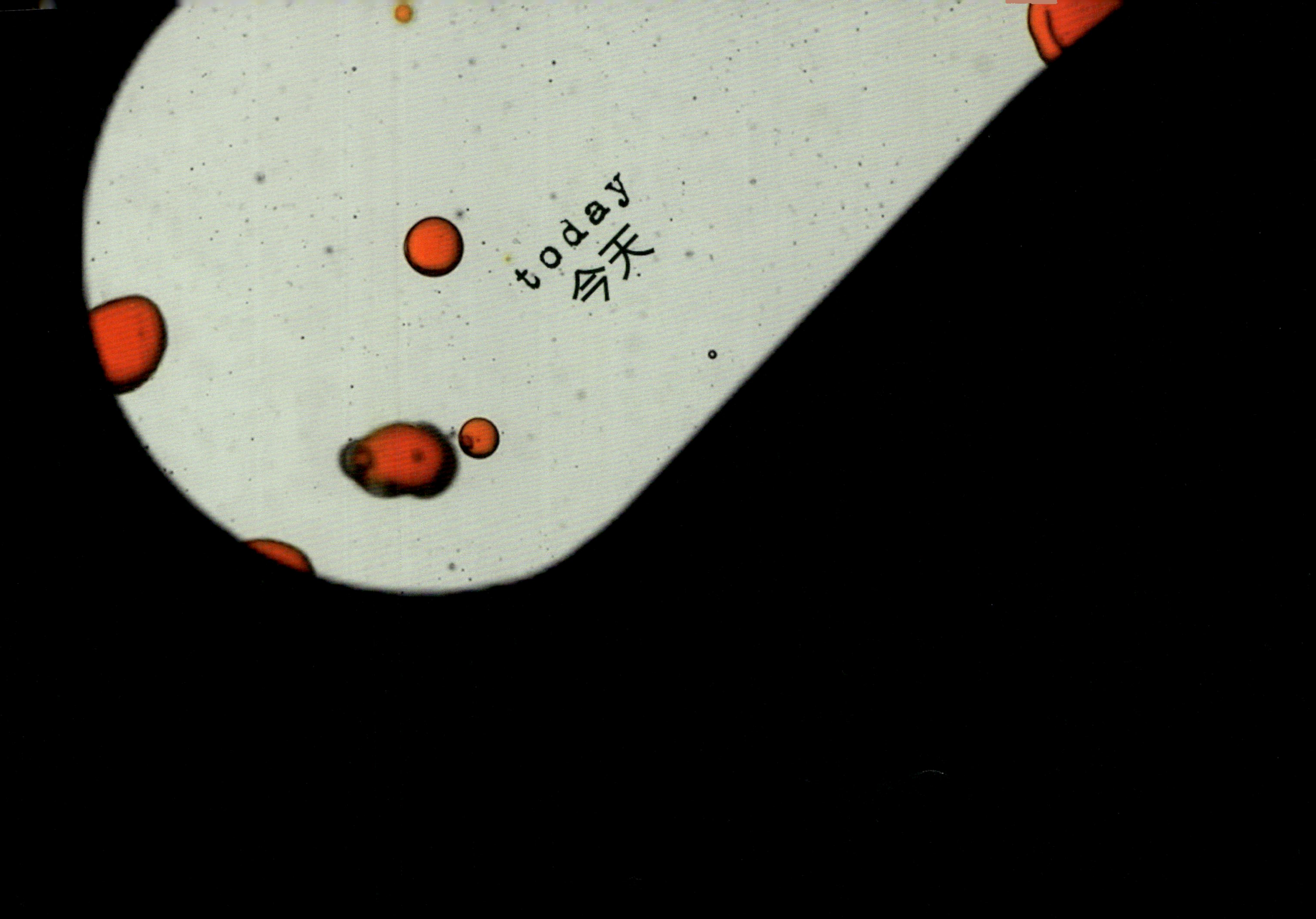
today
今天

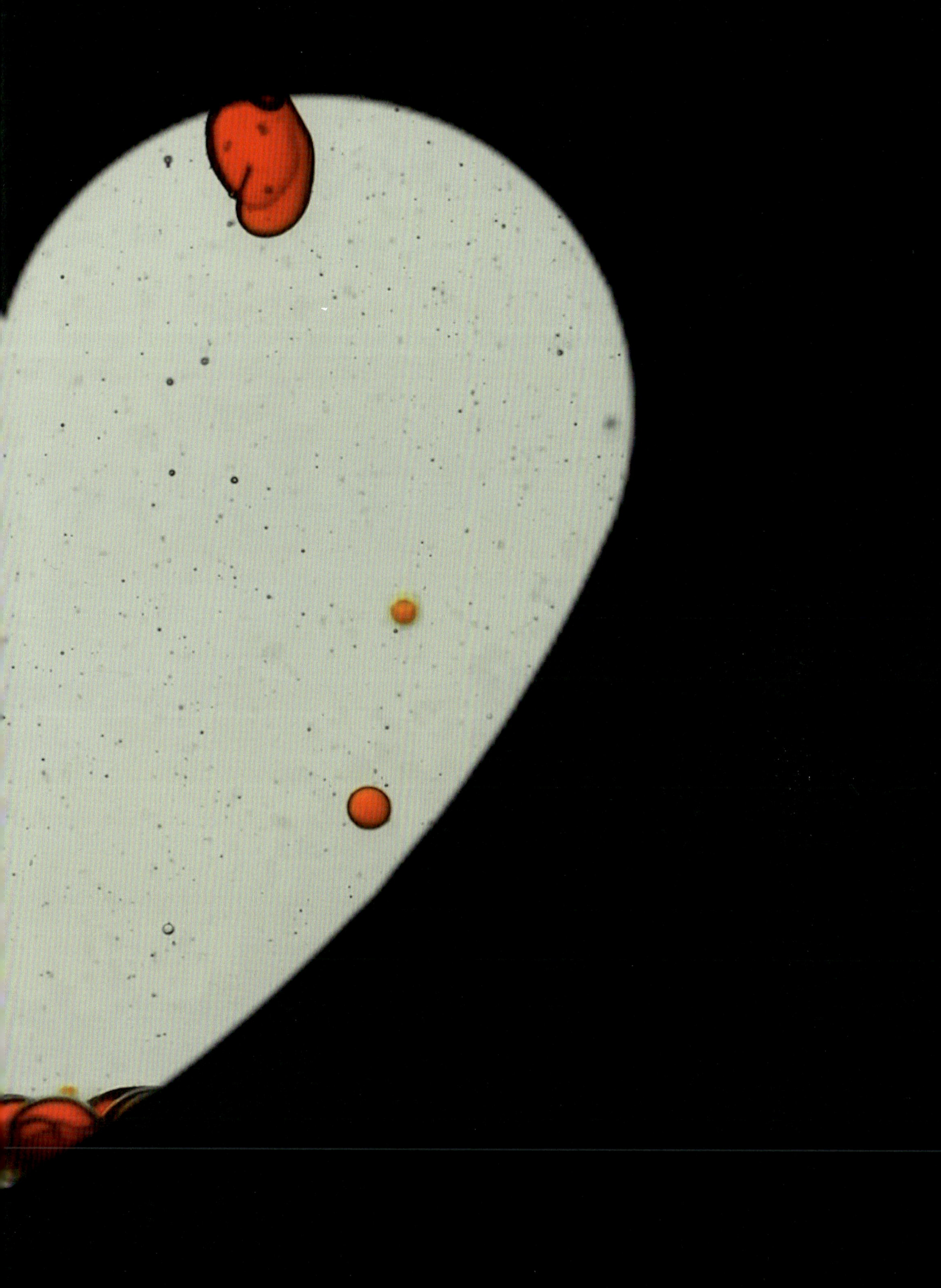

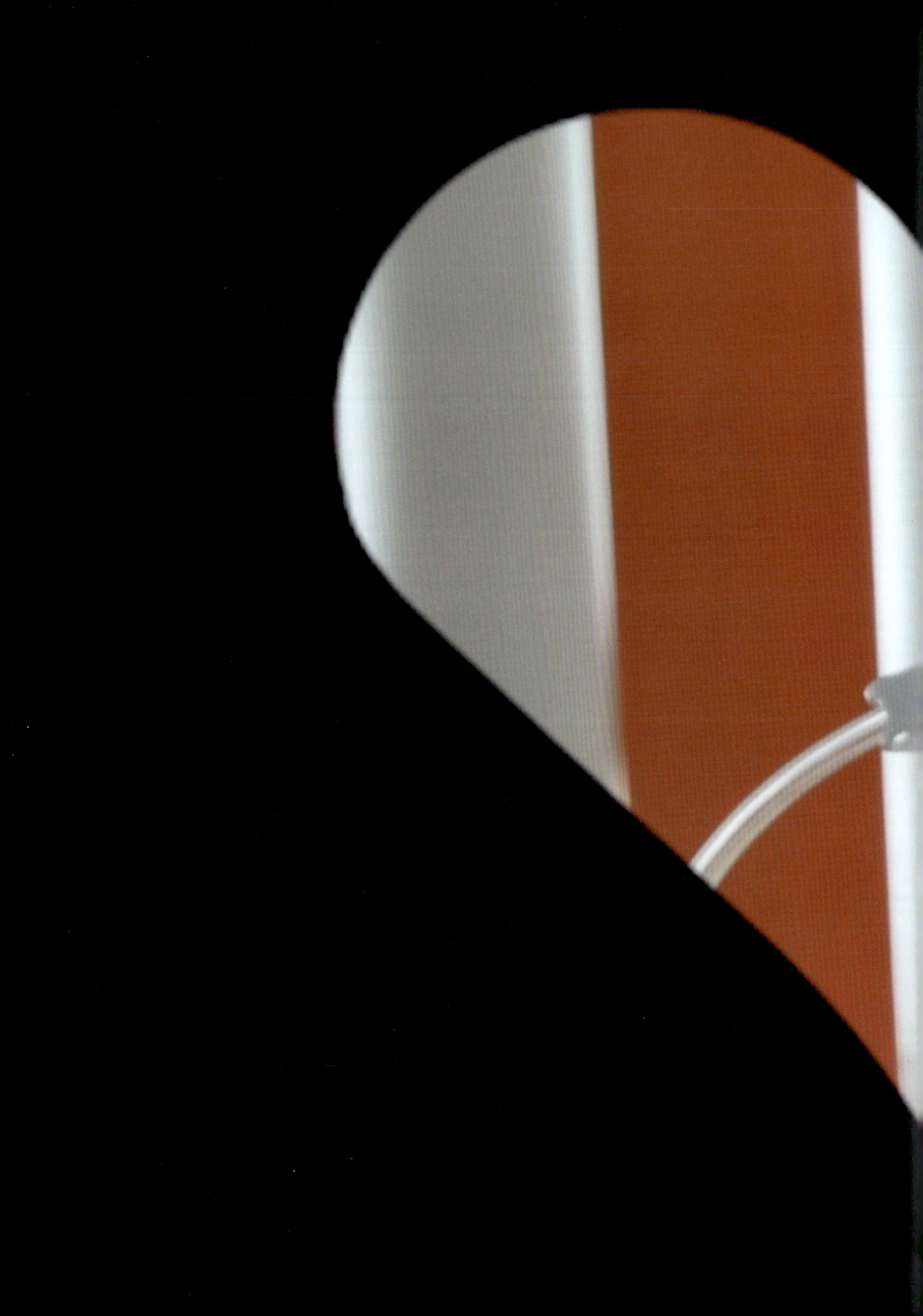

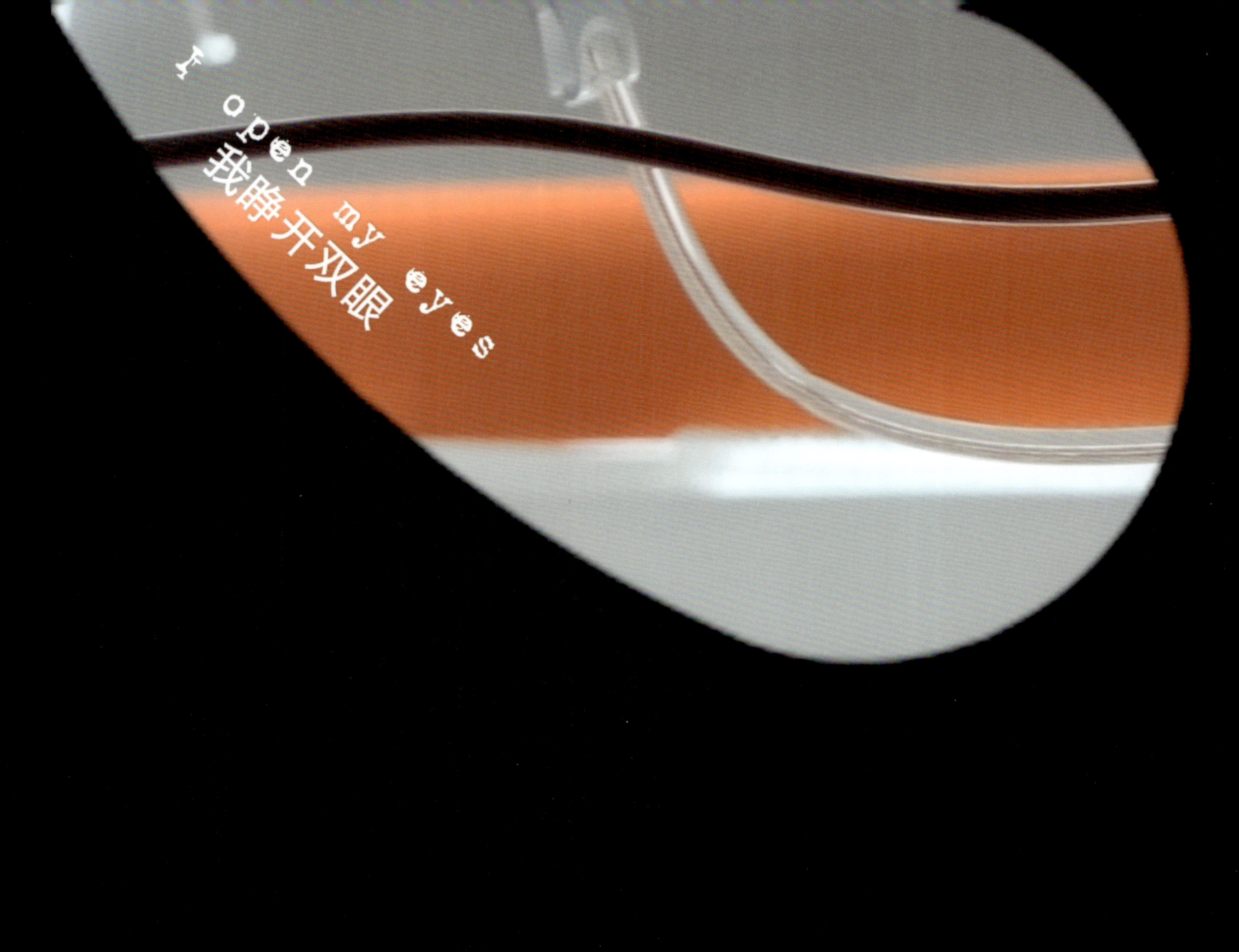

I open my eyes
我睁开双眼

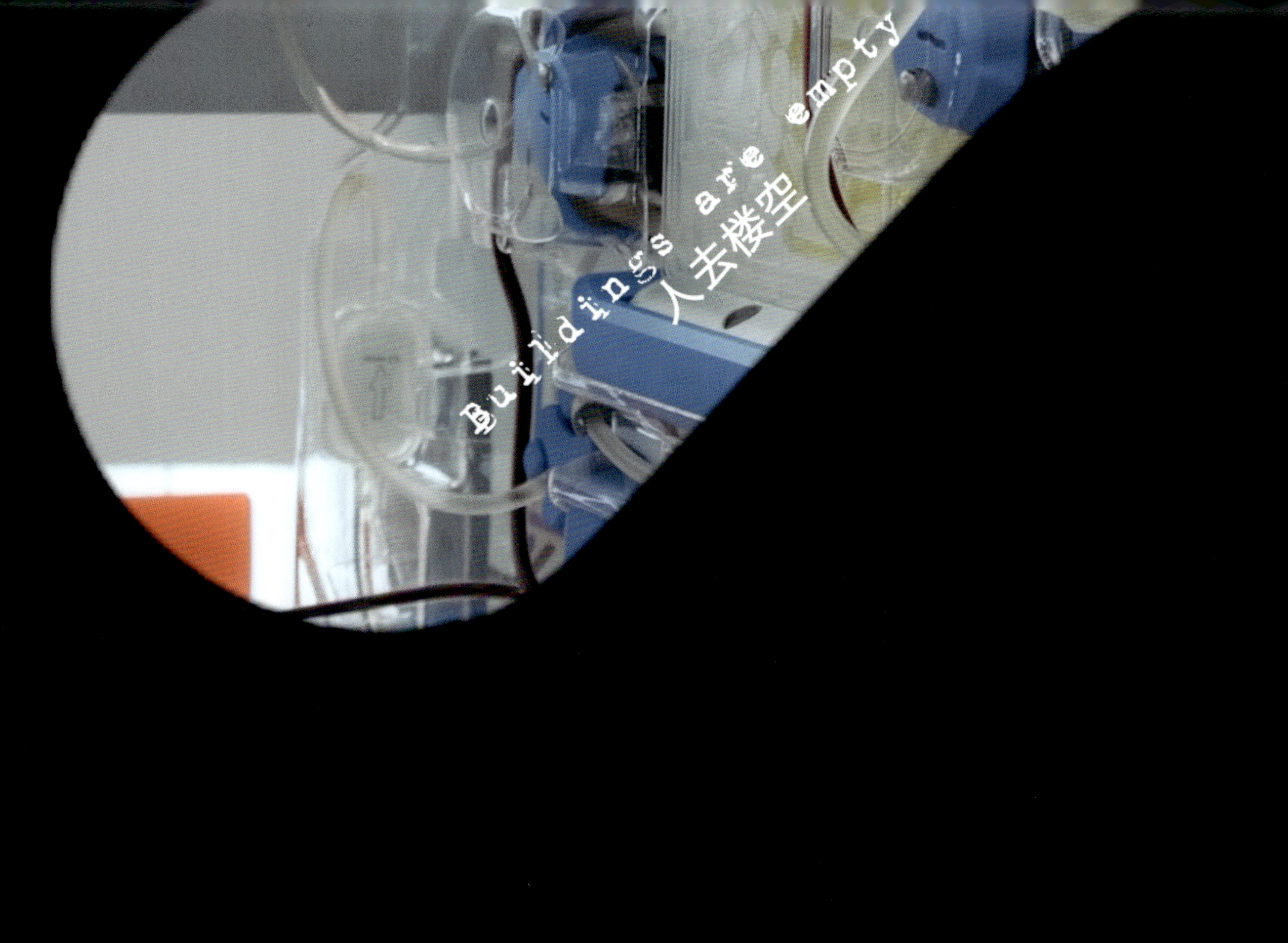

Buildings are 人去楼空 empty

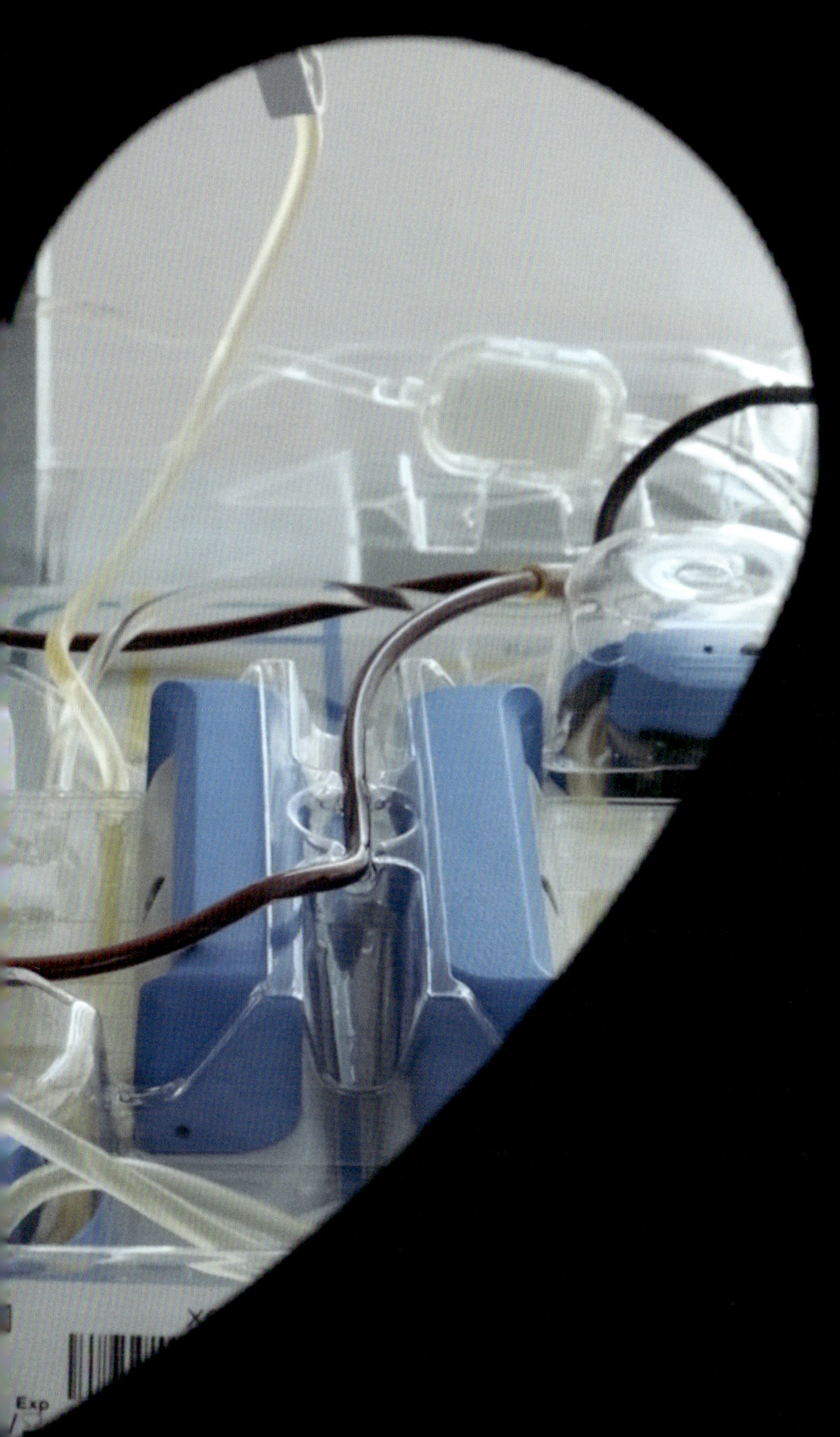

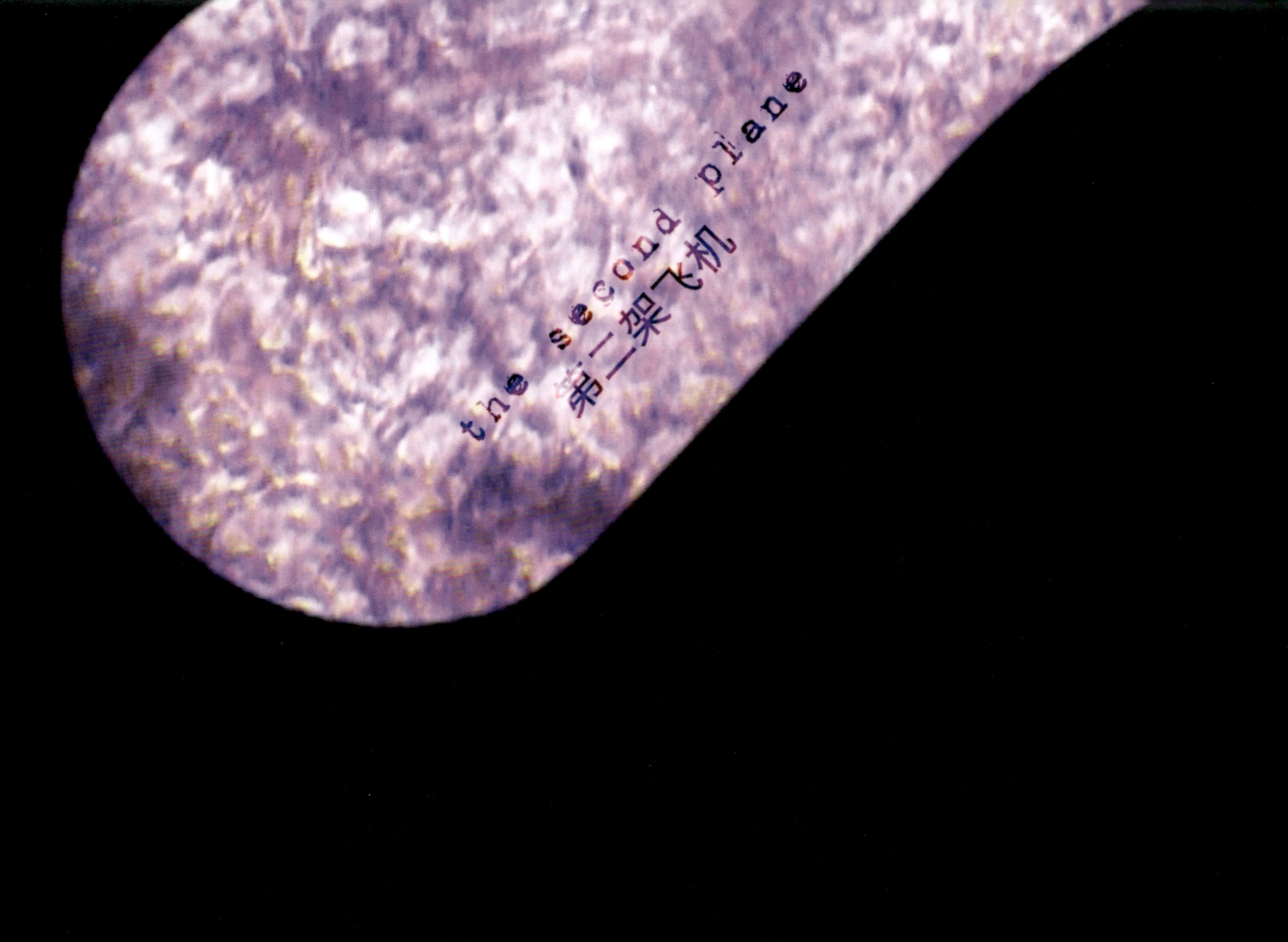

the second plane
第二架飞机

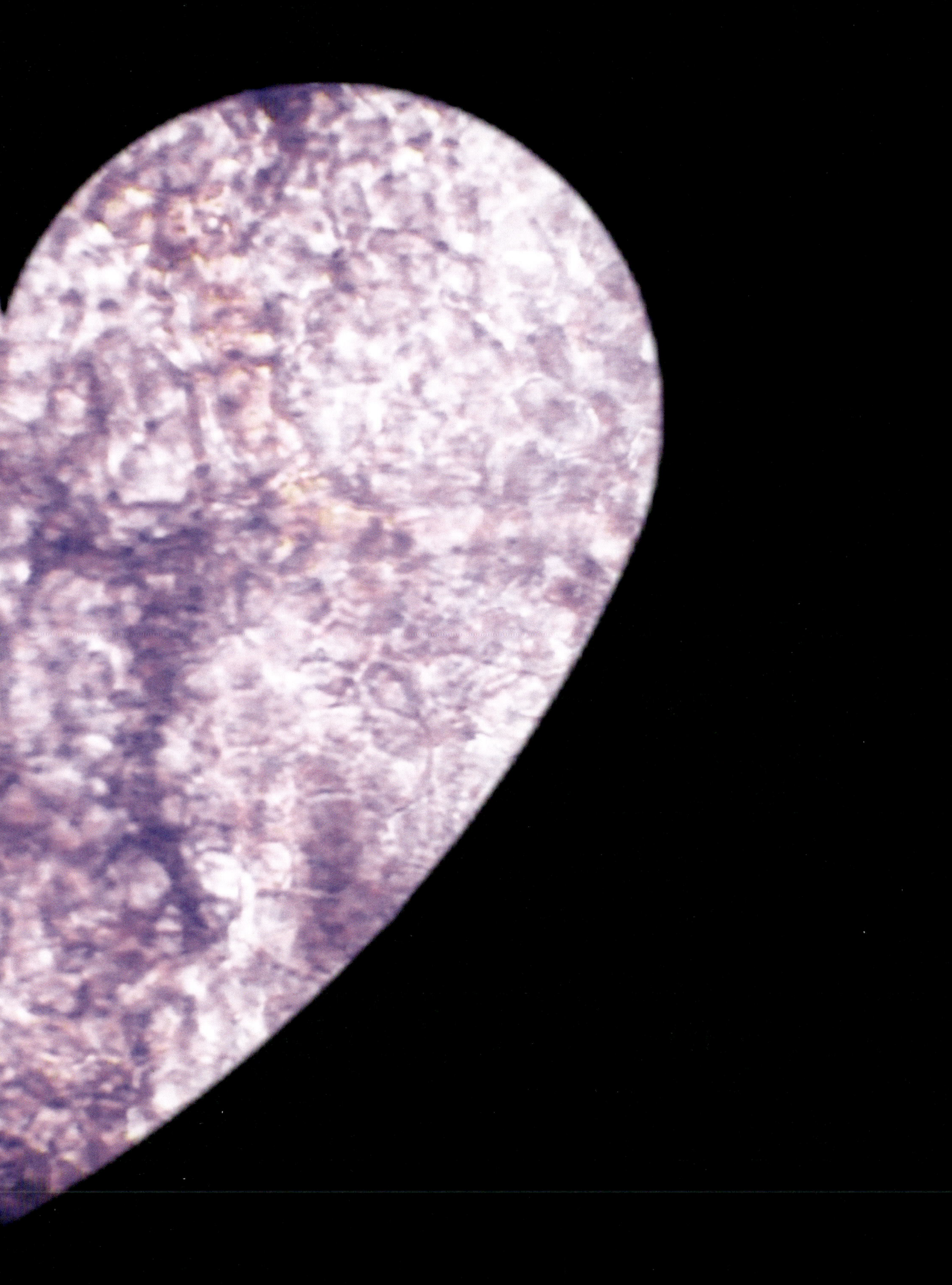

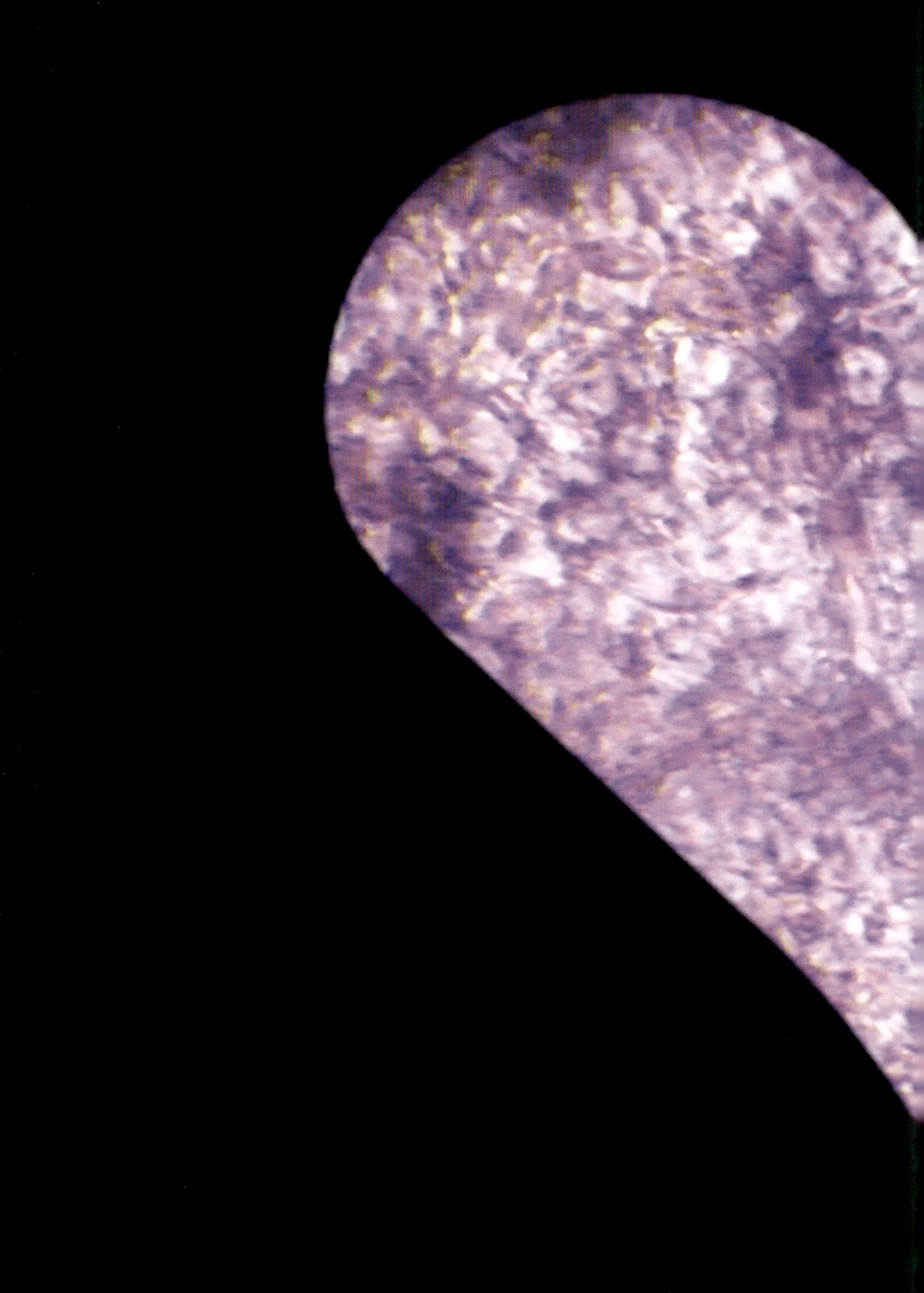

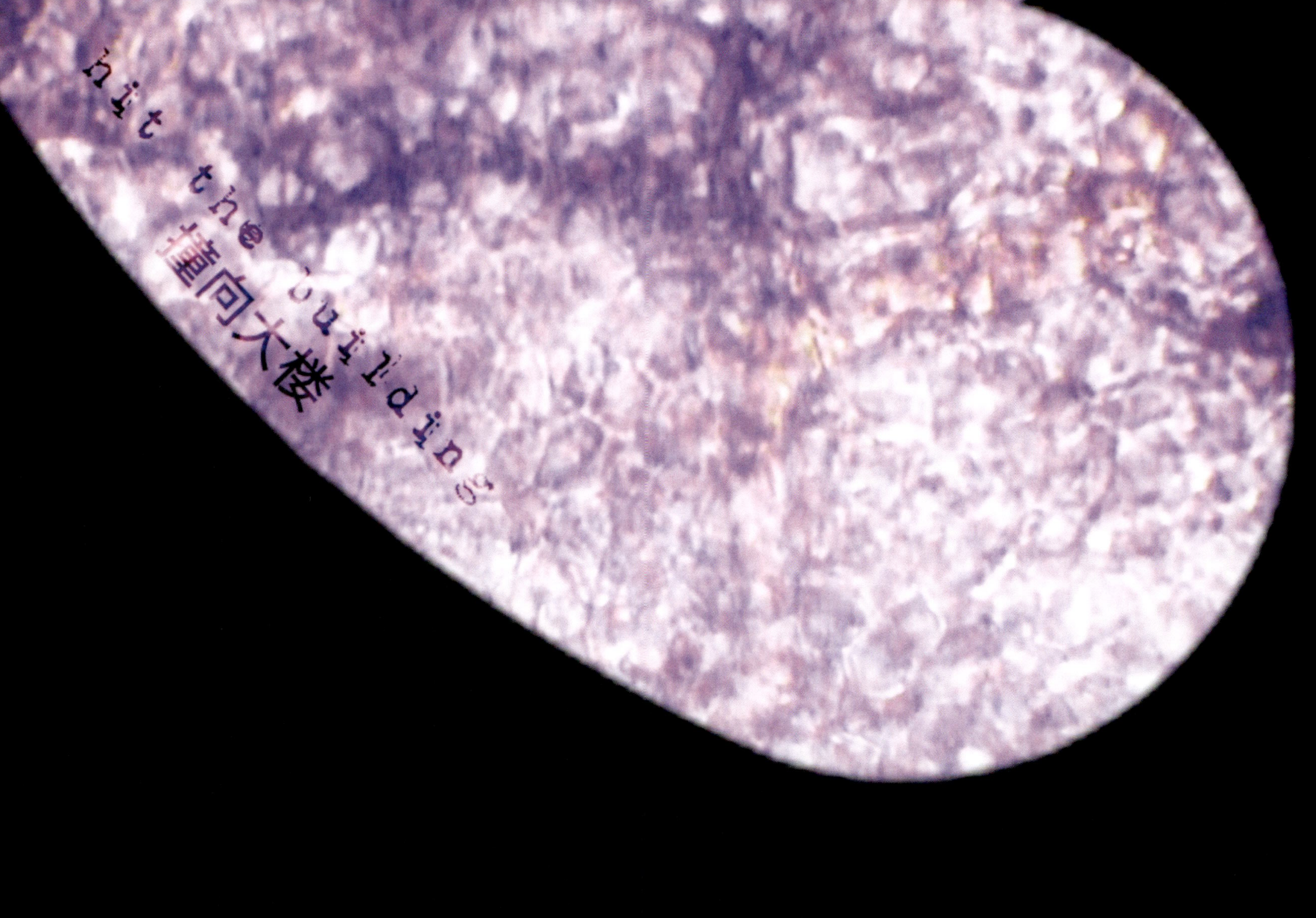

hit the building 撞向大楼

Shuang Li's solo exhibition, *I'm Not*, is a rumination on the power of devotion and the unexpected ways in which connection can take root. Similarly, this book is the outcome of the efforts and belief of many. The networks of individuals around the world who helped bring this project to life testify to the expressions of love inherent in Shuang Li's work. Our deepest gratitude goes to Shuang Li, an artist whose brilliant ways of seeing the world will continue to shape the minds of generations of art lovers. Both commissioning institutions are lucky to have embarked on this journey with you.

Thank you to the curators of the exhibition and editors of this book, Alison Coplan of Swiss Institute and Daniel Merritt of Aspen Art Museum. The collaborative spirit of the project was fostered by your adventurousness, curiosity, and deep insights into Li's vision.

We are grateful to Simon Wang of Antenna Space for his thoughtful and diligent stewardship of Shuang Li's practice. The exhibition was produced largely at Callie's in Berlin, and we are grateful to its outstanding team for their guidance in fabricating the outstanding sculptures. Alexis Colin, a key member of Shuang Li's studio, has been a leading voice in the development of this project and we are grateful for his support.

The texts in this book reflect the brilliance of their authors. We are grateful to Hanlu Zhang, Jeppe Ugelvig, and Olivia Kan-Sperling for going deep into Li's world and revealing important truths about her practice. Thank you to Sophia Al-Maria for her unforgettable interview with Li. Conversations between artists are precious and revelatory, and this dialogue is made even more special by your lasting influence on each other's work.

We are grateful to the fantastic team at Pacific, led by the magnificent Elizabeth Karp-Evans and Adam Turnbull, whose sharp eyes captured Li's distinctive approach across every spread. Many thanks to Joana Urtasun and Ayline Le Sourd of Pacific for ensuring no detail goes unnoticed. Miles Champion, as ever, deserves our utmost praise for his fastidious copyediting.

The exhibition at Swiss Institute was made possible through major support from Y.D.C. and the additional support of Shane Akeroyd and the Fonds cantonal d'art contemporain, Geneva. We express our sincere gratitude to Patrick Reynolds and the dedicated team of Swiss Institute for their support in realizing the exhibition. We additionally wish to thank the Board of Trustees, led by Maja Hoffmann, whose collective commitment to artistic excellence make this exhibition and book possible.

From Aspen Art Museum, we are grateful to Christine Egaña Navin, Anna Martin, and Simone Krug for their support in bringing the show to life. We are immensely grateful to our board of trustees, led by Amnon Rodan, for its exceptional dedication to art of the highest quality.

Shuang Li is an artist who inhabits distances with curiosity. The gaps and expanses between people and things, between words and their intended recipients, are vital territories for Li, ones in which wishes, fears, truths, and projections are cast into unknowable trajectories. In an expansive body of work that links video, sculpture, performance, and writing, Li traverses various in-betweens, paying close attention to the devices we use to minimize them and the ways in which they often fail. The relationship between these physical tools and the immaterial transmissions that course through them is often unresolved and entangled, leaving the user alienated and wanting. Within a desire to be closer lies a vulnerability, one that lurks throughout the internet, where we serve ourselves up to strangers. But love remains an overriding sentiment across Li's work, which tells stories of ceaseless yearnings for connection. The things we cannot say, the places we cannot go, the people we cannot see: all of this negation intensifies human life. Li celebrates defiant pursuits.

This book was made on the occasion of Li's first institutional solo exhibition, *I'm Not*, commissioned by Swiss Institute and Aspen Art Museum. Li delved into her own life as a fan to ruminate on how screen and internet technologies inform the social bonds and materiality of fandom, and the complexities of building a world predicated on a fervent love of something unreachable. Growing up in a small town in Southeast China, Li became (and remains) an ardent fan of My Chemical Romance, a band that introduced the possibility of subcultural belonging as well as the English language into the artist's life. MCR fandom served as a case study in the exhibition for an examination of faraway bodies and displaced desires. For the exhibition's title work, *I'm Not* (2024), Li rewrote the lyrics to the My Chemical Romance song "I'm Not Okay (I Promise)" in Mandarin Chinese and English, and the song was then covered by an a cappella group. In the resulting music video, a troupe dressed as an army choir conducted by a young girl melodically recites Li's version of the emo anthem. Li's lyrics line the book's inside cover, a surreal manifesto and a nod to the artist's own adolescence.

Three commissioned texts by Hanlu Zhang, Jeppe Ugelvig, and Olivia Kan-Sperling, as well as a revealing conversation between Li and fellow artist Sophia Al-Maria, give shape to this book. Zhang, a longtime friend of Li, maps the artist's early years in a personal address, drawing throughlines from her first artistic experiments in New York to her move to Shanghai and, later, Berlin, on the brink of the pandemic. Synthesizing histories of digital networks and the globalization of China, Ugelvig situates Li within the affective corners of the internet, noting her unique ability to find pathos in the Web. In a hallucinatory piece of fan fiction, Olivia Kan-Sperling tells the story of a rock band about to take the stage, and an airplane of singing schoolgirls crashing into a desert island. In a "post-pandemic cottagecore fantasy" that unfolded in the spring of 2023, Li speaks to Sophia Al-Maria, an artist whose work sparked a desire within Li to become an artist herself. The two discuss the nature of emo, high school bullies, Baudrillard, American mythologies, and advice to former selves. We are grateful to these exceptional writers and artists for their insightful contributions to Li's evolving world.

We first met Shuang Li in person in an empty, sun-soaked café in Geneva. The cream curtains lining the windows intensified the light so much that one needed sunglasses inside. The glow made the whole room drowsy and blissed-out; it felt like the way a dream might be depicted in a movie. Distance was acutely sensed by Li, who, by this time, had not returned to her home country of China for years due to COVID restrictions and a rapidly flourishing career that took her around the world. Over cake, we talked about the impossibility of her return and the creative silver linings of troubling fate. At the invitation of Mohamed Almusibli, Li moved into Cherish, the project space he founded with James Bantone, Ser Serpas, and Thomas Liu Le Lann. In 2021 she had a show as their first resident artist, and the house and city would soon serve as a backdrop for much of the work included in this book, including *ÆTHER (Poor Objects)* and *Déjà Vu*. Li thrives on indeterminacy, knowing the next destination is not of great importance. While making her shows in New York and Aspen, Li took road trips across the country, staying in clown motels in Nevada and small towns in Ohio. It is our hope that this book conjures the feeling of an unpredictable journey.

Throughout the book runs a poem by Li, set within the shape of a heart. In it, she tells the story of a girl who encounters the cracks of a fraught, rupturing world. These images come from Li's video *Heart is a Broken Record*, which appeared in both her New York and Aspen exhibitions. Projected into the rippling water of a heart-shaped fountain, a place to make a wish at the mall or in a public square, Li's words are interspersed with shots of crowds at My Chemical Romance concerts awaiting the performers, caught in an endless anticlimax of mounting cheers. At first encounter, the work is unnerving and absurd, yet the cries belie an infinite ecstasy only Li could evoke, a dissonant rapture.

We are forever grateful to Shuang Li, whose luminous mind graces every page of this book.

Right: *Distance of the Moon*, 2025
Installation view, Prada Rong Zhai, Shanghai

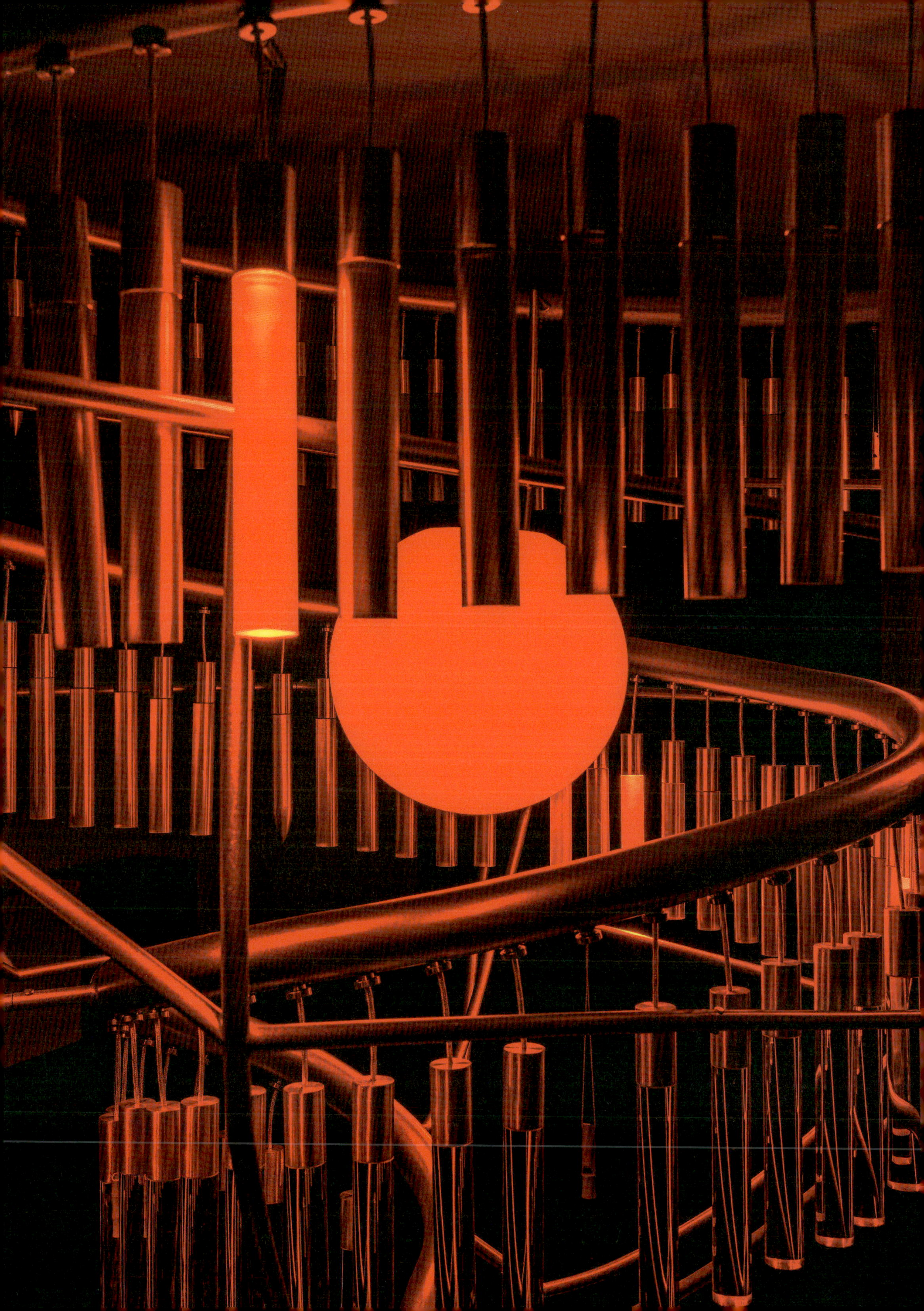

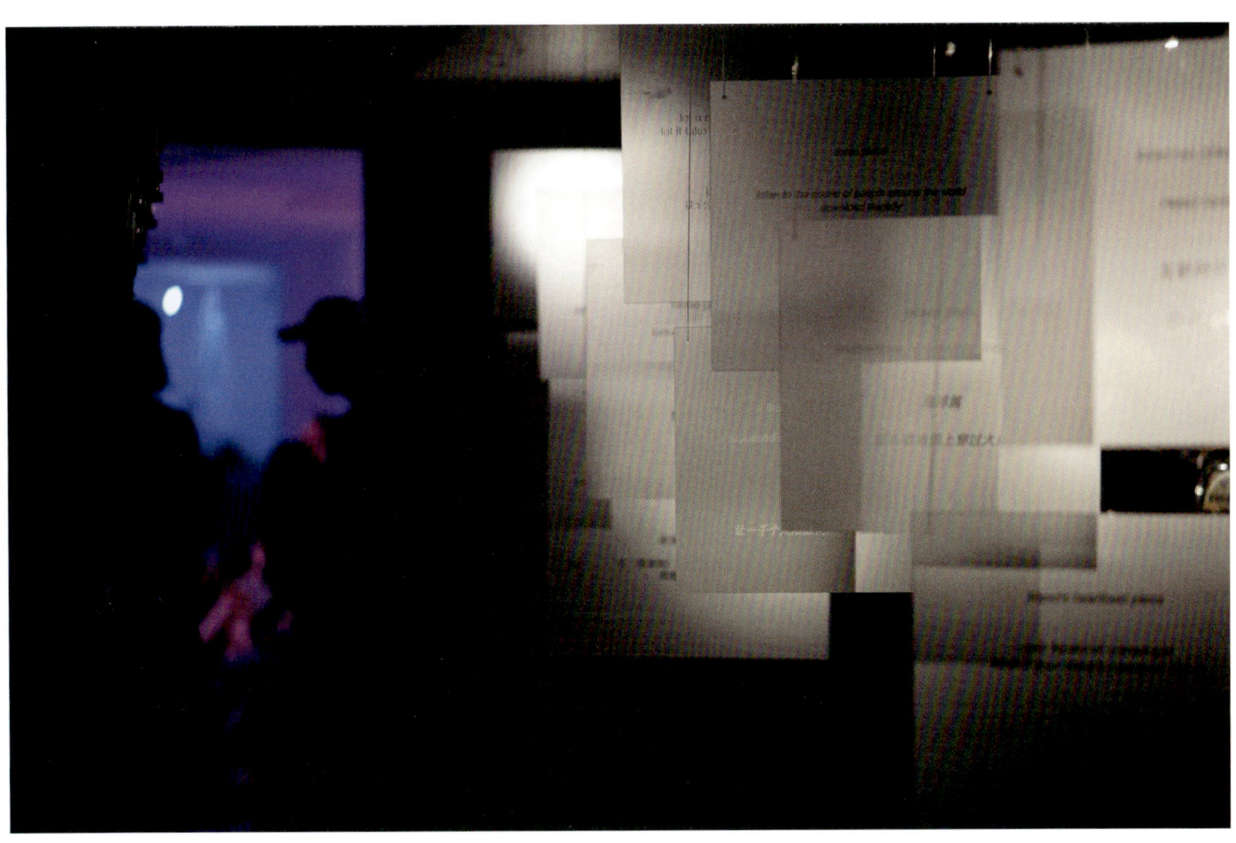

GЯΔPΣFRUIT, 2015
Installation view of *If Only the Cloud Knows*, curated by IDLE Studio
(Qiu Yun and Qiao Feifan) at SLEEPCENTER, New York, 2018

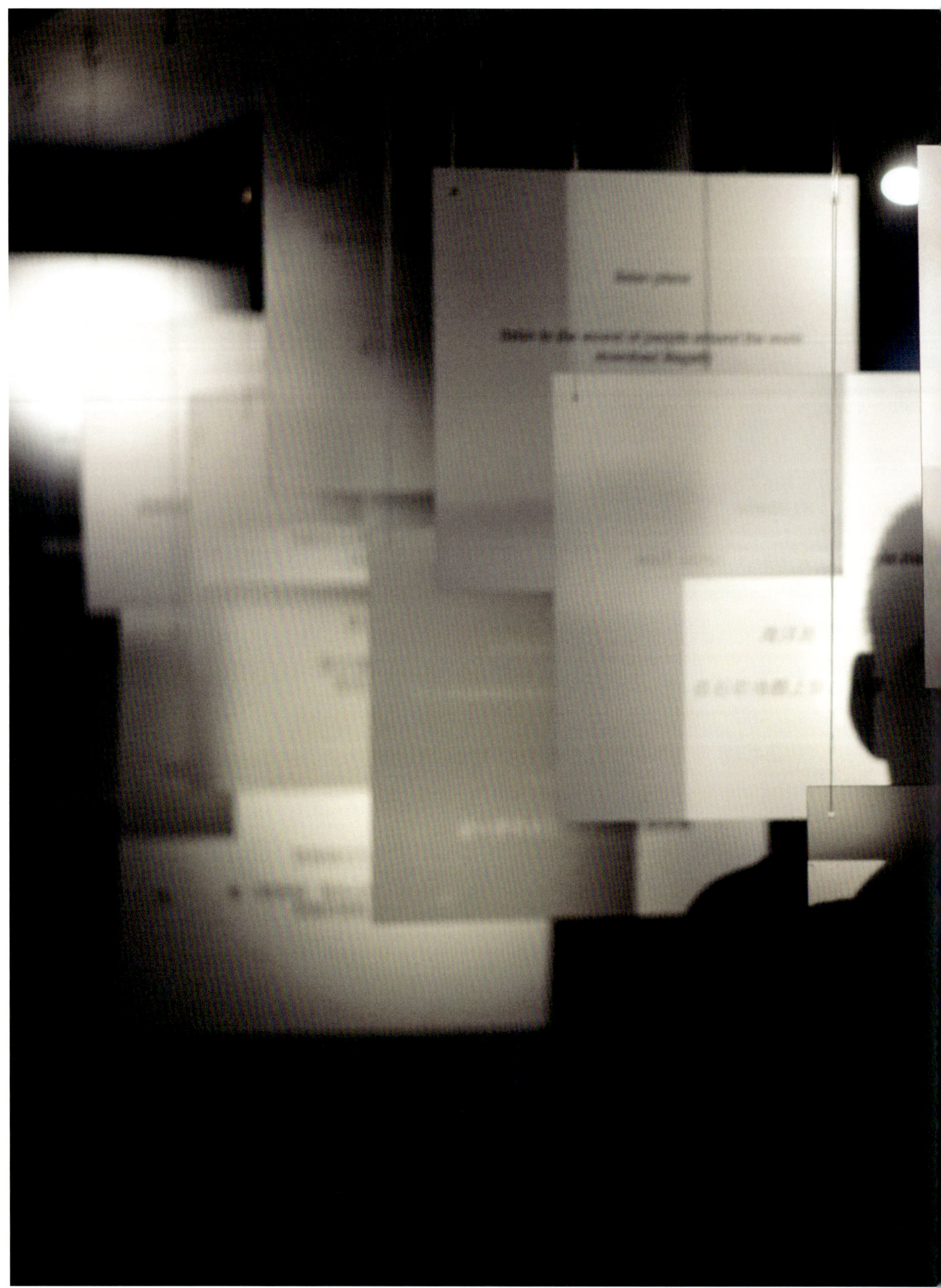

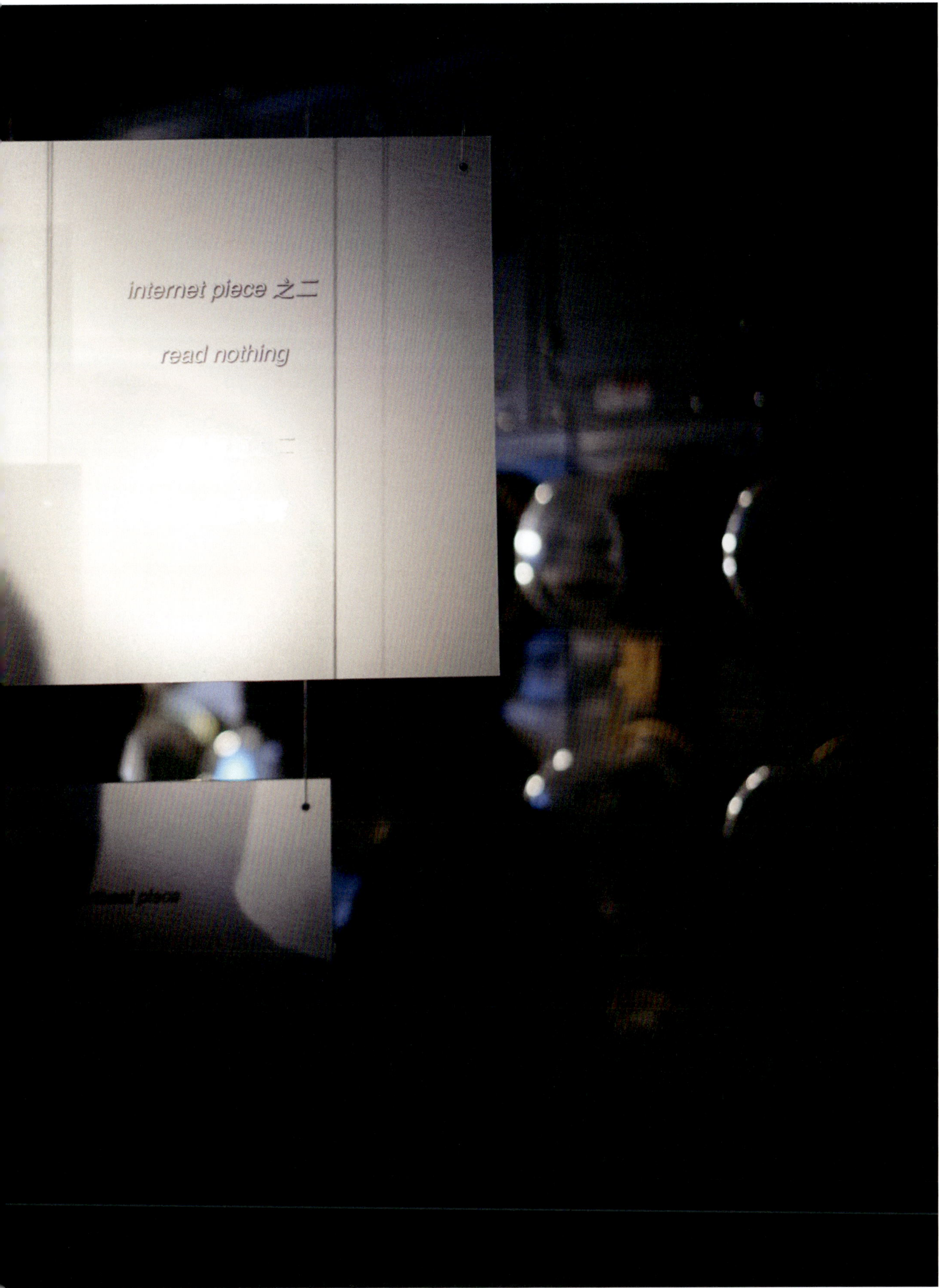

internet piece 之二

read nothing

internet piece

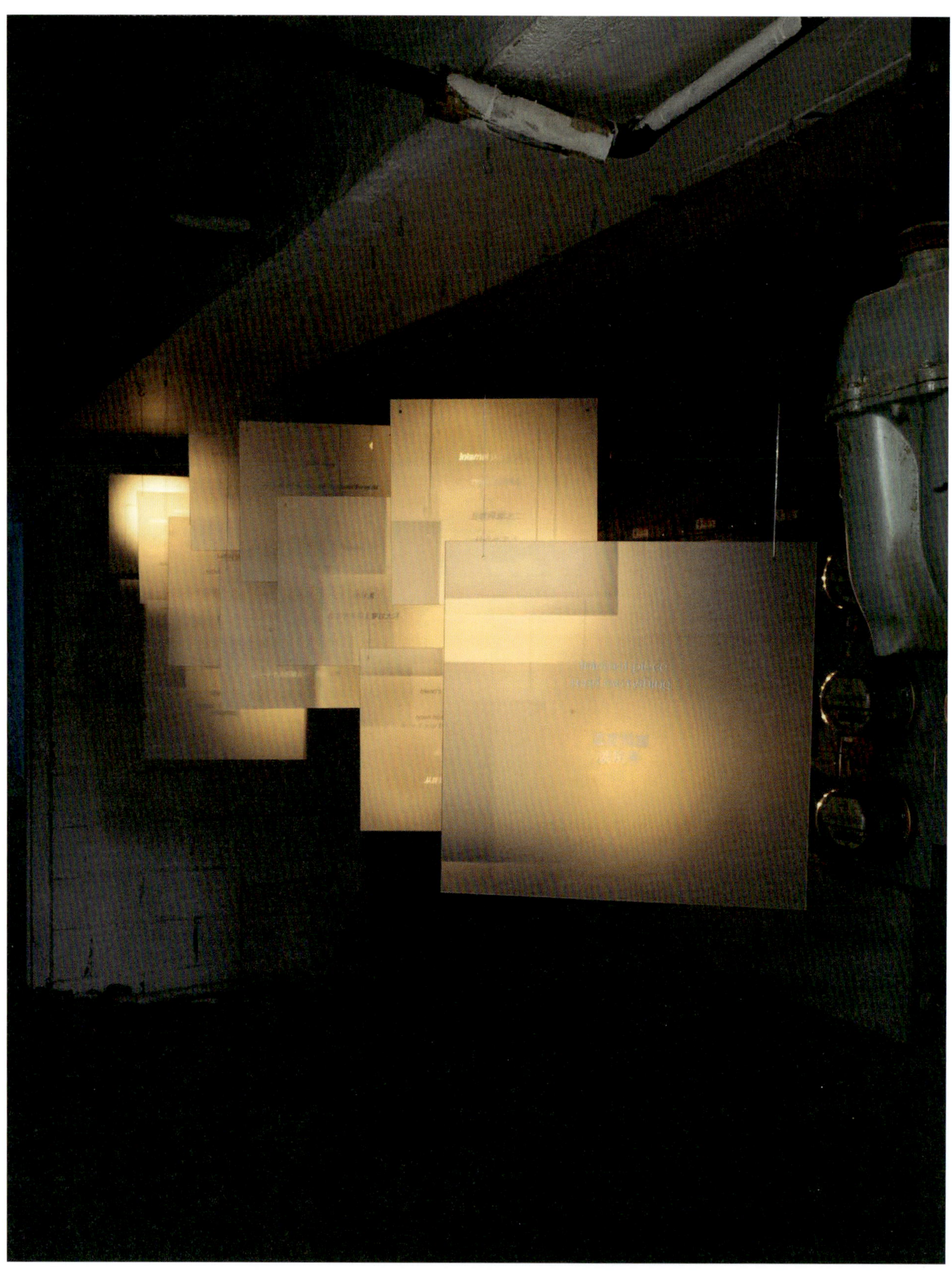

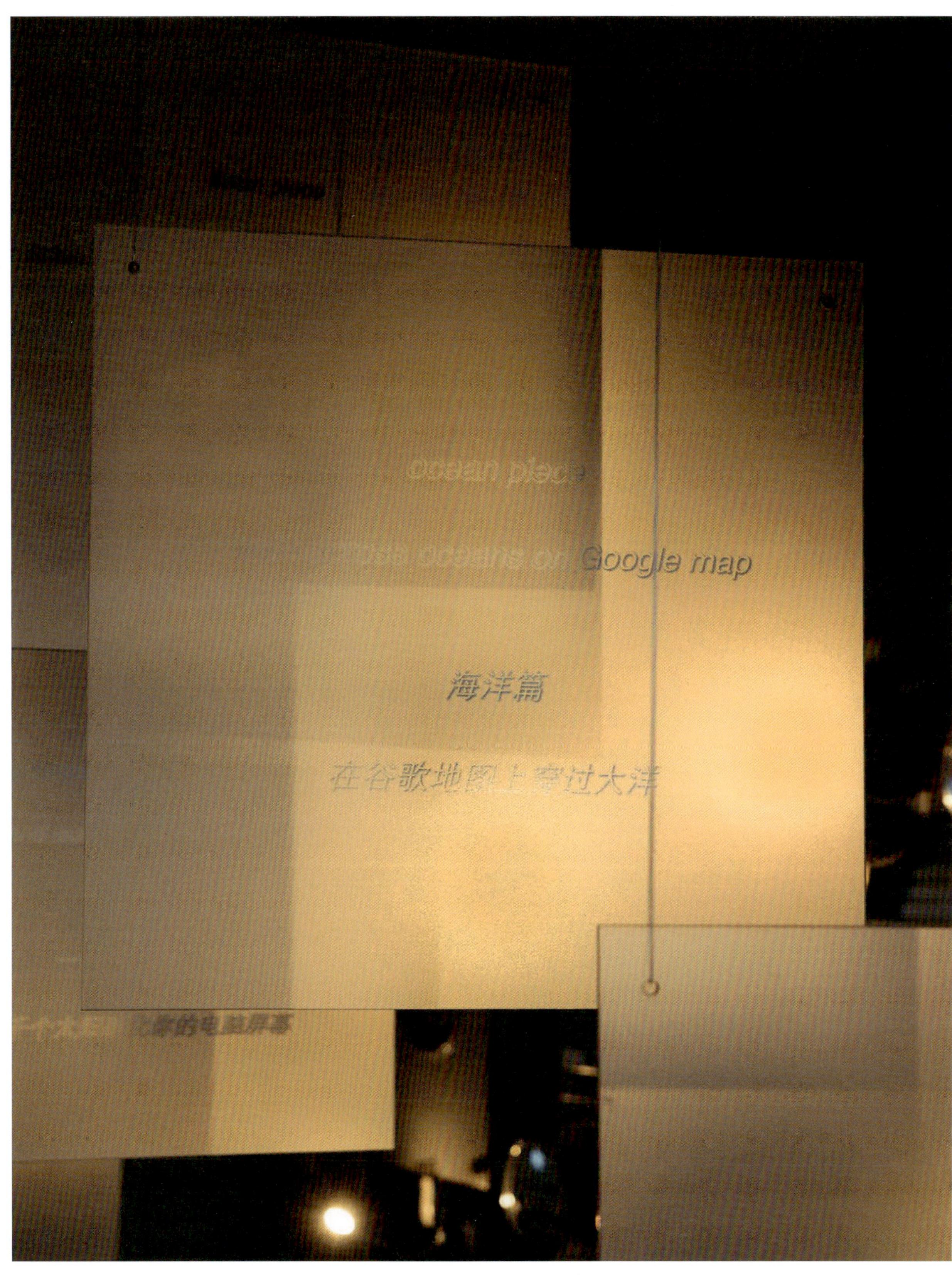
Ocean piece
cross oceans on Google map
海洋篇
在谷歌地图上穿过大洋
你的电脑屏幕

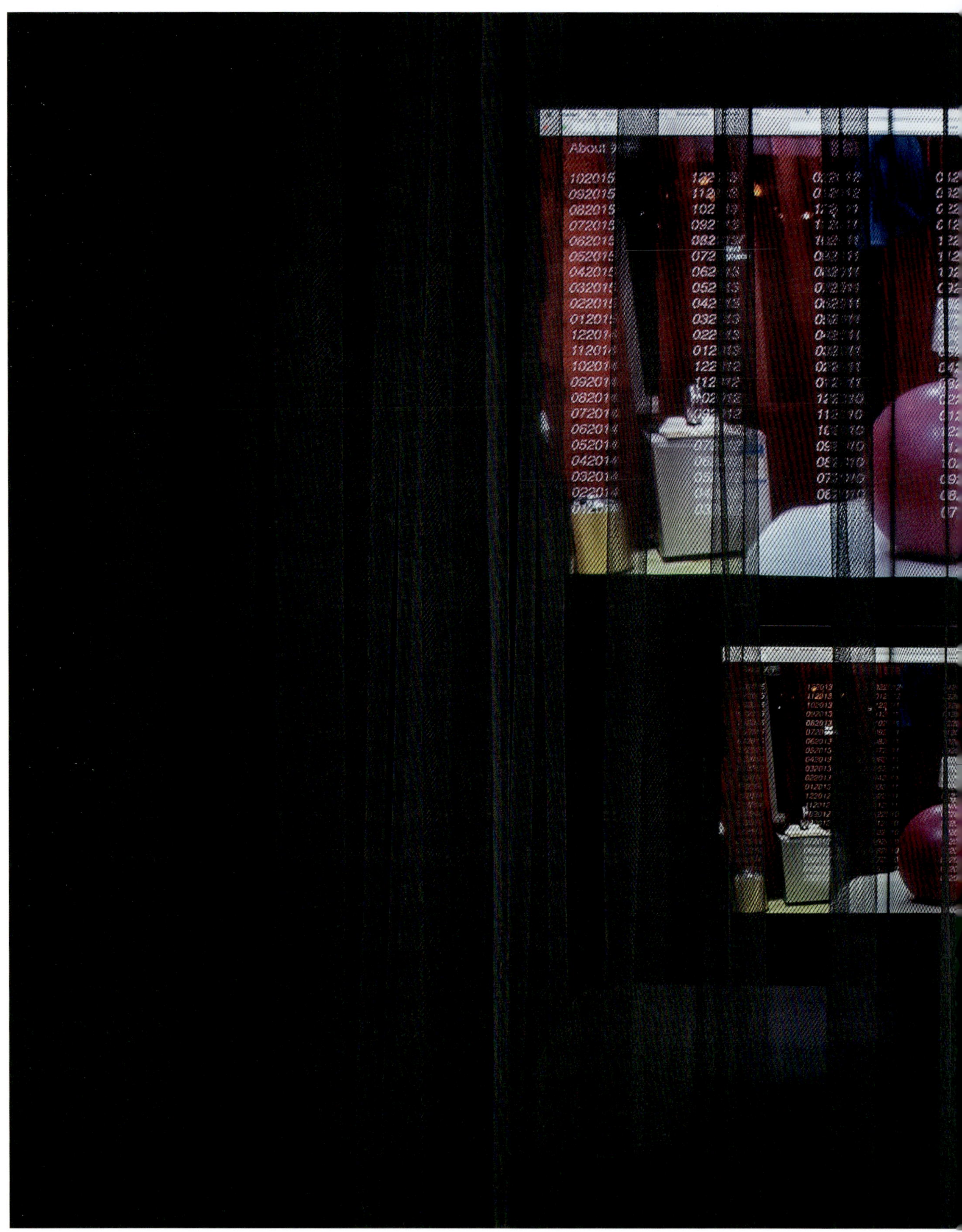

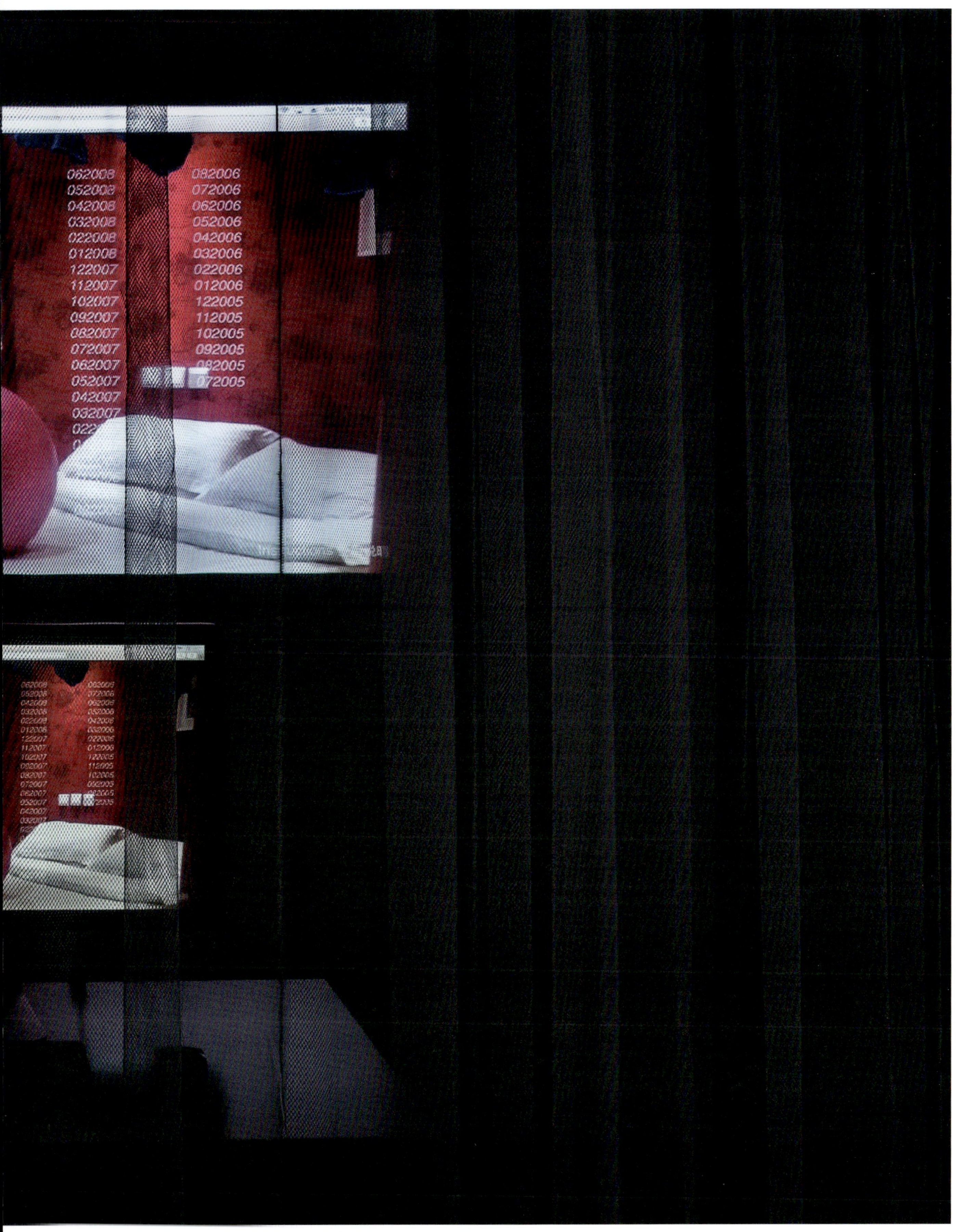

If Only the Cloud Knows, 2005–18
Installation view of *If Only the Cloud Knows*, curated by IDLE Studio
(Qiu Yun and Qiao Feifan) at SLEEPCENTER, New York, 2018

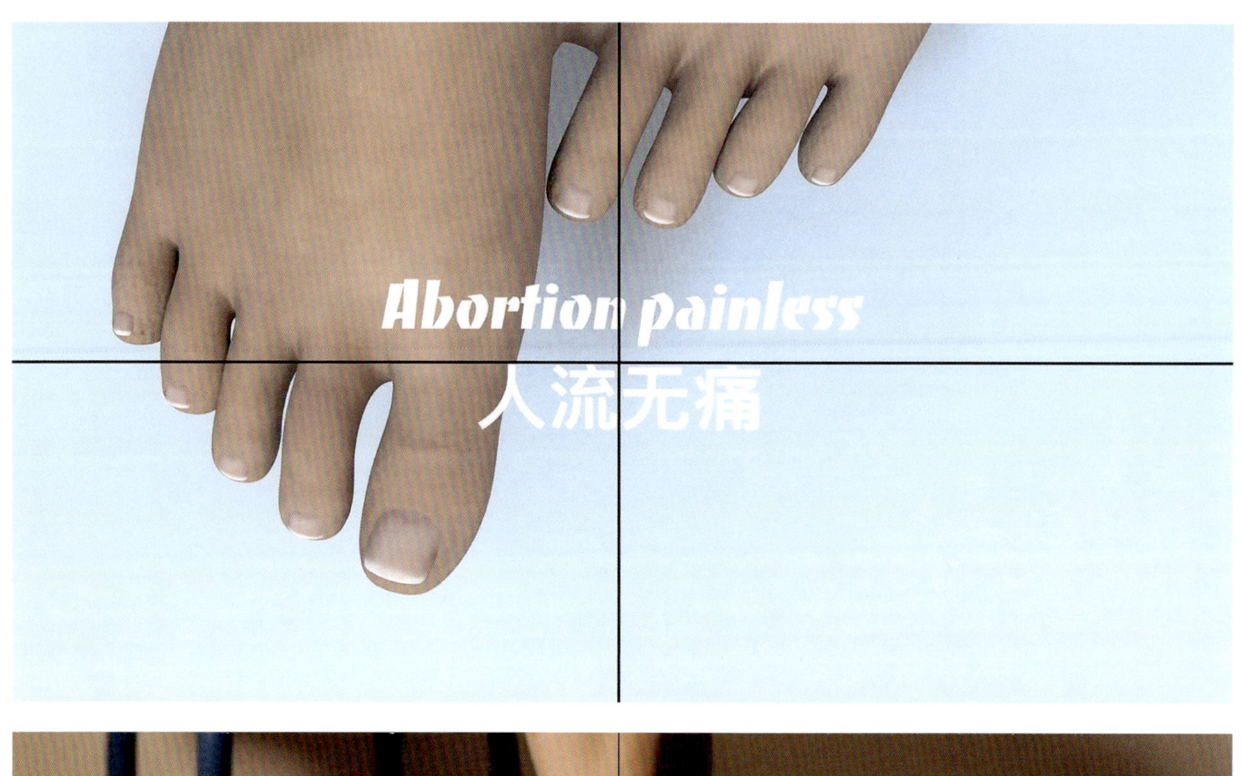
Abortion painless
人流无痛

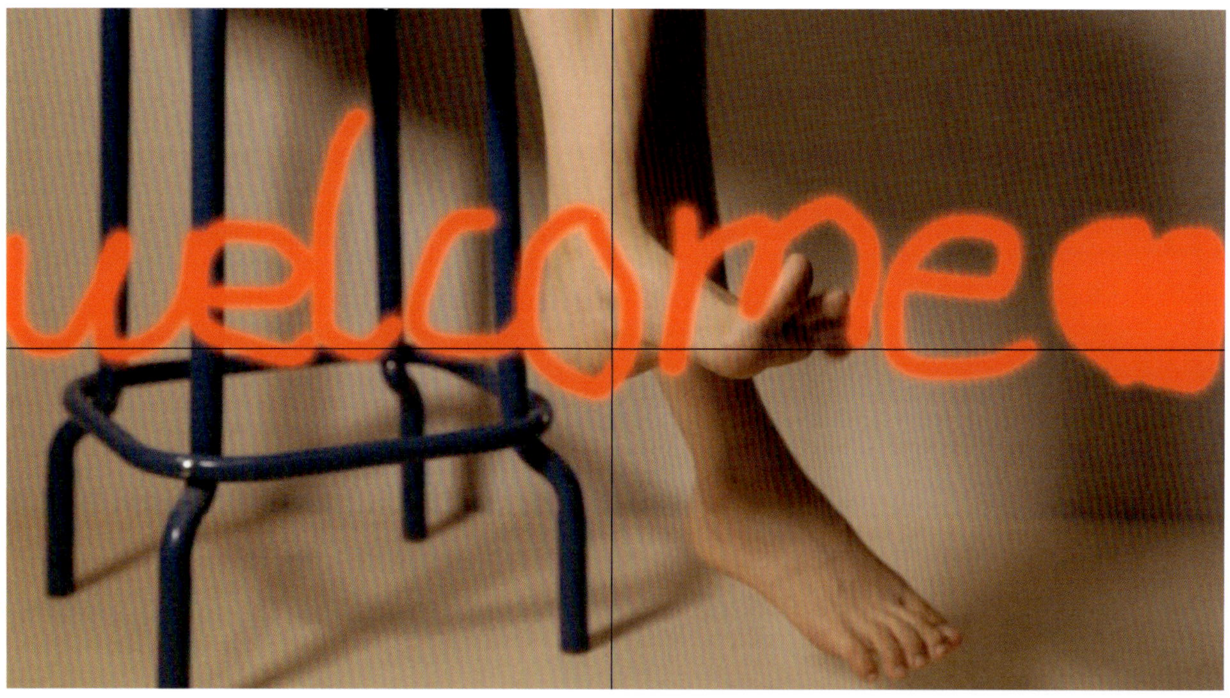
welcome

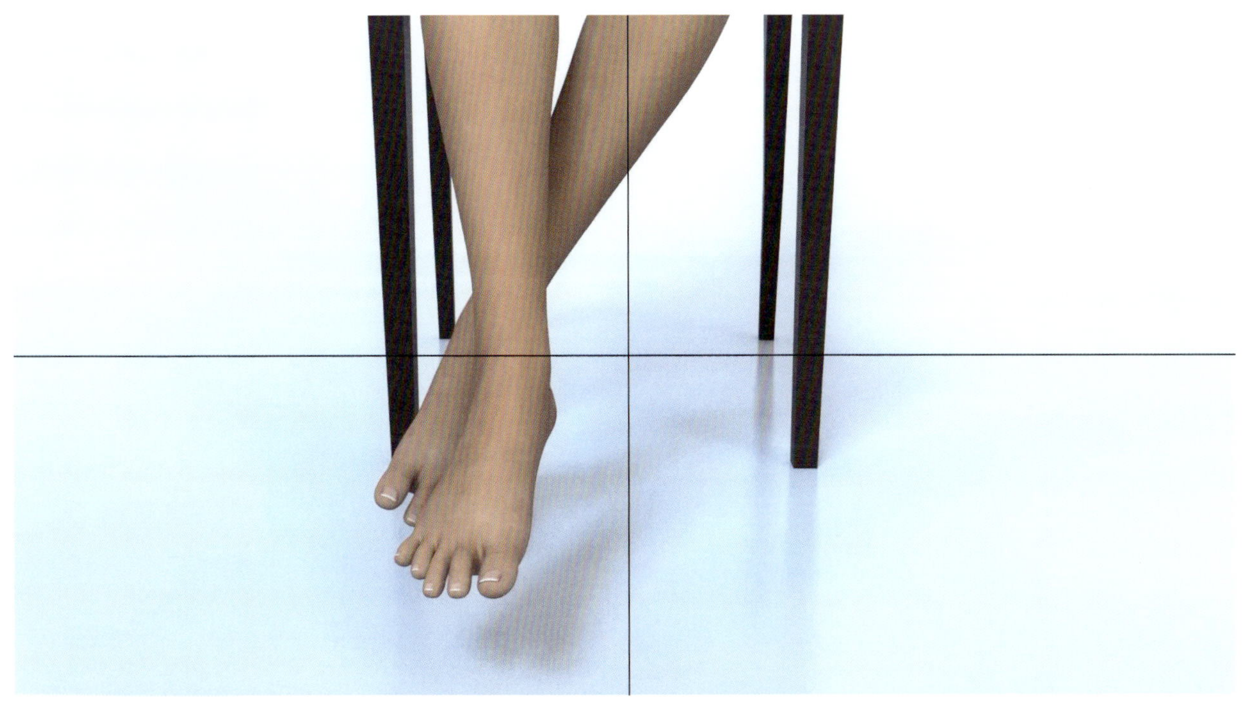
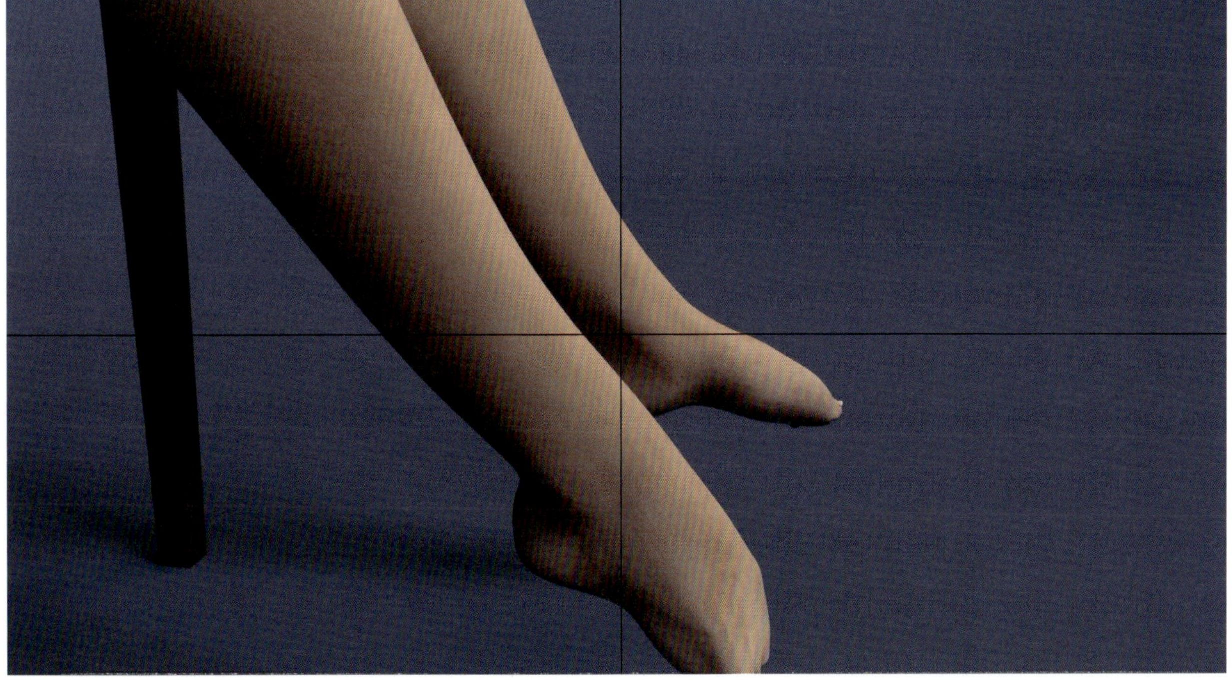

T, 2017–18

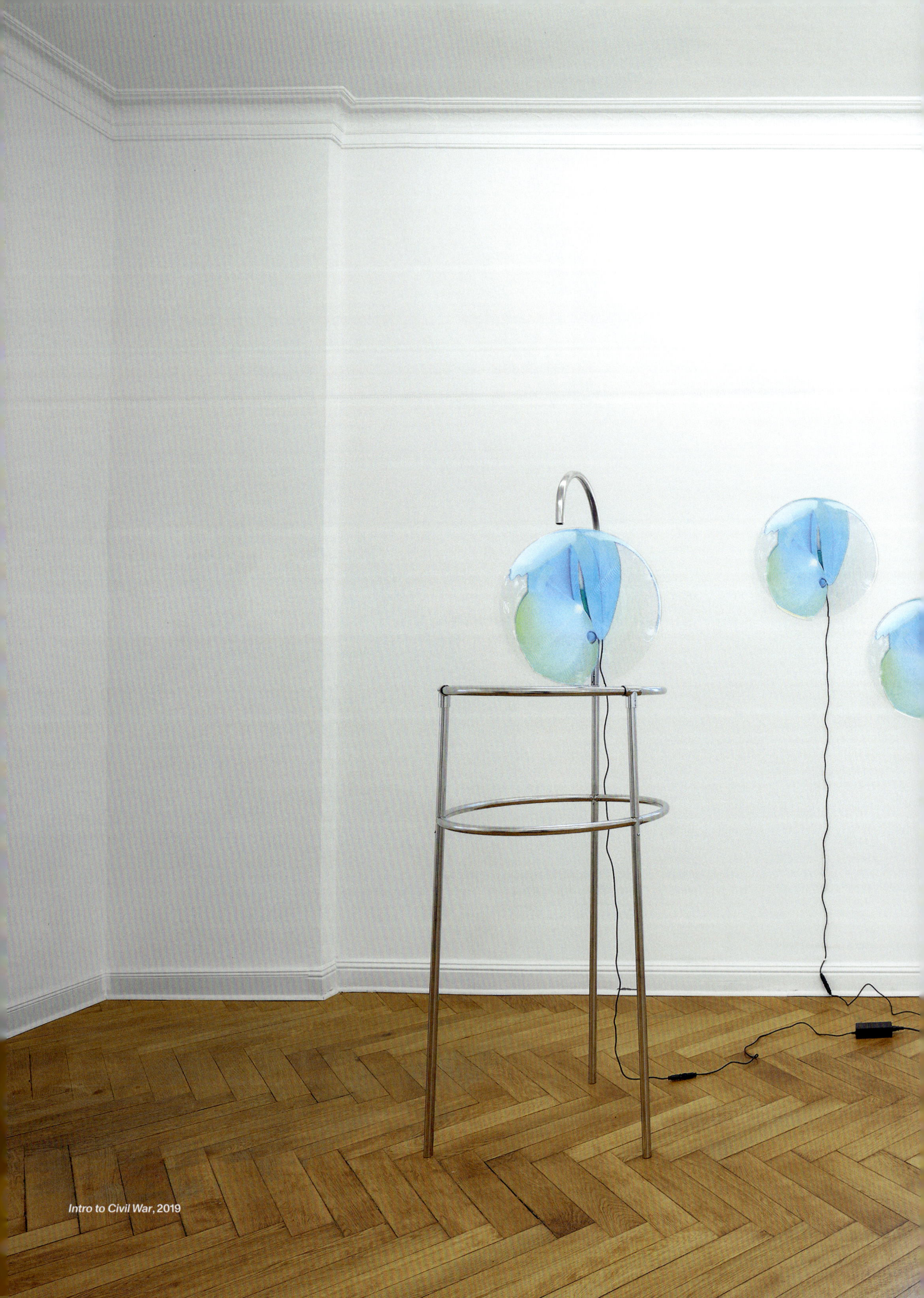
Intro to Civil War, 2019

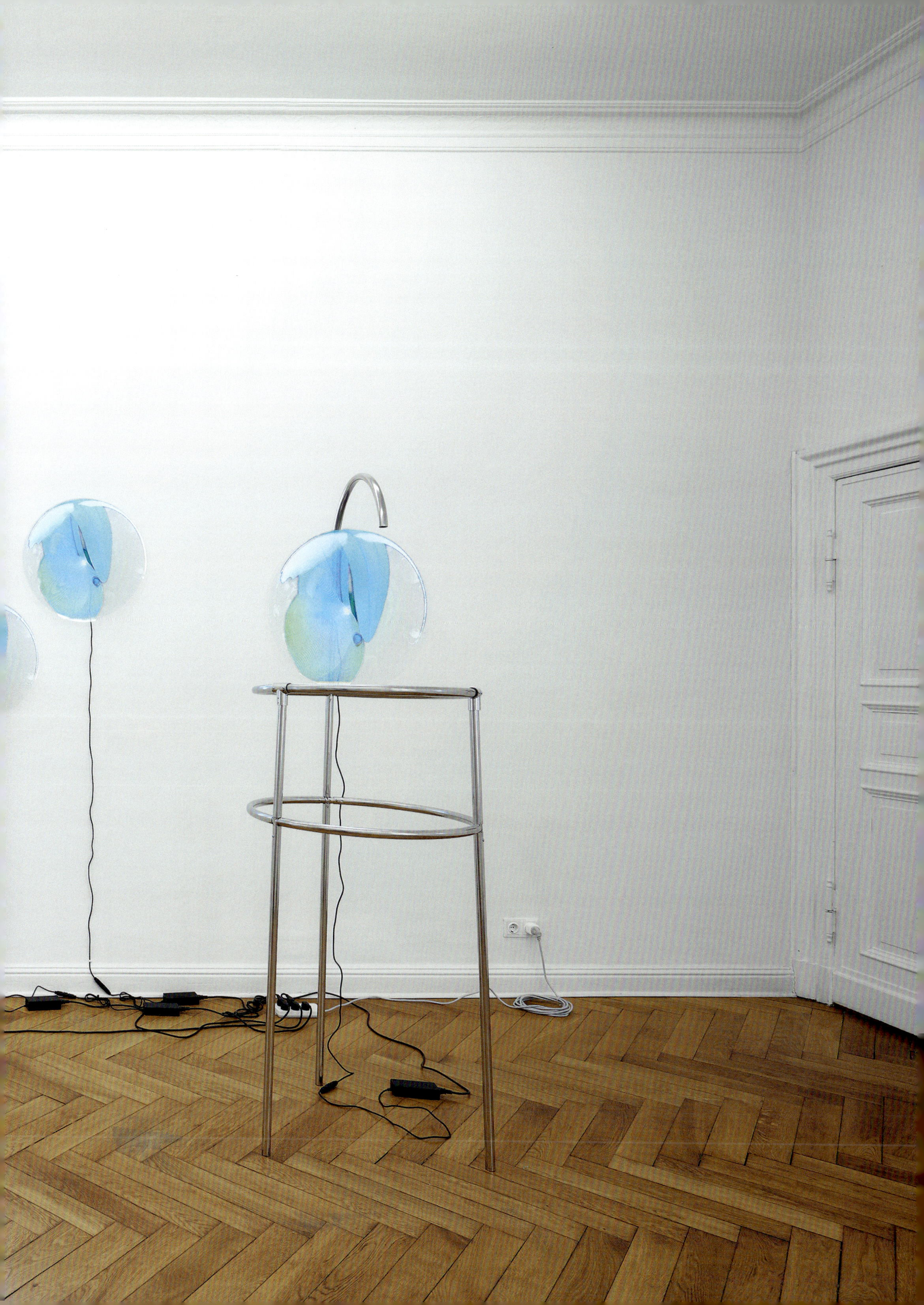

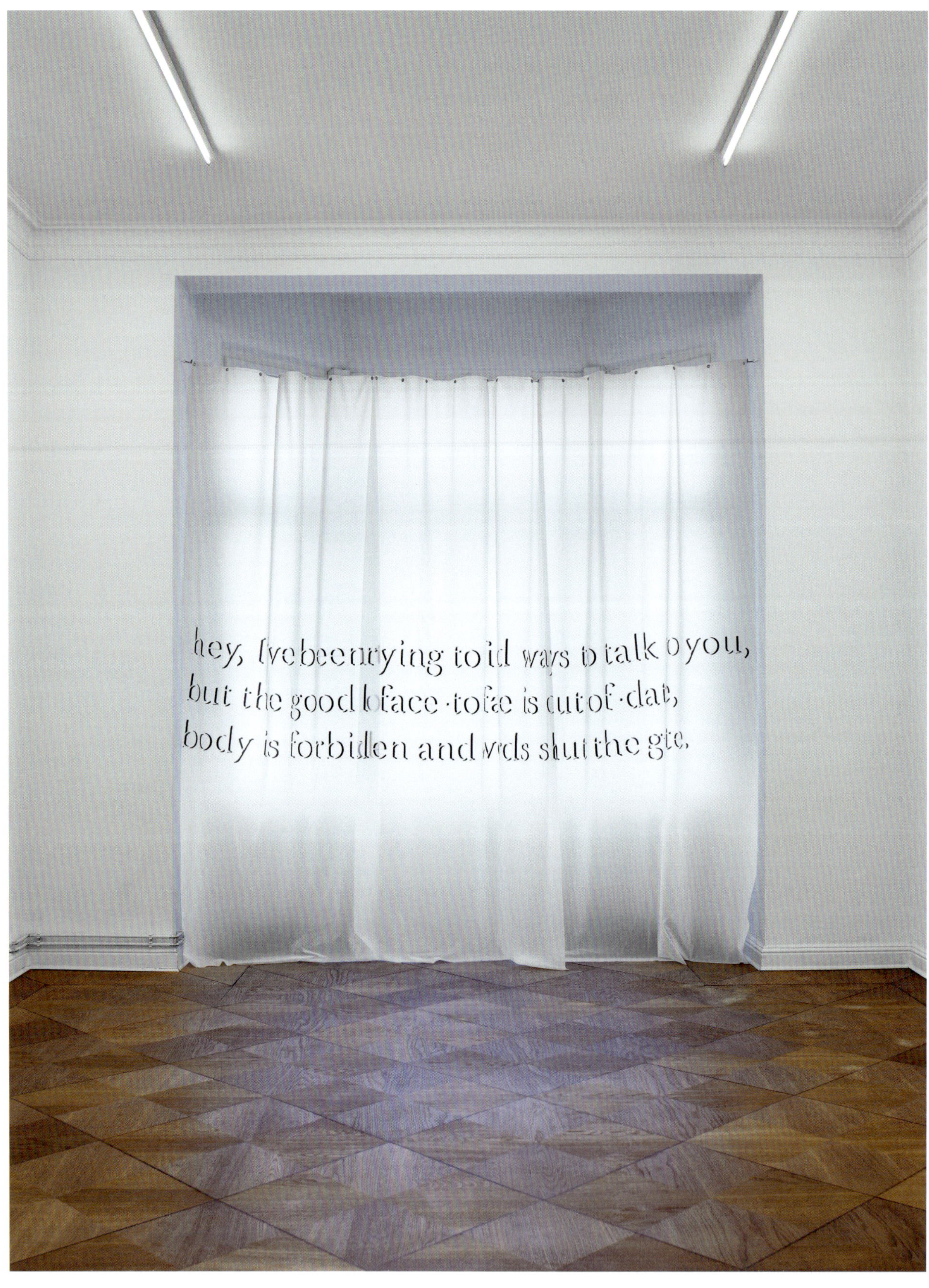

Intro to Civil War (Role Model), 2019

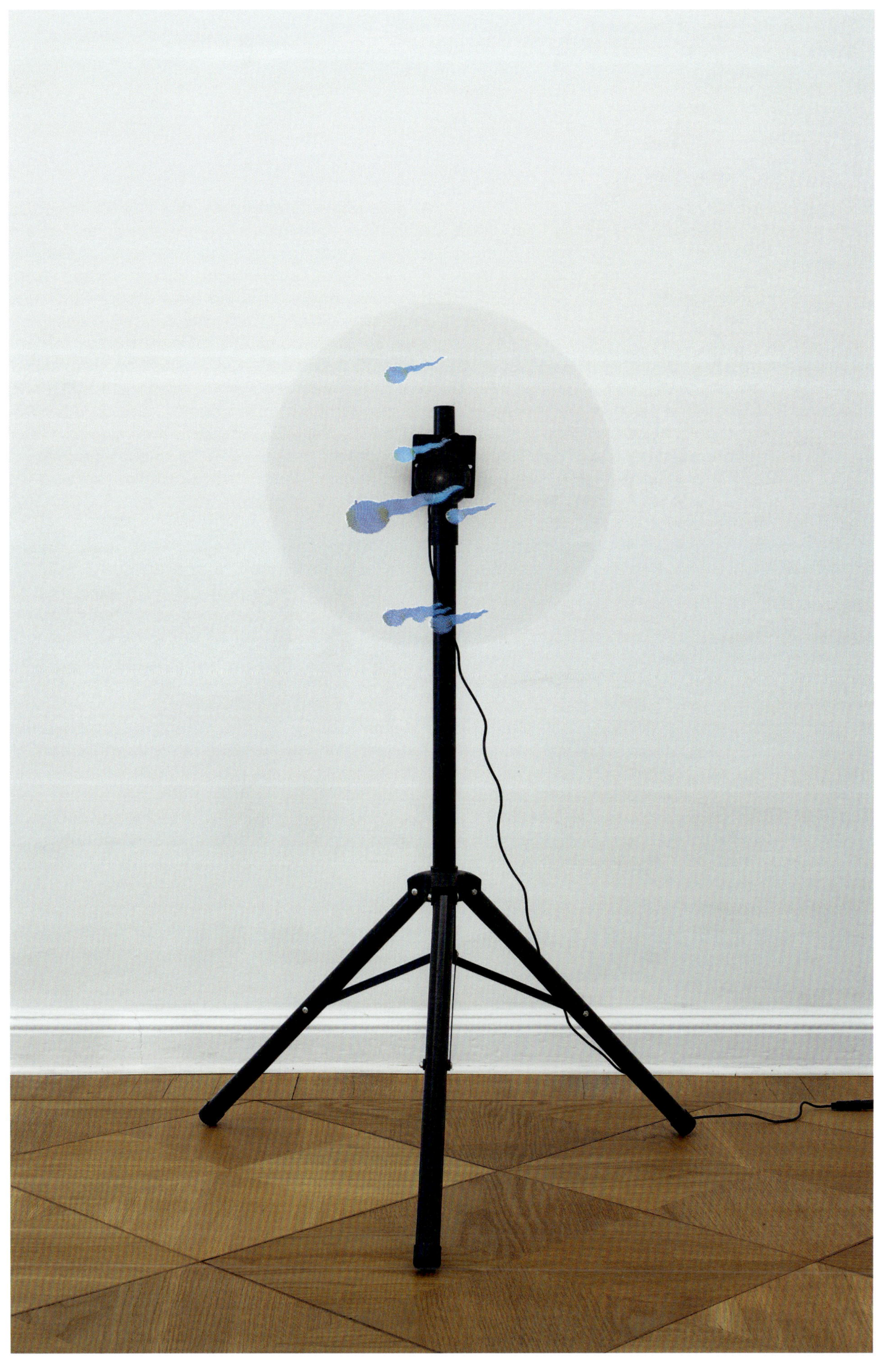

SHADOW OF REALITY
Every morning, one of the first things I see upon waking up is a translucent acrylic panel leaning against my bedroom window, inscribed with a two-line poem in internet slang.

open wechat
listen 2 yr fwend's heartbeat thru it[1]

It was early 2020. While packing on Shuang Li's behalf, as she had gone to Geneva for a residency and was then "stranded" there due to travel restrictions, I adopted this piece of hers and have kept it since. At the time, I was also leaving Shanghai to take up a curatorial position in Guangzhou, so I had to clear out the apartment we once shared and ship all her belongings to Nanping, her hometown.

This acrylic panel is a material test from Shuang's 2015 series *GЯΔPΣFRUIT*, created for the group exhibition *You Won't Be Young Forever*, curated by Bilijana Ciric. Shuang's inscribed panels are embedded within the old window frames of an abandoned building along Suzhou Creek in Shanghai. In 2015 the city was emerging as a hip international art hub, driven by a series of government-led real estate developments. Through Shuang's work, viewers could see the blurred reality outside, mixing old and new, rapidly changing every day, reflecting the unpredictability of the future. Earlier that year, Shuang had moved from New York to Shanghai.

GЯΔPΣFRUIT is a homage to and an "update" of Yoko Ono's conceptualist piece *Grapefruit*. Initially released as a publication, *GЯΔPΣFRUIT* comprises digital-age "instructions." Examples include the verse that greets me daily, "fwend's heartbeat piece," as well as others like "listen 2 the sound of ppl around the world / downloading illegally" (listen piece) and "set yr phone on fire / text yr mom wif it" (texting piece). Yoko Ono's seminal work was a commitment to dematerialization in a time when values in society and art were regenerating. Half a century later, facing a new wave of value disintegration, *GЯΔPΣFRUIT* instructs readers to perform a series of virtual acts, responding to our love/hate relationship with media and digital technology. These acts blend humor, sarcasm, and emo sentiments, shifting between self-mockery and self-redemption.

As somehow foreseen by the title of the 2015 exhibition, Shanghai's once-thriving art scene is now teetering, suffering from one of COVID-19's harshest aftereffects: disconnection from the world. And who could have thought that five years after *GЯΔPΣFRUIT* was created, messaging apps would become the primary means to hear a friend's heartbeat, stay updated on their activities, or maintain any kind of relationships? During the pandemic, mobile phones, social networks, and the digital economy were life essentials. The "instructions" in *GЯΔPΣFRUIT* might have offered some solace during the lockdown, serving as a mental survival guide.

After Shanghai, Shuang's work and career became more vibrant. Since 2020, I began to learn about her new projects from exhibition or commission announcements in my email inbox; whereas previously, when we were in New York and Shanghai, we would share and talk about ideas for a new work, even though discussions sometimes ended awkwardly in disagreements. For this essay, I incorporate second-person accounts. Writing about a close friend's work in a direct and personal manner feels natural to me. Additionally, Shuang often uses the second person in her works, directly addressing her audience or creating fictional introspective monologues. She enjoys playing with viewpoints, welcoming juxtaposition, amalgamation, layering, blurring, and fragmenting. I aim to emulate this polyphony of voices and perspectives in my writing here.

JUXTAPOSITIONS
Dear Shuang,

GЯΔPΣFRUIT was created under the pseudonym Yoko Nono, a playful nod to Ono. I share with you a fascination with language games, especially when they involve playing with words across different cultural and linguistic contexts, although we understand that fluency in language across cultures is a privilege.

We once contemplated starting an art duo called Pussy Rice. Another idea was to open an art space in Shanghai called Brooklyn Bagels. It was not technically an art space because no art would ever be exhibited. Around 2016–17, China's digital economy was booming at a breakneck pace, with nearly every aspect of life manageable via a mobile phone. We envisioned transmitting art via food deliveries, with the artworks traveling with orders to unknown audiences. And yes, Brooklyn Bagels would be an actual bagel shop.

T (2017–18) emerged as your artistic response to the explosive digital economy, delving into the then seldom-discussed issue of gender within the e-commerce sector. The main character of the videos is a customer service representative for a Taobao online store, who is required to adopt a cute, girly tone to boost sales of his goods: women's socks. The video presents a collage of images, featuring anime CGI close-ups of a female foot, juxtaposing contemporary fetishization with the ancient Chinese practice of foot-binding. Despite his initial resistance, the somewhat misogynistic protagonist ultimately embraces his virtual gender role. This gender confusion is intensified further by the fact that the male worker's voice is narrated by a female dubber, adding layers of complexity for both the character and the viewer.

After *T*, you made *I Want to Sleep More but by Your Side* (2019). Both videos adopt fiction as a discursive apparatus and feature young Chinese male workers as first-person narrators. *Sleep More* is about an online romance between a middle-aged French woman traveling to China and a young local factory worker. Despite their seemingly unrelated lives, one thing happens to connect their worlds: the yellow vests he manufactures in the factory, which are exported to Europe and become the symbol of a series of protests in France. The video is staged in Yiwu, where you lived for a year, and which hosts the world's largest wholesale market targeting the Global South.

Both works unfold through the inner monologues of their male working-class protagonists, which is a peculiar yet meaningful creative choice. Since China became the "World's Factory" after the 1990s economic reforms and 2001 WTO accession, the identity of Chinese workers is broadly represented; audiences everywhere have seen them in images accompanying sensational "Made in China" news stories. But they are usually nameless and speechless within the spectacle depiction of factories and assembly lines.

However, in the two works, through fiction, these identities suddenly gain a voice. They engage in lengthy introspection, discussing their coming-of-age stories, emotions, and social views, breaking away from the usually alienated and victimized portrayals of Chinese factory workers in mainstream media. These voices are invaluable because men, Chinese people, and workers are not identities typically recognized for their adeptness at self-expression.

The media's reduced representation of factory workers is often linked to polarized views on China's economic growth. The internal narrative of *qiangguo* (strong nation) and the Western "China threat" theory mirror each other, both overshadowing individual voices. Your fictions illustrate how economic globalization impacts Chinese society as a feedback loop of material production and cultural influence.

Your protagonists reflect on that. One mentions growing up playing World of Warcraft and learning about the world through another game, Uncharted Waters—the game that introduced you to wider geographies when you were little. The other recalls seeing images of blonde women in pornographic magazines. These depictions combine your personal experience, gender analysis, and attentiveness to how our desire interacts with global and technological influences. The works transcend traditional gender discourse, drawing on intersectionality to inform social critiques and to seek solidarity, albeit sometimes combined with elements of romanticization.

FROM LANGUAGE GAME TO
UNEVEN GLOBALIZATION
Discussing reality in China is like walking on a tightrope. Censorship from the state and the self has honed artists' knack for subtlety, but has also created a predominantly apolitical industry. Being subtle *and* political is the challenge. It is thus worth sharing some details hidden in the back stories of *T* and *Sleep More* that may be easily overlooked by audiences unfamiliar with the social context. These details demonstrate your keen awareness of labor conditions and biopolitics, set against the dual backdrops of authoritarianism and global neoliberalism.

In *T*, the protagonist's parents experienced the massive layoffs from state-owned enterprises, a historical event and trauma that remains unaddressed and unresolved to this day. Another character's father died in a mining accident, and his mother abandoned him as a child, fleeing from their hopeless rural village. Investigative journalism and sociological research about rural China are filled with tragic stories like these, which are difficult to publish or discuss openly. Fiction thus becomes a conduit for reality. The sacrificed civil rights, particularly of the rural population, represent the hidden costs of China's economic miracle.

In *Sleep More*, the protagonist insinuates resonance with Xu Lizhi, a migrant worker-poet who tragically committed suicide by jumping off a building at the Foxconn factory complex, which is Apple's major manufacturer. The narrative of the video also sheds light on the vast, precarious newer class of delivery workers in so-called post–assembly line China. Although these are not the main storylines in the two works, these hidden plotlines almost form an outline of labor history since the founding of the People's Republic, creating a profound parallel that echoes the mention of the yellow vest movement in France.

Social critique in these works extends beyond the Chinese context. In *T* and *Sleep More*, one protagonist is forced into gender fluidity to meet the demands of cheap emotional labor in the e-commerce world, while the other is exploited to manufacture the protest symbol of a social movement on the other side of the globe. Is a non-binary narrative of gender inherently progressive? Are the yellow vest protesters aware that their visual identity depends on cheap foreign labor? These inquiries emerge from the fictional setups of your work, broadening the discursive scope of international progressive movements, such as the America-led "woke" movement and European leftist positions.

The plots of these two works juxtapose diverse social contexts and underscore the interconnectedness and disparities of our modern economic and social systems. They frame discussions on gender and labor within the uneven networks of globalization and advocate for a more inclusive discourse that integrates both identity politics and economic justice.

In *Sleep More*, there is a poignant scene where the Chinese worker finds out about the yellow vest movement. After another long workday, the young man eats dinner "with one hand holding chopsticks and the other scrolling through protest images online. Despite not understanding or caring about the protests, [he] find[s] a glimmer of hope in these images, seeing the exit of the black hole." This moment, though optimistic in the reality of our deeply fractured world, attempts to tie the destinies of workers worldwide together.

TRANSLUCENCY
You became interested in globalization early in life, prior to studying in the United States. Born in the final phase of socialist-collectivist China, our generation grew up in the early and more rosy stage of economic reforms. Global mass culture flooded into the newly opened-up country like water through a lifted gate, via both formal and informal channels. We're children of pirate and *dakou* tapes, illegally downloaded art movies, knock-off video games, the list goes on. You were fascinated not only by the content of these new things, but also their format and medium, which revealed the undercurrents of globalization's informal networks. That has clearly evolved into the backstories of many of your works.

Later, the influences we received growing up, especially those from the West, would be critically examined during our education in the United States through canonical theories in the humanities such as postmodernism, colonial studies, and globalization critiques. Additionally, the experience of living between two power-competing countries often put us in situations where we found ourselves simultaneously critiquing and defending the same "side," for either side.

Such a background of cultural amalgamation results in your willingness to embrace ambiguity or even self-contradiction, as reflected in your works with layered narrative and open ends. This penchant for juxtaposing faraway contexts and allowing unexpected, meaningful collisions to guide stories recurs as a conceptual approach in your creations. In *Intro to Civil War* (2019), you facilitate a dialogue between ancient Chinese courtesans and an AI sex doll. In *ÆTHER (Poor Objects)* (2021–22), you reference the prototypically feminist goddess Nu Wa, who creates the human species and saves it from a catastrophe, alongside uncanny depictions of female influencers doing mukbang streaming and vlogging, and a solar eclipse that overlaps with a ring light commonly used by social media influencers. This work discusses the ramshackle physicality of our body in today's world.

Coming from a background of media studies, you make art with the brush of our time—the filter. For you, filters are not limited to image tools on-screen but are, rather, a more pervasive reality. Filters are translucent. With them, reality is visible but not 100 percent clear. Throughout the years since *GЯΔPΣFRUIT*, you have tirelessly embodied translucency in your work, both formally and conceptually. Translucency, to you, is a metaphor for our relationship with the world: as human perception and media technology infiltrate each other, reality becomes a slightly blurred or distorted version of itself.

After all, "realism isn't reality," as it says in *ÆTHER (Poor Objects)*, hence your fondness for capturing abstract images of reality or editing reality toward abstraction. This consistently manifests in your art pieces through the materials you feature and techniques you employ: fish-eye lenses, all kinds of reflections, footage taken by a GoPro tied to a duck, resin-cast objects, overlaps, CGI images…

Your take on technology, unlike that of some other artists who explore the virtual and often veer into nihilism, is imbued with sensitivity and warmth. This is because you are particularly concerned with the place of the body, human emotions, and desires within this reality, or quasi-reality. You continuously investigate the ever-evolving relationship between body and screen, as you often grapple with the diminishing yet inescapable presence of your own body.

Lord of the Flies (2022) stages a truly memorable confrontation between you and the physicality of your own body. In this work, you remotely trained twenty performers to act as your avatars. They dressed like you, walked like you, and interacted with your friends as you would. The image of twenty Shuangs appearing together evokes the mythical Monkey King, one of whose numerous

superpowers is to multiply himself by blowing on a strand of his hair, while also recalling modern technologies of cloning or cloud-based data replication. You once again juxtapose the ancient with the sci-fi. More importantly, you finally achieve the paradox of being both absent and omnipresent—the metaphor for our bodily condition in the digital age. Watching this work from afar through social media, I was struck, as your personal styling aesthetics of layering and mix-matching, so familiar to me that I sometimes gave my playful comments, coalesced into a powerful performance blending contemporary surrealism, dystopian imaginations, and post-COVID reflections on self- and mutual care.

ABSENT BODY
In *Lord of the Flies*, your chosen self-representation includes wearing a My Chemical Romance T-shirt, something you often wear in headshots and photos. You take every opportunity to tell the world that you are an MCR fan. In the "adult world," fandom is often associated with adolescence, fervent and immature. You nevertheless have remained loyal and patient with the journey of becoming who you are today. You even made an exhibition about it.

I'm Not, the exhibition at Swiss Institute in New York and Aspen Art Museum in Colorado (2024), feels like a homecoming show for you. It serves as an official homage not only to My Chemical Romance but also to the tumultuous and repetitive process of growing up, which involves constant self-construction and destruction. This process is so universal yet equally unrecognized. The title of the exhibition and the eponymous video piece is taken from MCR's hit "I'm Not Okay (I Promise)," a song you were obsessed with during your teenage years.

You said why you felt such a profound connection with an emo band from afar was because you both shared a desire to escape—escaping boring suburbia for the band members, and escaping a typical, controlling East Asian family environment in a fourth-tier city for yourself. While crediting your scarcely accented English to the emo band, you also stress that language is not important to understand the sentiment of their music.

The exhibition goes beyond the conventional fan–idol dynamic of fan art with its transformative adaptation from "I'm Not Okay" to "I'm Not." *I'm Not* (2024) is the music video of your cover of MCR's original emo anthem. In this piece, a group of androgynous Chinese youth dressed in army uniforms alternates between singing in a choir and crawling dreamily across the floor. The ambivalent and haunting visuals starkly contrast with the music, which is a cheerful and resolute a cappella rendition with lyrics that blend Chinese and English.

The phrase "I'm Not" holds at least three layers of meaning. First, it reflects a dissatisfaction with reality and the comfort and resonance found in distant fantasies, which is the reason MCR's music reverberates so strongly for you. The second and psychoanalytic reading is that, according to you, the absence of the idol's physicality is the foundation of fandom; the idol becomes an endless projection of desire because they are unattainable and unachievable: I'm not who I am a fan of. Lastly, within the negation of "I'm Not," a subtle affirmation emerges; the rewritten lyrics resonate like a manifesto, embodying a collective voice that challenges the stigma surrounding fandom.

With artworks rich in discourse, introspection, and sincerity, the exhibition's portrayal or, rather, reification of fandom is dialectical, offering thoughtfulness and dignity to a typically marginalized identity. Its message is critical yet free from cynicism.

In the video, the same MCR T-shirt you like to wear is pushed from a balcony to the ground below by an unknown hand, possibly symbolizing a step toward personal growth. Speaking of the growth of a fan, the exhibition is accompanied by a heartwarming and inspiring anecdote. During your encounter with one of the band members in New York, you exchanged autographs with him, blurring the line of being a fan and a fellow artist. You redefine fan art and fandom.

FIFTY SHADES OF DESIRE
I'm Not continues your long-term inquiry into mechanisms of desire and how it functions in the world, particularly how it intertwines with sociopolitical structures. This exploration can become really dark but yours is not entirely deconstructive and bleak because your work raises another question: Amid the cracks of mass culture, media, and consumerism, is there any agency, autonomy, or subjectivity left in people's desires? *I'm Not* strives to address this question through both the work and your own experience as a fan.

I'm reminded of the year 2015 again. On Valentine's Day, you made your debut as a professional artist with a performance titled *Marry Me for Chinese Citizenship*. In the work, you navigated the urban maze of Midtown Manhattan wearing a sandwich board marked with the titular sentence. The reactions were diverse: some people appreciated the humor; others laughed at the twist; yet many completely misunderstood the message, responding with scolding, demeaning remarks, and catcalls. This work, too, scrutinizes desire.

Marry Me for Chinese Citizenship again plays with language and displaced cultural contexts, and it highlights the fact that our desires are entangled with consumerism, paradigms of nation-state politics and cultural power imbalances. It is hard to break free. But back to the question at hand: Amid these constructed and problematic desires, do we retain autonomy?

I believe this work has provided an answer. The sentence you carry is an imperative, a command. It is firmly proclaimed to everyone around you, as you boldly throw yourself into the streets. You made yourself a testing ground for desire. The varied responses on the street speak volumes to the dilemmas and precarious status of women and immigrants in society. While our desires tend to project onto absent bodies, your body here is so present that it turns public space into an active place for debate.[2]

I was also there that evening, walking alongside you from a distance and observing the too-typical-to-be-true reactions of passersby. Just as I followed you on the street during that performance, I also aspire to follow your instinct in being true to yourself; remaining loyal to desire while having the courage to dissect it, recognize its impurity and complexity, and bravely throw yourself into the world as an invitation.

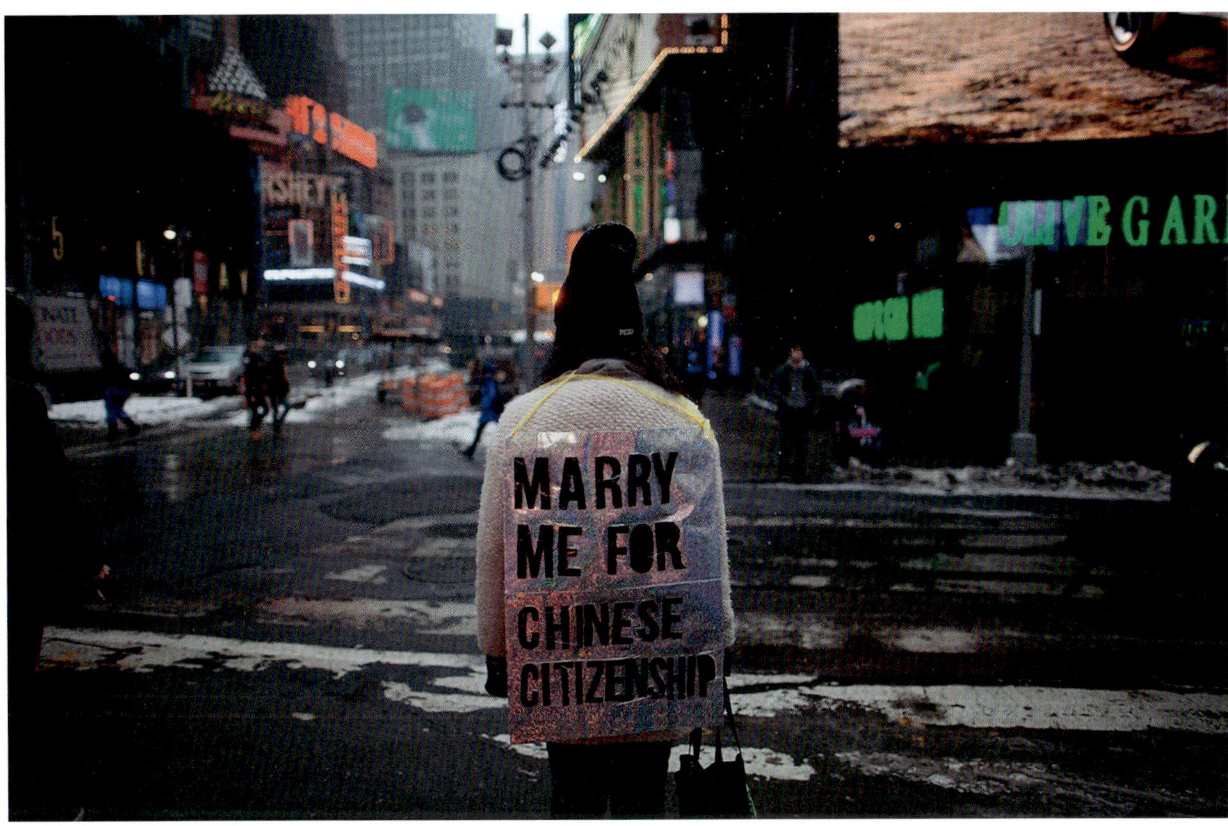

Marry Me for Chinese Citizenship, 2015

Notes

1   The poem is bilingual. In English: open facebook messenger / listen 2 yr fwend's heartbeat thru it. In the Chinese lines, "wechat" replaces "facebook messenger." Shuang and I talk on WeChat.
2   Additionally, this piece has long-lasting reverberations. A mutual NYC friend recently shared that she only dared to start using the "Marry Me for Chinese Citizenship" tote bag (derivative presentation of the performance) again this year because she felt that Asian hate finally began to fade after four years since the beginning of the pandemic.

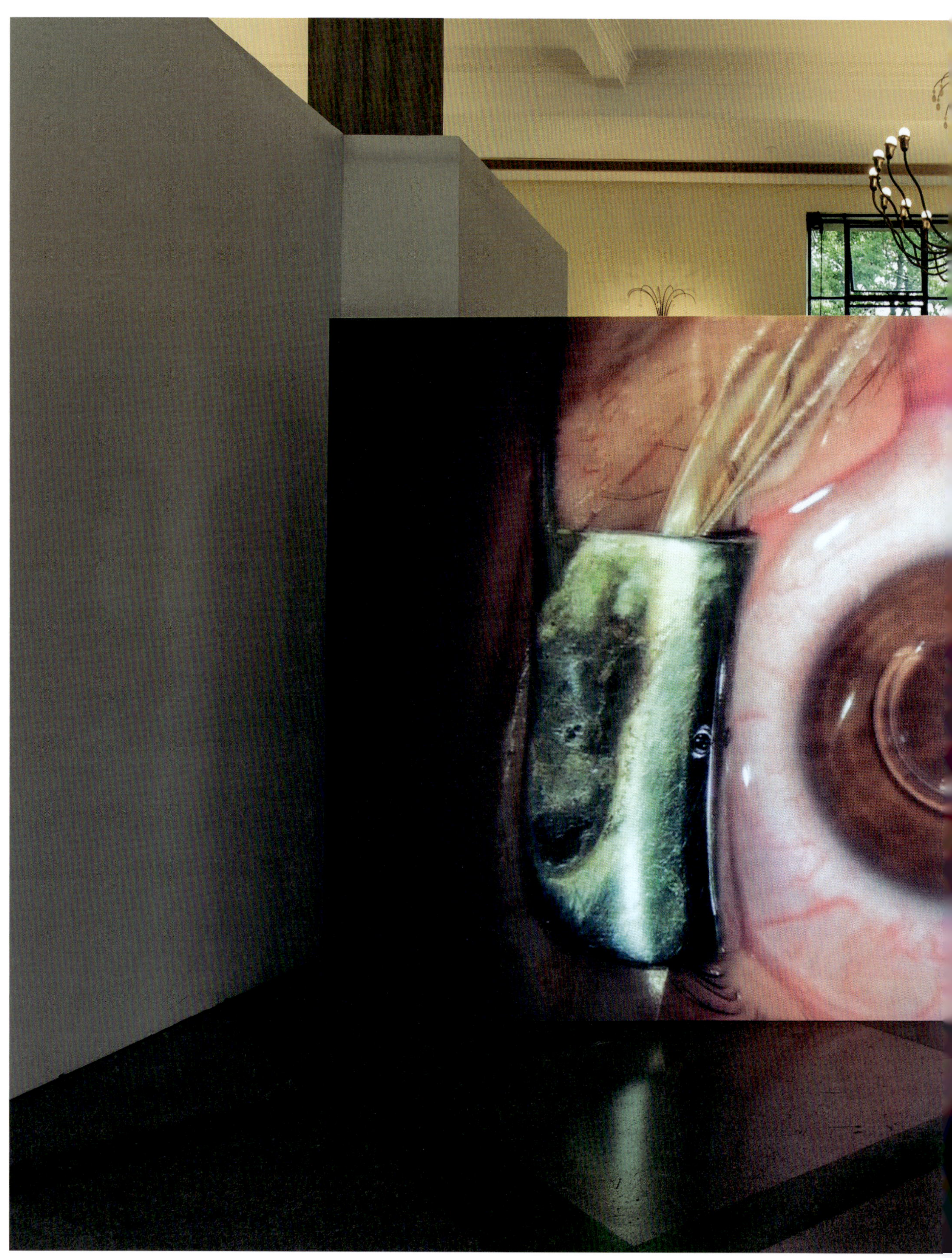

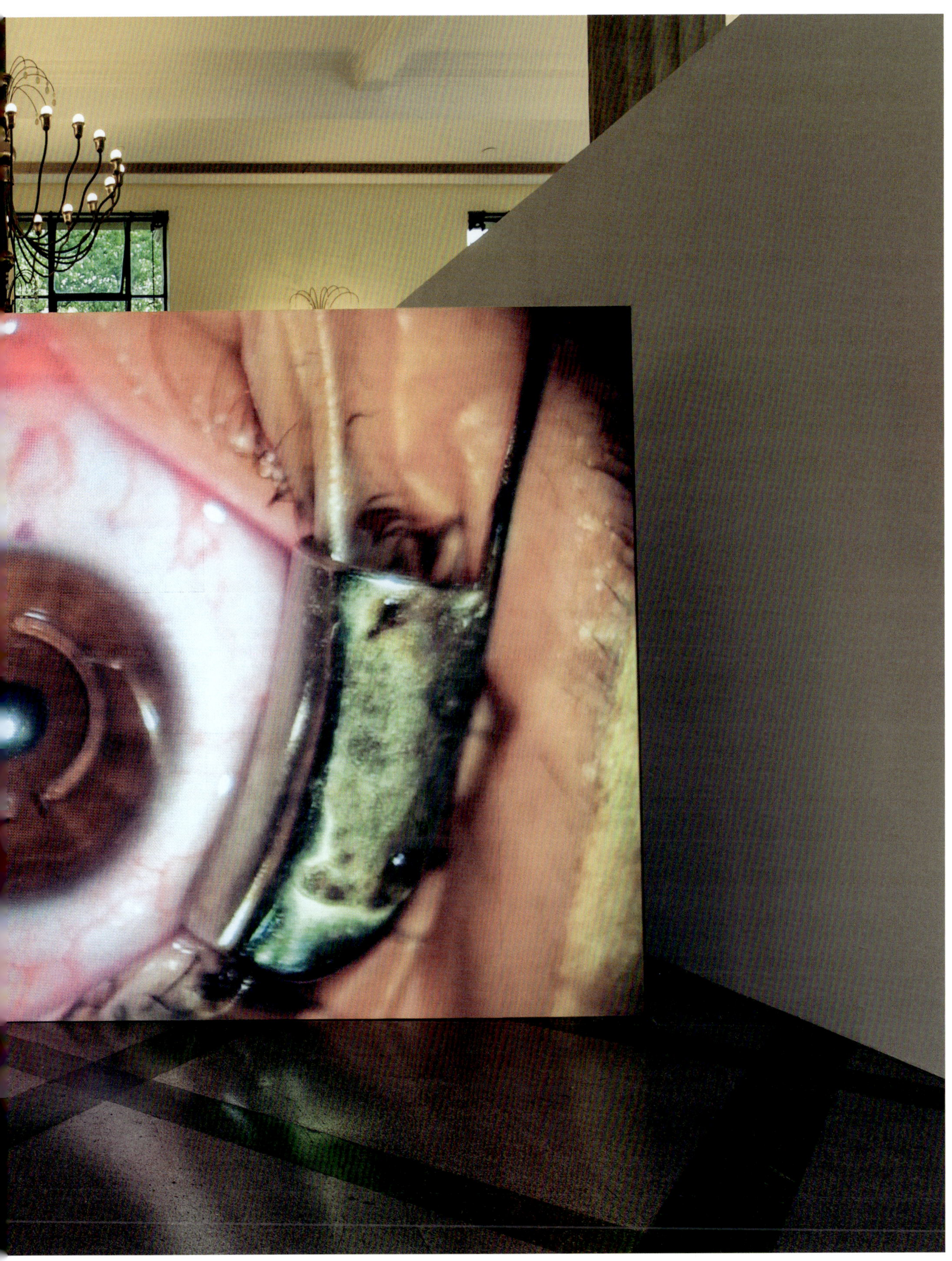

I Wanna Sleep More but by Your Side, 2018–19

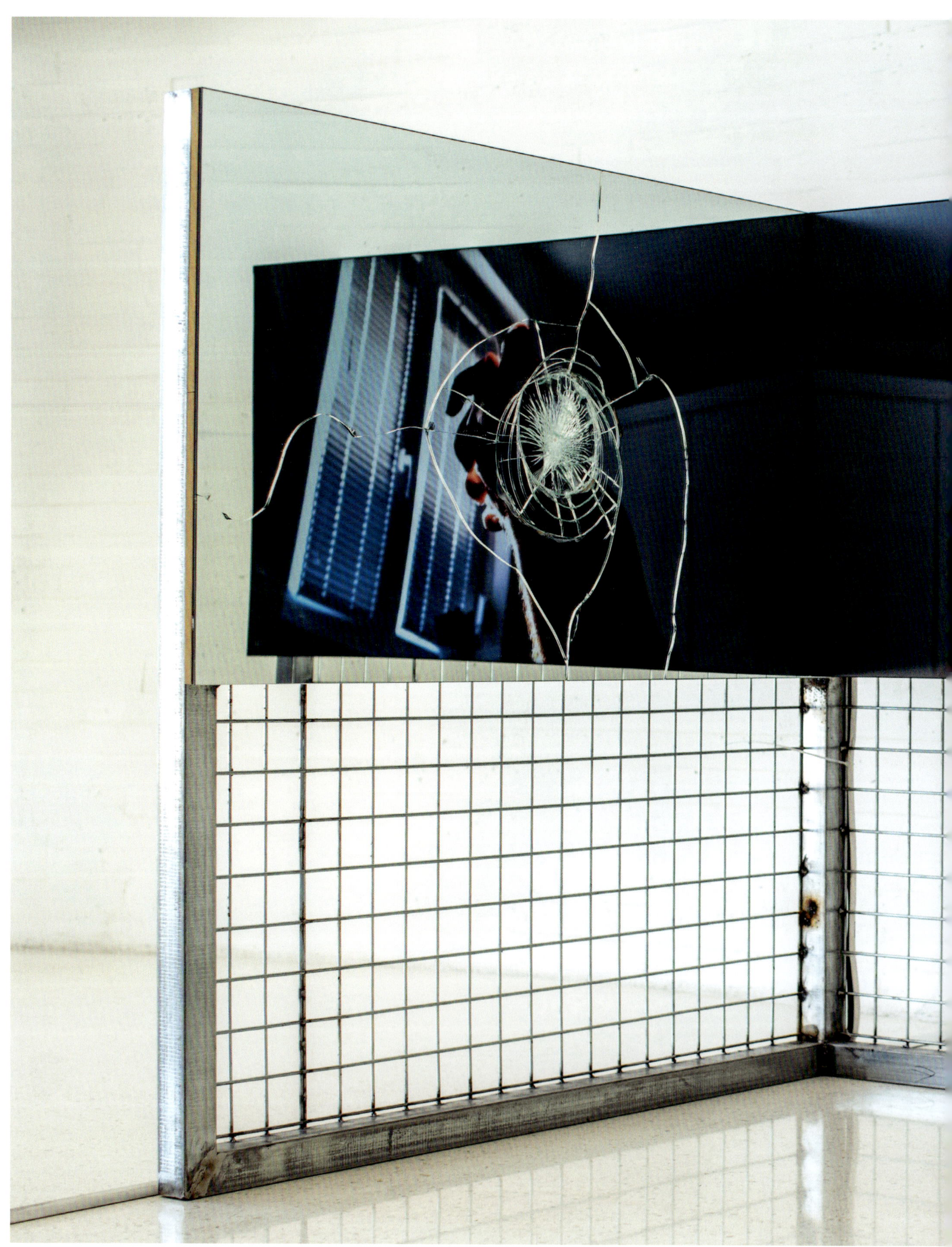

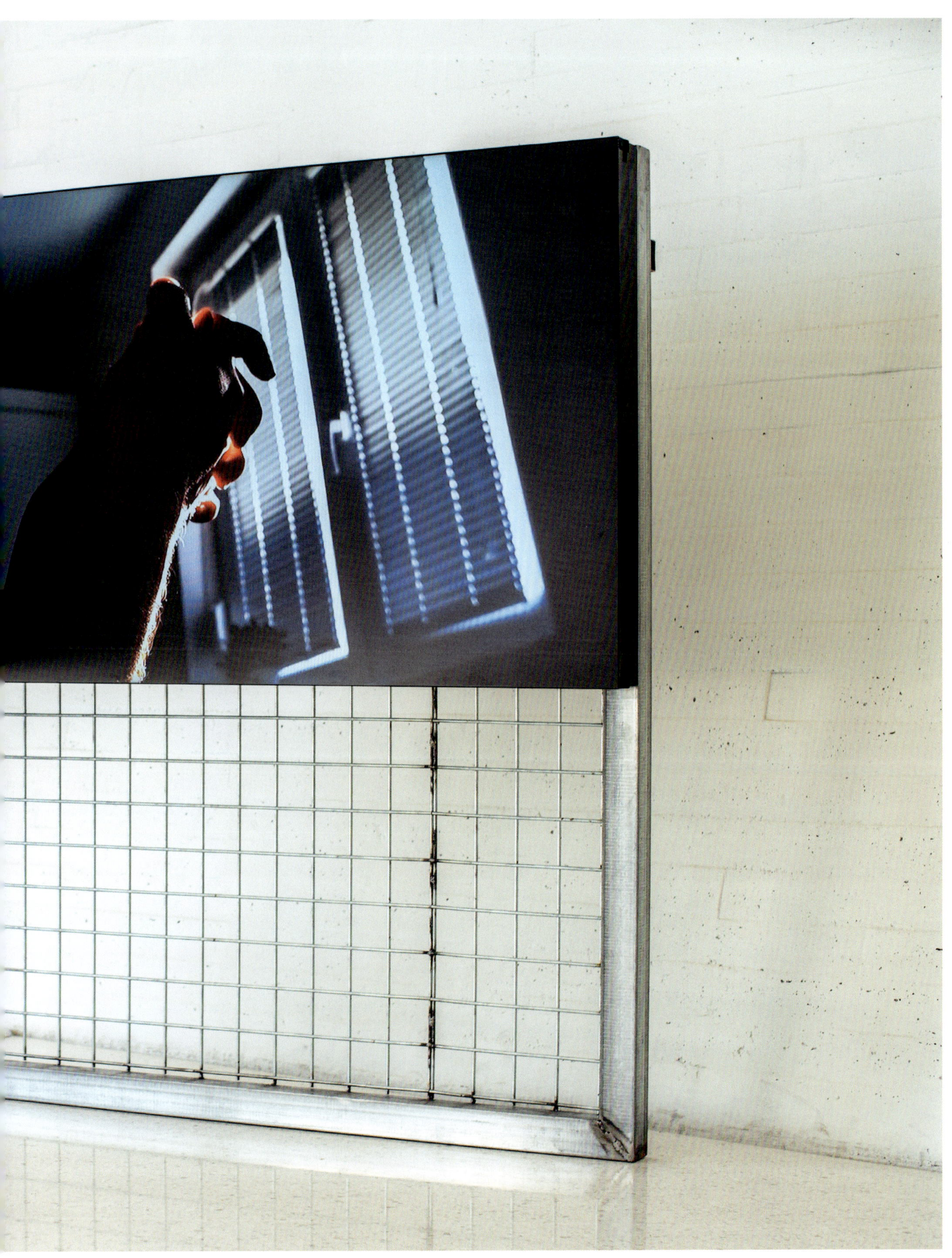

I Wanna Sleep More but by Your Side, 2018–19
Installation view, UCCA Dunes, Aranya, 2020

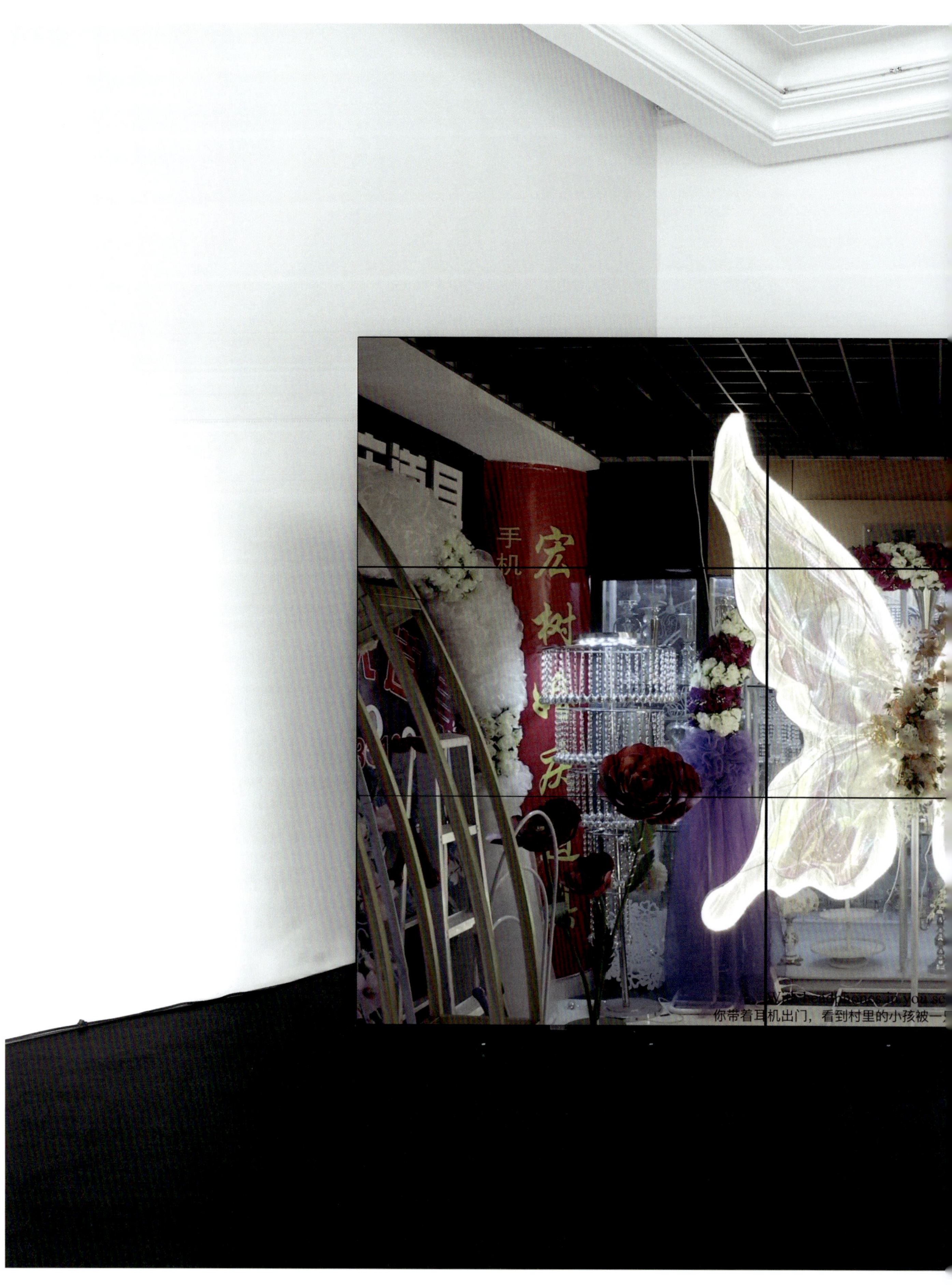
手机
宏树
你带着耳机出门，看到村里的小孩被一只

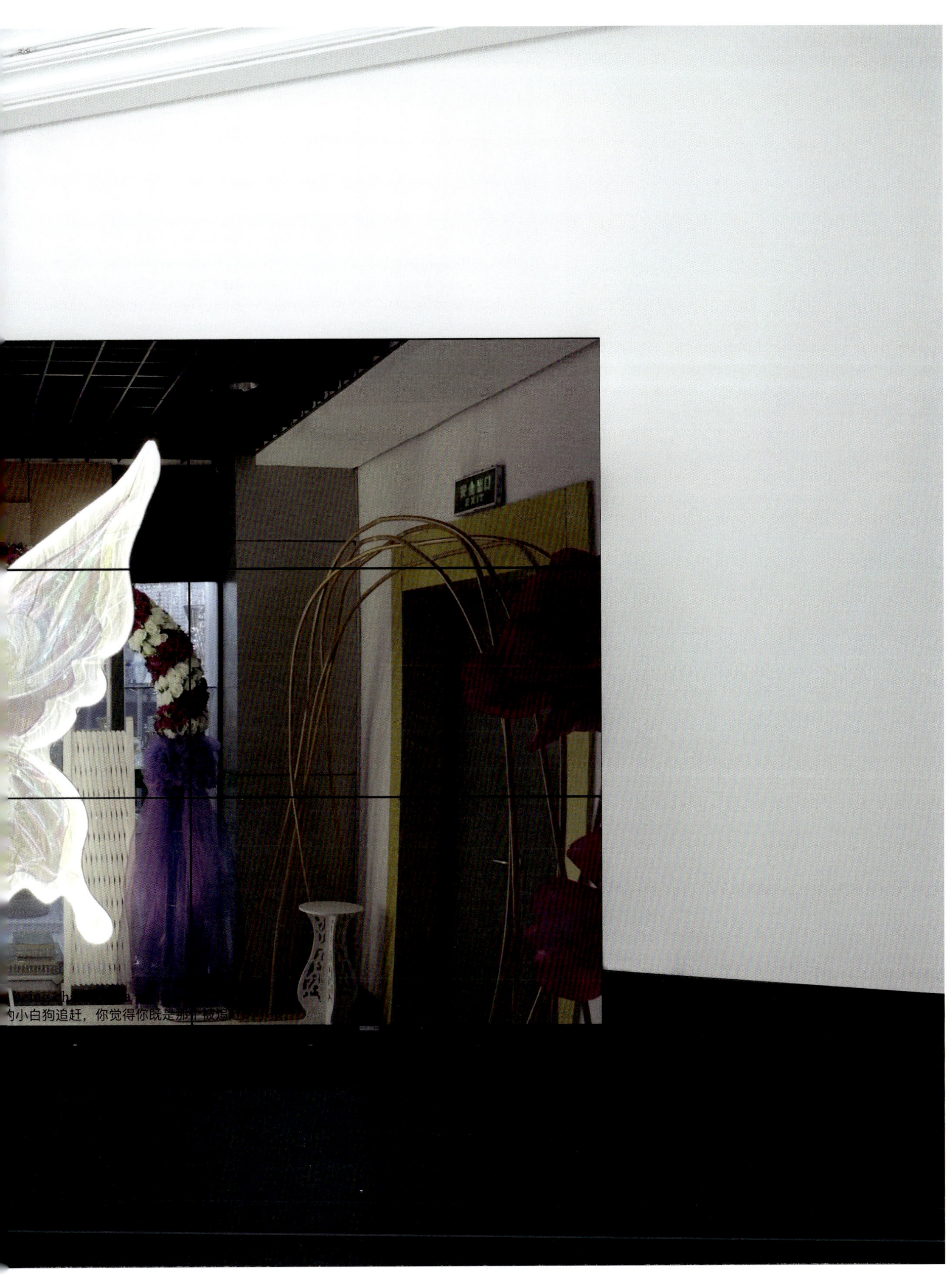

I Wanna Sleep More but by Your Side, 2018–19

"What would it mean for us to be sincere without authenticity
—to be perhaps, more like a bot?"
— Tung-Hui Hu

The internet is an intense place, that is to say, a place of countless intensities—measured not only in the velocity of images and information but in pure affect. To traverse the Web's informational architectures and social networks is guaranteed to produce a range of sensations, some namable as emotion (excitement, fear, desire, ennui) and countless beyond language.[1] These affects are not only virtual but also intensely visceral, corporeal: implicating and pertaining to a body.[2]

"Surfing the Web" is one of those linguistic artifacts of the early internet that wonderfully conjures an image of the virtualized body engulfed in the ecstasy of cybernetic movement, caught in the center of a data centrifuge, its gargantuan whirlpool of images. But with the coming of the smartphone and the "handheld" internet, surfing has largely been replaced by scrolling, which shifts away from a metaphor of the virtualized body and re-centers the physical—flesh-and-blood—body of the internet user, thumbing away on individual screens at a ferocious pace. In this era, terms such as "doom-scrolling" have emerged, which evokes a very different, negative image of internet consumption, one characterized more than anything by a sensation of lethargy, where the wonders of the Web are ambivalently linked to a pervasive sense of ordinariness, boredom, passivity, and disassociation.[3] Here, social media seems to have paradoxically produced new *asocialities*—renewing an old tirade about the waning of affect in postmodern society. On the contrary, others speak of an *excess* of affect, but an affect which may just struggle to find its object or medium in data systems intended primarily for lucrative data-harvesting and surveillance.[4] Yet the internet remains as that circuit where people compulsively go looking for something otherwise absent or missing in their lives, where they go looking for themselves or a self even as many digital platforms produce a perverse sense of denial of this very feeling.[5]

These terminological shifts in the relatively short history of the internet suggest a reconceptualization of the internet user in interconnected technical, corporeal, and affective terms: as Web technologies change, so do our bodily and emotional entanglements with them. Shuang Li is an artist and avid internet user, and her work tracks the aesthetics of these changes—how they unfold across our unevenly connected planet. Born in Wuyishan City in China's Nanping prefecture in 1990, Li belongs to a generation of artists that came of age in the era of Western post-internet art, but she has continued to elaborate its themes beyond the Euro-American discourse that largely produced it. If I insist on this characterization of core Western post-internet art, it is less in terms of historical periodizing or the identities of its protagonists, and more in regard to which internet is in question in post-internet: indeed, in cybernetic theory as much as art history, there is a tendency to falsely approach the internet as a universally open, monolithic, decentralized network. In fact, there is nothing but a multitude of networks, and what Tung-Hui Hu describes as "non-Western internets" continue to birth other post-internet aesthetics through other devices, finding other mythologies and other cultural images to metaphorize the sensation of using them.[6] To put it simply, it all depends on the user: her location, her devices, her predilections, abilities, and affective commitments.

Shuang Li's own technological primal scene is a case in point: China at the turn of the millennium, during the erection of the Great Firewall (防火长城). Here, early users such as Li (then still a child) were free to navigate the still wildly unregulated Web as the Chinese Communist Party developed ways to control it politically, fearing potential influence from outside agents such as the US, or worse, the domestic China Democracy Party, which assembled in the late 1990s in the wake of the Tiananmen Square protests. But the Great Firewall was no overnight feat, and in fact took years to build: Between 1998 and 2008, as more than 40,000 government officials were employed under the instruction of computer scientist Fang Binxing, Chinese users such as Li were free to move around in its open construction site, slowly encountering new scaffoldings, blockades, and sealed perimeters—information obstacles that, in turn, countless countermeasures such as the now ubiquitous VPN[7] would attempt to open. For Li, this period was a thoroughly cyberpunk time of vernacular, glitchy media: a time when using global telecommunication systems inevitably meant subverting them, a cyberculture made up of bootlegs, tenuous torrent downloading, lagging YouTube clips—"poor" images and commodities, in the words of Hito Steyerl.[8] The artist spent her childhood gaming on her knock-off Nintendo or listening to American punk rock and emo music through locally sourced *dakous*: overproduced music discs shipped to China for material repurpose but redirected to black markets and sold to curious consumers, who accepted their variable errors. Each disc would have a hole punched through it to strip it of its value as a commodity, giving it the Chinese name meaning "CD with a hole." These consumer idiosyncrasies, the result of far-reaching transnational trade deals and copyright laws in constant flux, had vast affective implications: *Dakous*, for one, produced a generation of Chinese punk rock fans who transculturally tuned in to the affective sounds of American post-industrialism, making it theirs by recoding its signifiers. For the pubescent Li, the angst of American emo band My Chemical Romance solidified in the urbanizing landscape outside her teenage window, where high-rises sprung from the ground at a fervent pace while others, inexplicably, were marked for demolition. The Chinese real estate bubble (2005–11) profoundly refashioned the brick-and-mortar landscape of the nation, sending millions of middle-class nuclear families such as Li's into an unspoken ritual of weekly real estate showroom visits and frequent moving, frequent shifts between homes that oscillated surreally between render and habitat.

In Li's 2024 exhibition *I'm Not* at Swiss Institute in New York and Aspen Art Museum in Aspen, we meet fragmented mediations of this memory in the shape of a sculptural environment of scaffoldings and screens. The viewer is invited to navigate the ruins of what appears to have once been an architectural model of a housing complex, only now, enlarged to fit the audience. The anonymity of the gallery white cube emphasizes the sitelessness of these haunted and inherently phantasmagorical interiors, but various ephemera offer clues as to whose dream this was. American emo rock ephemera lies engulfed in epoxy floors or ceilings of scaffolding; scattered around the

rooms lie ossified plateau raver boots, a wardrobe turned into stone, relics lost to the obsolescence of history. Shrouded behind one scaffolding structure, a video (*I'm Not*, 2024) plays across a grid of monitors; in it, a Chinese choir dressed in fake PLA army costumes sourced from Taobao performs a cover of My Chemical hit "I'm Not Okay (I Promise)" (2004). Li's choir stand stoically in what appears to be a film studio, but as they begin to sing, the video quickly fades into a reverie of stock-like images of crowded concert venues (MCR's, presumably). Contrary to the fever-paced intensity of the 2004 original, Li's version is somber and wistful in comparison: a melancholic angst pervades the film, as if adding other emotional depths to the emo genre. *Remember when we were there, together?* the media seems to ask, uncertainly: the only proof we have are blurry JPEGs of crowds that look like countless others. In Li's adolescent reverie, material atmospheres of collective affects fuse and flux across dispersed rooms, devices, and countless geographies. Here, physicality is a mere signifier that can be forever negotiated by image cultures in circulation: to "have been there" is a state of mind rather than an event.

For if the Chinese real estate bubble of the new millennium produced a sense of placelessness, this would only be amplified through Li's media consumption. Background imagery in video games such as Grand Theft Auto offered access to semi-fictional rendered environments, mash-ups of historical areas and cultural geographies from far-flung places, game spaces transporting users to generalized "New Yorks" or "Los Angeleses" and asking them to embody it for hours on end. Li, for one, was on board, thrust into the virtual by an acute desire to "escape … [her] immediate surroundings but also … [her] own body"[9]—a media trope that, for all its geographical site-specificity, is close to universal. In retrospect, the artist understands these media journeys as when she "got to see the world for the first time. Of course, it was a highly mediated one, but no less mediated than how life is today."[10]

Li is right, for when scholars popularly pinpoint movement as the central characteristic of modernity, they mean of both persons and information, and across material and data networks. This is an epistemological challenge to a swath of concepts (place, migration, travel, communication, relationality) because their definitions have historically assumed a material concreteness that has since been revealed by cybernetic theory as only ever partial, enmeshed in a number of virtualities. This not only pertains to the computer user sitting by her device, "linked up" to the network: as Zygmunt Bauman argued already in 1998, the screen joins other structures such as the airport, the shopping mall, the freeway, the tourist precinct, the theme park, the resort, and the modern city itself as "expressions and outcomes of this effect of cultural globalization"[11]—namely, a sense of interlinked homogeneity and smoothness. Yet Li's work reminds us that this process never actually delivers what it promises: the artist negotiates the virtual accessibility of concrete distances, of heavy space felt by the lightness of instant media (or vice versa) through the prism of affect. Li's work is filled with stock imagery, ripped YouTube clips, and digital renderings of phantasmagoric intensity—but also webcams, ring lights, discarded CD players, and unmade beds that call upon that ubiquitous material environment of the individual internet user, the fleshy cyber-I that exists in a fantastic virtuality all the same. Digital content (still) circulates fueled by the affective response of human users, who, as a result, exist in complex states of bodiliness in far-flung corners of the universe, between flesh and data.[12]

It was appropriately upon arrival in New York—the carbon-based version—that Li turned her Web usership to the medium of art. She cites an exhibition by artist Sophia Al Maria, another thinker of digital globalization's heterogenous aesthetics, as a key moment of inspiration and awakening. Li shares Al Maria's curiosity for digital networks, of which she should be considered an archeologist as well as an auto-ethnographer, propelling a variety of digital personas on journeys, into systems—systems that are so informationally immense that they are only palpable in/as affect.

In *I Want to Sleep More but by Your Side* (2018–19), Li charts the vastness of such journeying, following a single commodity, a neon traffic vest, manufactured in Yiwu, a city in the Zhejiang province of China. The film recounts the story of the vest from the physical manufacturing infrastructures, wholesale retail enterprises, and logistics systems that realize the ubiquitous vest and transport it into global circulation, traveling all the way to consumerist end points, where it becomes available as a material signifier—in this case, as a symbol of the *gilets jaunes* social movement in France, which began in 2018 as a series of populist demonstrations against an unprecedented cost-of-living crisis. In the film, Li weaves together images of China's industrial infrastructures but overlays a fictional online dialogue between a French mother and a young Chinese factory worker, an unlikely epistolary coupling considering their vast distance both in terms of geography and social reality. Here, one individual labors away manufacturing vests for the other individual's labor protest—a bizarre but completely conventional motif of global consumerism, if you really think about it. Li's fiction surveys human desire and relationality at all scales, across psycho-geographies and systems topographies (material–virtual–bodily–social) while disjointed sounds and images flicker in front of us with poetic effect. This cinematic layering, inspired by Surrealist and Expressionist cinema, points to the disjointed nature of human affect itself in the network, a network that always fractures but never fully disconnects. As Travis Jeppesen has written about the work's two characters, "likely never to meet in person, and further distanced by their inability to speak the same language, they nevertheless partake in a strange communion, brought together via abstract and disembodied flows of global capitalism."[13]

Li's practice attunes us to the scalability of affect, its inherently networked nature, connecting the vastest with the most intimate. Consider *If Only the Cloud Knows* (2005–18), finished in the same period as *I Want to Sleep*, constituting a kind of sister work. Reflecting upon the ubiquity of electronic storage (e.g., cellphones, hard drives, cloud storage) and its influence on human memory, Li uploaded all of her electronic photographs and text messages produced from 2005 to 2015—between the ages of fifteen and twenty-five—to the peer-building Web platform builder commandx.kim and proceeded to remove all backup storage. Visitors to the artwork were given not only total access to the data of Li's private life but, effectively, the freedom to delete it—that is, if they agreed to leave a message in its stead. During the active phase of the artwork, a few clicks on numerated lists would expose anything from text messages about coffee plans to low-res holiday photos, diary entries, and food orders. Slowly, Li's data biography was literally overwritten—with new writing, from the network, producing a social architecture of writing, a *digiarchitext* of sorts.[14] The archive of the project, which remains online, is characterized by entire sections left empty by user-driven erasure, a playable metaphor of wetware amnesia and entropy in the age of the digital, where prosthetic memory is revealed as enormously fragile thanks to perpetual software updates and hardware malfunction. In fact, this became apparent at the beginning of the work's active life, when it was intermittently hosted on another URL, which the artist forgot to pay, causing its reentrance to the market. Consequently, for a while, people who clicked on the link would end up on a porn site. Here, Li's heroic act of feminist self-exposure (evoking historical performance art pieces by Yoko Ono and Marina Abramović) is lost in the internet's immense data soup, which, despite massive surveillance infrastructures, (still) offers other kinds of agency, namely the privilege of hiding or partial disappearance via fragmentation. Or as the artist offers in a poetic prelude to the piece published on the site, even after total exposure, after a full leak:

YOU STILL WOULDN'T KNOW ANYTHING ABOUT
  ME
FOR HEART IS NOT A METAPHOR
NEITHER IS CLOUD.

This short verse points to how the fleetingness of feeling (intimacy, safety, secrecy) mirrors the fleetingness of data. Inversely, Li appreciates the key fact that the banality and intimacy of personal digital experience nonetheless offers entryways into the unfathomably systemic and networked— that bewildered place where individuality disintegrates and multiplicity spawns through feedback loops, glitches, duplicates, and copies. For as Hu writes, under digital capitalism, "being yourself" is the absolutely dominant moral and technological regime, in which user accounts are equated with personhood, choice with agency.[15] Indeed, much of Li's work departs from the position of the individuated user who, confined to their rooms alone with their devices, experiences the angst of virality along with the fleshiness of usership: an oscillating

identity position where singularity and multiplicity exist in constant negotiation. Who, after all, can be sure where the/one's/a "body" is when watching POV concert videos on YouTube; or cat videos, or gameplay, or video art, for that matter? Is there not a sense of embodiment at work here? But while the authenticity of physical location goes flimsy, the unmistakable reality of affect retains its evident power (not least when measured in circulation of data). Hu asks us directly: "What would it mean for us to be sincere without authenticity—to be perhaps, more like a bot?"

Li explores this lacuna of corporeal uncertainty in a string of works realized during COVID-19, when the artist—who, at the time, was living in Yiwu—got stuck in Europe, where she had traveled to install an exhibition. Left to fend for herself in a continent to which she had only tenuous connections, Shuang drifted between Switzerland and Berlin, between couches and sublets of friends and acquaintances, for several years. The experience resulted in work that thematizes placelessness and homesickness as registered in/as media consumption—hers, others, and those strange in-betweens. In *How Come an Image* (2022), the artist goes looking for herself in the doom scroll to cope with homesickness, while *Among Us* (2021) uses the eponymous space-themed online multiplayer video game (which surged in popularity during lockdown) to revisit the social and reproductive politics that marked her childhood (the Chinese one-child policy). *Exit Wound* (2020), in turn, experiments prosaically with media recording and projecting in the artist's new physical environments, examining how the fleshy body relates and reacts to such environments through devices and screens.

For the internet user Shuang Li, the dispersion of the self is always impending in consumption and immersion, and is, in fact, an inevitable and even joyful part of the internet experience. *Lord of the Flies* was an instruction-based performance staged at the Shanghai gallery Antenna Space in 2022. During the opening of a group show that Li was included in but (still) not able to physically attend, she sent twenty doublegangers in her stead, dressed in her distinctive usual attire: ponytail and blunt-cut fringe, a My Chemical Romance T-shirt over a white shirt, a black blazer, tartan skirt, black boots, legwarmers, and a silver

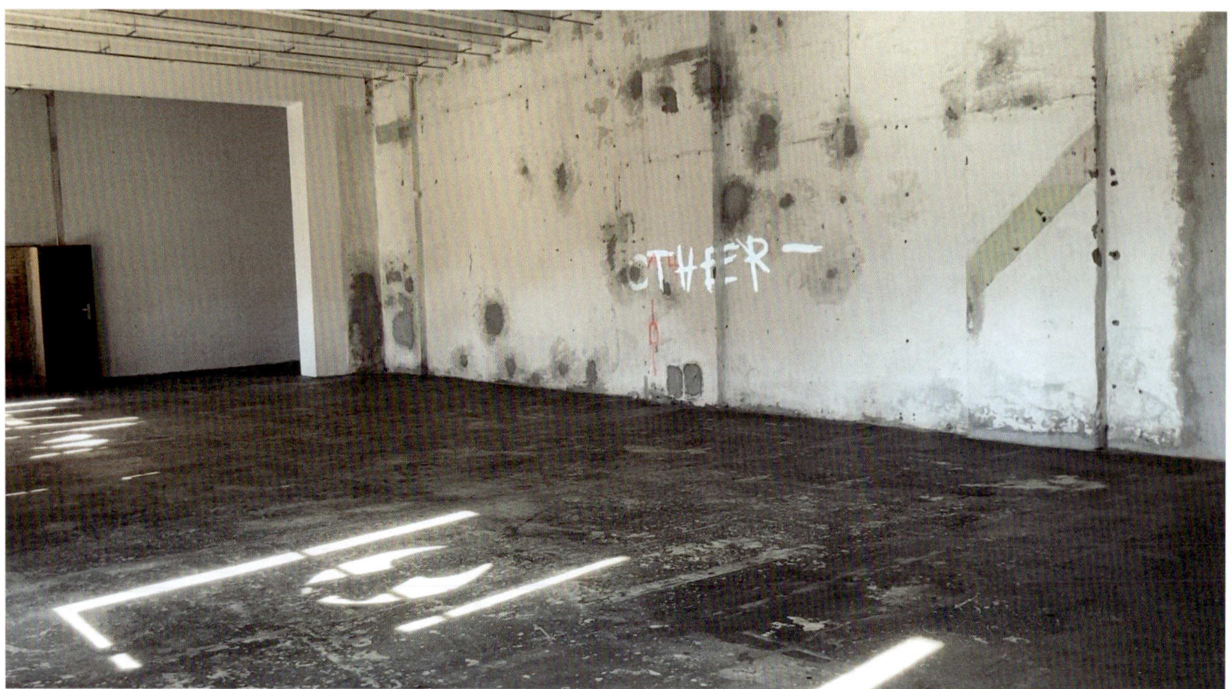

Exit Wound, 2020
Installation view, Callie's, Berlin, 2020

backpack. Li had instructed these local performers remotely, training them to interact with gallery visitors using pre-drafted scripts. She also trained them to identify particular friends in the crowd, who they would approach, address by name, hug, and proceed to read personal letters that she had drafted, concluding with an official goodbye on behalf of the artist.

Formally, Li's army of me most immediately recalls Italian artist Vanessa Beecroft's notorious performances from the 1990s, where groups of identically styled women stand silent and immobile for hours on end, producing a styled live tableau vivant reminiscent of a photo shoot or a doll factory. At the time, Beecroft explained these works as variously dealing with her own identity, with her childhood, and with her sexuality. Similarly engaged in forms of self-duplication, if not actually self-portraiture, Beecroft's displays, Christine Ross writes, "disclose the contemporary subject as an individual preoccupied with identity, with both the erasure of self and the related need to continuously re-create the self through processes of idealized identifications."[16] But whereas Beecroft's performances duplicate the independent self as a kind of narcissistic self-absorption, ultimately seeking to *disengage* the other, Li's is distinctly communicative and social, with doppelgängers employed as postal tools of affective messaging, comparable to an email or WeChat call. Under the site-specificity that was the COVID-19 pandemic, Li's performance showed deep appreciation of the power of fleshy bodies in the relaying of love and tenderness for one's friends in an age of forced distance, but it also questioned the need for an originary body (namely, Li's own) to be engaged in such relay. Beecroft's women are idealized spectacles—silent, noninteractive, expressionless—while Li's are on a mission, live proxies for emails and phone calls that themselves are proxies for Li's own presence, which she attempted to spread across the network navigated by nothing less than love. So what is the status of these human proxies? Are they but fleshy bots, coded by an author in the network? Does that diminish their affective intensity? When the artist's doppelgängers reappear in the 2022 *Déjà Vu* (which also serves as the documentation of the original *Lord of the Flies* performance), it is as a confused mob in the streets, anxiously crowding together like a school of fish. At one point, the camera catches the sunglasses-clad gaze of one particular figure and slowly begins to zoom in on her face; the group reacts to this gaze, and robotically begins to circle around her. This proxy is clearly unique yet indistinct from her multiplications; it is "her" yet not Shuang Li herself (we think). Poetic subtitling offers an illuminating paratext:

It All Started
With Characters Forming a Word
Becoming Interchangeable
Then Words Become Interchangeable Too
As a Result All the Objects
Are Interchangeable at this Point

Is a person more than a word, a stable sign? As the film progresses, Li's doubles disperse from their source and begin to live increasingly individual lives, all documented by the cameras hidden in their spy sunglasses that capture encounters and conversations with gallerygoers as well as with each other. This constant multiplication of motifs produces a visual swarm-like effect of being totally surrounded. Here, Shuang Li is nowhere to be found yet everywhere to be seen—spread out in a network like a virus, or a meme. It is by spreading out, cybernetic theorist Erica Scourti writes, that "the specific and generic, singular and multiple are always hopelessly confused—but … this might be a productive site of possibility."[17] Hu picks up on this idea and uses it to contemplate different models of subjectivity offered by the digital, those that see "identity [emerge] as much from the network and infrastructure that we inhabit and are entangled with, as [they do] from any sense of a coherent interior essence."[18] If the individuated mode of the Web produces lethargy, we should work to spread out across the mass of data in the digital environment, leaving behind a topographic model of the self as a private interior that should be protected from mass culture (perhaps by camouflage or by disguising oneself within the crowd). It is, Hu writes, resonant of philosopher Édouard Glissant's call for when "one consents not to be a single being and attempts to be many beings at the same time:"[19] "If one sets aside the insistence on the uniqueness of the individual, collectivity would be no longer tied to an idealized form of network publicity that would rely on the mutual exchange of individual interests but rather something more lethargic."[20]

Affect is the central nexus for these revolutionary modifications of the digital because affect relies on and is nourished not by bodies but by connectivity. Affect, we learn, is an inherently subjective force, wherein individual humans—users—appear as "envelopes of possibility" for deeper affective flows. Media amplifies affect, and affect is highly contagious, producing positive feedback loops across vast geographies and across systems.[21] And thus we arrive at Li's most recent topic of exploration, fan culture, which culminates in the before-mentioned *I'm Not*. Since *Lord of the Flies*, which indirectly became a homage to the self-styled (and globally ubiquitous) My Chemical

Romance fan, Li has explored how global fandom produces models of affective togetherness across the "long voids of the internet," to paraphrase Kris Cohen, author of the seminal book on digital group dynamics, *Never Alone, Except for Now*.[22]

In assemblages such as those found in the *I'm Not* installation, Li layers fan letters, posters, friendship bracelets, and other fan ephemera in a transparent resin, producing a gooey surface of signifiers that could be taken from any MCR fan anywhere in the world—in New Jersey, Poland, or Tokyo. Li knows this, for it was the American emo genre that first thrust the artist into the world, a fleeting transfiguration of the genre's suburban escapism to the distant locale of Wuyishan City. Fandom taught her English, taught her love, taught her pain: it trained her affective capacities. This is evident in the retrofitted lyrics in *I'm Not*, which, in a casual mix of English and Mandarin, journey its listener far away from American suburbia, into an abstract plane of Shanzhai poetics:

I'm Not the Earth – I'm Not Autumn – I'm Not a Metaphor – Everything Must Go – Until the Blood Went Cold – I Cannot Tell You the Definition of Romantics – In a Time Like This

Which social contexts once gave these fragments meaning? Which bodies uttered these words, and how did they end up here? Fandom points to the difficult but important truth that there is a huge affective pull or relief to being in a mass, because a mass, as Tiziana Terranova argues, "is by definition asocial (rather than antisocial); it is a group of people who simply figure as intensities of feeling."[23] This also applies in the realm of the digital, where user individuality is constantly leveled by a feeling of immersion into the diversity and vastness of the Web population. The digital mass alleviates us from the prison of individuality, if only for the duration of a YouTube clip: it offers a chance to sing the same song, even if the lyric is a little different. Shuang Li's work attunes us to the deep affects that are found within the networks we call home; the wonky translations, half fractured, dispersed, mutated—but never inauthentic or insincere.

Notes

1   J. MacGregor Wise, "Community, Affect, and the Virtual: The Politics of Cyberspace," in *Virtual Publics: Policy and Community in an Electronic Age*, ed. Beth E. Kolko (New York: Columbia University Press, 2003), 120.

2   "Affect identifies the strength of the investment which anchors people in particular experiences, practices, identities, meanings and pleasures but it also determines how invigorated people feel at any moment of their lives, their level of energy or passion." Wise, "Community, Affect, and the Virtual," 119.

3   Tung-Hui Hu, *Digital Lethargy: Dispatches from an Age of Disconnection* (Cambridge, MA: MIT Press, 2022), xxi.

4   For, as Fredric Jameson has argued, apart from the destruction of the grand narratives (and with them ideology), one of the hallmarks of the postmodern era is the waning of affect. Brian Massumi writes of an excess of affect in society. See Fredric Jameson, *Postmodernism, or, the Cultural Logic of Late Capitalism* (Durham, NC: Duke University Press, 1991), and Brian Massumi, "The Autonomy of Affect," *Cultural Critique*, no. 31 (1995): 83–109.

5   On digital lethargy, Hu writes: "There's a recalcitrant set of feelings here—of being passive, or wanting to disassociate and be anyone but yourself, or avoiding decisions—that I call digital lethargy. Because they go against the sense of agency and liveness that digital platforms produce, and against the permission they tout for users to simply be themselves, these feelings can seem perverse, or even self-defeating." Hu, *Digital Lethargy*, vii.

6   Hu, *Digital Lethargy*, 7. I want to propose a more complicated theory of post-internet vis-à-vis the variety of global internet infrastructures, which, importantly, are not virtual but intensely physical, as Li's work indeed so beautifully alerts us to. See, for example, her 2022 fashion show installation for Miu Miu, on the history of oceanic internet cables.

7   As historian James Griffith recounts, by the early 2010s, the Great Chinese Firewall—once "little more than a glorified porn filter"—had evolved into "the most sophisticated system of online censorship in the world," thrusting hundreds of millions of users into "another" internet. James Griffiths, *The Great Firewall of China: How to Build and Control an Alternative Version of the Internet* (London: Zed Books, 2019), 7.

8   Hito Steyerl, "In Defense of the Poor Image," *e-flux Journal*, no. 10, November 2009, https://www.e-flux.com/journal/10/61362/in-defense-of-the-poor-image/.

9   Alex Greenberger, "Artist Shuang Li Embraces Digital Technology's 'Wrinkles' to Combat Corporeal Alienation," *Art in America*, June 13, 2023, https://www.artnews.com/art-in-america/features/shuang-li-art-venice-biennale-interview-1234671107/.

10   Shuang Li, interview with the author, December 2023.

11   See Zygmunt Bauman, "On Glocalization: or Globalization for some, Localization for some Others," *Thesis Eleven* 54, no. 1 (1998): 37–49. For a discussion of Bauman, see David Holmes, introduction to *Virtual Globalization: Virtual Spaces/Tourist Spaces*, ed. David Holmes (London: Routledge, 2001), 4.

12   On this topic, see Jeppe Ugelvig, "The Digiarchitextual Body – or: *Brandon*'s Corporeal Virtualities," *Parallax* 25, no. 2 (2019): 155–73.

13   Travis Jeppesen, "Openings: Shuang Li," *Artforum* 60, no. 1 (September 2021): https://www.artforum.com/features/travis-jeppesen-on-shuang-li-250453/.

14   See Ugelvig, "The Digiarchitextual Body."

15   Hu, *Digital Lethargy*, viii.

16   Christine Ross, *The Aesthetics of Disengagement: Contemporary Art and Depression* (Minneapolis: University of Minnesota Press, 2006), 52.

17   Erica Scourti, "Expose and Repurpose: Opposing Self-Commodification," Haus der Kulturen der Welt, Berlin, January 30, 2015, YouTube video, 20:44, https://youtu.be/sYPd-CTwrzA?si=On4Xjs7Ewn71zMgD.

18   Hu, *Digital Lethargy*, 127.

19   Édouard Glissant, "One World in Relation: Édouard Glissant in Conversation with Manthia Diawara," *Nka* 2011, no. 28 (Spring 2011): 5.

20   Hu, *Digital Lethargy*, 127–28.

21   See Anna Gibbs, "Affect Theory and Audience," in *The Handbook of Media Audiences*, ed. Virginia Nightingale (Oxford: Wiley-Blackwell, 2011), 251–66.

22   Kris Cohen, *Never Alone, Except for Now: Art, Networks, Populations* (Durham, NC: Duke University Press, 2017).

23   Tiziana Terranova, *Network Culture: Politics for the Information Age* (London: Pluto, 2004), 138.

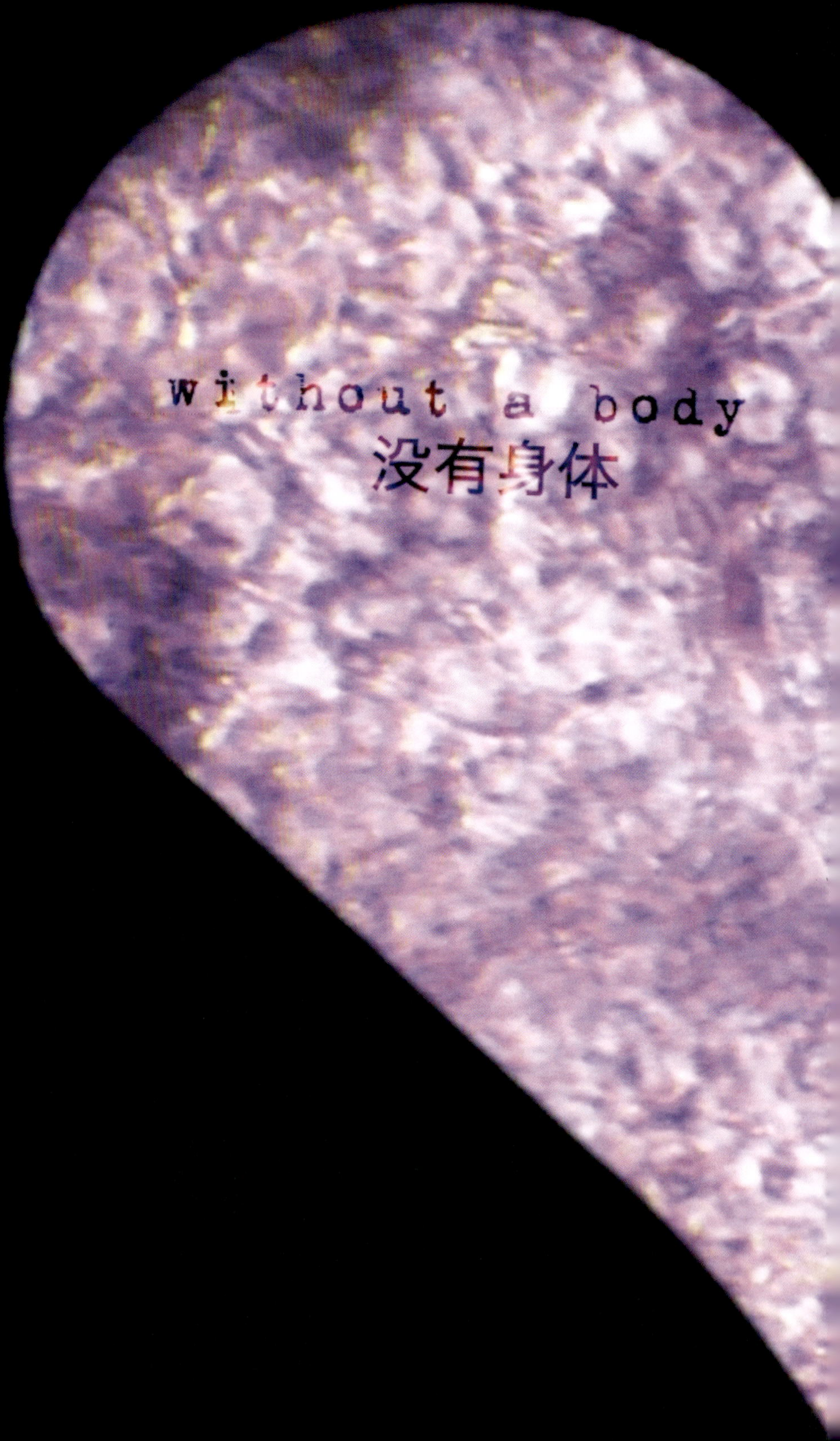

without a body
没有身体

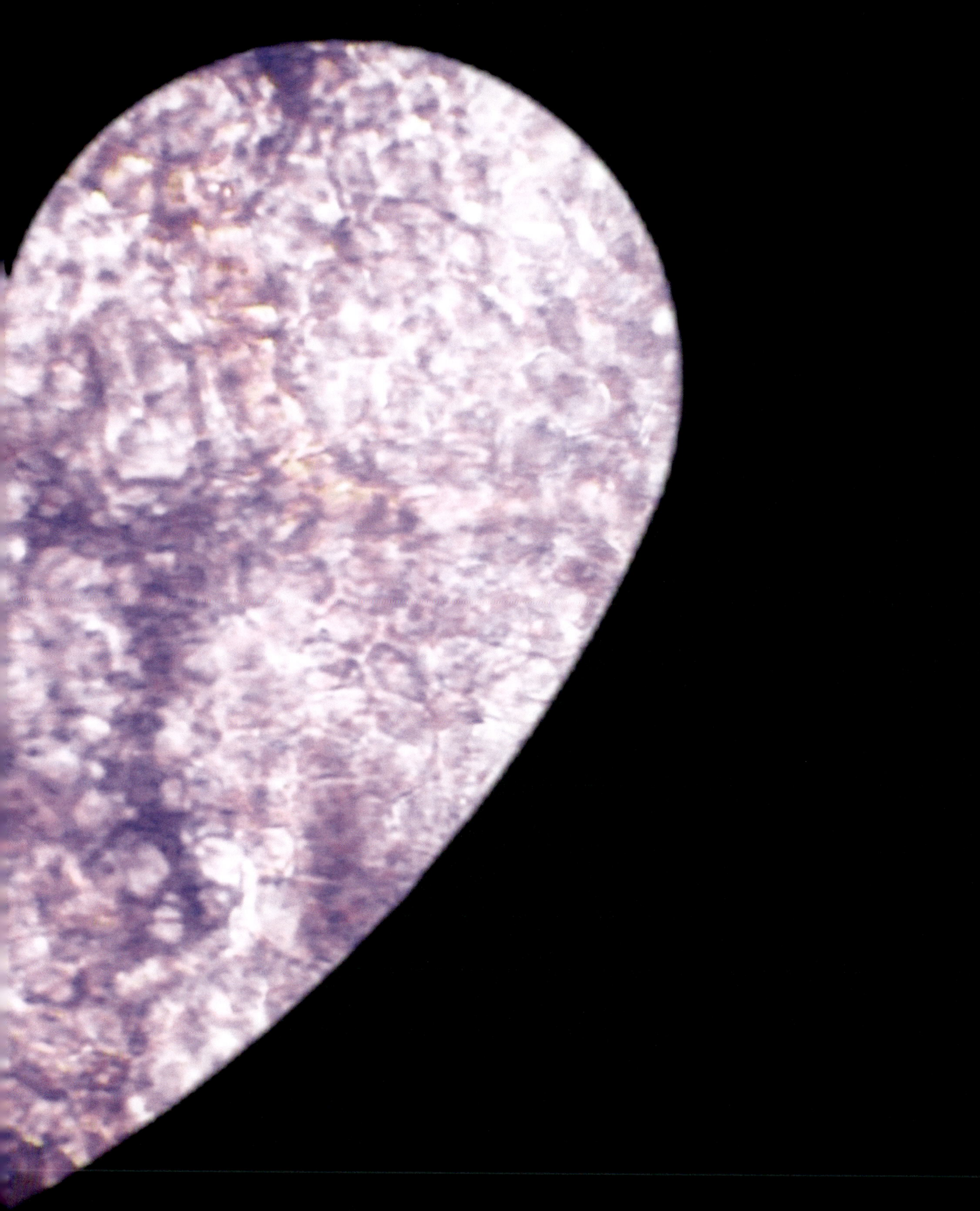

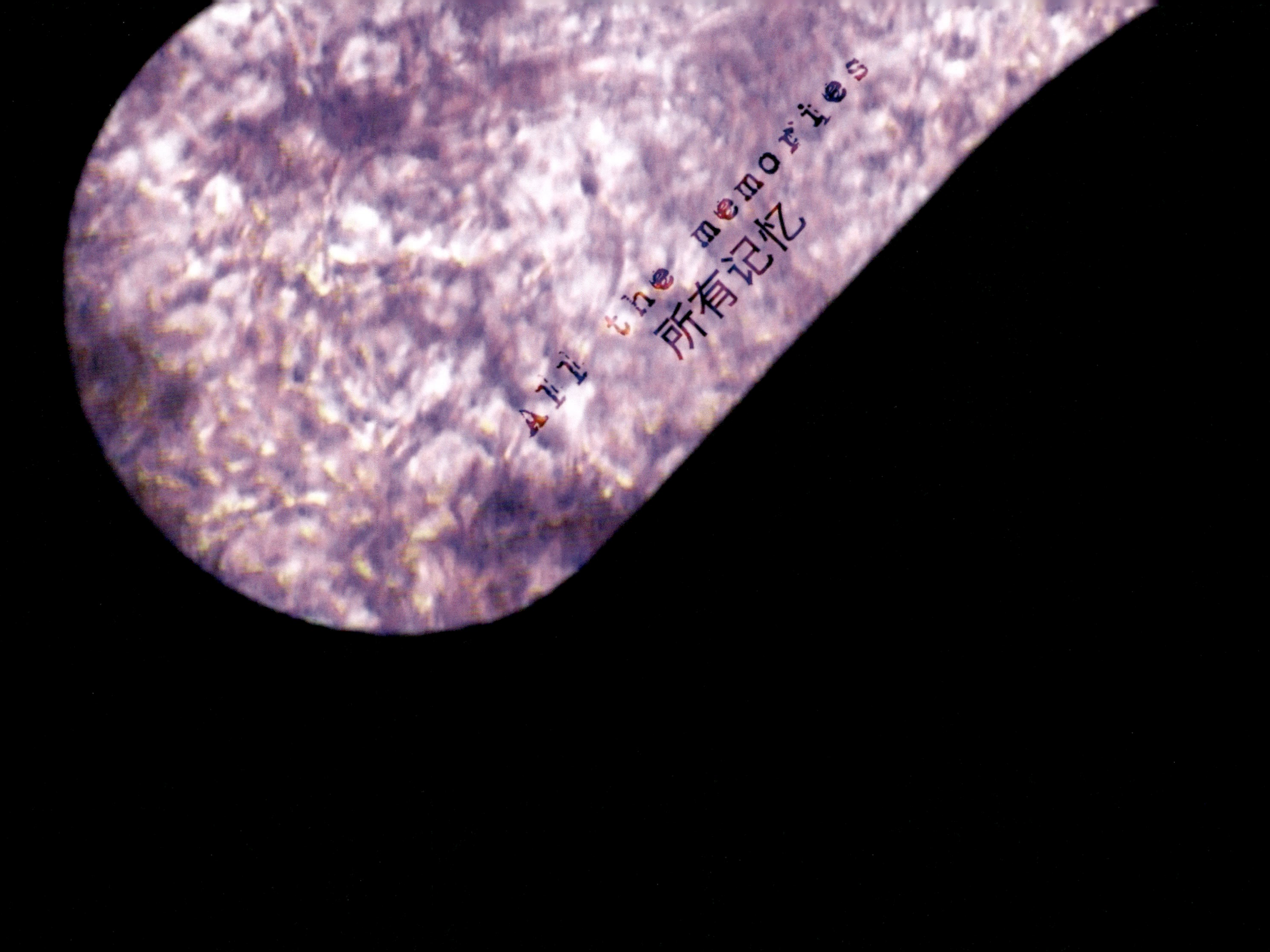

All the memories
所有记忆

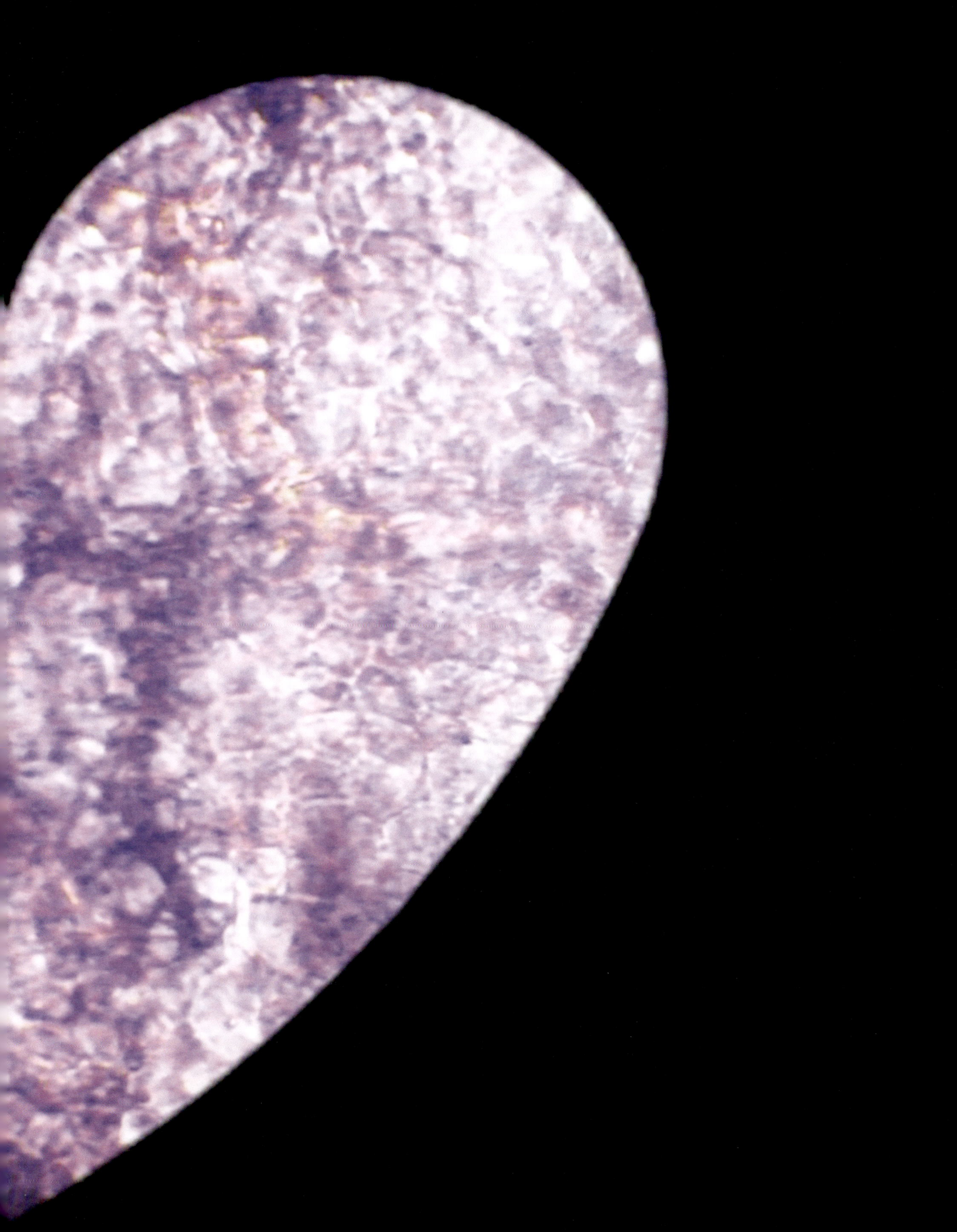

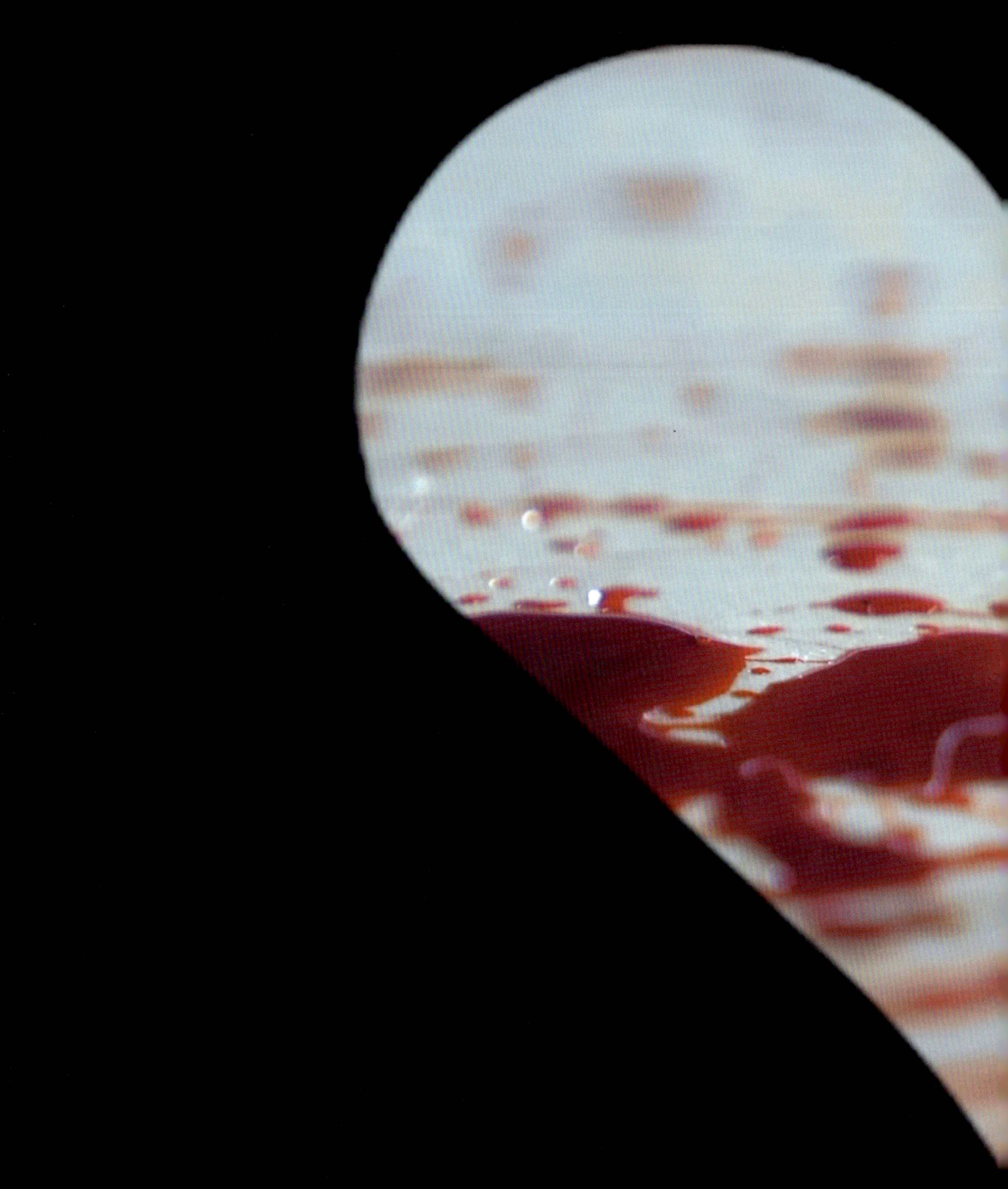

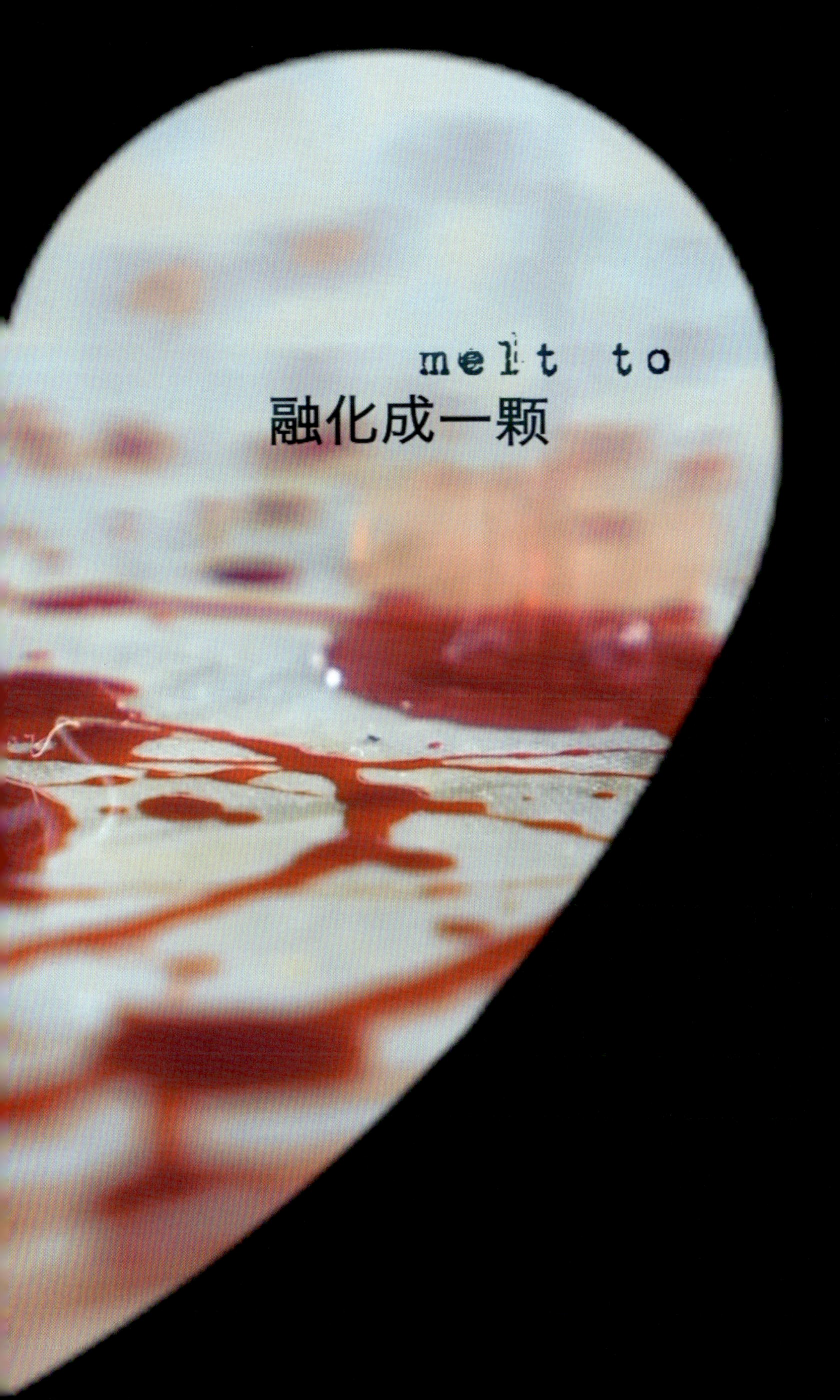
melt to
融化成一颗

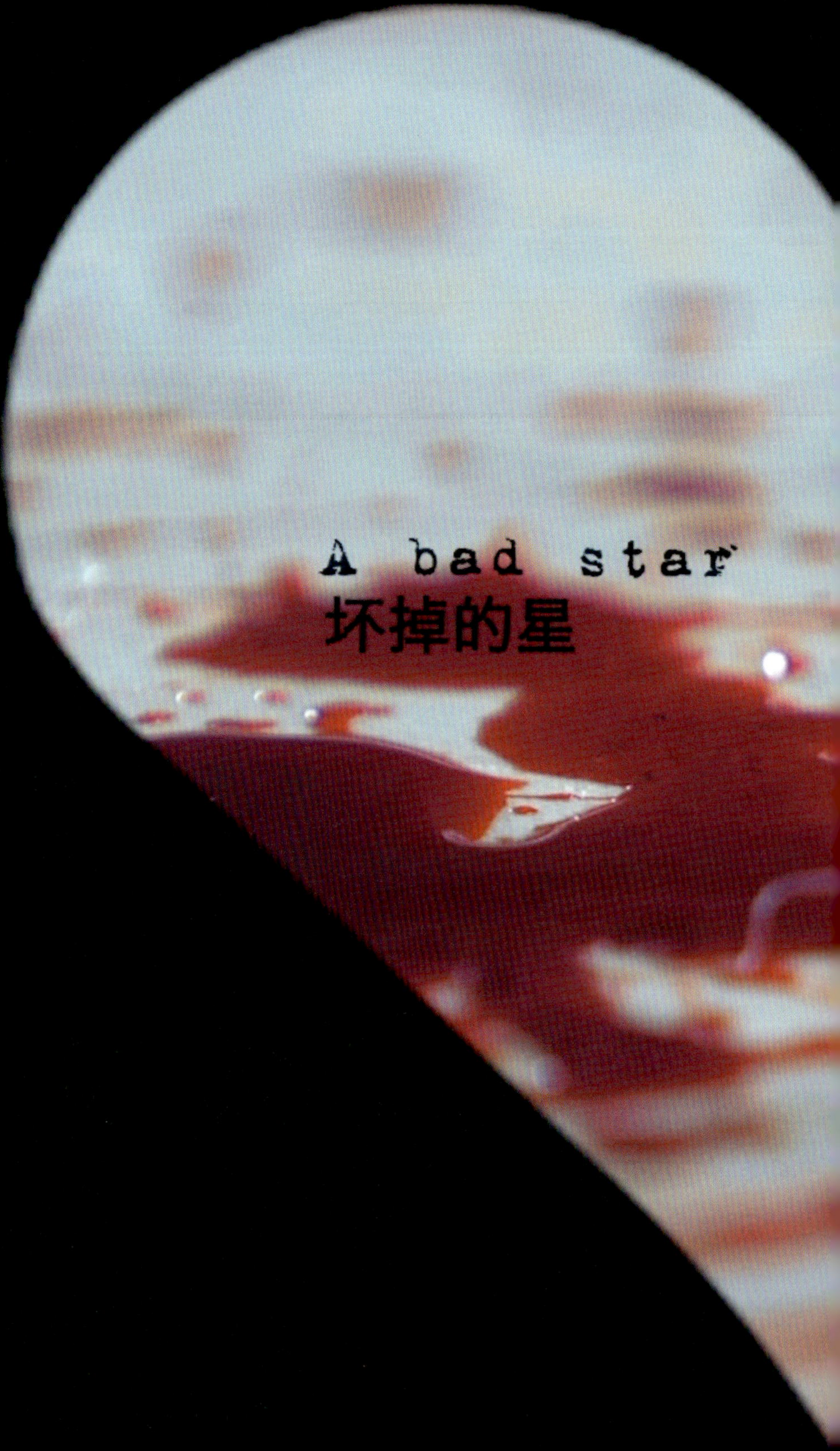

A bad star
坏掉的星

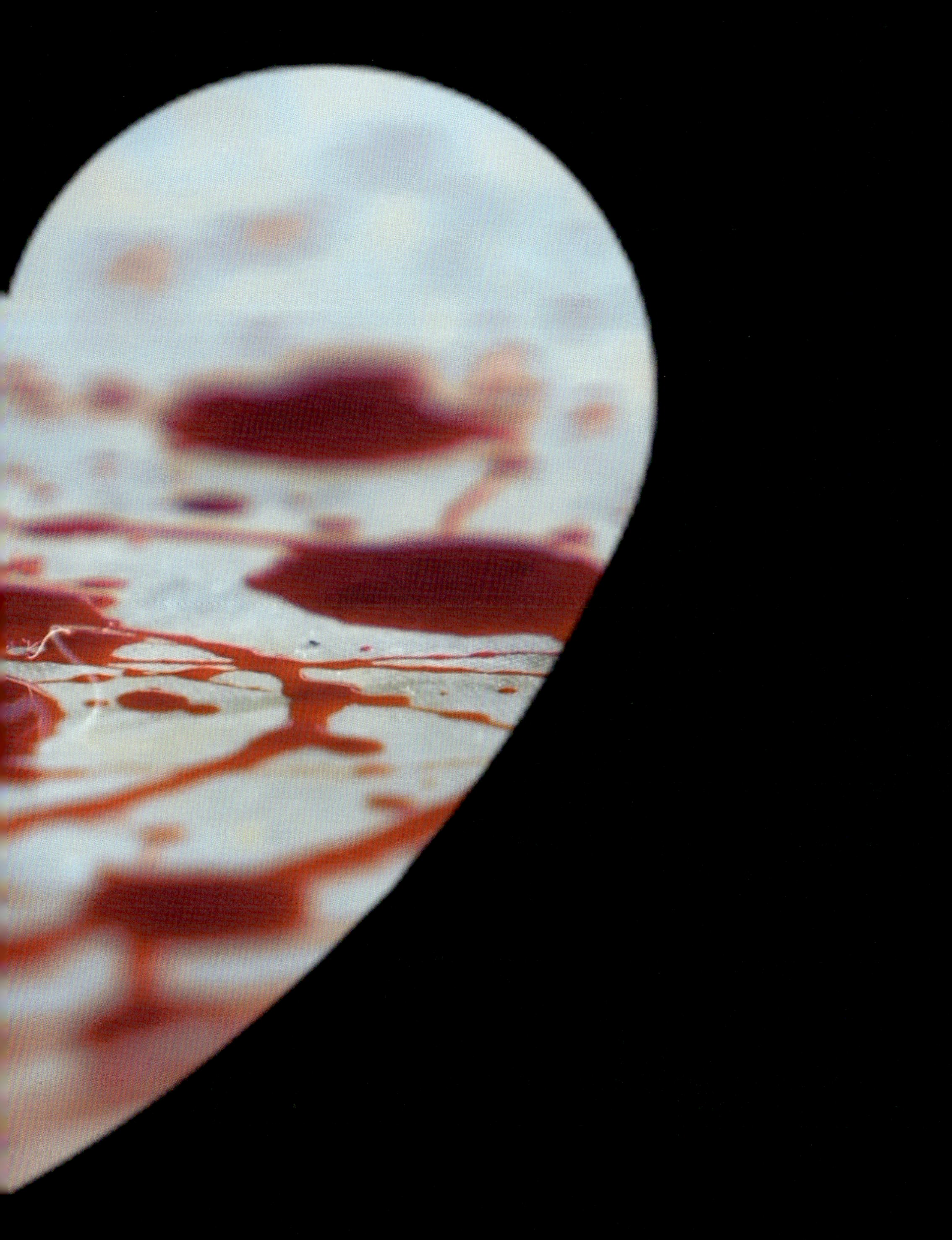

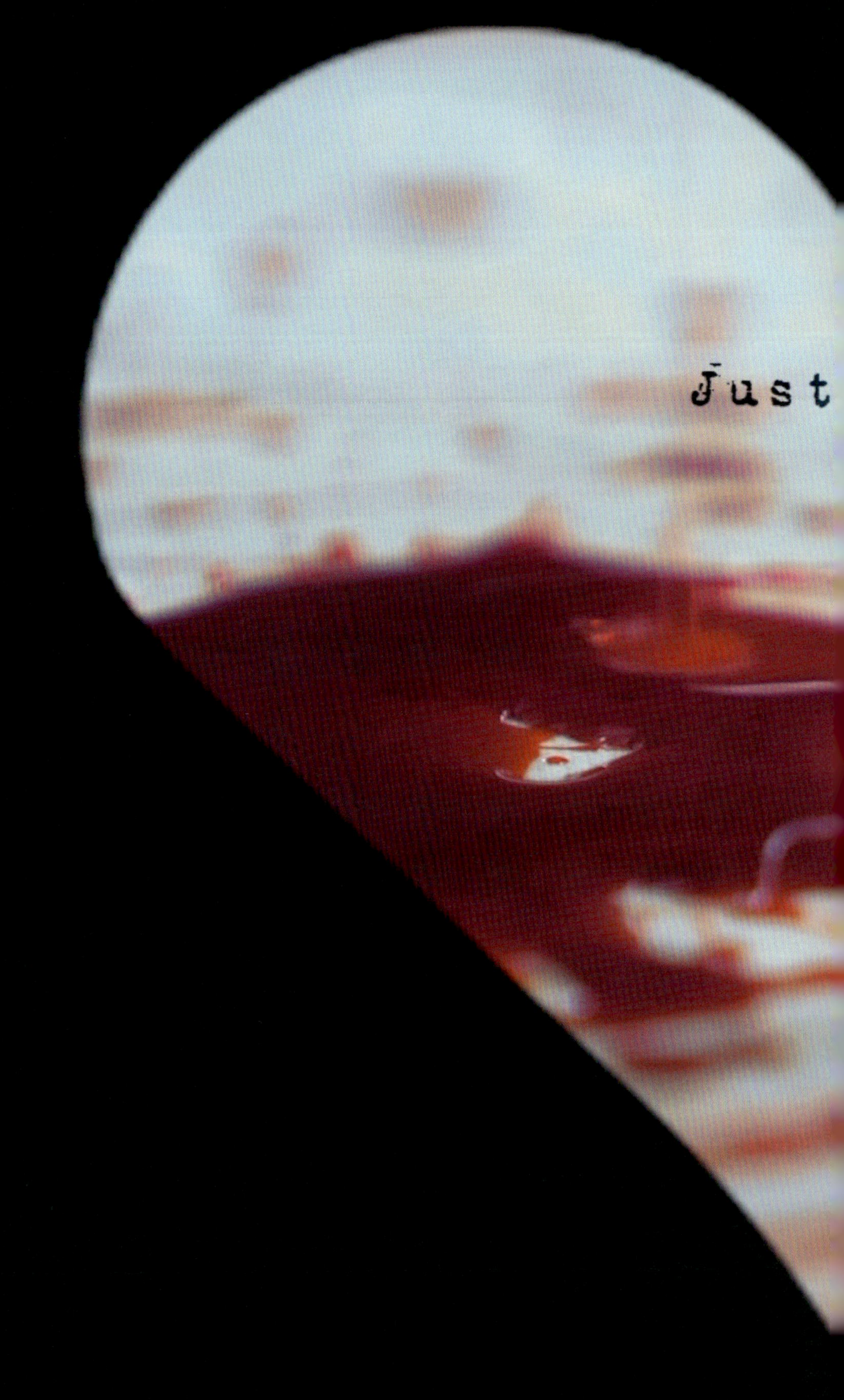
Just

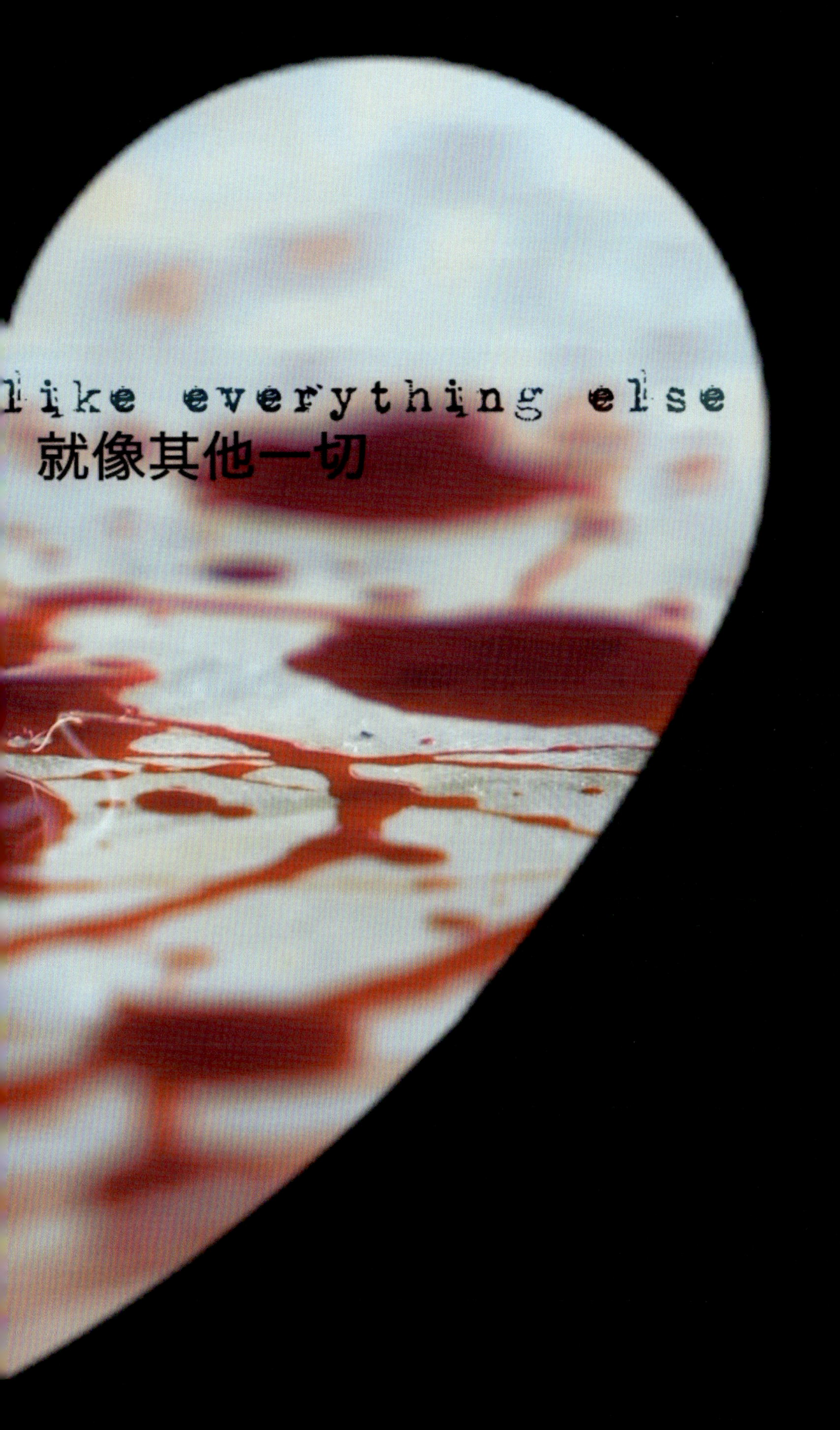
like everything else
就像其他一切

that has

been diluted
被稀释

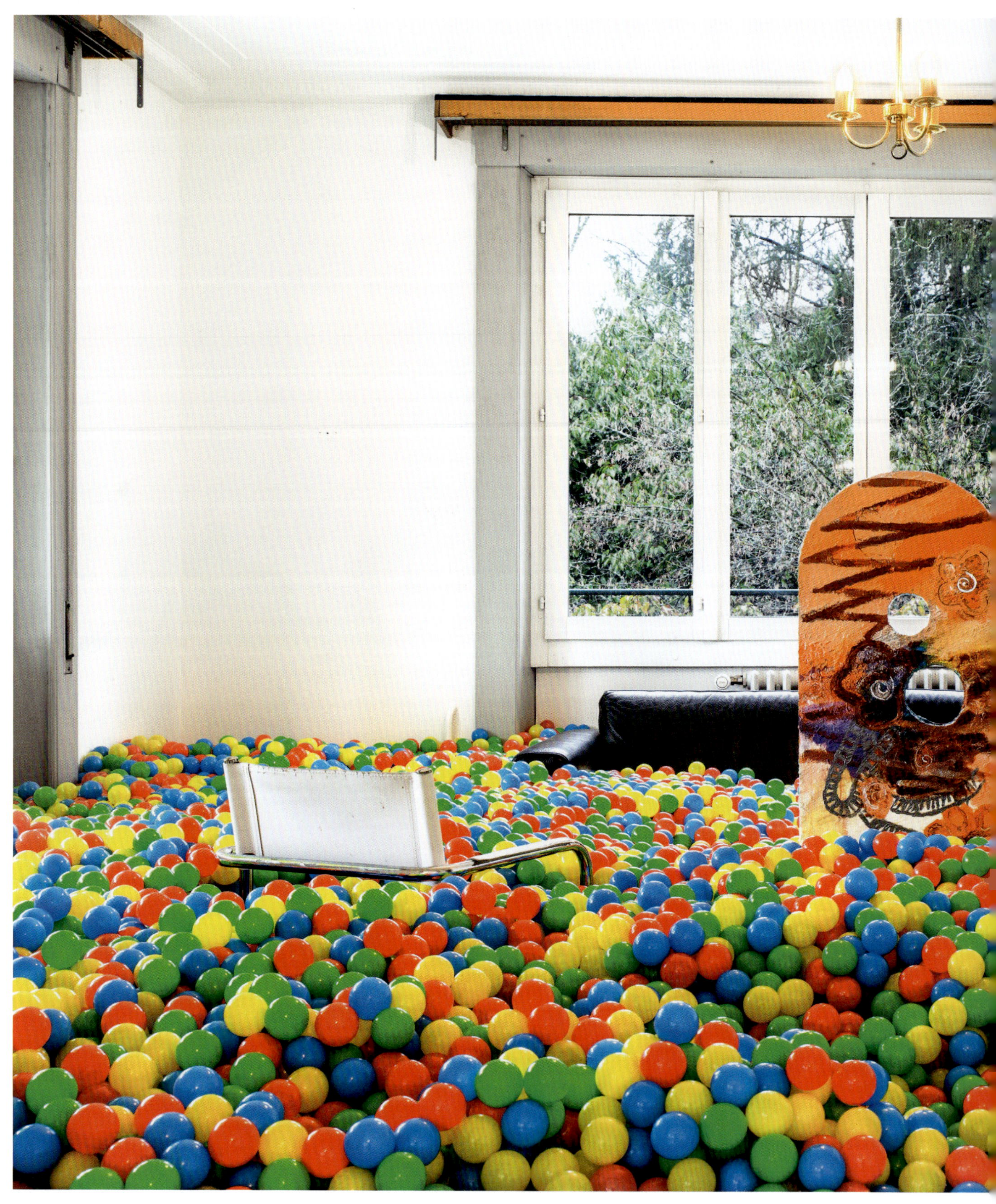

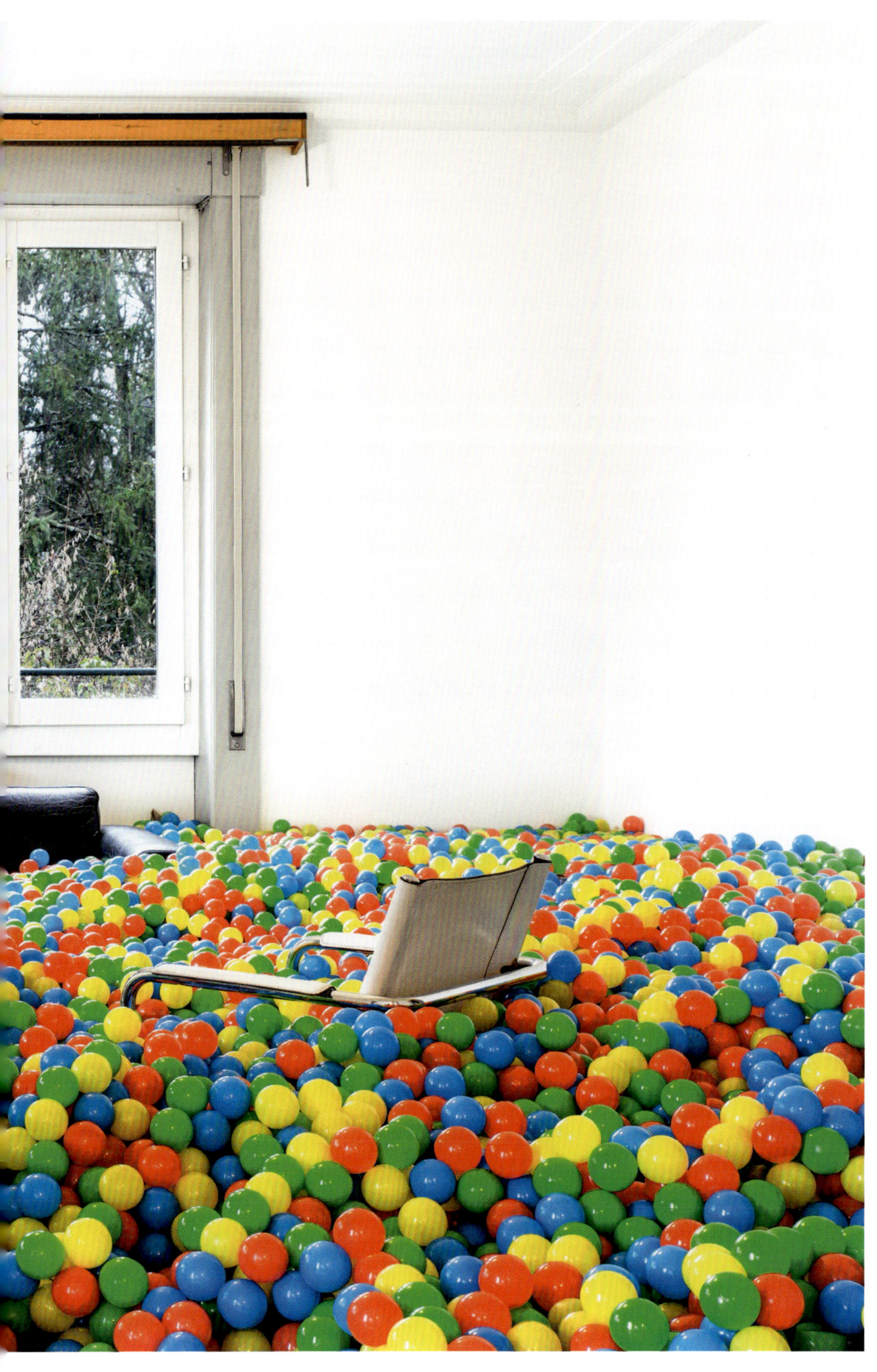

Kim, 2021
Installation view of *Among Us* at Cherish, Geneva, 2021

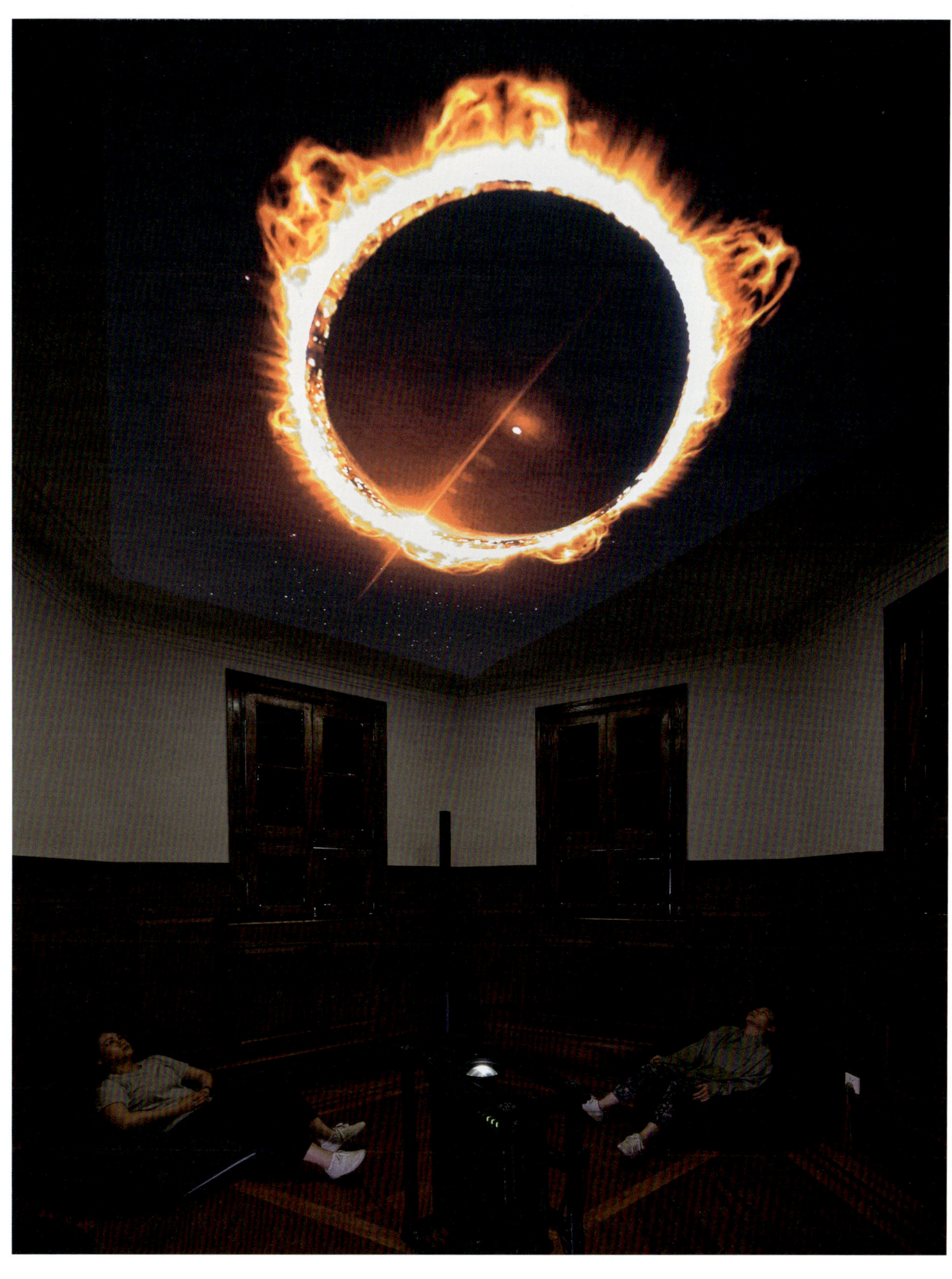

ÆTHER, 2021
Installation view, Kiang Malingue Gallery, Shanghai, 2021

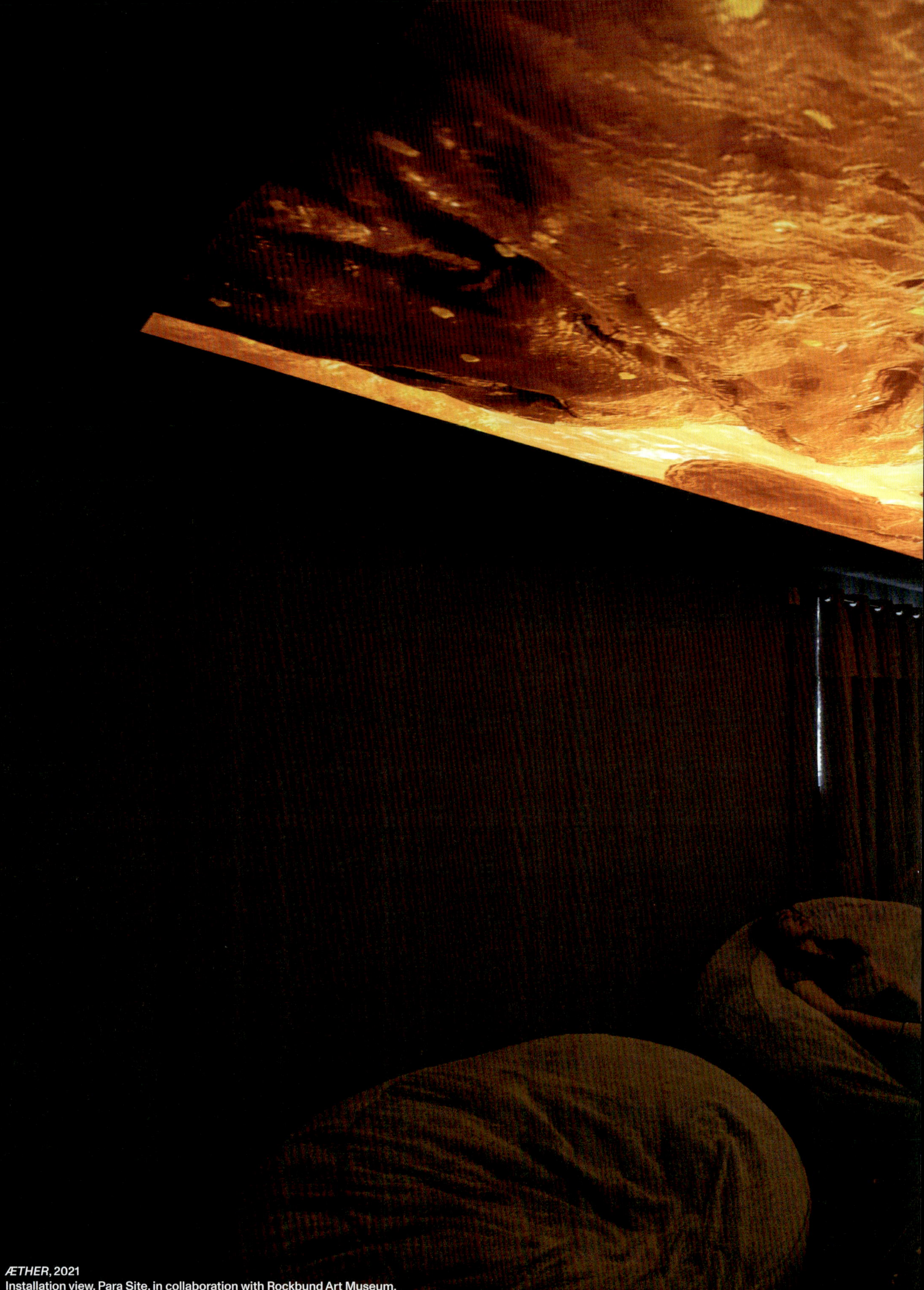

ÆTHER, 2021
Installation view, Para Site, in collaboration with Rockbund Art Museum.

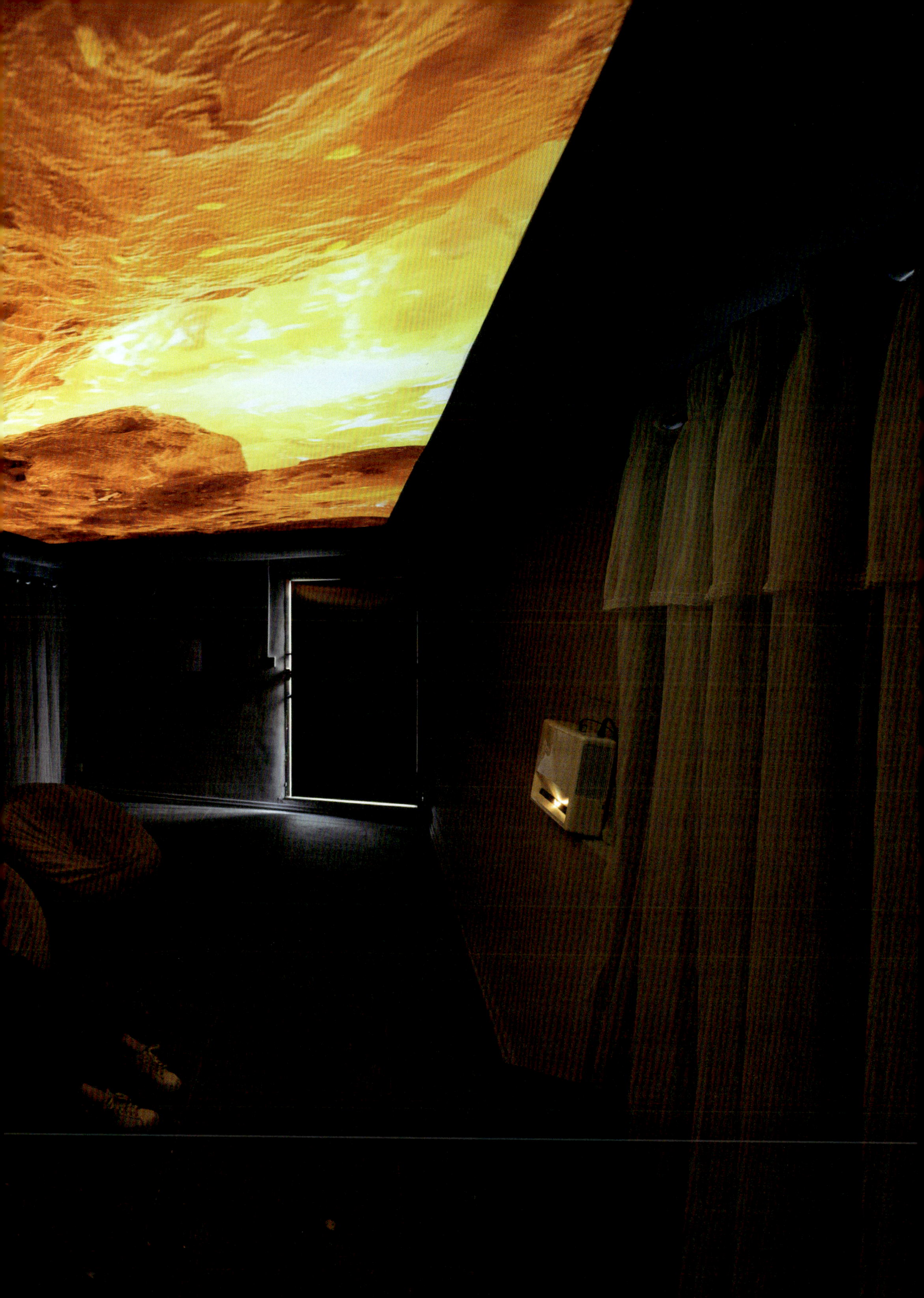

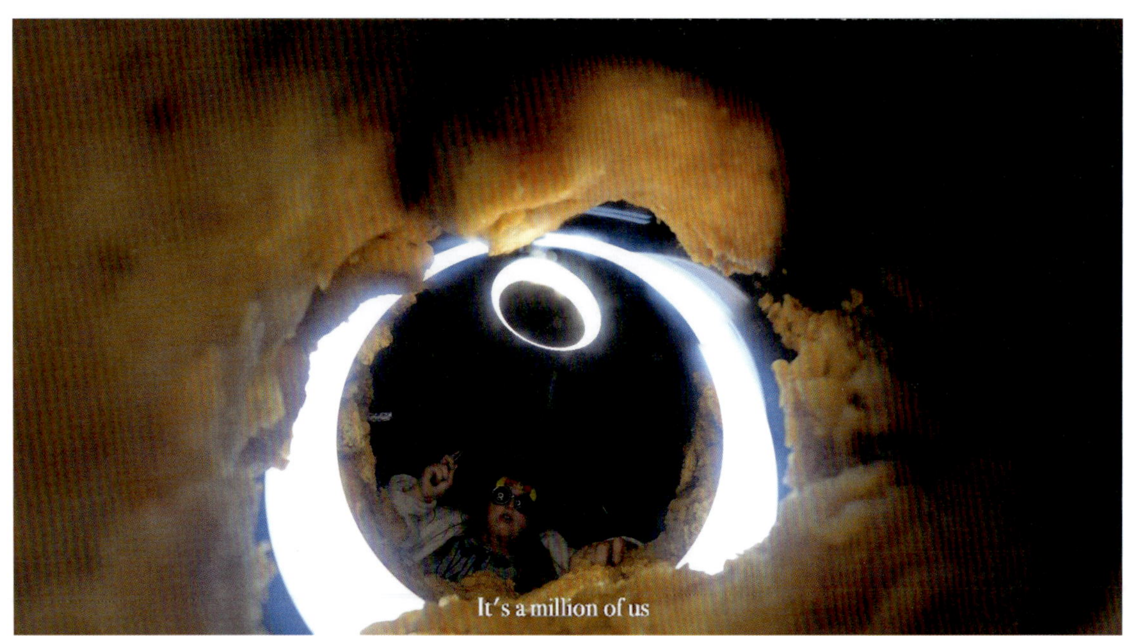
It's a million of us

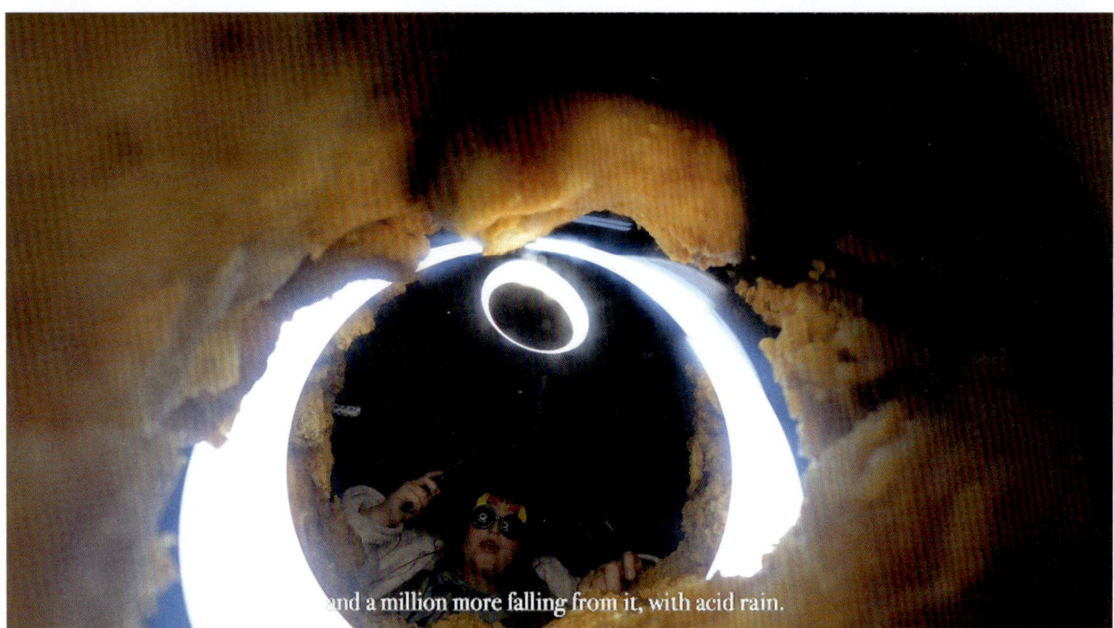
and a million more falling from it, with acid rain.

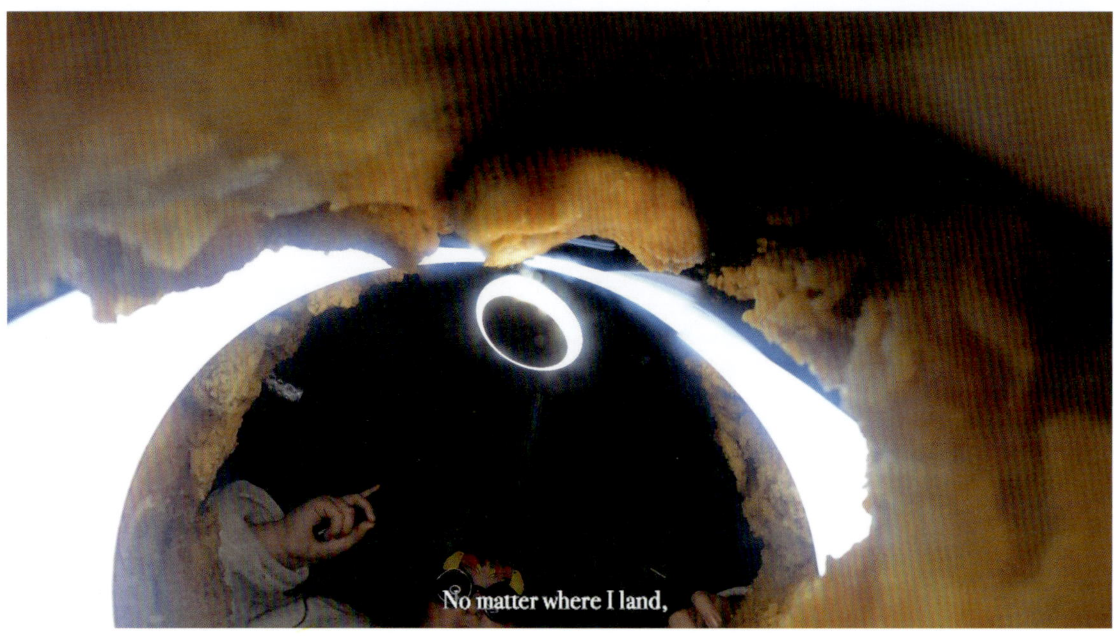
No matter where I land,

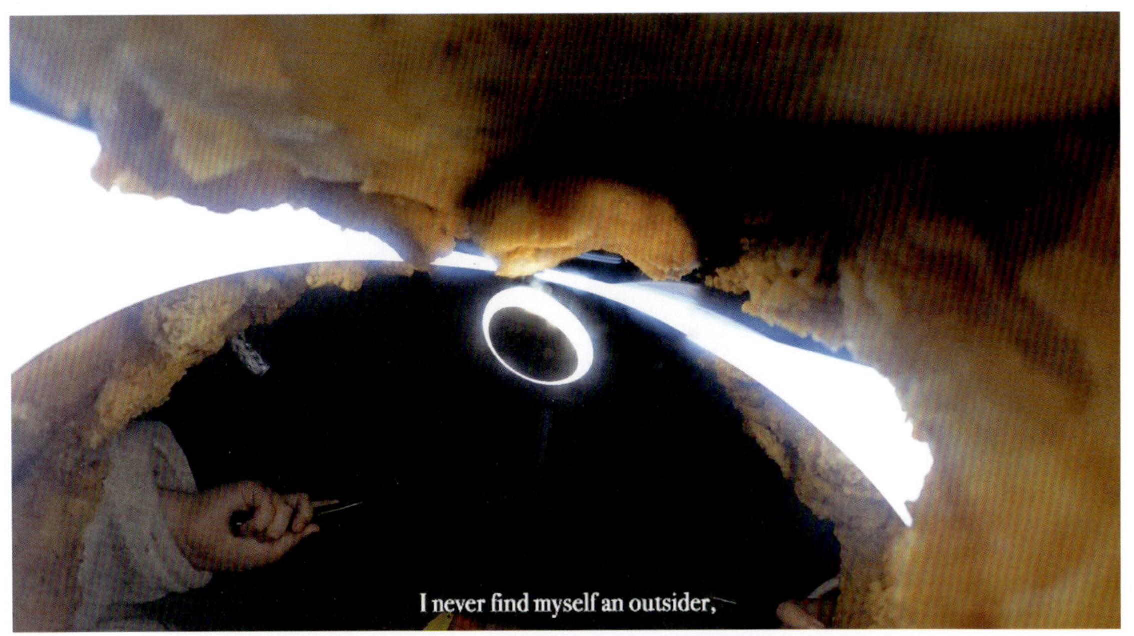
I never find myself an outsider,

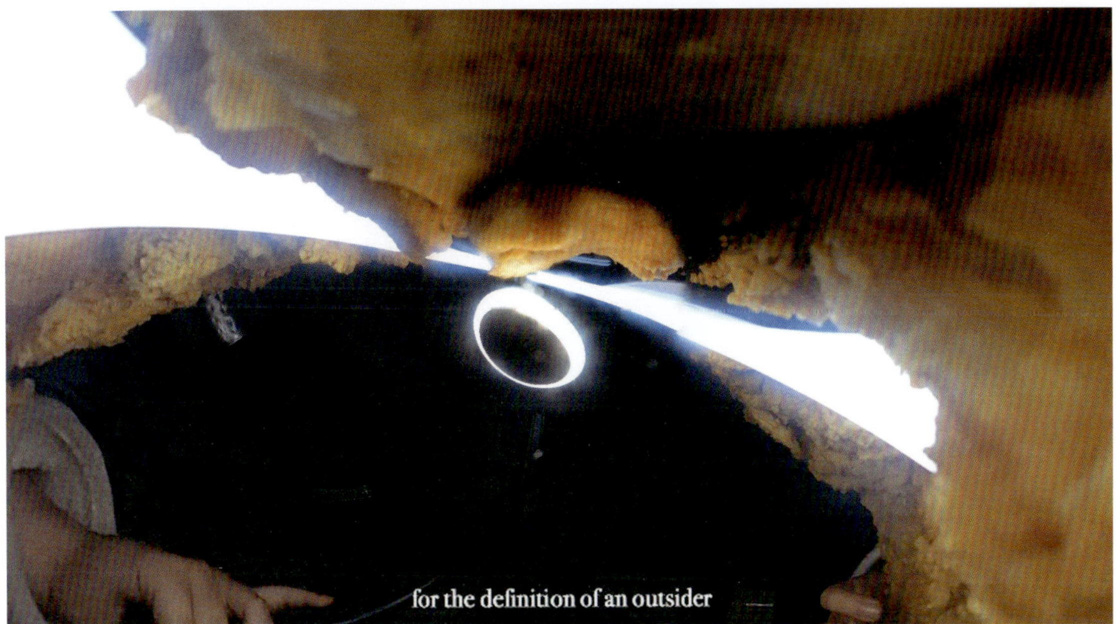
for the definition of an outsider

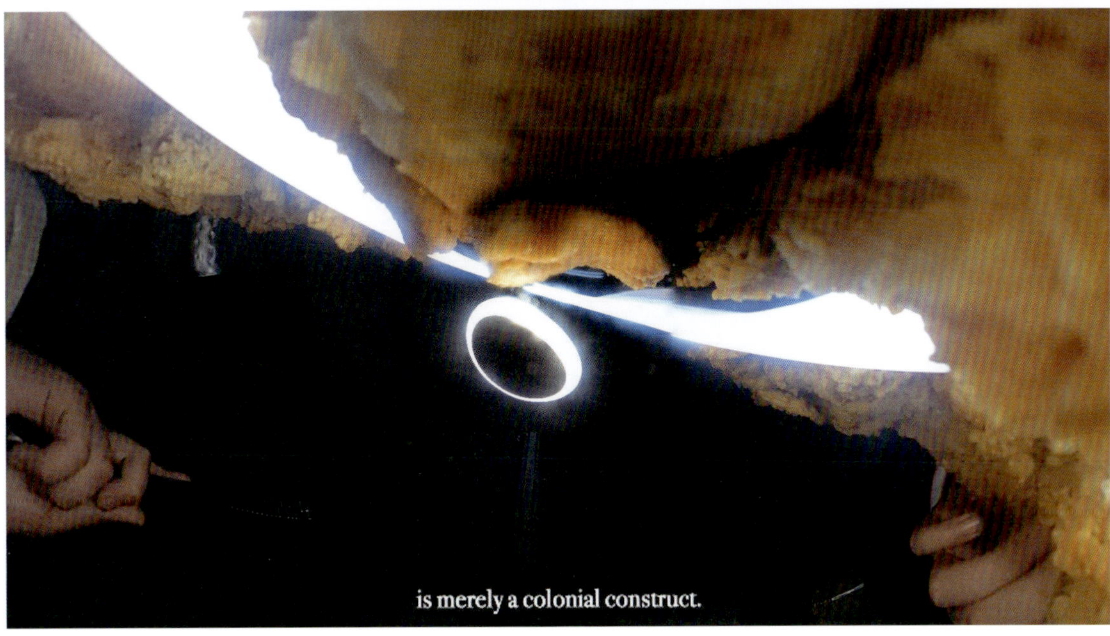
is merely a colonial construct.

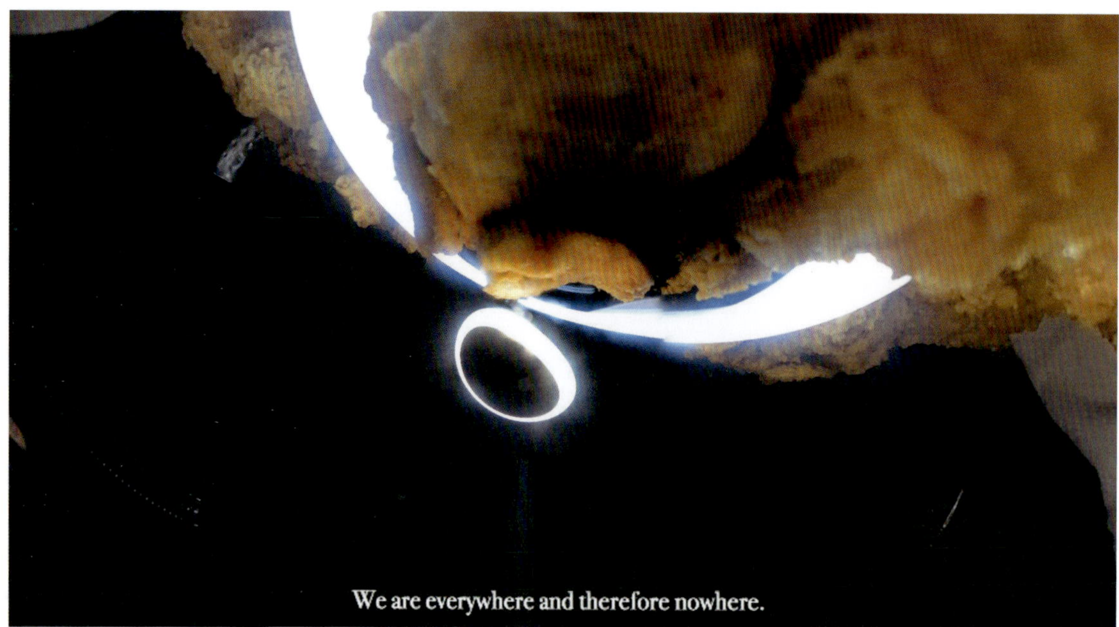
We are everywhere and therefore nowhere.

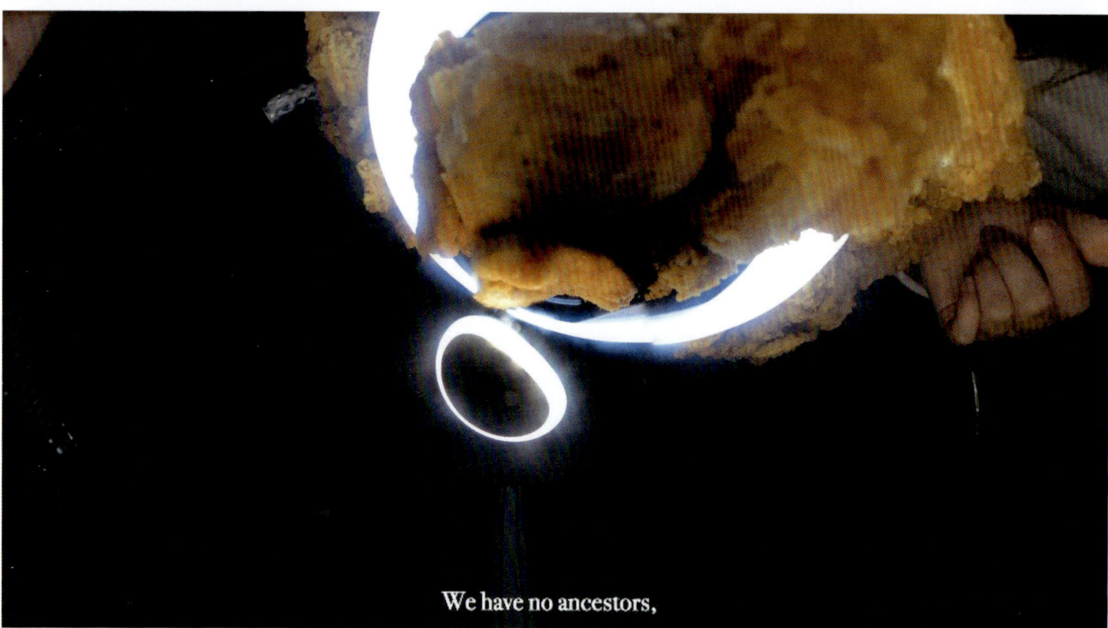
We have no ancestors,

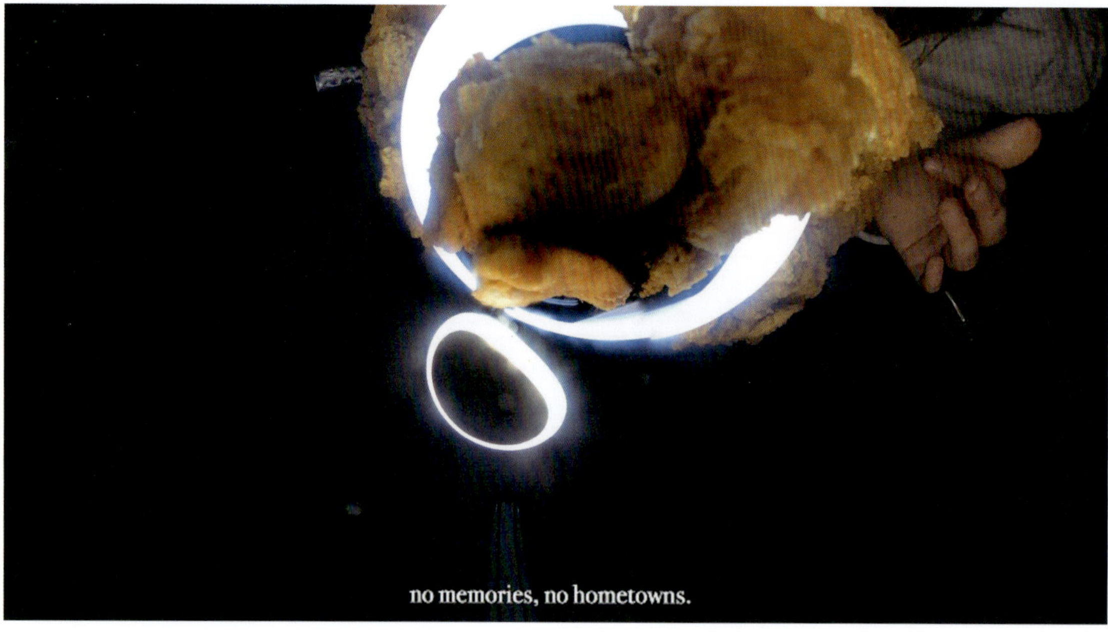
no memories, no hometowns.

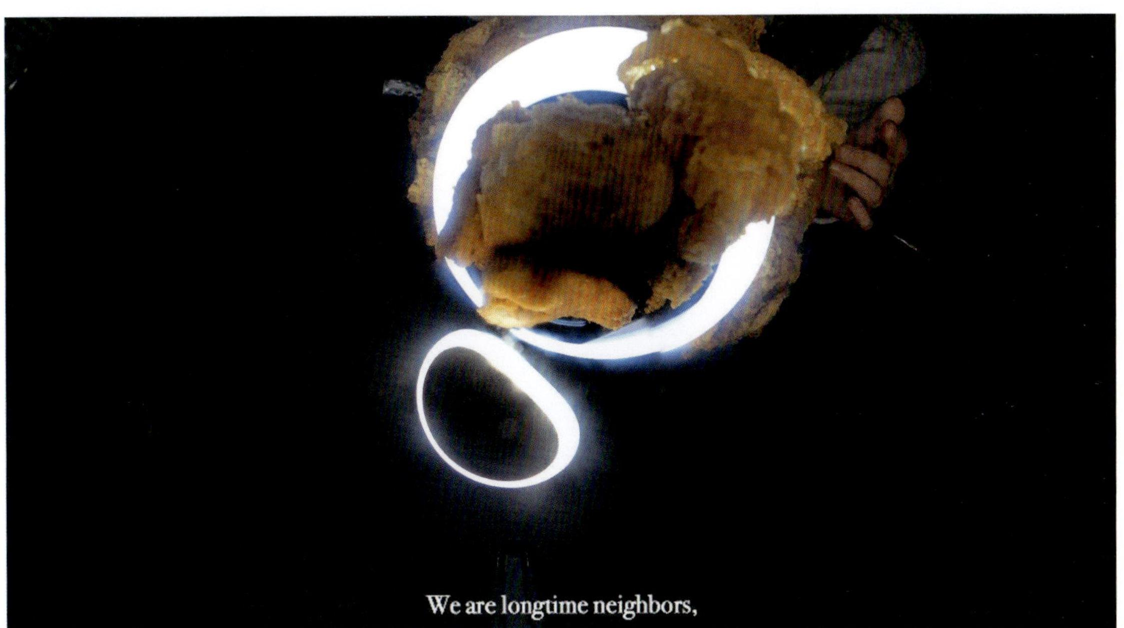

We are longtime neighbors,

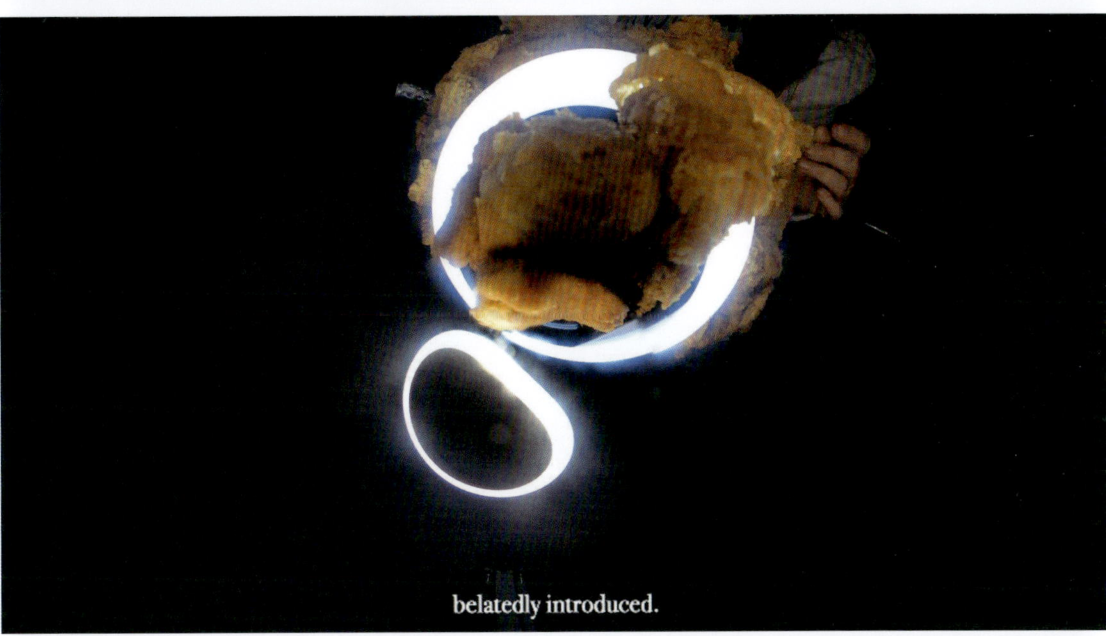

belatedly introduced.

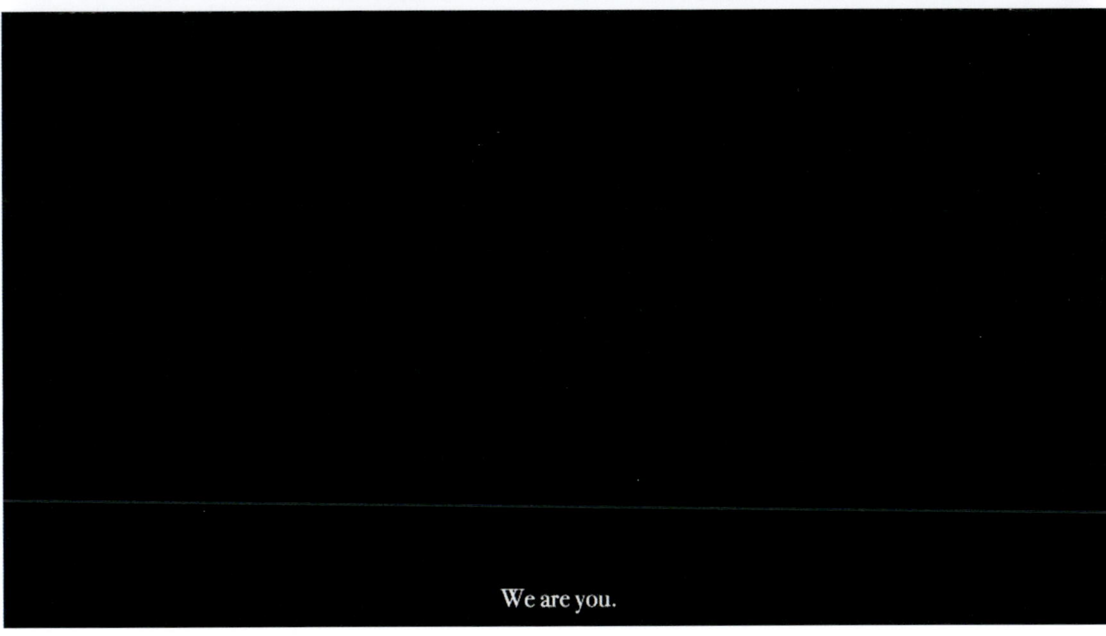

We are you.

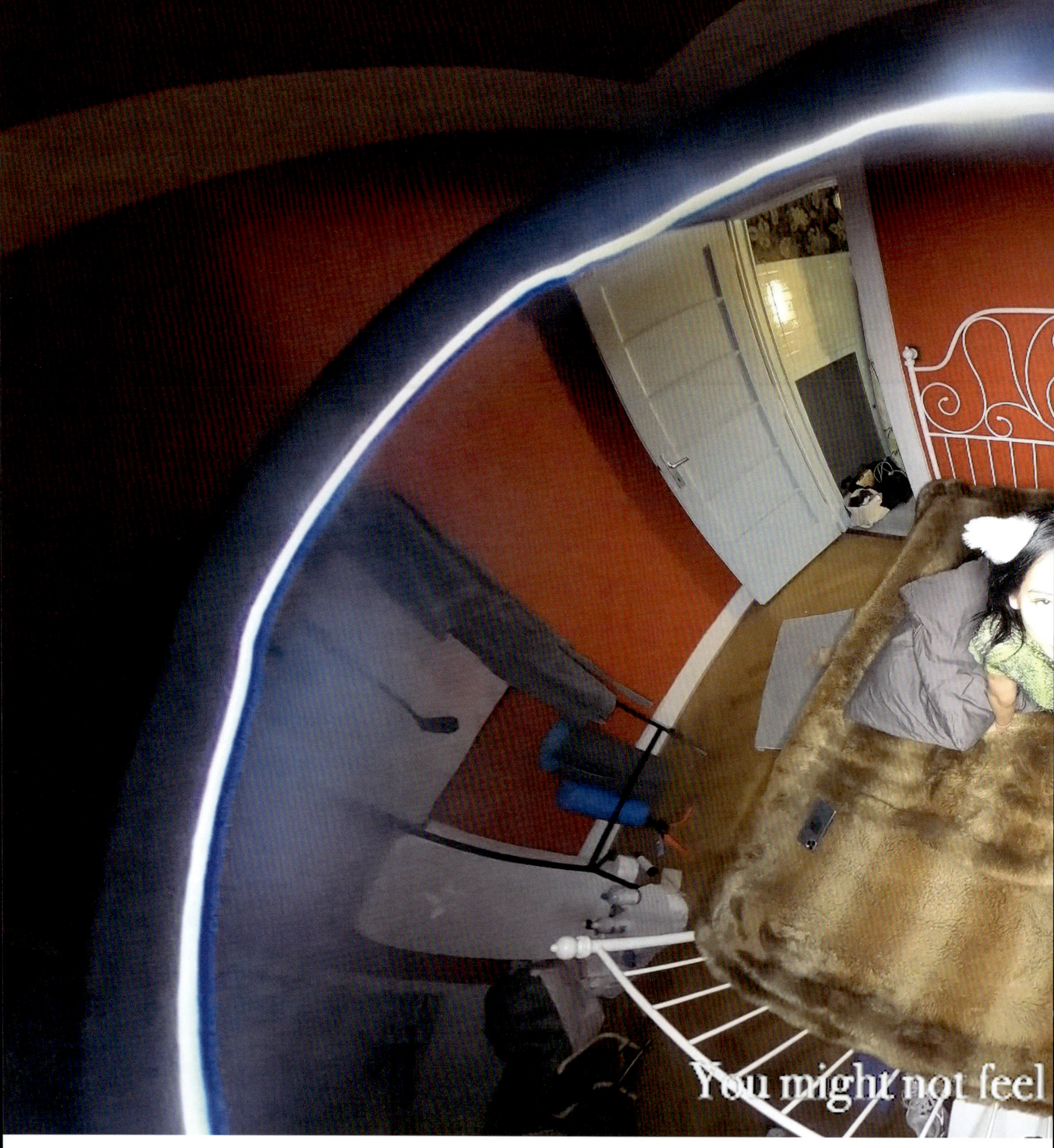
You might not feel

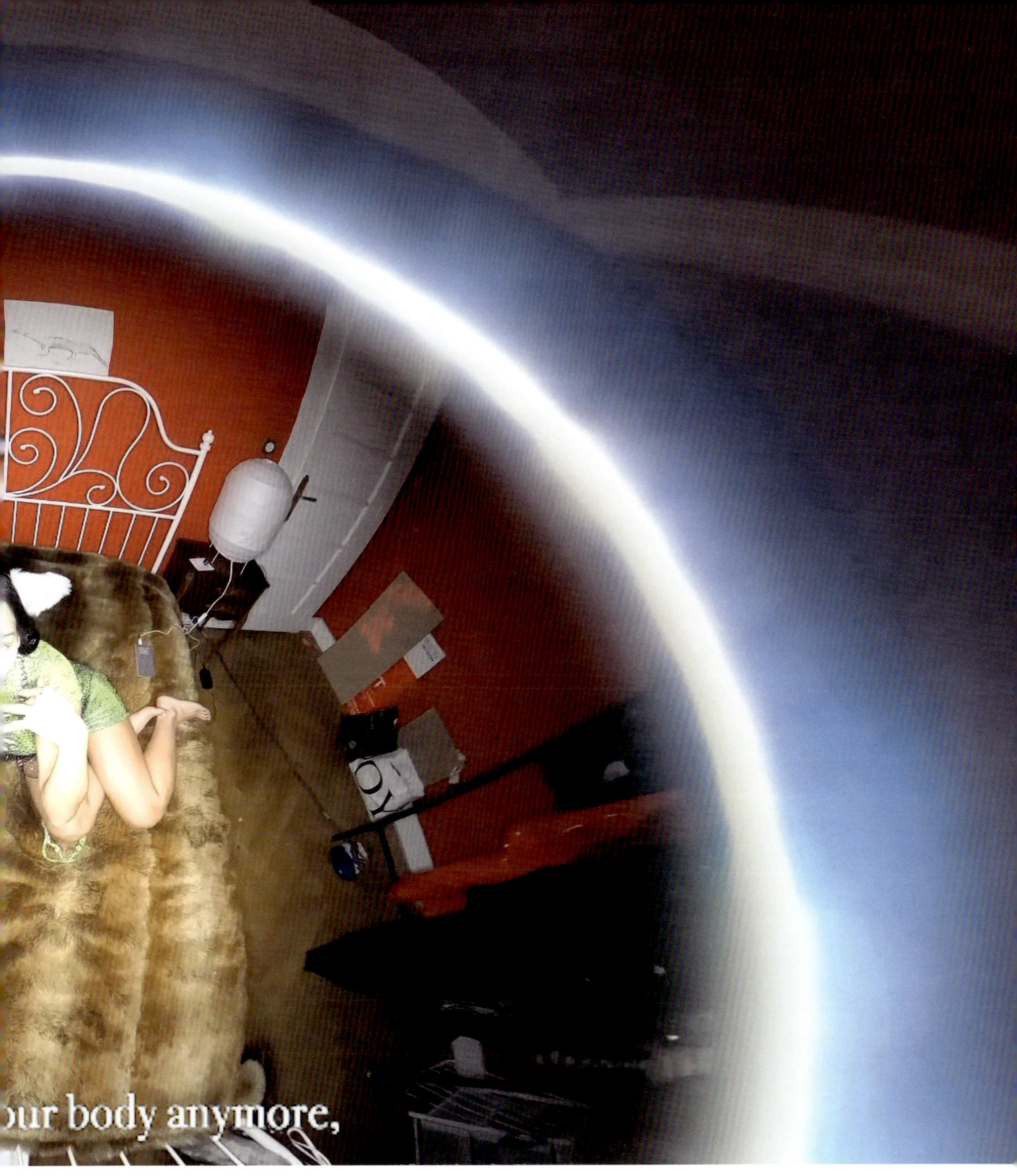

ÆTHER (Poor Objects), 2021–22

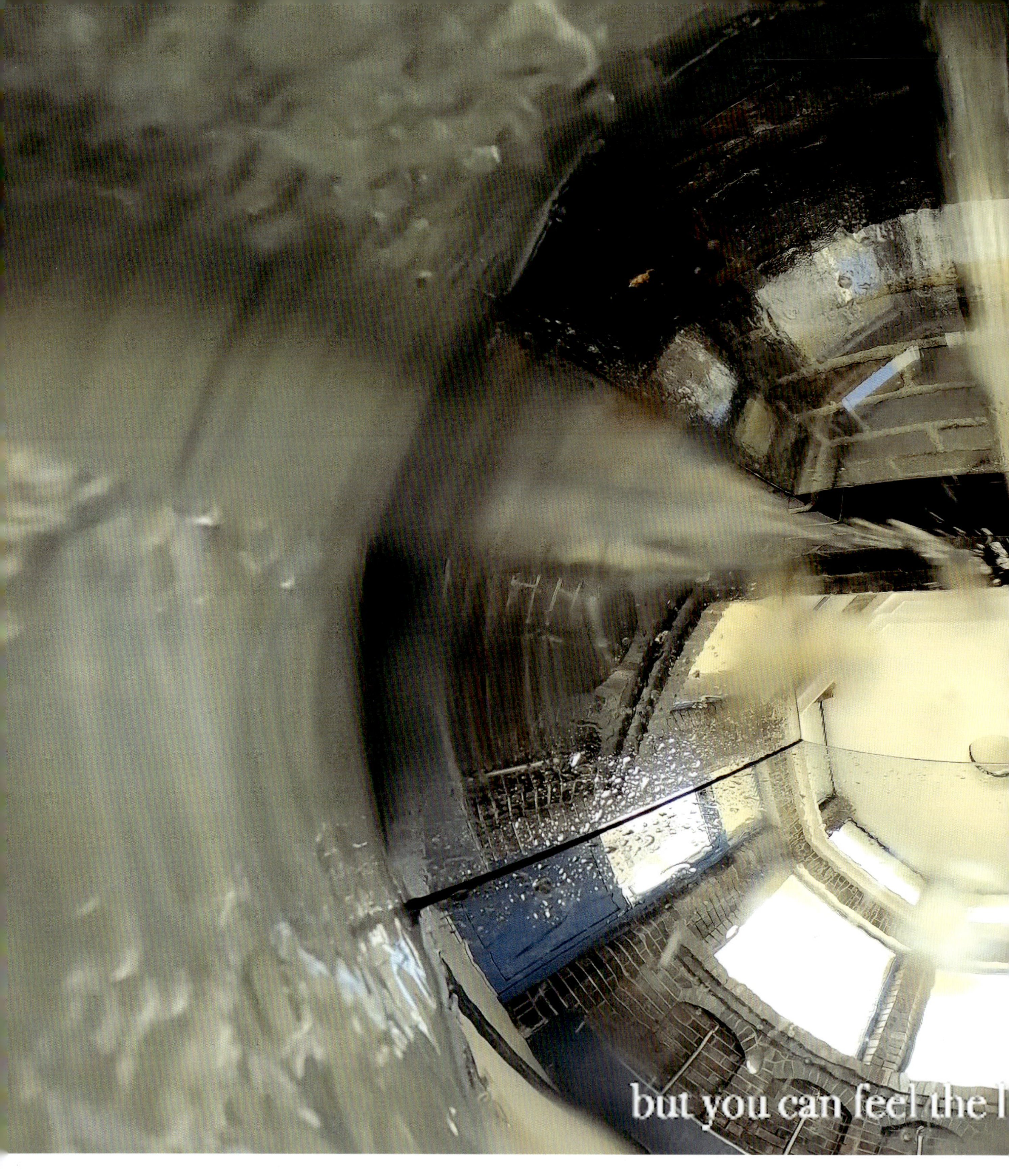
but you can feel the l

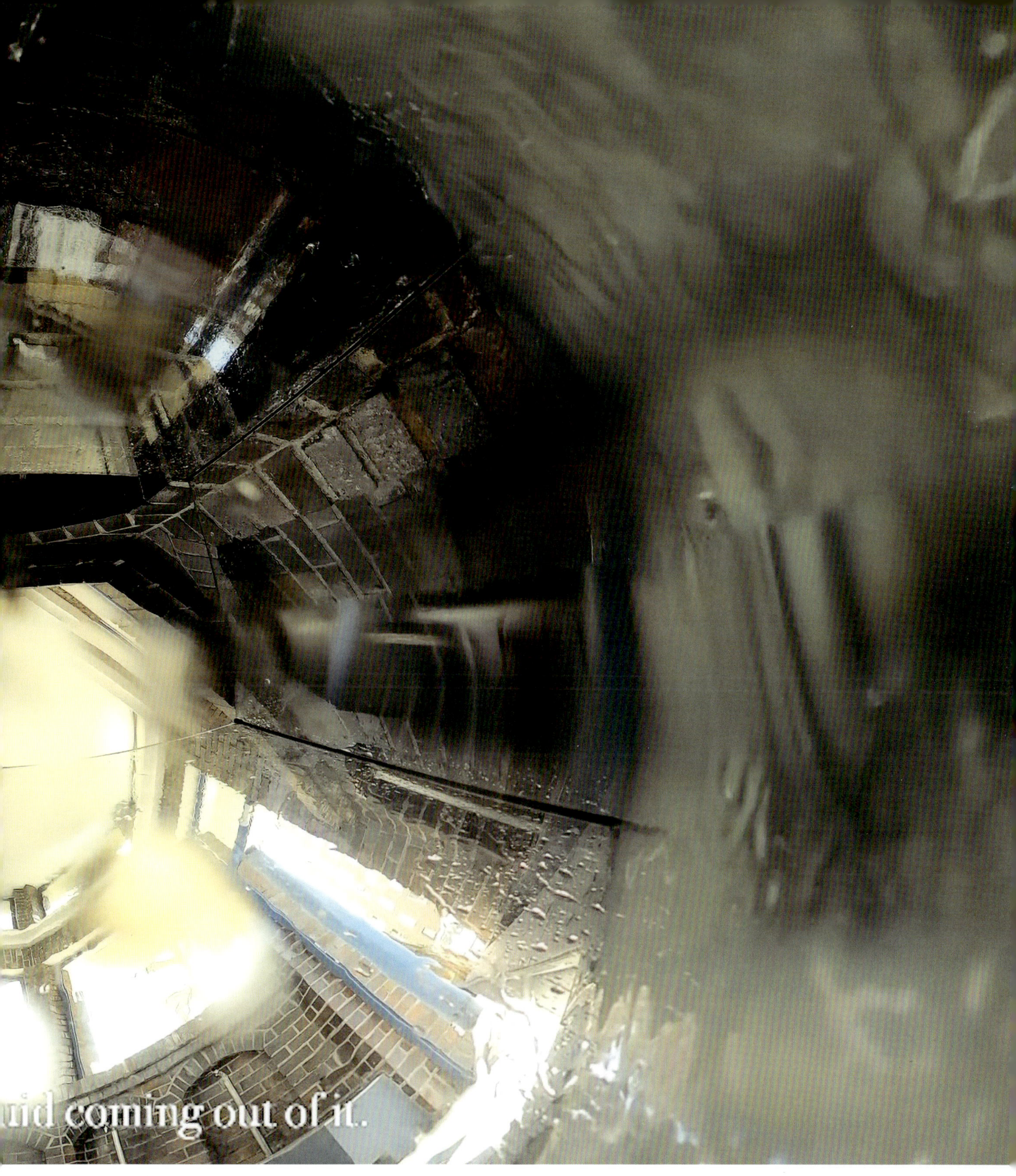
nd coming out of it..

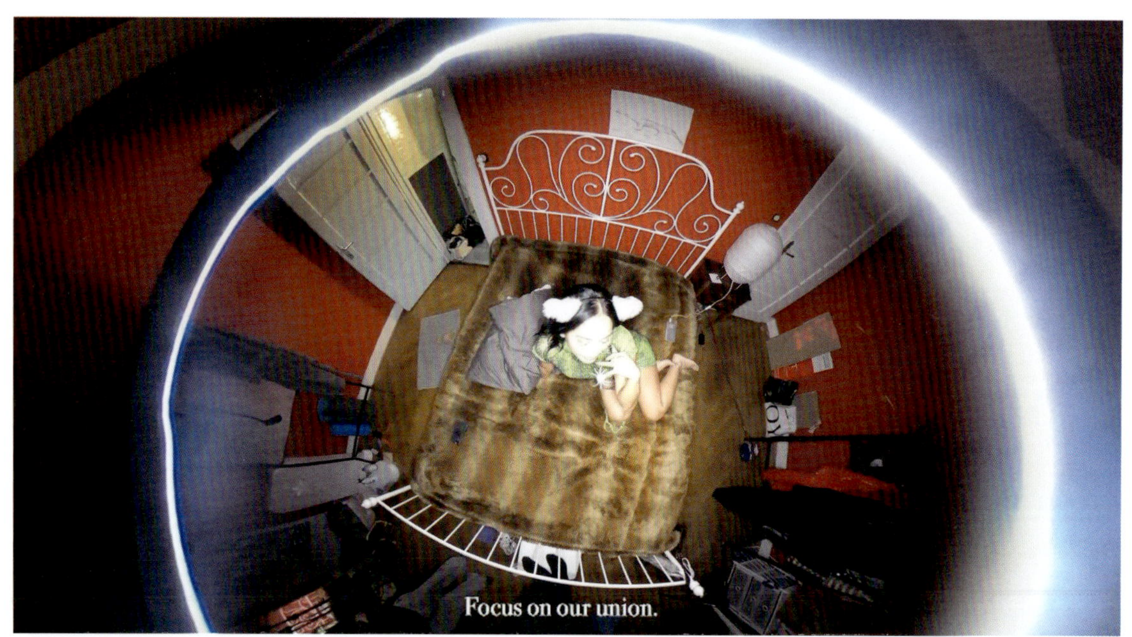
Focus on our union.

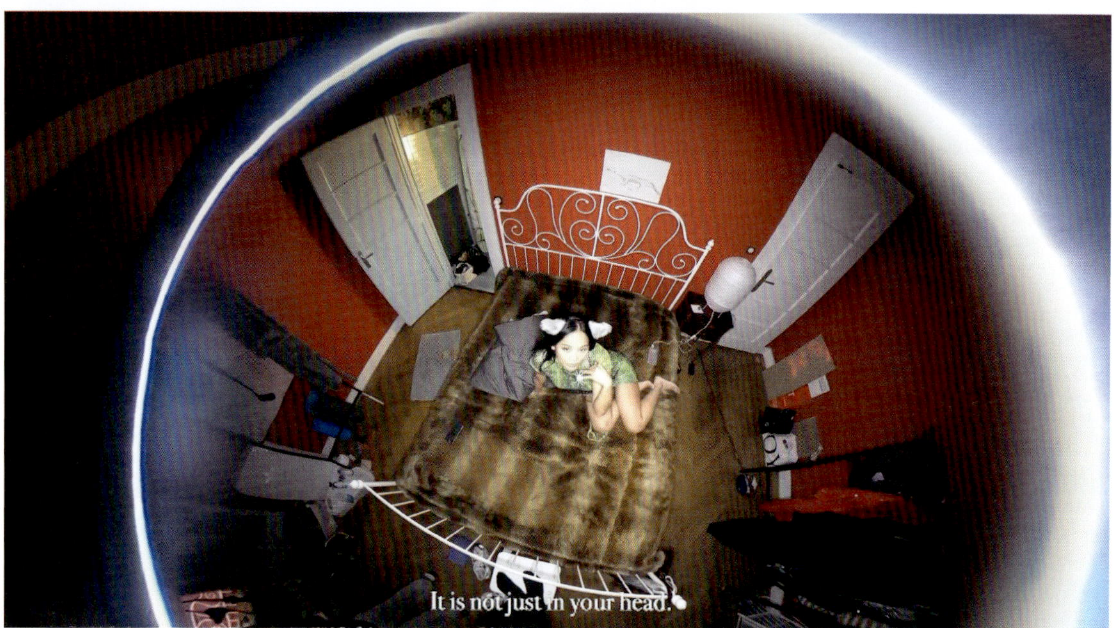
It is not just in your head.

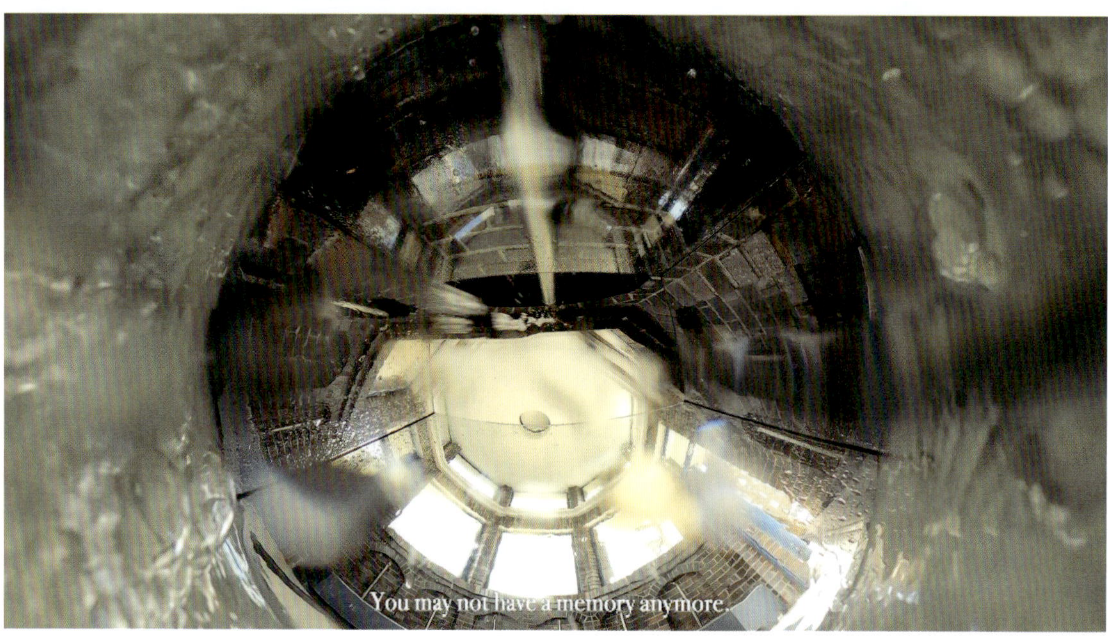
You may not have a memory anymore.

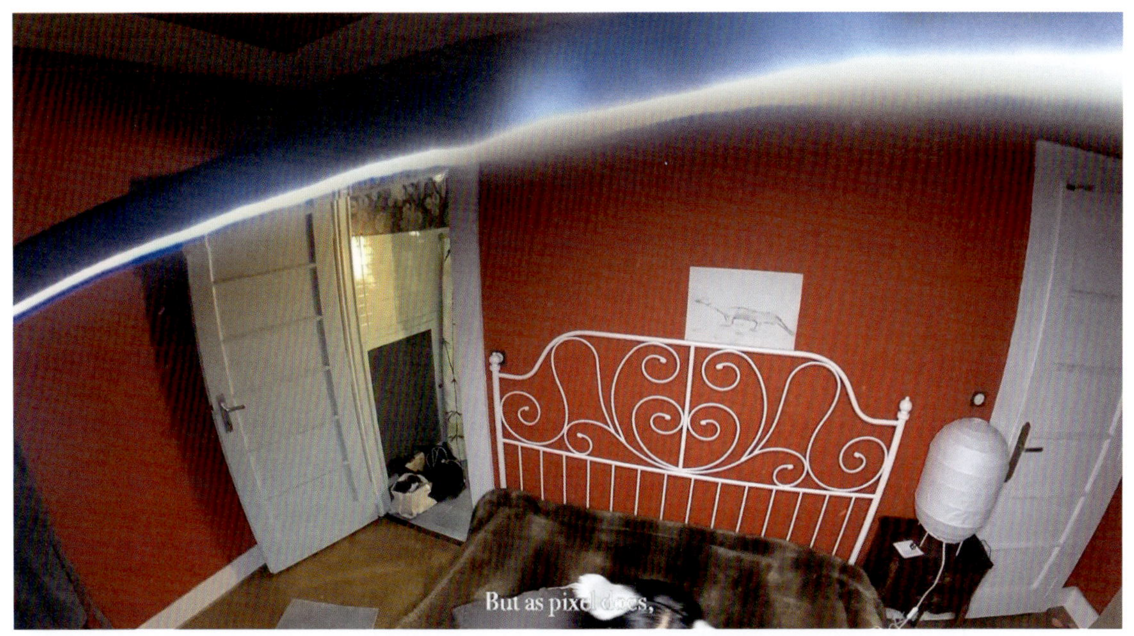
But as pixel does,

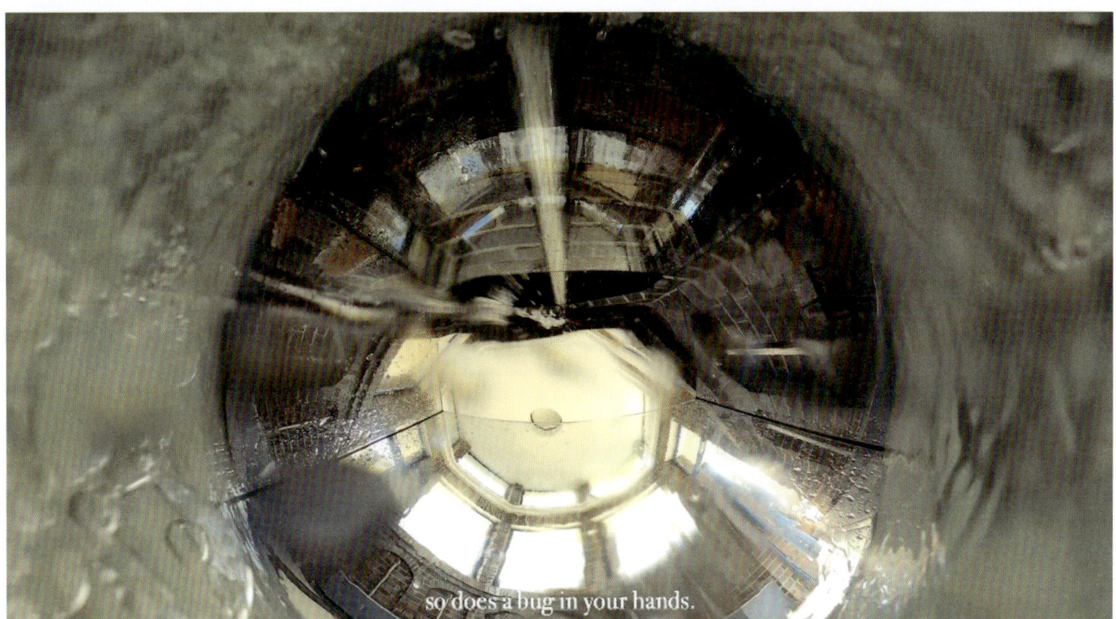
so does a bug in your hands.

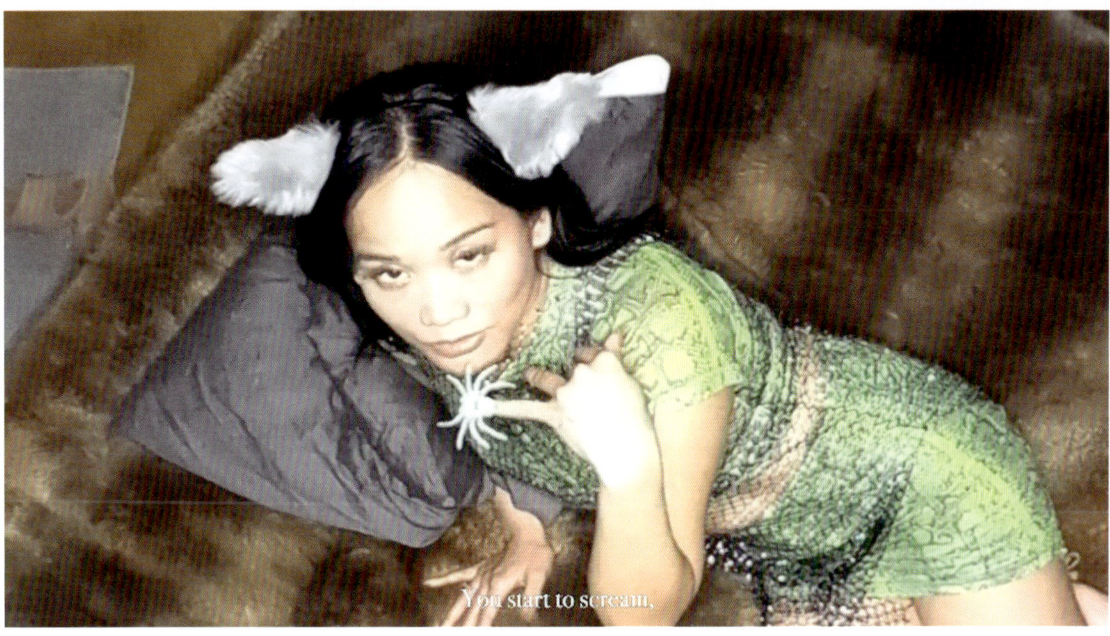
You start to scream,

I was a fan once. But somewhere along the way, I got bored. Life felt desperate. Everything was exhausting. Nothing was fun. I went to an aura reader who said, "It's giving greige." What happened to being "Obsessed!"? Where was my enthusiasm for new ideas or bands or artists or books (or banned artist's books, for that matter)? Had millennial adulthood just knocked the wind out of me? Was I having an allergic reaction to living in the West? To capitalism? To gluten? Had I sold out? Let the man get me down? Lost myself? Was this real life? Is that all there is? If so, how depressing. Finally, one day I admitted to myself: "I'm not okay!"

And shortly after that I met Shuang, a comrade, accomplice and friend who sorted me out. She said, "It's okay. You're just going through an emo phase."

And then played me "I'm Not Okay (I Promise)" by My Chemical Romance.

We listened to music, read books, made art and were fangirls of many things together (including Mia Goth in the role of Pearl) but mostly we became fans of each other. I hope you will enjoy the following conversation that was recorded between Shuang and I in the spring of 2023 while living a post-pandemic cottagecore fantasy together in the middle of nowhere for two months. It has been cut for brevity and edited for clarity.
— Sophia Al Maria

SOPHIA AL MARIA: Getting to know you and getting to know your work made me appreciate fangirldom. Or is it scene girl–dom? You introduced me to My Chemical Romance and your origins story via a love letter you wrote to the band, and I became interested in the way you relate to them. So, I wonder if you could share the story of how you found MCR, which a lot of your work revolves around.

SHUANG LI: I learned about My Chemical Romance totally by accident. I grew up in a small town in the southeast part of China. It was so small and boring, there wasn't even a shopping mall where we could hang out. But then there was this shop called Dakou CDs. It sold music labels' dead stock, overproduced CDs. To save on storage, record labels punched a hole in the disc and shipped it

off to Asia as digital waste. Somebody figured out that the hole only hurt one song, and sometimes the hole missed the disc completely. So the CDs started circulating again within the context of East Asia. But they weren't a commodity that was sold front and center at a record store. They were something that people sold in back rooms. You would have to know to go into the back to look. And this was before the internet, so it was all transmitted by word of mouth. So you just went to the back and you could see whichever album cover appealed to you, and you bought it. It was like two dollars for one. And they came punched with an extra hole.

SAM: Can you describe the place?

SL: It was a small magazine shop. In the front there were the usual magazines and stuff. At some point you would arrive at a curtain. You went past it, and there were boxes of CDs. That's how I found My Chemical Romance.

SAM: Which album?

SL: *The Black Parade*, the one where they went mainstream.

SAM: That's probably around the time when people started downloading music. So American record companies would have been getting rid of CDs they weren't selling.

SL: Yeah, true. I never thought about that.

SAM: How old were you?

SL: Fifteen? Fourteen? I never thought about the broader context before, but, yeah, around the same time, my parents bought a computer and I could go online, but I only had one hour of computer time per week. So, I would just go on YouTube. This was before China had the firewall thing, so you could search for whatever, but it was still very slow. I would go to YouTube, and I would download one album or one music video to put on my mp4. A tiny one. And I would just watch the few music videos on it when I woke up, the same way I watch TikToks these days.

SAM: What video was it?

SL: "The Black Parade." I had a couple, "Famous Last Words," "I'm Not Okay," "Helena." And there are some other bands that were completely random to me, too. I just liked their album covers.

SAM: So, Shuang Li. Li Shuang.

SL: Not my government name!

SAM: I'm sorry. Am I being a bully? I should know better than to bully an emo.

SL: That's exactly the person you should never bully.

SAM: I was bullied. Trauma trickles down. Were you bullied as a kid?

SL: No.

[Note from Shuang, months after our conversation: OK, I lied, I was bullied a little. But my knee-jerk reaction has always been, "I'm not a victim"—I can't help it.]

SAM: Interesting . . . I'm curious about the things that draw people to certain genres of music. I was definitely drawn to things due to my geolocation. Embarrassingly, my first cassette tape was a country tape. I enjoyed Dwight Yoakam. The original rat boy of summer. Kurt [Cobain] died right before I went to middle school. So it was the fading echoes of the '90s. Green Day, Offspring, but very grunge inflected. When I got older, I got into a lot of British stuff. Bollywood songs. New age Gregorian chants. French Ye-ye. Whale songs. At that age, I think it didn't matter what it was, on some level; I would have listened to anything from far away. I always felt like things were happening elsewhere. Like I was a spectator not a participant.

SL: Because you were in Cairo?

SAM: No, because I was in Puyallup, Washington.

SL: Who would you hang out with when you were a teenager?

SAM: I wasn't really allowed out much. My best friend, Rita, who you kind of remind me of actually, and I would just play pranks, go to thrift stores and make up characters and skits and shoot them with an old camcorder. I heard about dirty girls later and realized, that was us. I don't really know what it was about that time … it was sort of post– riot grrrl really but I think there was a quasi-gay, unconscious anti-capitalist, punk adjacency and grunge cantankerousness that has influenced me as a person probably … and the country music. [*awkward silence*]. *Anyway.* To go back to that "special emo something"—what do you think it was that attracted you to MCR? Did you know when you saw the album cover? Was it when you went home and you listened to it? Was it months later, you picked it up again, and then you played it?

SL: With My Chemical Romance, it was immediate. As soon as I heard them, my life was changed forever.

SAM: Welcome to the parade. How do you feel? How do you know you're feeling what other people are feeling? When you're dancing together or when you're jumping together or … ?

SL: In the case of emo, definitely crying together.

SAM: Crying together, we share the same tears, which is, incidentally and randomly, a Sailor Moon song.

SL: Really?

SAM: At least, that's the translation . . . Were you a depressed child?

SL: Yeah. It's depressing being an only child with an entire generation of only children born in the one-child-policy era of China.

SAM: You made a whole work [*Lord of the Flies*, 2022] around bringing your live avatars together in MCR T-shirts in Shanghai. Were all of those people fans already?

SL: That was when I was locked out of the country due to COVID-19. At the beginning, I was living on a month-to-month basis between residencies, friends' places, and short-term rentals. After around a year of failed attempts I had come to terms with the fact that I wasn't going to be able to go home, so I settled down at Cherish in Geneva.

I had this show with Ad Minoliti in Antenna Space, Shanghai, a city where I used to live. So I trained twenty people to dress up as me to go to the opening; they all had individualized scripts, as well as personal letters to read to my friends to say goodbye. A close friend, Dre Romero, worked with me on this performance for wardrobe direction. She got a letter read to her from a performer, too, which she didn't expect. She had the genius idea to put everyone in the MCR shirt, since that's what I wear all the time. We weren't thinking about fandom, per se, but when twenty people showed up in the same band T-shirt, the imagery of fandom was evoked regardless. So, to answer your question, they weren't fans, they came as performers.

SAM: And they left as fans!

SL: Maybe.

SAM: What a result. I think that would be a video I would want to see, two My Chemical Romance fans seeking each other out to make a video together.

SL: I did have many friends from various My Chemical Romance message boards. There was a Chinese My Chemical Romance fan forum where I made many friends and, as a teenager, it was so special. You encourage each other to write and to make fan art together. I think that marked the beginning of me wanting to make art, to be honest. Gerard Way from My Chemical Romance went to the School of Visual Arts. He wanted to be an illustrator and he was working at the Strand Bookstore. One of his comic series was called *The Umbrella Academy*, by the way, which I read back in the day; it was recently adapted into a TV show. So, in the beginning, I was trying to make comics, but it didn't really speak to me.

SAM: There were also a lot of other things happening around the music then, like Myspace and everything.

SL: That was the era when the internet could have literally talked to someone.

SAM: One of the things I really love about the way you think about the world and also reflect it in your work is through the lens of a very specific time.

I feel like most artists that I love and go back to all the time, across centuries, are reflecting their time and their experience honestly, and reflecting where they come from. But also, they're mirrors, not native informants.

SL: I was thinking about it recently, actually, when we went to Marseille, when I met Ryan [Trecartin]. We were talking about this, and I was telling him that I thought his work was really, really ahead of his time. It's not reflecting his time, it's reflecting what's about to come. If you look at TikTok today, you see his shadows everywhere. He was the first one to put all his videos on YouTube and everything.

SAM: His works inspired me greatly, I saw the videos on YouTube first.

SL: The same way you inspired me!

SAM: When?

SL: When I graduated from NYU, I was so lost. One day I was just walking around in New York, and I walked into your solo show *Black Friday* at the Whitney. It was the first time I ever saw anything like that. And that's the moment I was like, maybe that's something I would want to do in this lifetime!

SAM: Really?

SL: Full cycle.

SAM: I don't know what to say, so I'm going to change the subject. There are certain major global events that shape your exhibition, *I'm Not*. Can you talk about a few key moments that you think have influenced your worldview and the prism through which you're making your work?

SL: 9/11.

SAM: Could you expand on that?

SL: 9/11 has a butterfly effect for My Chemical Romance. Gerard was working at the Strand at the time. On the day of the attack, he had a morning shift and as he was leaving work, he witnessed the explosion and saw bodies falling from the sky. The next day he founded My Chemical Romance, on September 12, which is my birthday.

SAM: The band was founded on your eleventh birthday.

SL: Yes, my eleventh birthday is My Chemical Romance's day of birth. It was really incredible when I learned about this. At that time of 9/11, we had a school program, and every day a kid would go to the front of the class to do a presentation of major news that happened that day. I will never forget that morning, this girl—she was really cute with a round face and pigtails—she went to the front and started talking about 9/11. I think, at that time, only one plane had hit, but she was delivering the news with a very joyful, TV presenter type of disposition because—I can only speculate—she believed that's how you should do this kind of presentation and that's how everyone was doing it. So she did it in such a joyful way, including when she said that a second plane had just hit one of the towers. And, of course, nobody in the class, including the teacher, understood what she was talking about. I guess nobody in the world did, at the instant it happened.

SAM: It must have been so abstract.

SL: Yeah, it's true. But maybe because I couldn't really go to these places. Like, I lived in New York, but I wasn't able to live in Ohio. Maybe New Jersey, but not Nevada. So I really fantasize about other places because of the Midwestern emo bands.

SAM: Have you ever read that Baudrillard book about America?

SL: No, which one? I need to read it.

SAM: That's what I should have gotten you for your first institutional solo show there. We should look at it because I feel like you might be into it. Basically, Baudrillard was really obsessed with America because he felt like it was a reflection, a matrix, I think he did a road trip. I remember thinking his obsession with this manifest accelerationist destiny of "America!" was so much about myths and aesthetics, it was riding alongside Orientalism as a mode of othering. My father literally went to America because he wanted to drive a truck and be a cowboy in America because he saw it on TV. When I started trying to unpack my own history, it got deeper and deeper. When I understood the

reason my dad ever even saw that stuff, it was because of oil. Because of Saudi Aramco TV. Because if Roosevelt hadn't made a deal, like you saw in *Bitter Lake*, television wouldn't have been showing *Rawhide* and all these cowboy movies where they used to rock up. My dad would literally go to the bar and order cold tea. Even though it was whiskey in the movie, in Arabic, it was cold tea. It would be translated. And so much is mistranslated. There's an uneasiness to America. Like, white people with a bit of sensitivity to vibes or knowledge of history know the feeling of not really belonging there. Which is why it sort of makes sense that emo came from there.

SL: Why?

SAM: *Rebel Without a Cause.* James Dean comes from there. All of the outsider rebel stuff is from American ideology and self-mythologizing as revolutionary. There were people from all over the world there before European colonization and genocide. I mean, it was colonized by Asia through the Bering Strait. I wonder if there were prehistoric emos. I'm sure there were, because in the 1400s in Europe, there were much bigger cities in the Americas, St. Louis in Mexico. These cities were way bigger than they were in Europe. London was small compared to these cities. But when they started to collapse, you must have gotten emos. I feel like that's what happens when civilizations start to fail. Like after the French Revolution, young people basically became nihilistic goths. They were super morbid. They had earrings like guillotines. They had seen so much violence. But they didn't call it goth or emo in the eighteenth century. But they would literally paint their faces to look like they were dead. The girls all wore really transparent garments to look like shrouds, but it was really scandalizing because they would basically be naked. So it's something that's in the human culture of the empire maybe? The mourning period expressed culturally. When you first showed me *The Black Parade*, the first thing I thought was, this reminds me of Napoleon. It's very martial but they're the underdogs. I don't know if I trust the image. They always wear kind of military-looking clothes. It freaks me out. I remember staying in your room at Cherish (before I knew you), there was a coat with epaulettes hanging next to the bed. I remember wondering, "Who is this baby dictator!?"

SL: Me.

SAM: Can you explain the martial thing?

SL: That's a good question. There's military content in the show—for the video *I'm Not*, where I covered MCR's "I'm Not Okay (I Promise)." I rewrote all the lyrics, some in Mandarin Chinese and some in English. Then I had an a cappella group perform it. I wanted to film a military choir for the video, so I bought military-ish uniforms from this website, Taobao, to dress them. Then I intercut it with footage of crazed fans from MCR concert footage, to form a contrast between stern-looking military people and frenetic fans. I don't really know where the military aspect comes from in terms of MCR, but, for me, I always associate the image of the army with fans. And that's all that an army should be.

SAM: Did Gerard come from a military family?

SL: No, I don't think so. Green Day also have songs where the music video is about the war. "Wake Me Up When September Ends," remember the video? It was this couple, the boy signed up to join the military without his girlfriend knowing, then she got so mad.

SAM: That happened when I was in senior year. I almost joined the US military.

SL: Really?

SAM: Yes. You don't know this?

SL: No. Why?

SAM: Scholarship. It was '99. My mom was really pushing. She wanted me to join. She wanted me to stay in the States. My dad was meanwhile saying, you can go to Qatar, I think you can get a scholarship. My mom was like, the US military is a done deal: you can get a scholarship after you serve for two years. If I had served for two years after graduating in 2001…

SL: Oh my god, you would have gone to Iraq.

SAM: I don't like thinking about it, but I do sometimes. Many people who I went to school with went to Iraq and Afghanistan. I saw one of them in the

mall in Qatar once. That's in *Black Friday*. It was probably around 2004. I was with my little sister. My mom had sent these little T-shirts for her that had an American flag on them. And she was, like, four or five years old. She was mortified. I was trying to hold her hand so she wouldn't get lost while she was trying to cover up the flag on her shirt. We were outside of a Nando's or something. And I see this kid I went to high school with, because the biggest American military base is in Doha, and he was dressed down. But you could always tell people from the base by their boots. And of all people it was this kid Dusty Miller from my high school in America, and I was wearing hijab. Even though we dissected a fetal pig together in AP Biology, five years later, I looked like the kind of person he was trained to kill. Isn't it ironic?

SL: Yeah.

SAM: OK. My next question is, what made you decide to pursue art? People who decide to run away with the circus and do art (unless they come from a family of collectors or artists) have to push beyond the boundaries of what their family thought was possible. At least, that's my observation. So I'm wondering if you could talk a little bit about the first piece of art you saw and how it changed things for you.

SL: The first one I saw, I don't remember, to be honest. But I do remember the first piece of contemporary art that really left a huge impression on me. I was in college, and then I went to this museum in Beijing. At the time, there was this retrospective of a Chinese artist who was very active in the '80s, Gu De Xin. He's part of a group of artists called Star Collective, which is really funny because another one of them has the exact same name as me, but she's a painter, and she's actually, like, the OG it girl. The ticket to enter the museum was really expensive for me at that time, so I just went to the gift shop. I saw this one thing, it was like a thick postcard. On the cover it had a kind of soviet or communist propaganda style of big red font that said, "We kill men, we kill women, we kill children, we eat men, we eat women," and so on. But when you opened it, there was a picture of a blue sky and it said, "we can go to heaven." That was the first time I was like, wow, art. But to this day, I still haven't seen this artist's works in person, because at the peak of his career, he just decided to quit, and nobody heard from him ever again.

SAM: Legend.

SL: I know. I think he also had this piece that was just an entire room of apples, but they rot as time goes by, as the show goes on, and if you go at the end, it would just be rotten apples and their smell. Really nice. Very digestive, death-focused work. I think, looking back, it might be my first installation, because I was living in a dorm at that time. It was actually like a semi-military school. I can't believe I went to a semi-military school.

SAM: This was in Shanghai?

SL: No, it was a town outside of Beijing. You had to get up in the morning at 6:00 a.m. to jog.

SAM: No.

SL: Yes. And then you couldn't stay out. The dorm closed at ten and there were people checking if everyone was in their beds. So it was a bunk bed, on top was the bed, on the bottom was a desk space. I drew this sign on a piece of paper—in China there's constant construction and destruction happening, so there were a lot of buildings that were always marked 拆, which means "destroy." So I drew that sign in red and put it on my wardrobe, so when you opened it, you broke the sign.

SAM: So when you say *destroy*, do you mean like condemn, the way they put on buildings?

SL: Yeah, it's like a mark. Like this building will be destroyed tomorrow.

SAM: Wow. So every time you opened your wardrobe, it was like walking into a condemned building. But a condemned outfit. A condemned look. *A way of seeing*. I love the way you have such a specific viewpoint on the world, like each work is filtered through the prism of a particular moment that seems to change things for you.

SL: I mean, right now is definitely one of those periods. I assume it's pivotal for everyone. To watch genocide on your phone from your bed and not be able to do anything about it. Yeah, but to

be honest, it's really against how I live to assume this point of view. I always want to find a way out, maybe not just out, but more like against it, which I realized recently, because, at the beginning, I didn't really see how my work and technology interacted. Of course, my work all comes from or talks about technology, but it's not until recently that I realized it's actually, in essence, rebelling against technology. It's not just about using the most advanced screens or the most advanced technology but it's about finding a way out of here. But it's also like the only way out is through. So I guess we have to live through it to think about a way out. I think it's important not to give up. There must be something we can do to help besides reposting, besides protesting, besides donating. There must be things we can do.

SAM: Boycotting.

SL: Yeah.

SAM: Physically going there. I've been thinking a lot about how artists and writers went to the Spanish Civil War. Are the screens what stop us from being the kind of people who get drawn to a cause to physically go? I do feel concerned that we're all so entwined with comfort and capitalism that making that break and devoting yourself to something physically has become totally alien. Whereas before, you probably weren't that comfortable where you were anyway, so you might as well go do *something*. But that's a larger conversation about mass bourgeois ideology. Maybe it was yesterday we were talking about how your work, and I really relate to this, the way that you don't really want to shoot anymore. You want to just reuse found footage. You made that incredible piece [*Heart is a Broken Record*, 2023] that's just the eternal anticipation of right before My Chemical Romance comes out, which, in a way, is a sort of archival piece. It reminds me of stuff like Christian Marclay's *The Clock* (2010), or just revisiting archives or revisiting collective memory, or the many different perspectives of a fan video, which is why that piece is so brilliant. It feels like a real, perfect example of why and what your work touches on. That's extremely moving to me. But with technology, there's this thing that was happening maybe in the mid-2000s, which was very mid, in my opinion, salvage punk which was such a white bro extinction crisis thing. But just reusing old stuff or using hacks to reboot old pieces of technology still feels relevant. I think knowing how to hack and reuse and reboot old tech is important. Not knowing how my devices are functioning makes me feel like a domesticated animal.

SL: True.

SAM: Does it make sense to think that domestication is bad? Is ignorance bliss? Is laziness bad? I read something—no—I saw a TikTok about the just-lie-down generation and that sort of youth culture developing an ideology of resistance to the current dominant paradigm. And in a way, I thought—resisting in a way that offends society is basically what punk was. Is it punk to "just lie down"?

SL: It is quite punk, but, for me, it just seems too easy. I feel that most days, I have to go against it because I can lie down forever. My iron deficiency makes me sleep twelve hours a day easily.

SAM: The other day I was listening to something about how, in the civil rights movement, a lot of white young people went to the South, many of whom died or were injured on the front lines of the civil rights fight in the South. There were buses going down there in similar ways that there's been talk of convoys going to Gaza or at least being at the Rafa border.

SL: I remember my dad was also talking about the Vietnam War, about how he really wanted to go, but at that time it was like you had to be part of the Chinese army first, and then they would send people together to Vietnam. So he tried really hard to enlist in the army, but they didn't pick him. And he was really mad about not being picked.

SAM: I guess everyone in the army is a pick-me girl.

SL: I'm the last one to be chosen for that team, I hope. I remember when he was telling me, he's like, I'm so sad I didn't get enlisted. I was like, why? You were gonna die. But in light of today's events, I think differently now. It just appears that history is just literally repeating itself in all the ways possible. I remember, for me, personally, growing up in China in the early 2000s, having witnessed this very different period than before when the country

opened up and embraced capitalism, the market economy, and we had a chance to study abroad and travel abroad and do all these things, and you would think, history was just history. It wouldn't happen again. But during COVID it's exactly the same things, if not worse.

SAM: So you've ended up based in Europe. Now you're going back to New York, but via a Swiss Institute show, and you live now partially in Switzerland. What do you think this show is going to be saying to an American audience or a New York audience? And what about it is maybe different from your other work?

SL: I haven't thought about it. How did you feel when you had the Whitney show? Where were you living at that time?

SAM: I was living in Doha. No, I had just moved to London.

SL: How was that show for you?

SAM: I wanted to talk about shopping malls to an American audience because I was interested in that architectural structure, which, actually, was designed by Victor Gruin, who was an Austrian architect who disavowed it at the end of his life. He was sorry that he made these traps, but it was very explicit that those buildings and the way they're built are meant to disorient. For a person who walks into them, it's a scripted environment. It's a ritual. There's a sort of religious aspect to them. You have to pay your alms to get out. Like, you use your card or pay in cash. Go into the changing room and you have to face yourself, confess the truth, when you're trying things on. So I find them to be very fascinating, and also I get lost in them easily. Even though I can be aware of them being manipulative spaces, I also feel totally open to manipulation—you can know someone is gaslighting you and still participate.

SL: Totally. That's capitalism.

SAM: Yeah. In one sentence. That's what I wanted to talk to America about, I guess, specifically how that's a soft-power way of having colonial power. You can insert your shops and places to recoup your money. And it's also related to disaster capitalism. That's, I think, a Naomi Klein idea. She used the example—which I think about a lot—of Iraq, where the US magicked a market out of the chaos they had created and the reality Iraqis were condemned to. Condemned … destroyed. Can we go back to your first ever installation?

SL: When I was making *Heart is a Broken Record*, at one of the first meetings with the producer, all I had was a basic drawing. I didn't even think about what it actually looks like. He asked what kind of finishing I wanted to have for the fountain. Without thinking, I said I wanted it to look like a fountain in the shopping mall. Emo was the first music generation that was labeled a sellout. And they even hang out at the shopping mall all the time.

SAM: Going to Hot Topic. I wonder if it's a ghost shopping mall.

SL: It could be. Actually, I heard there are already some museums in China that have become ghost museums. A lot of museums in China are privately funded and backed by real estate companies. So, after the bubble burst, a lot of these real estate companies went into bankruptcy. As a result, some museums closed. And there are some that just turned into abandoned ghost museums.

SAM: Sounds like a cute date to take a big titty goth gf to. What even is goth? It's a riff of a tribe that capitalized off the disaster of the fall of the Roman empire but—I digress. I associate goth and emo and even, to an extent, lying down with grief and not so much nihilism as much as a humble acceptance of death, and it's like there's a bit of humility in it that I feel strongly attached to whatever the ways it's monetized or popified.

SL: Wow, that's such a beautiful reading of emo.

SAM: Thank god. But do you think it's just these two genres, or do you apply that to other genres?

SL: Is shoegaze also lying down?

SAM: I feel like shoegaze is pretentious even if I do indulge in a melancholic navel gaze now and then. Does melancholy have a place in your work? Sorry. That's a yes or no question.

SL: Yes.

SAM: How does grief manifest for you?

SL: I think, as I grew older, it became more and more necessary for me to keep making art because otherwise I wouldn't know how to process anything. Making work is my way to actually cope with the world, with what I'm going through. So, yeah, it starts with grief, for sure. Like this performance that I did was the grief about not being able to go home, not being able to see or even just say goodbye to my friends properly. It's the grief of being trapped in this physical body.

SAM: I'm going to bring in an American reference, really a fucked-up one. It's Tom Sawyer. Do you know the story?

SL: No. What's the story?

SAM: Well, he's a naughty boy. A naughty white boy in the Antebellum South. But in one of the stories—it's so crazy that we had to read those books at school—he fakes his own death and goes to his own funeral. But he's watching from above, enjoying watching everybody cry and grieve for him, which is, I think, such a white-boy fantasy also. I mean, maybe it's a child fantasy, but it's very emo, I have to say.

SL: Yeah, it is.

SAM: I want to go to my own funeral. I actually have a playlist called "Play This When I Die."

SL: What are the songs?

SAM: There are many. You can look at it, if you want. I started making it when I did this death doula course, which was kind of an extreme way to deal with my fear around loved ones passing away, in retrospect. But it was interesting to think in a group around practical preparations for such a thing.

SL: Both my grandparents passed away during COVID. China was going through a draconian lockdown till the last moment where the economy was collapsing. People were really living in hell, and they just opened up overnight. There were no measurements or prevention of any kind. So obviously, a lot of the old people got it immediately and died. My grandma was one of the first people that got COVID after this opening up. When I finally got to travel back, we went to visit her and my grandpa's grave. I'd never been to a Chinese grave-yard before. It's very different from the European ones here, where every tombstone is so beautiful, with all these different sculptures. In China, it was just like an entire mountain. And it looks like a real estate model, too, because every single tomb-stone is the same, and just the name and picture on each one is different, and every stone is at an exact distance from the neighbouring ones. An entire mountain of them.

SAM: You mean like a planned development?

SL: Yeah.

SAM: American-style compound.

SL: Yes, totally.

SAM: City of the dead.

SL: Mountain of the dead.

SAM: So, Shuang Li, what would the 2005 you think of the 2023 you?

SL: Wow.

SAM: I stole that from a Gerard Way interview.

SL: I don't think she would understand anything.

SAM: What would you tell her?

SL: I would tell her I met Frank Iero and he told me my work is awesome, and he asked for my autograph. Yeah. She would understand this. She would die.

SAM: She can't die because then you wouldn't exist.

SL: But what would you tell, how would you describe yourself to a fifteen-year-old you?

SAM: I would tell her that she's gay. Maybe save some time, some bad experiences.

Give her advance warning about that, I think. That even if everything isn't necessarily going to be OK, she should just lie down more, resist the urge to please her overlords of people-pleasing.

SL: Where do you think that comes from?

SAM: I think it comes partially from being pro-grammed and raised as a girl. But I think part of it is a survival strategy. Easy and trying to stay or be comfortable.

SL: In the fields of art or exhibitions, do you make different works for different continents or how do you usually go about it?

SAM: Well, whenever I do new work that's for a specific show, I definitely always feel it's import-ant to not just plunk ideas or stuff that was for a particular audience or even a particular time and place, because then it's not really the same as trying to talk with people. But my practice has changed over the years from being quite closed in a way, to being more open, involving more people. It was hard for me to move toward that openness of working with people, of having conversations open. There's also a fear element of losing control, I suppose, which is one of the reasons why I really love the idea of just doing something like drawing, but also wanting to do things like the exquisite corpse project that we did together, which is not the first exquisite corpse film ever, but it is like an attempt to undo this very rigid, hierarchical way of thinking that the art world has about an artiste or whatever. We talked about how the institutions often won't let you put your collaborators' names on the wall of yours. In my Doha show I had an artwork that was just the names of everyone who contributed in any way.

SL: That's so good.

SAM: To go back to the question, which was how would I make different works for different conti-nents, I guess it feels like presuming a lot to just do the same work in multiple places that maybe it has nothing to do with. That's why I stopped doing Gulf Futurism stuff when I stopped living there, because I was like, I'm not going to just be a diaspora person who's capitalizing on some-thing that I'm not experiencing anymore. But that split was very specific because I left Doha. I didn't consider myself diaspora before that. And then I left in my twenties after working there. And I was like, I should just make work about where I am now and what I'm interested in now. But in a way, it still totally informs everything. And weirdly, I'm going back to Gulf Futurism now, even though I don't live there. Because I've been working there on and off and I have more observations, I guess.

SL: I only started working with things that are very specifically China-influenced after I was taken away, but I don't consider myself diaspora. I consider myself a person in displacement. I think maybe because of this context of being violently taken away, it forced me to process it. Going back to your question from before, what has this show meant for me in New York, I think people usually talk about how New York influenced them, the same way it did for me. The most formative periods of my life are my early twenties in New York and early thirties in Geneva. I can't believe they are coming together perfectly in one show. Everything in New York happened through this lens of MCR. When I first started going to school at NYU, I would walk down the street and think, wow, this is where Gerard saw bodies falling from the sky. In some songs he talked about it. On the first album, there's one song called "Skylines and Turnstiles."

SAM: What are the lyrics of that song?

SL: "This broken city sky like butane on my skin."

SAM: It's quite sort of tragically romantic sounding.

SL: Yeah, that's my kind of romance.

"This broken city sky like butane on my skin
Stolen from my eyes, hello angel, tell me
Where are you?
Tell me where we go from here
And in this moment, we can't close the lids, on
    burning eyes
Our memories blanket us, with friends we know,
    like fallout vapors
Steel corpses stretch out towards an ending sun
Scorched and black, it reaches in and tears your
    flesh apart
As ice-cold hands rip into your heart
That's if you've still got one that's left

Inside that cave you call a chest
After seeing what we saw
Can we still reclaim our innocence?
And if the world needs something better
Let's give them one more reason, now
Tell me where we go from here"

SAM: Where does emo go from here? What comes after emo?

SL: There are people on TikTok talking about how they do a full circle in life through different phases, and go back to being emo, listening to the same playlist from when they were teenagers. These circular tracks of life seem to bring us back to where we were before, but they can also be seen as markers of cycles, like in numerology. I'm comfortable staying here.

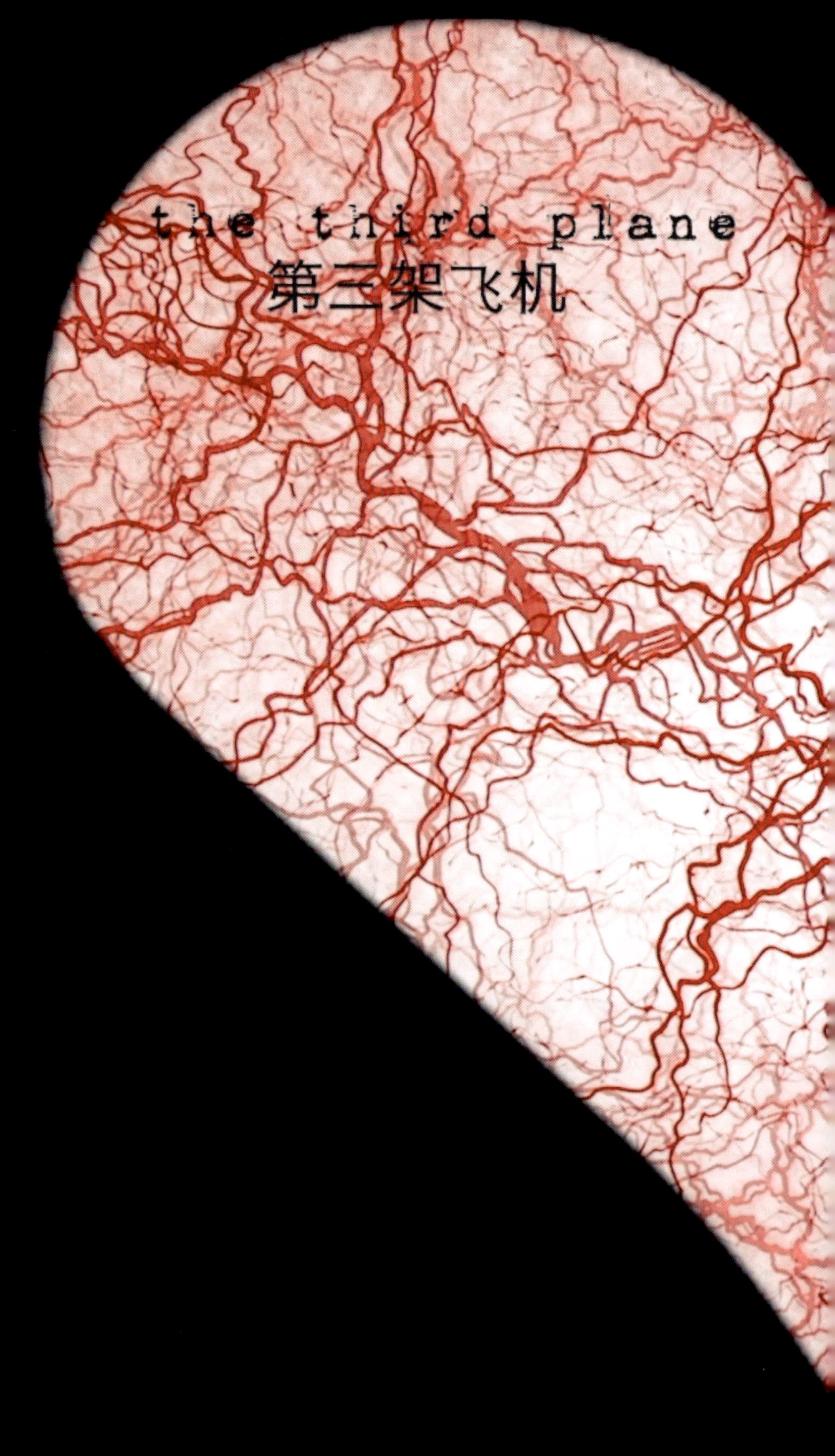
the third plane
第三架飞机

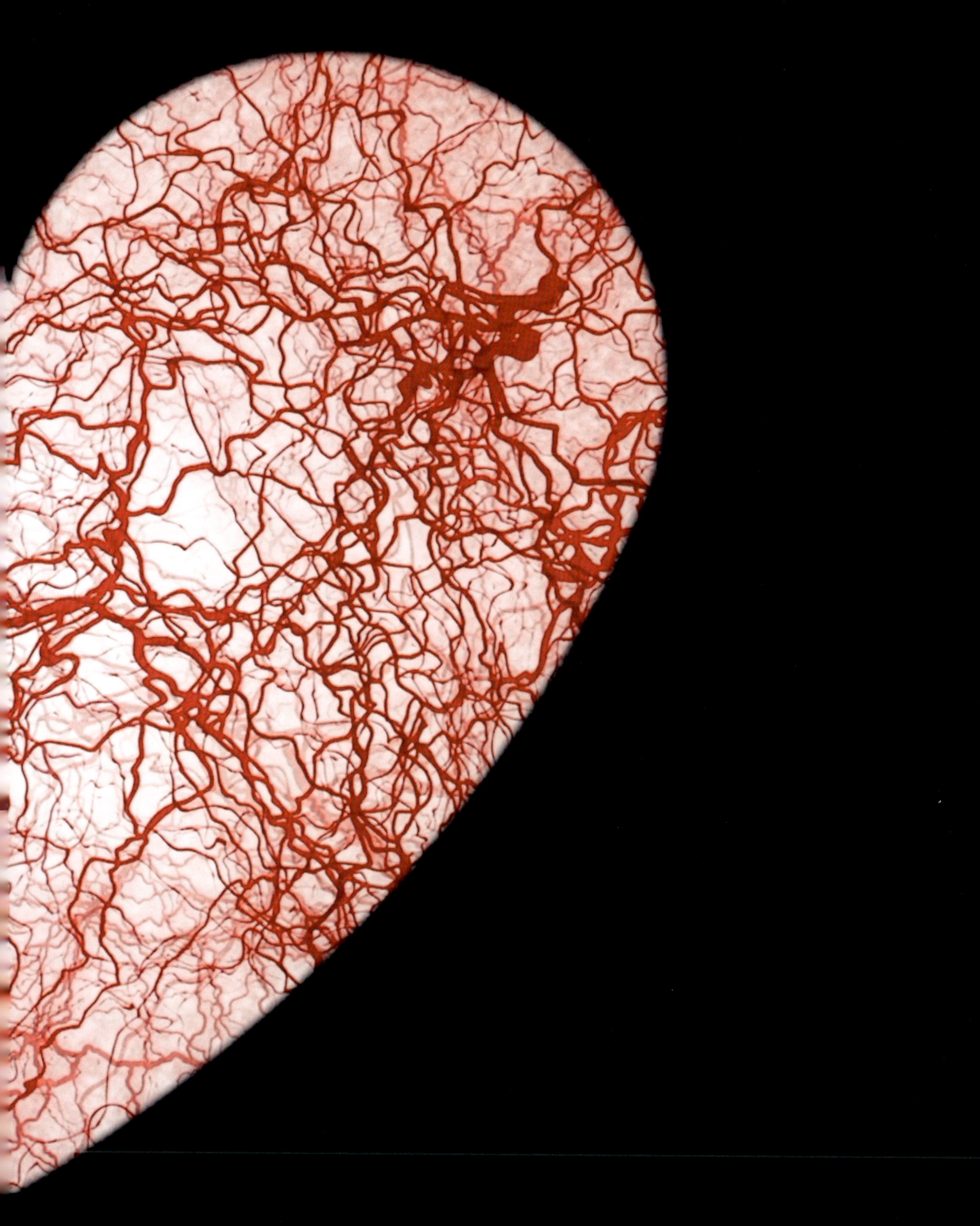

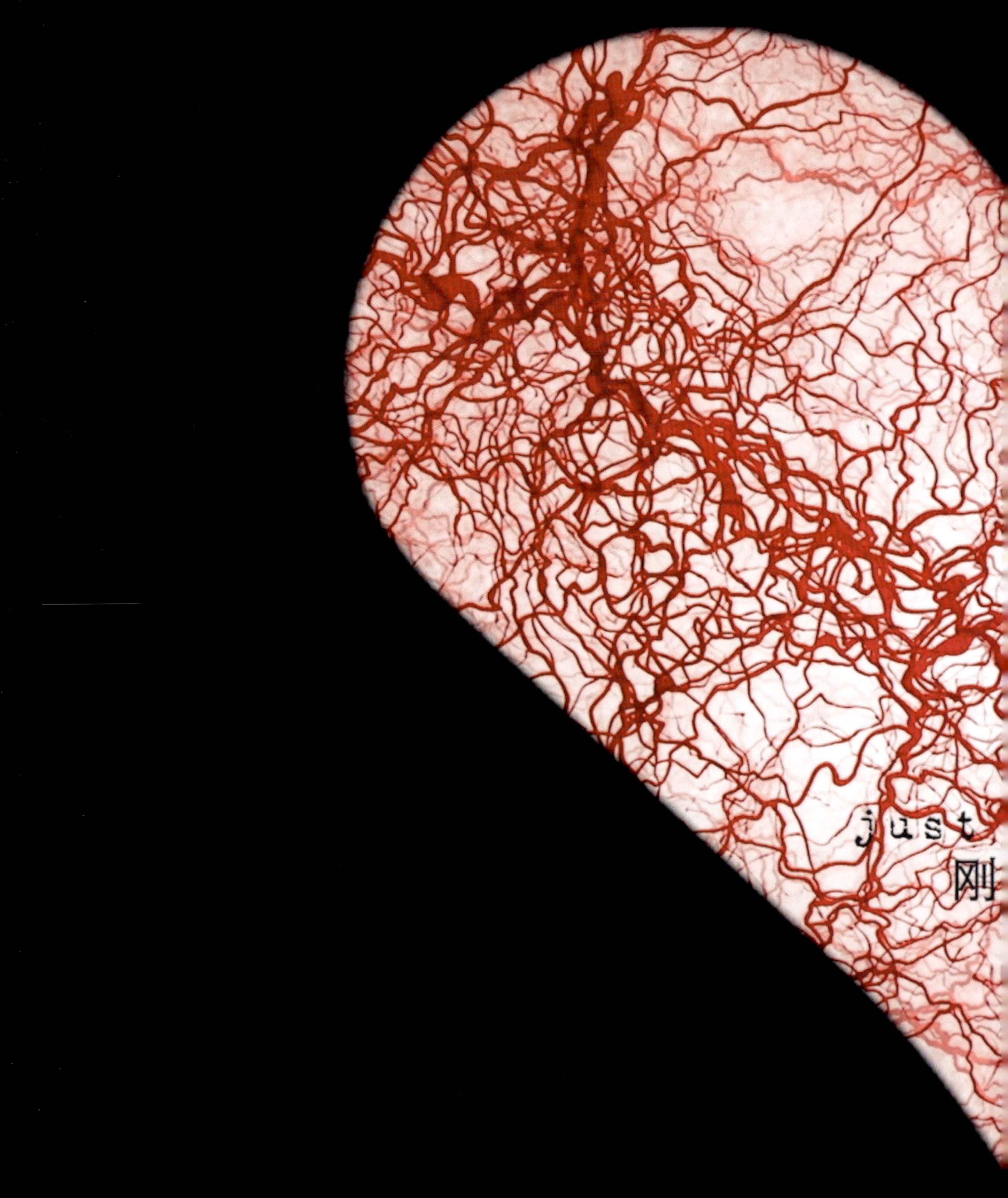
just
刚

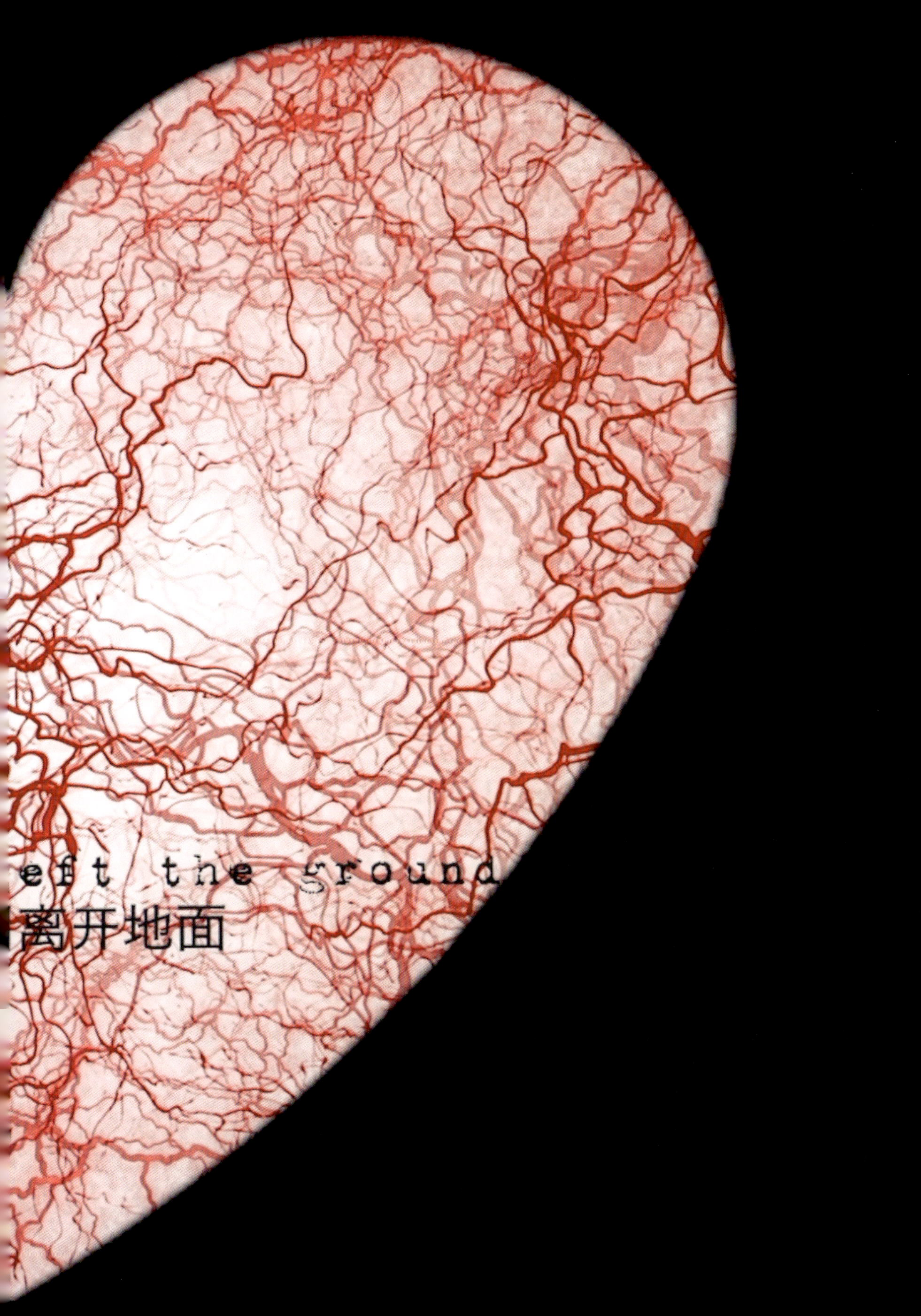
eft the ground
离开地面

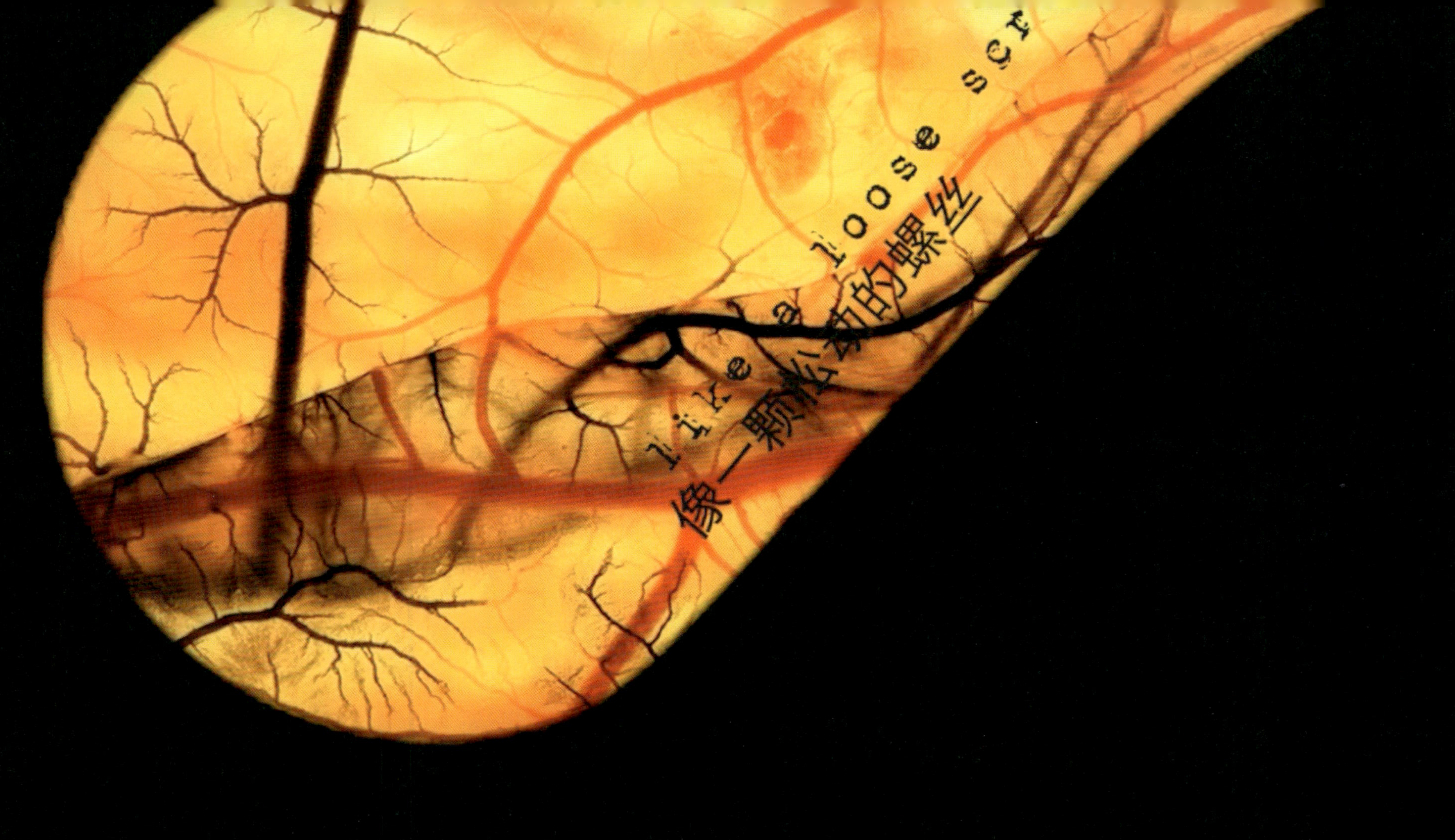
like a loose scr
像一颗松动的螺丝

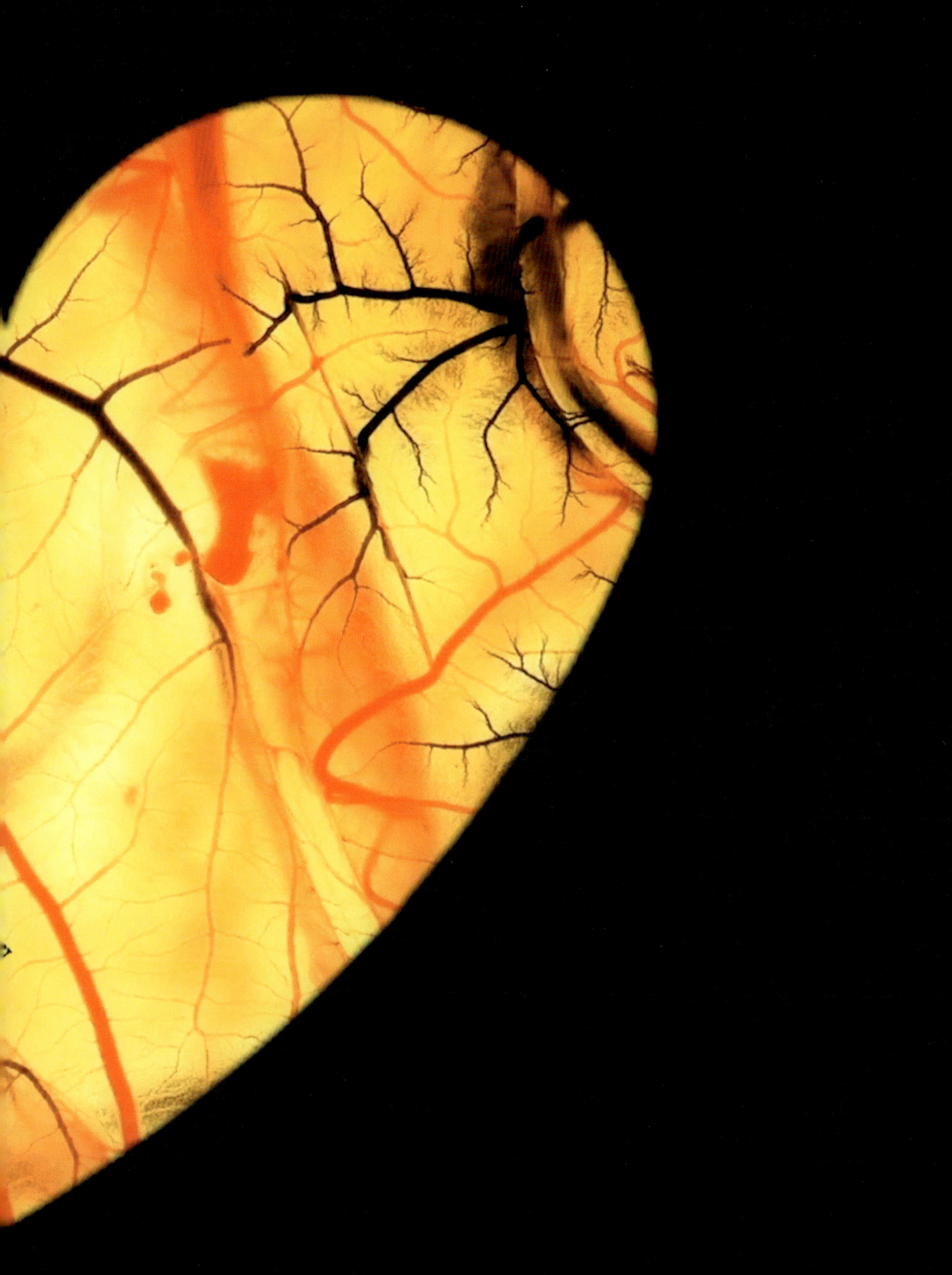

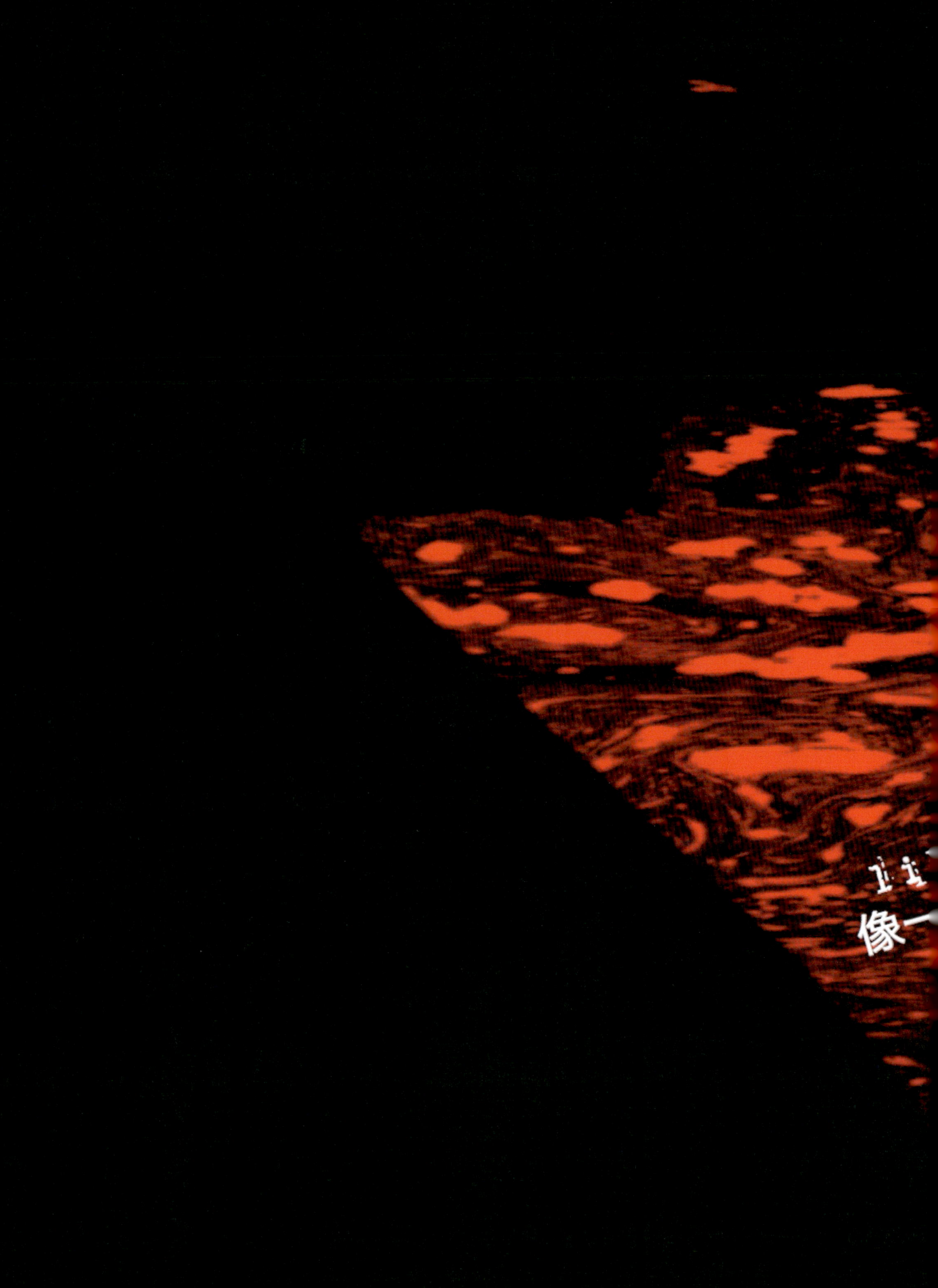
像一

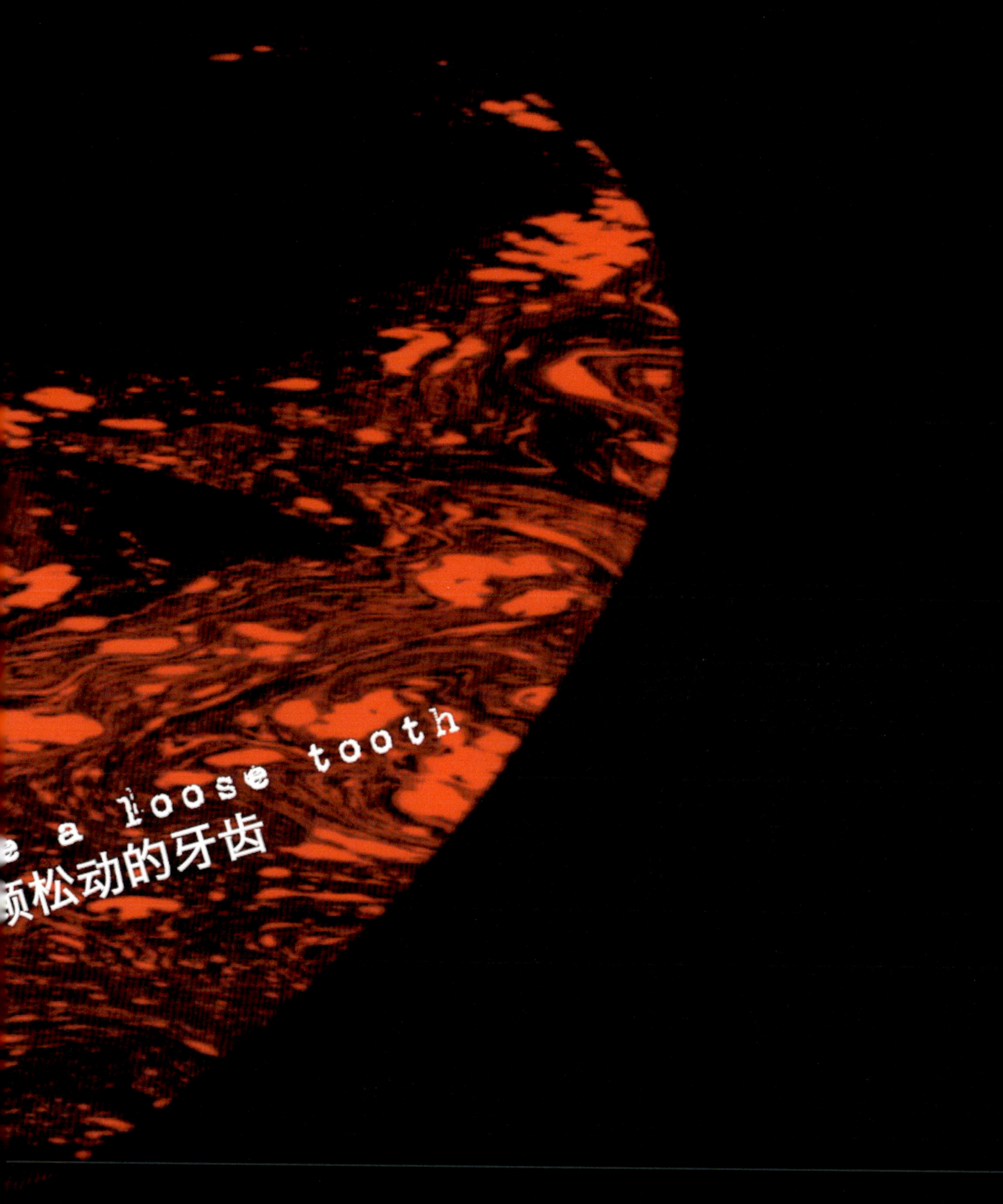
e a loose tooth
一颗松动的牙齿

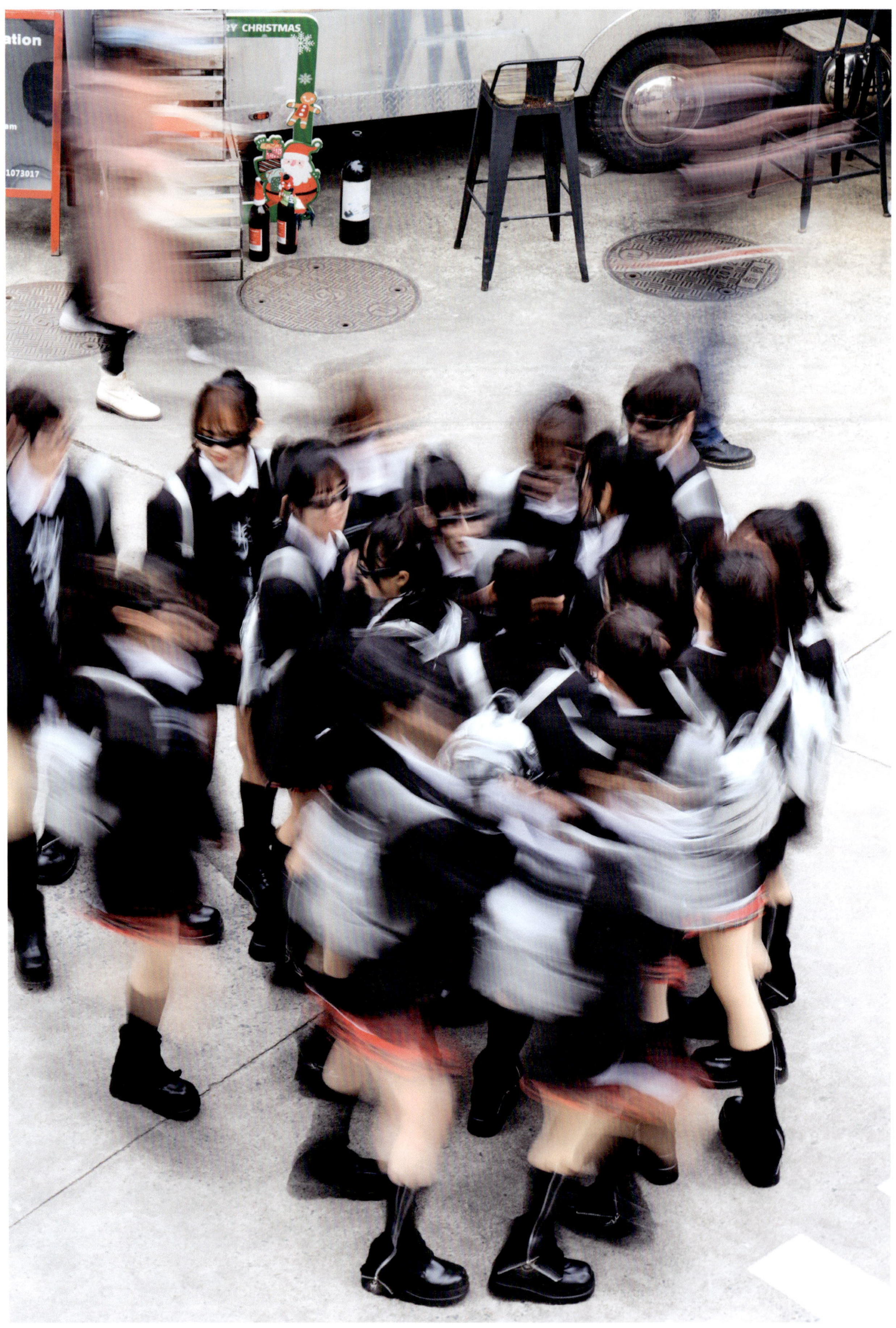
RY CHRISTMAS

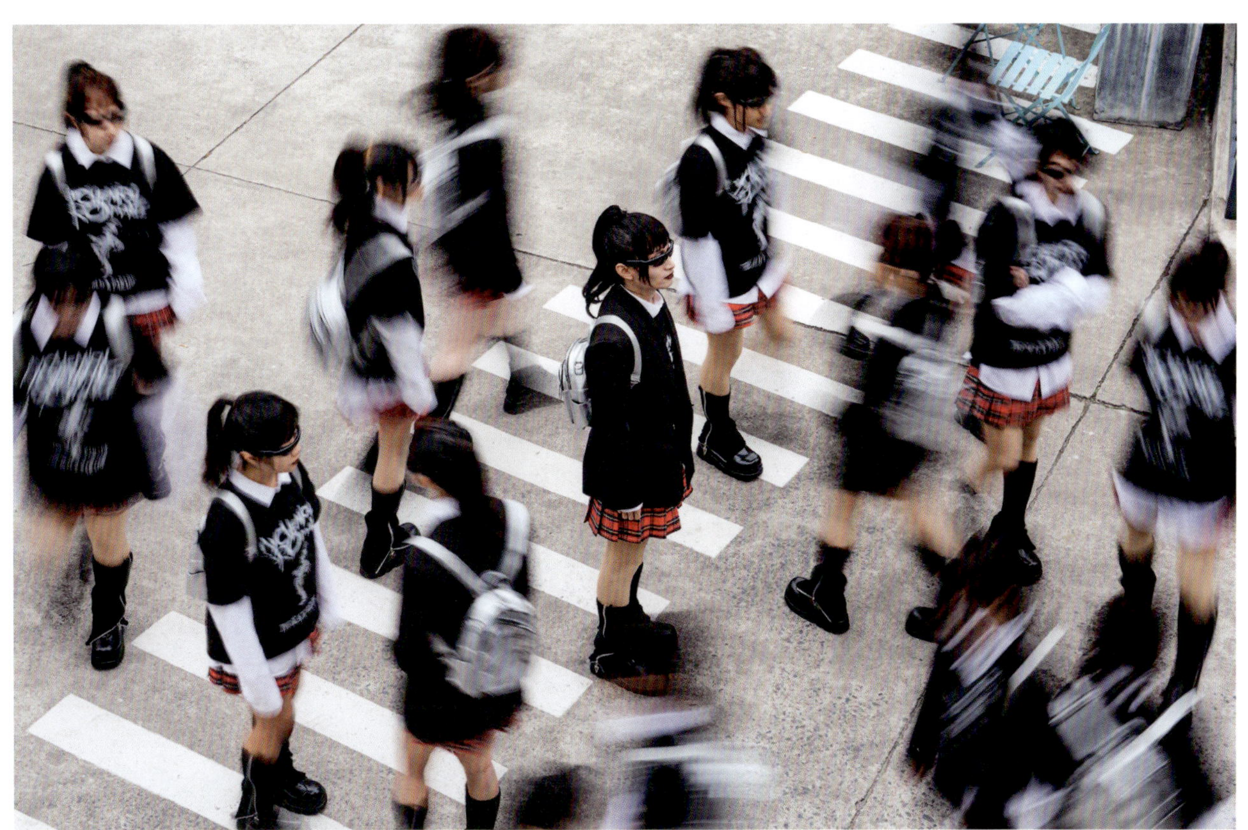

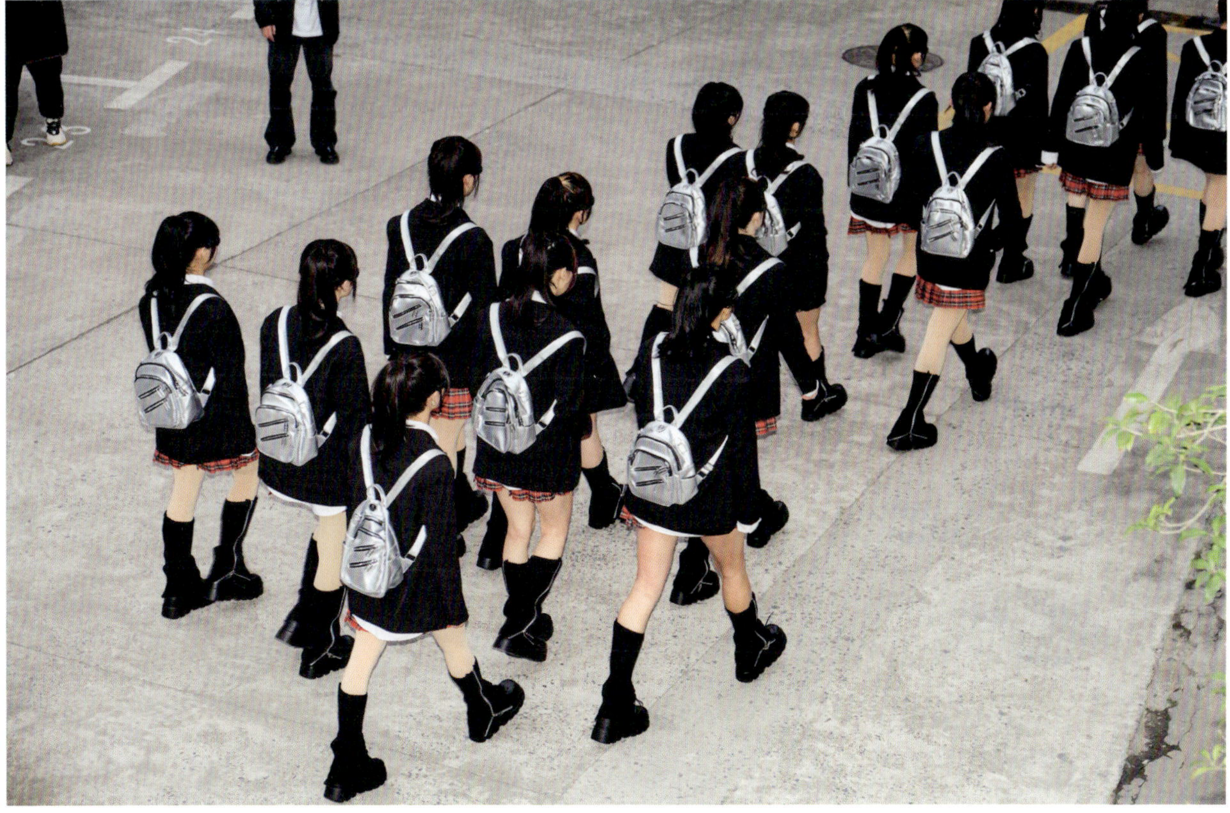

Lord of the Flies, 2022
Performance view, Antenna Space, Shanghai

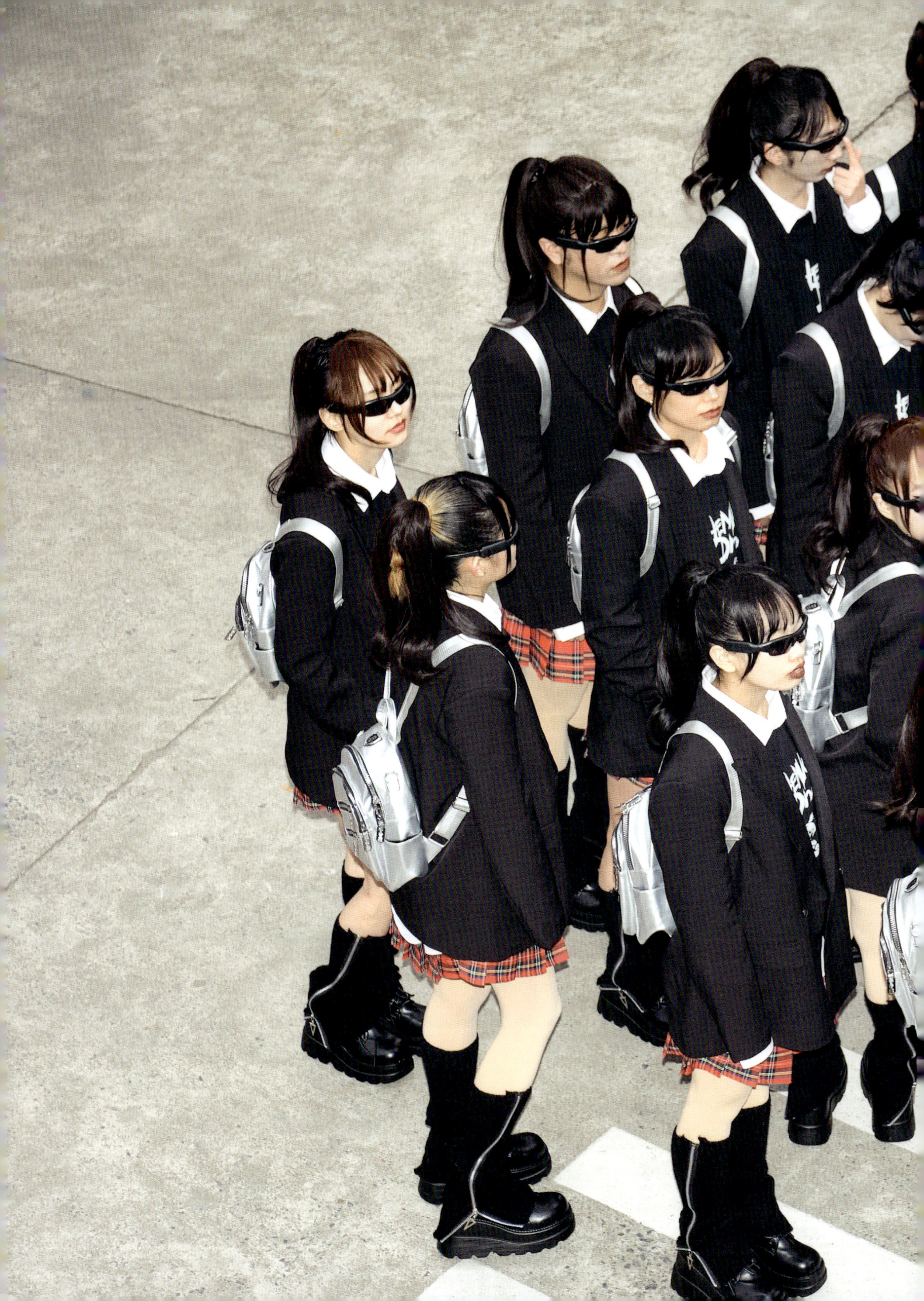

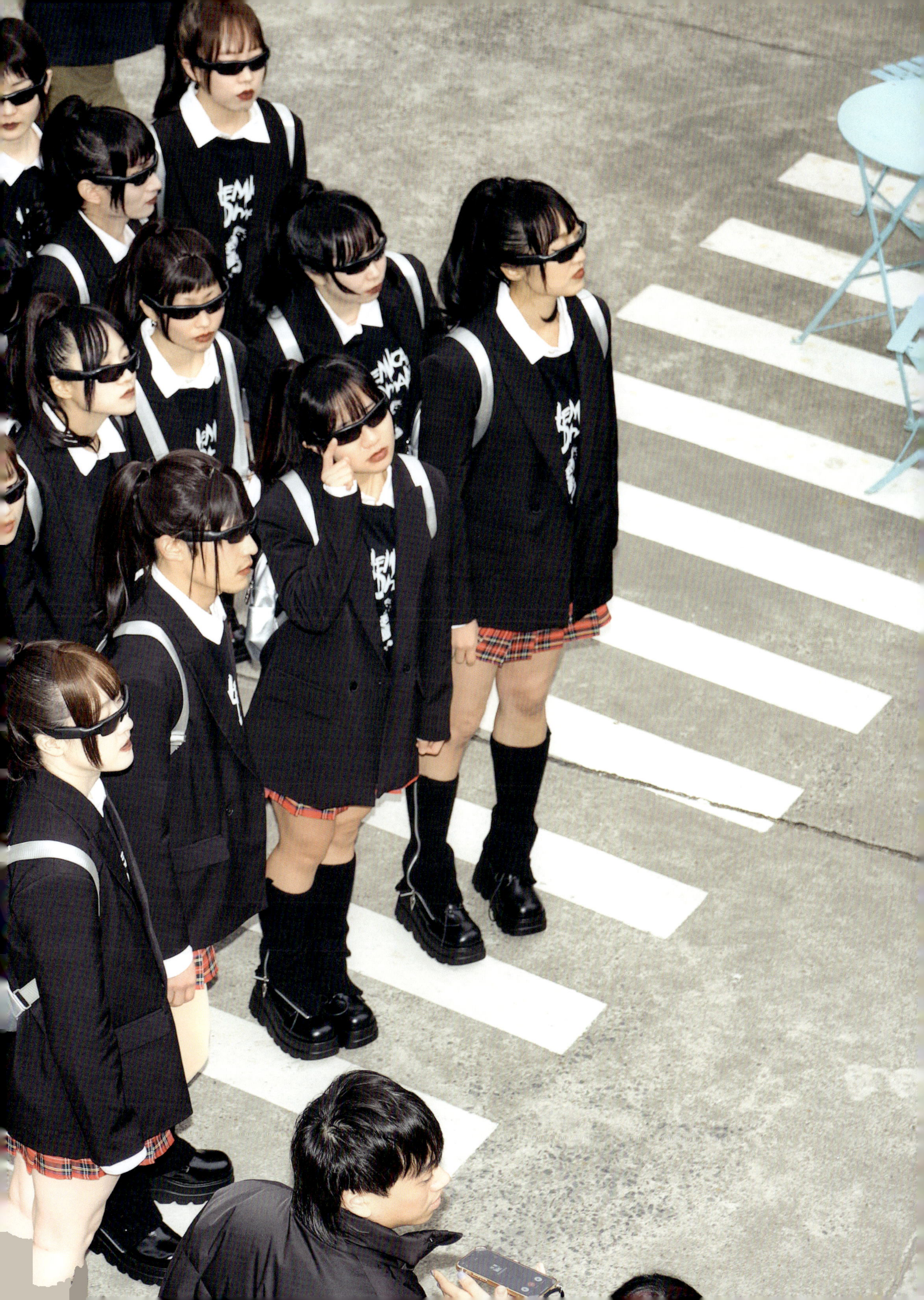

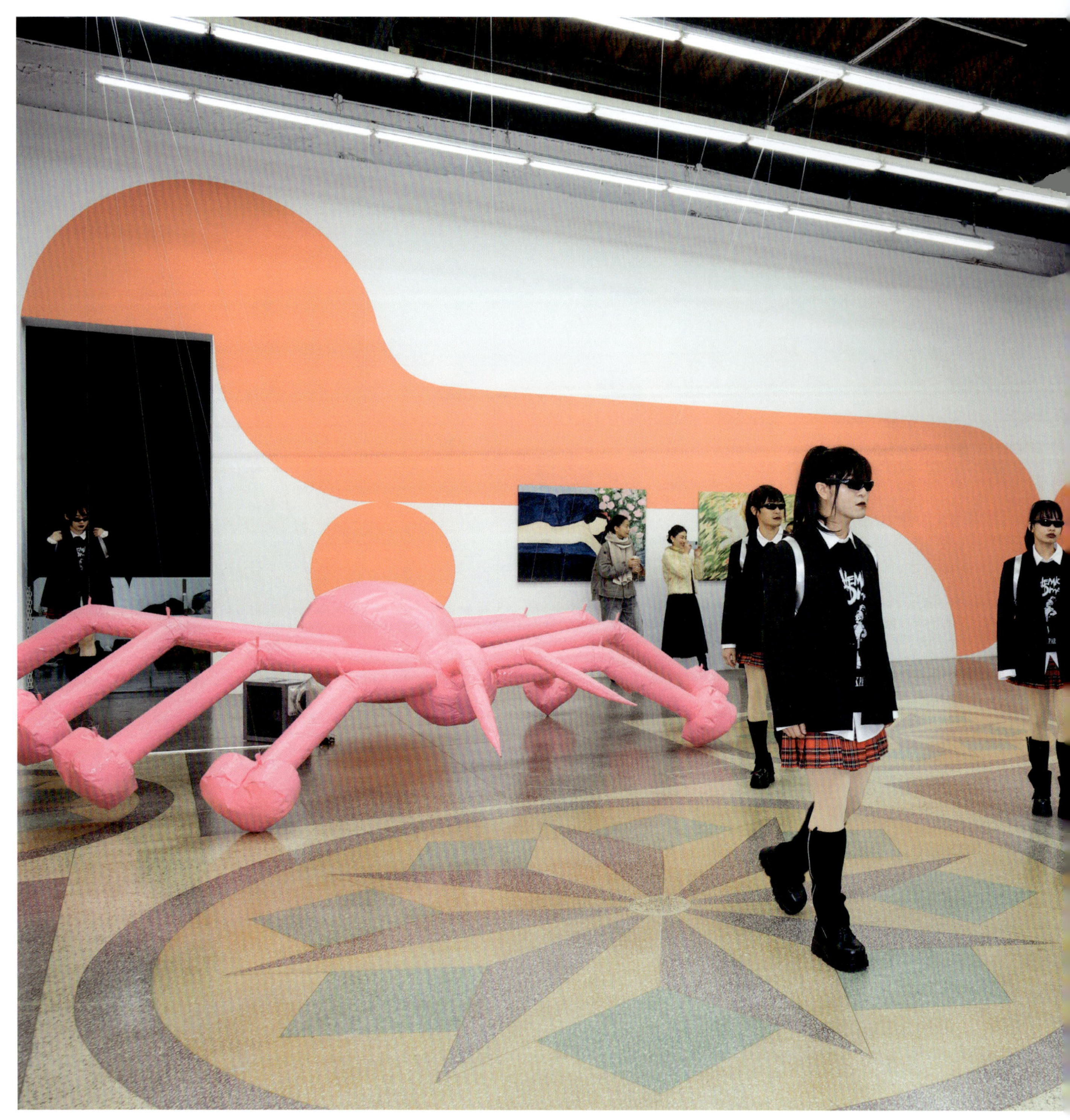

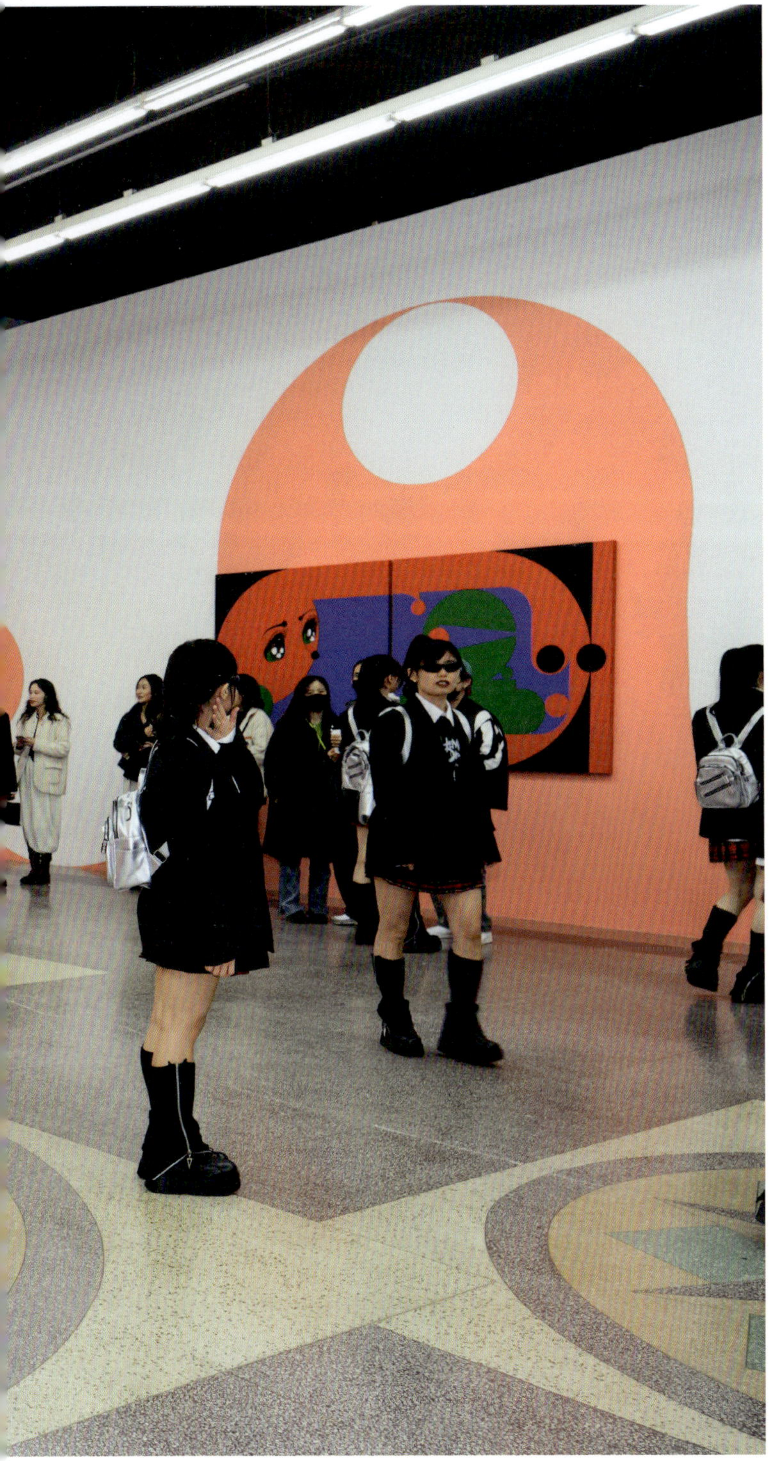

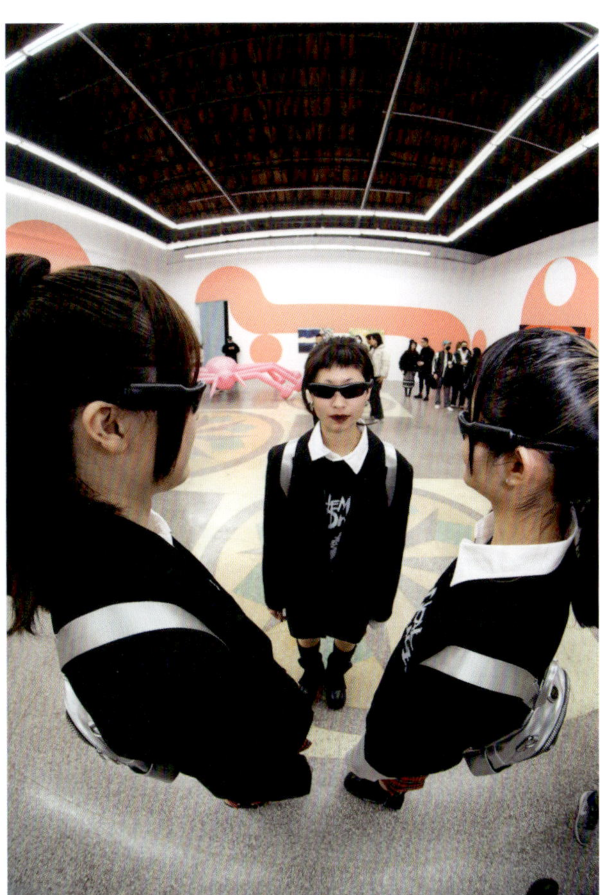

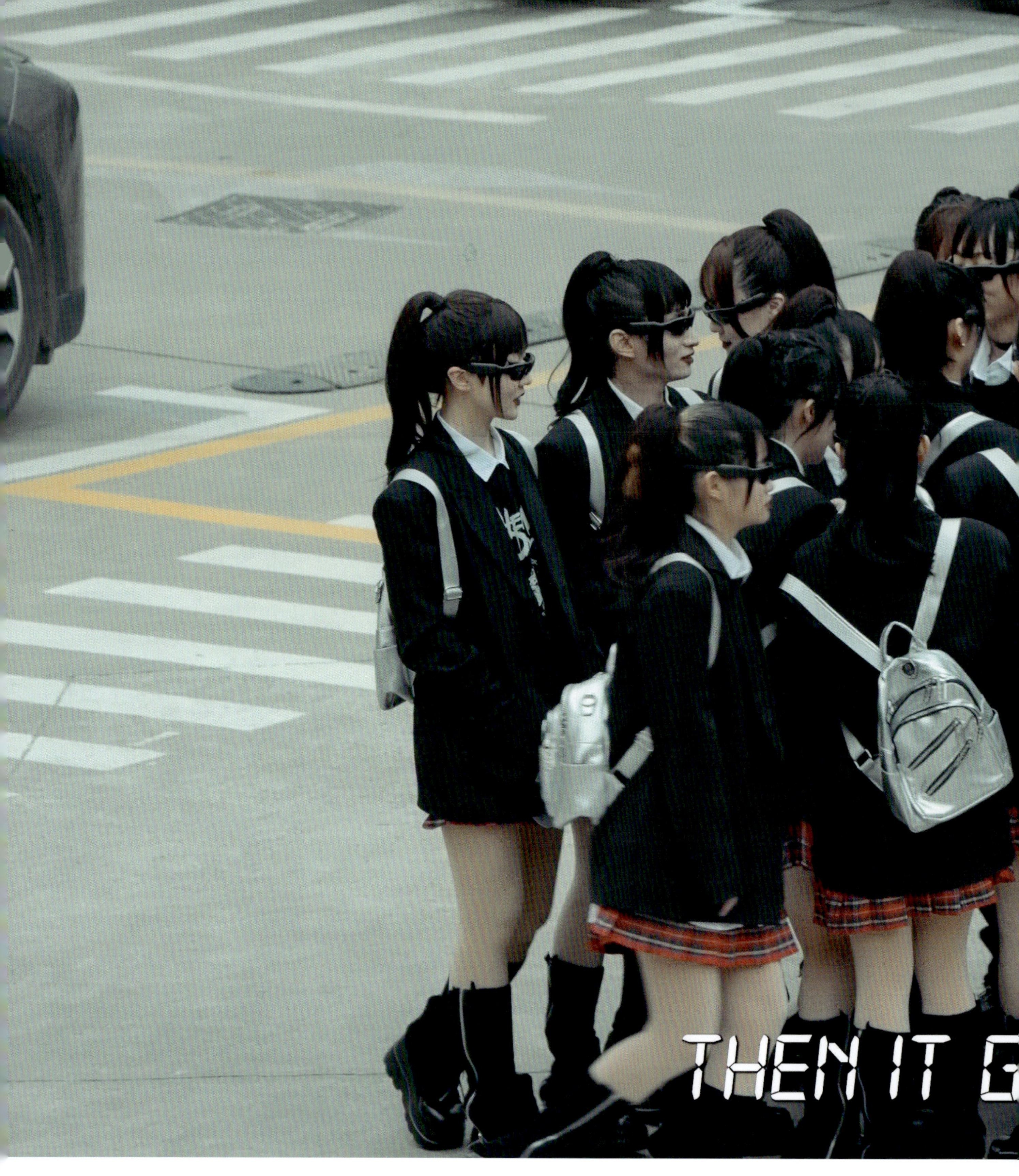
THEN IT G

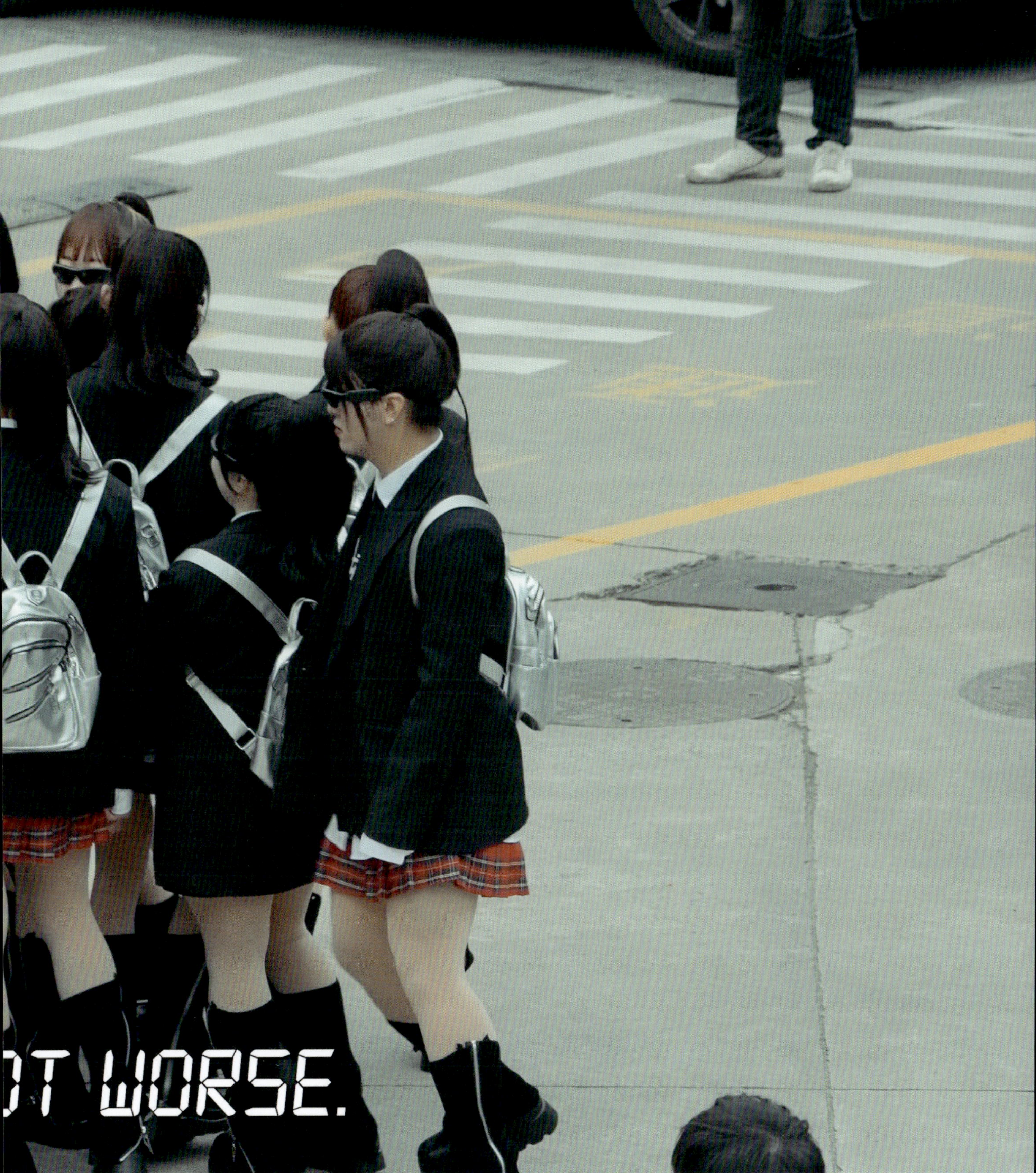

Déjà Vu, 2022

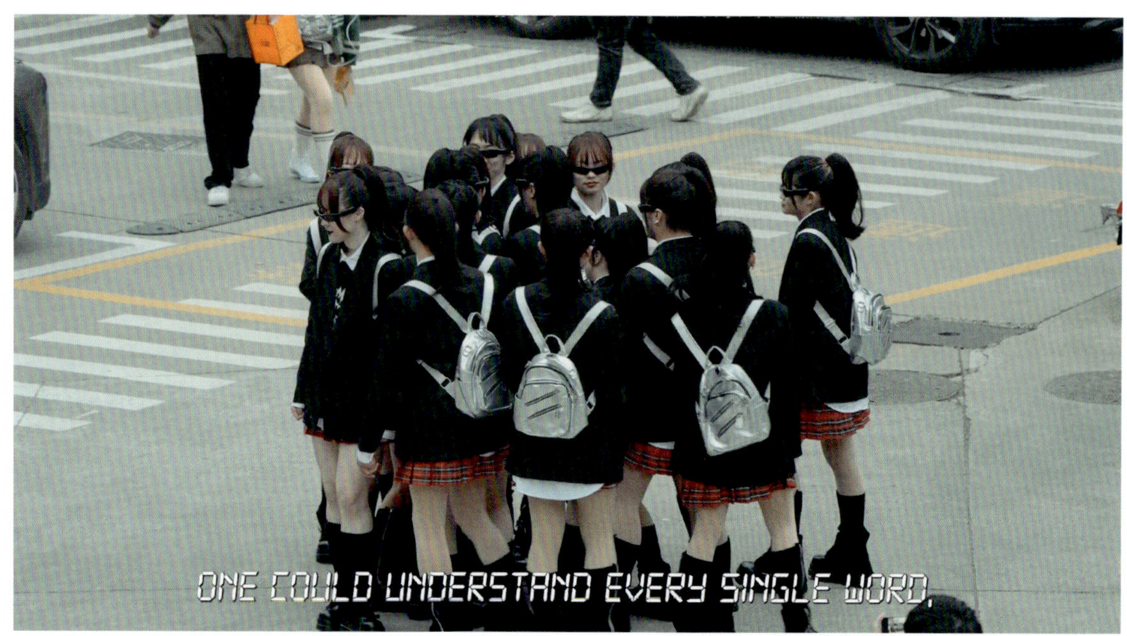
ONE COULD UNDERSTAND EVERY SINGLE WORD,

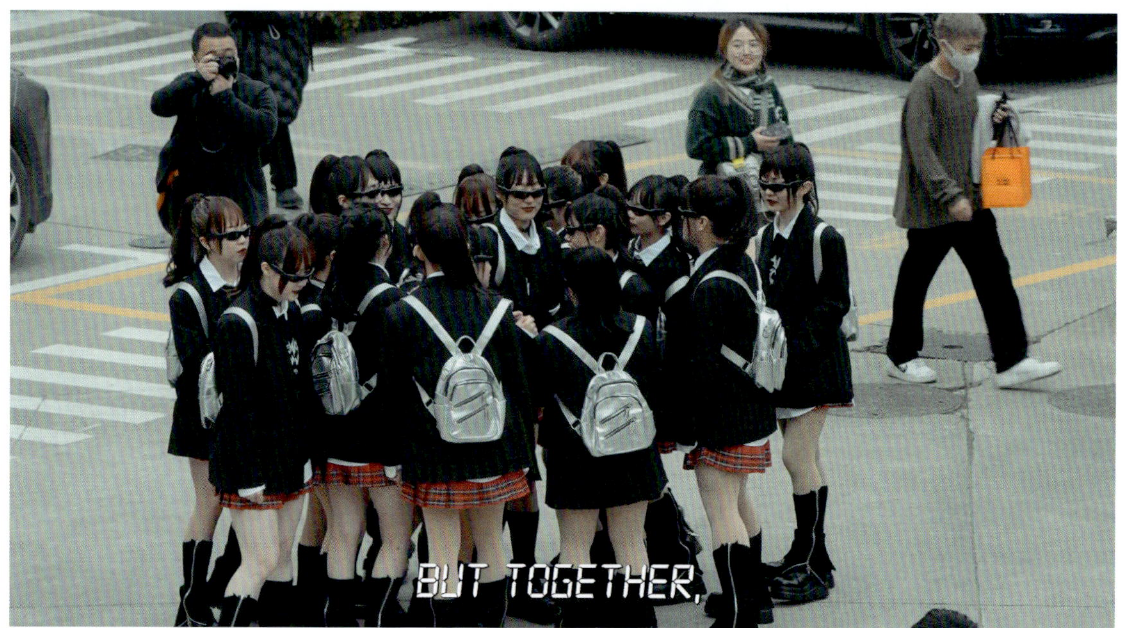
BUT TOGETHER,

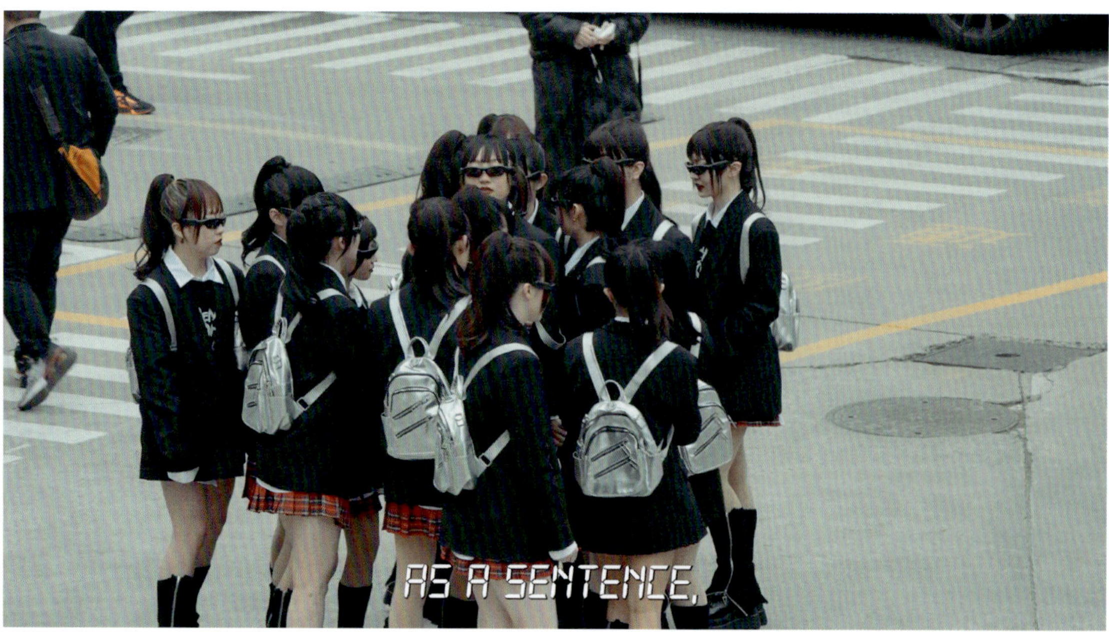
AS A SENTENCE,

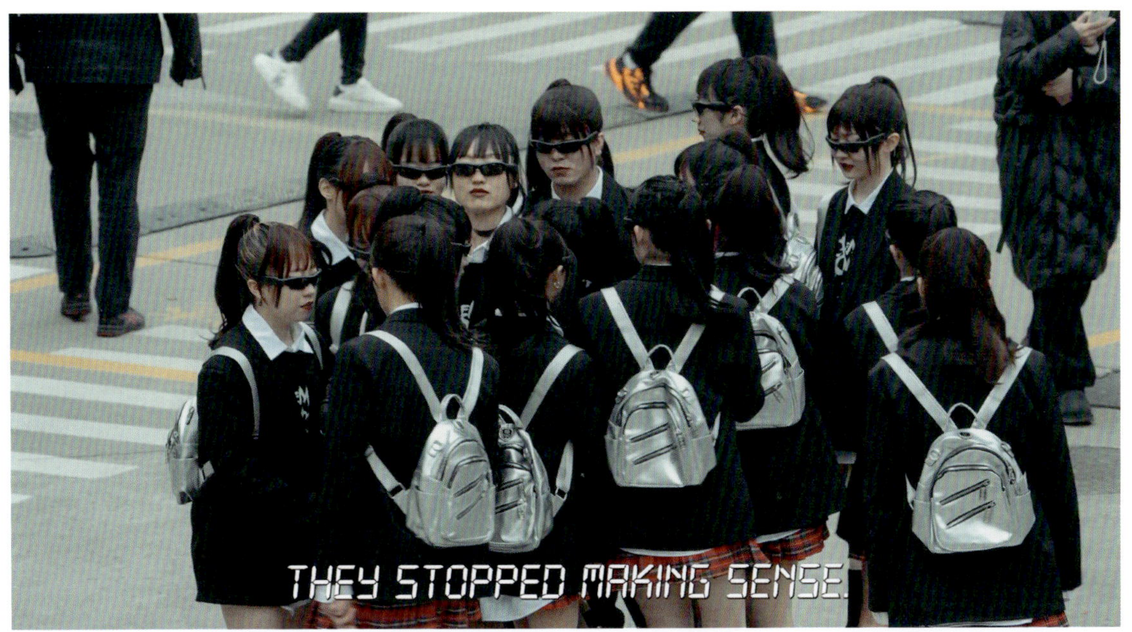
THEY STOPPED MAKING SENSE.

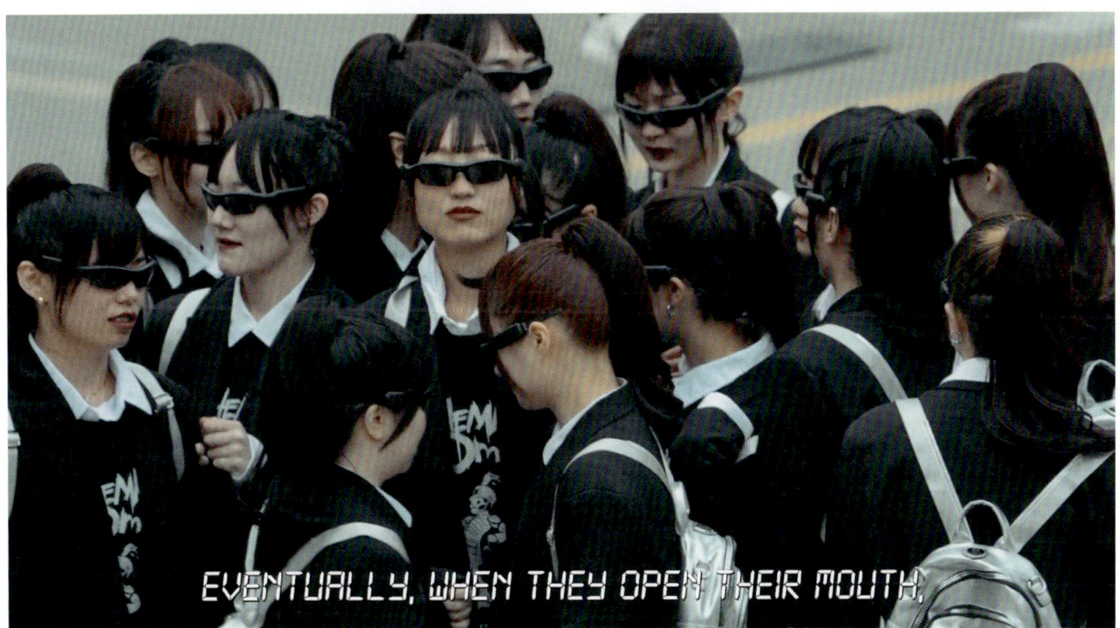
EVENTUALLY, WHEN THEY OPEN THEIR MOUTH,

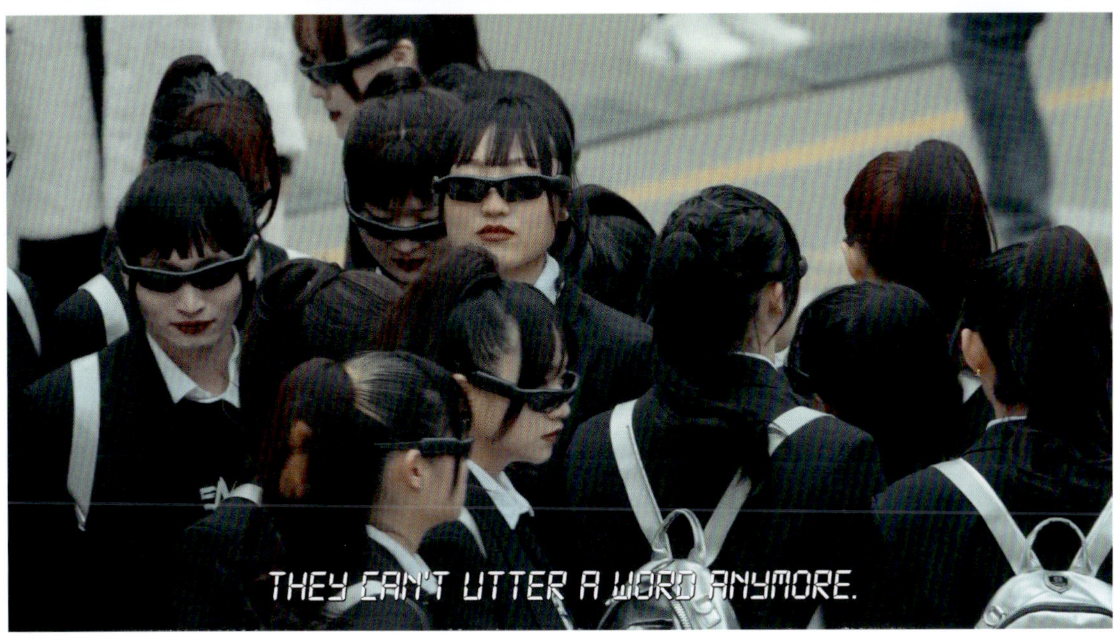
THEY CAN'T UTTER A WORD ANYMORE.

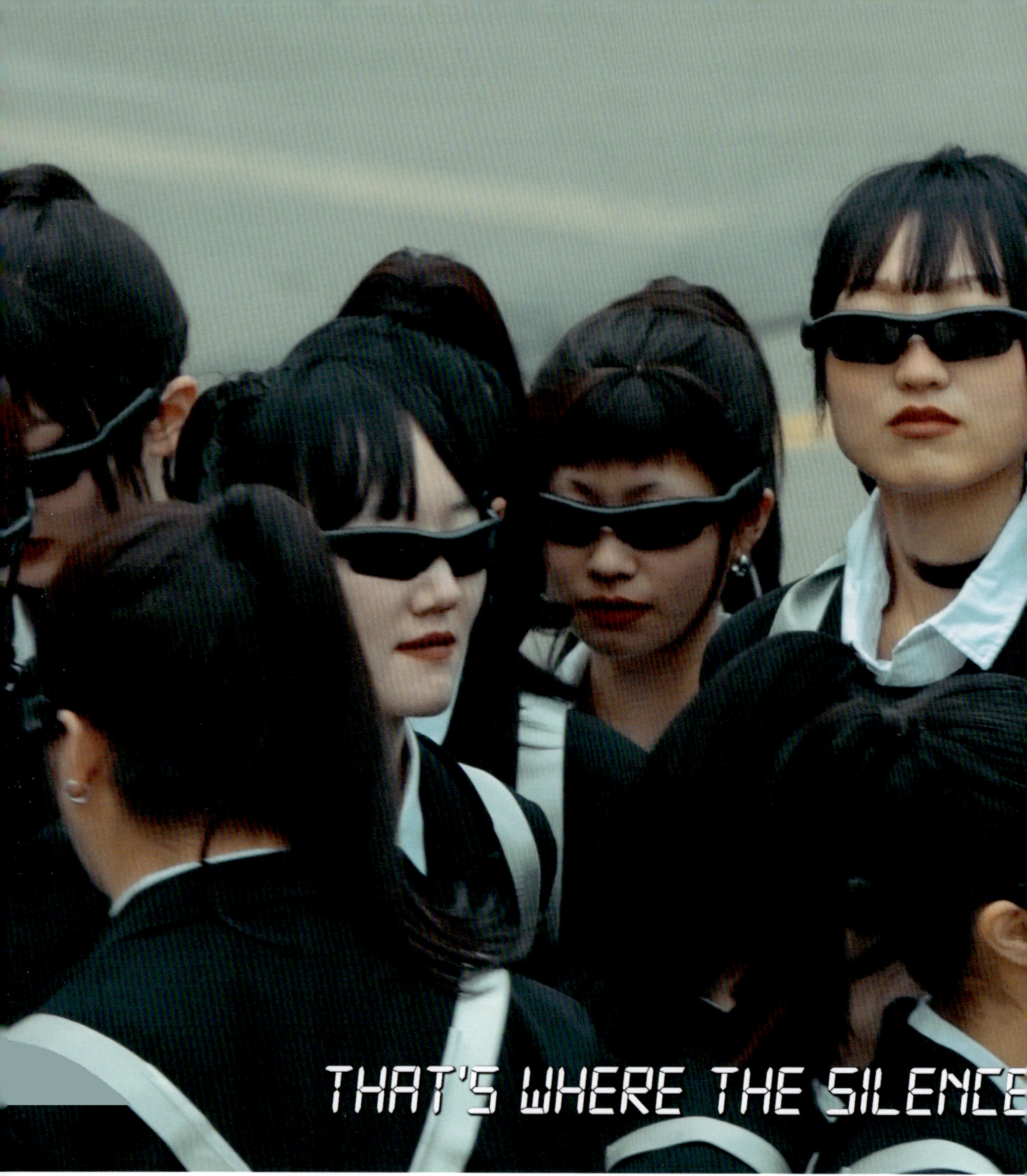
THAT'S WHERE THE SILENCE

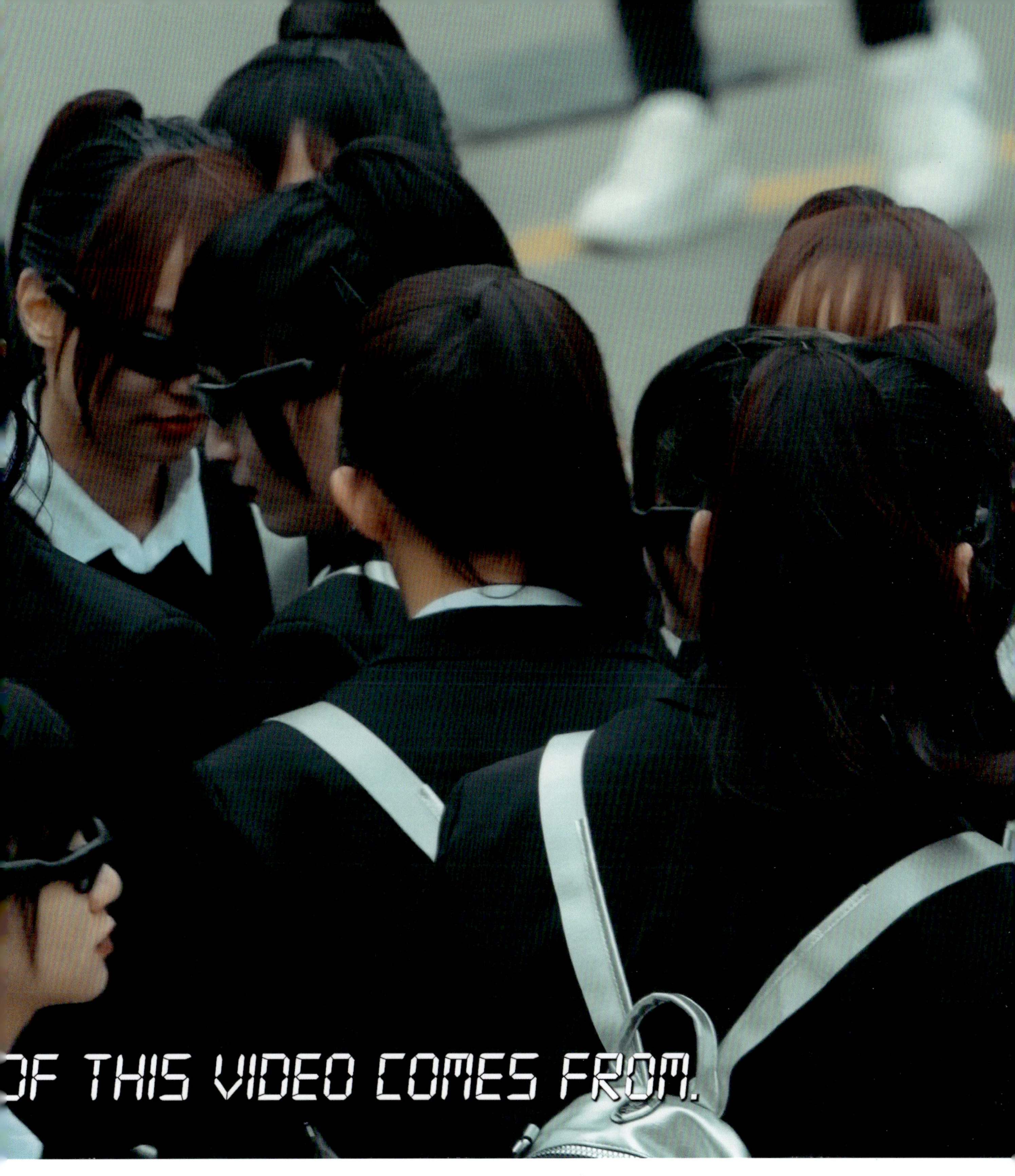

OF THIS VIDEO COMES FROM.

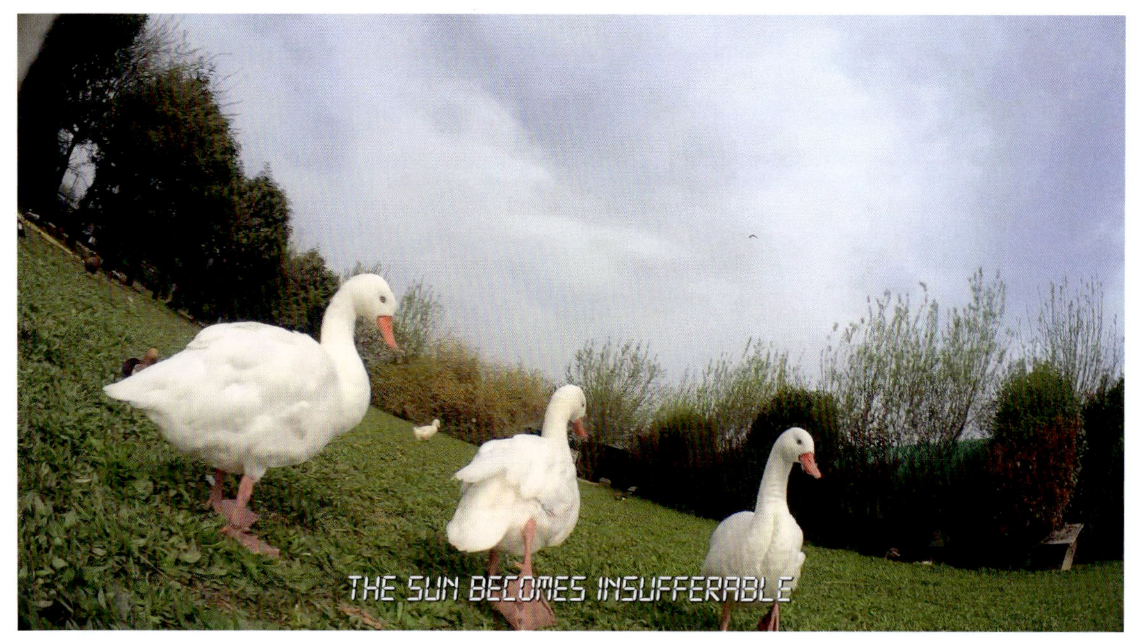
THE SUN BECOMES INSUFFERABLE

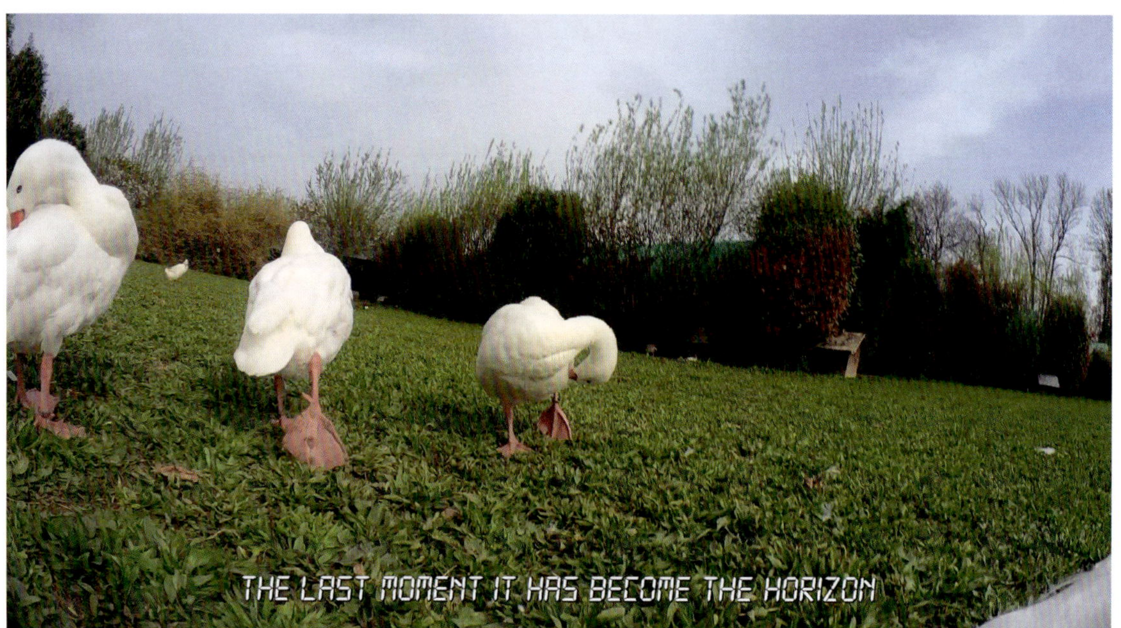
THE LAST MOMENT IT HAS BECOME THE HORIZON

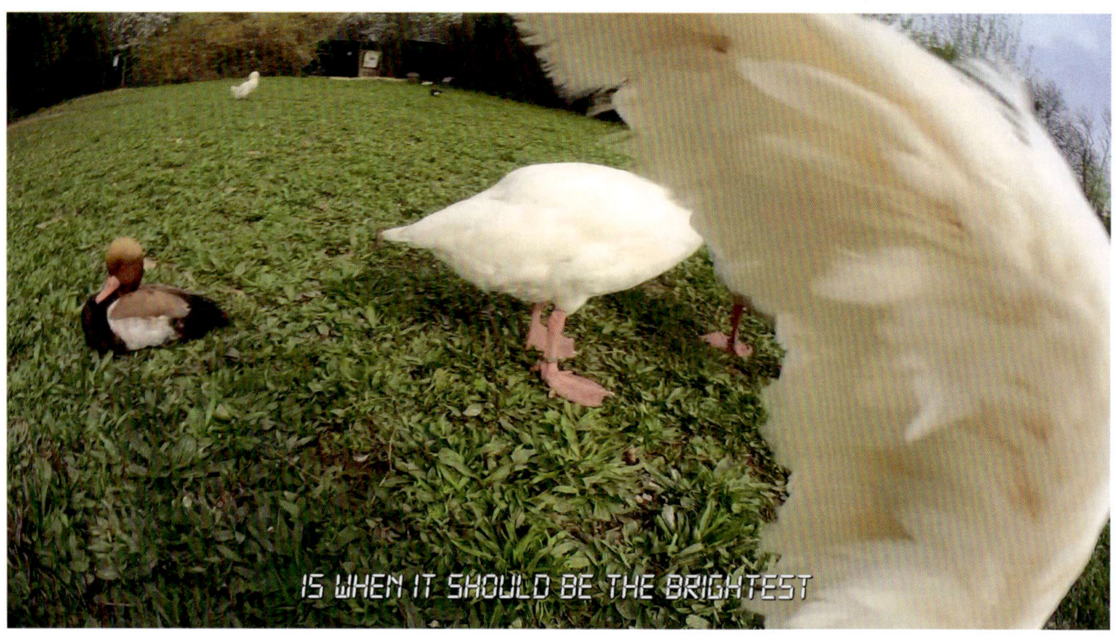
IS WHEN IT SHOULD BE THE BRIGHTEST

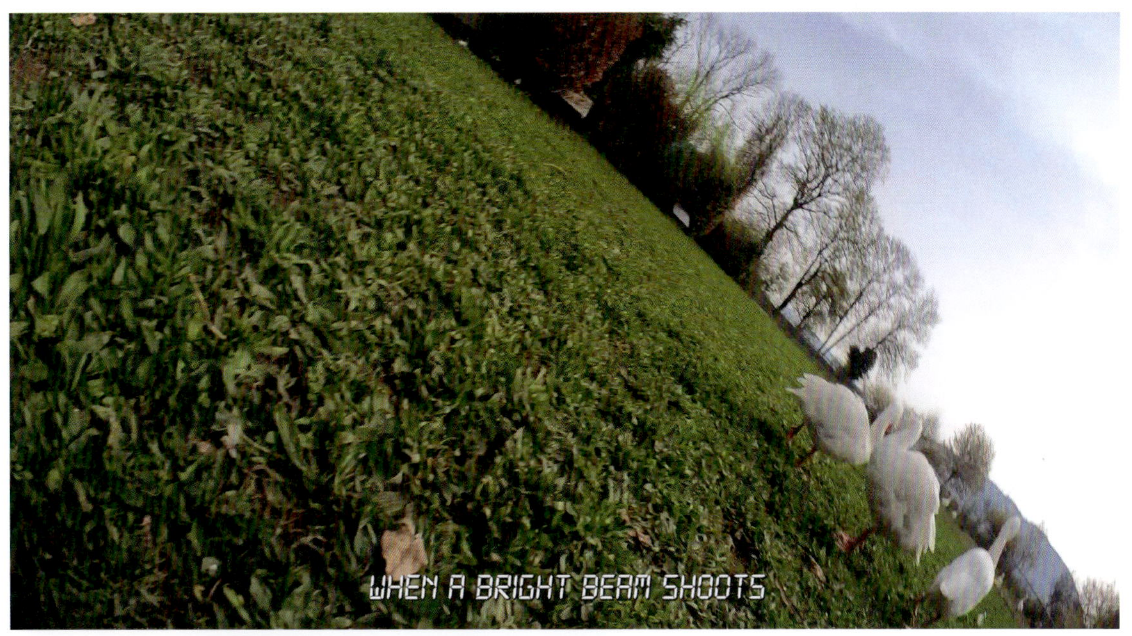
WHEN A BRIGHT BEAM SHOOTS

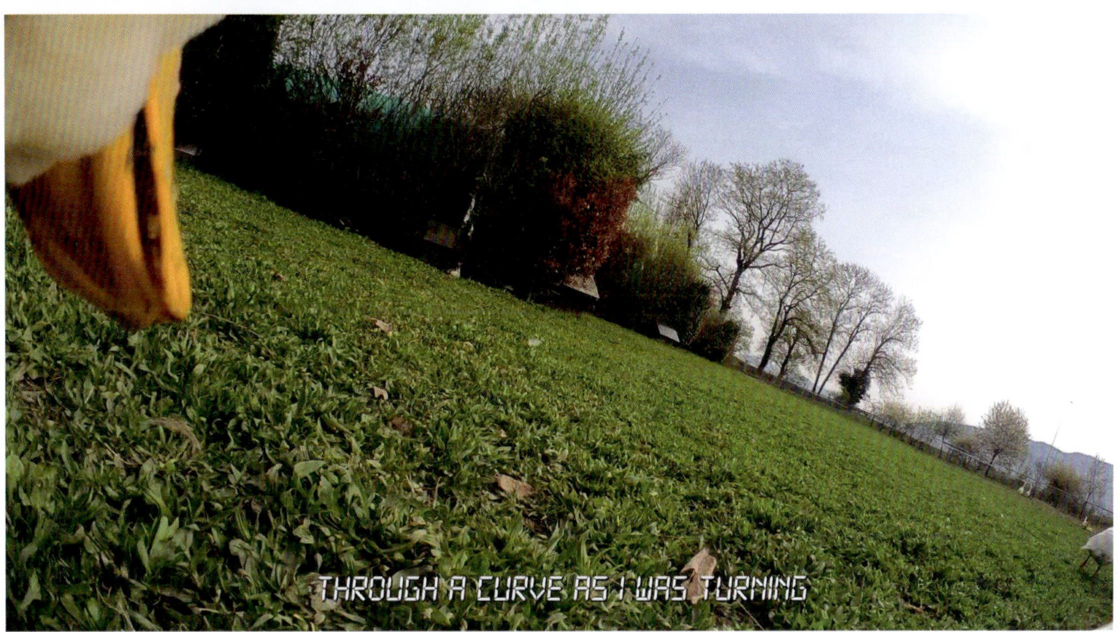
THROUGH A CURVE AS I WAS TURNING

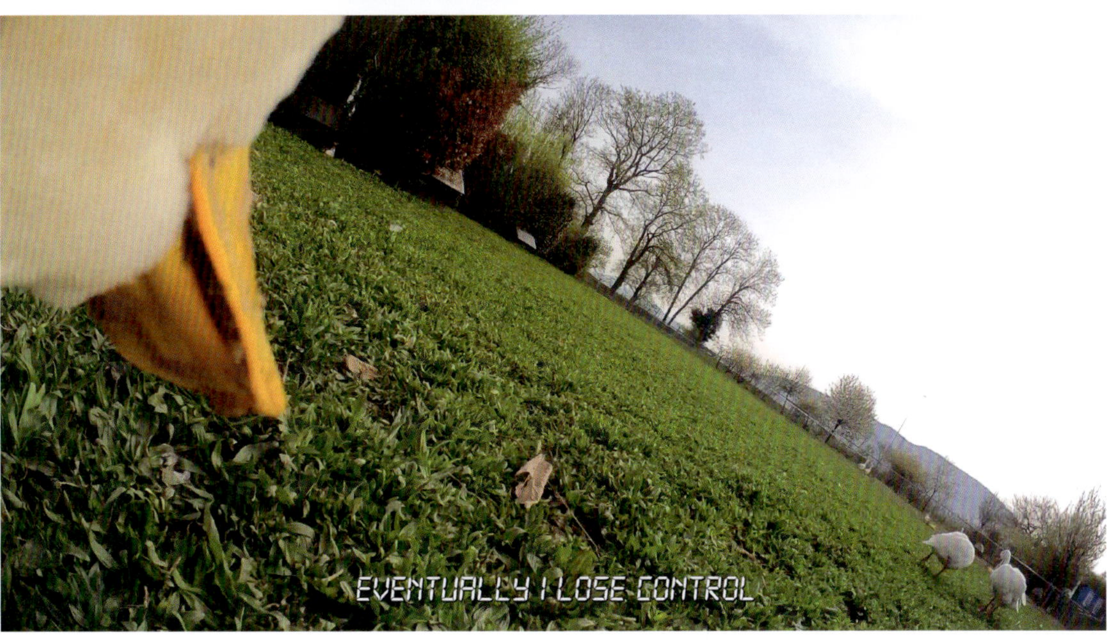
EVENTUALLY I LOSE CONTROL

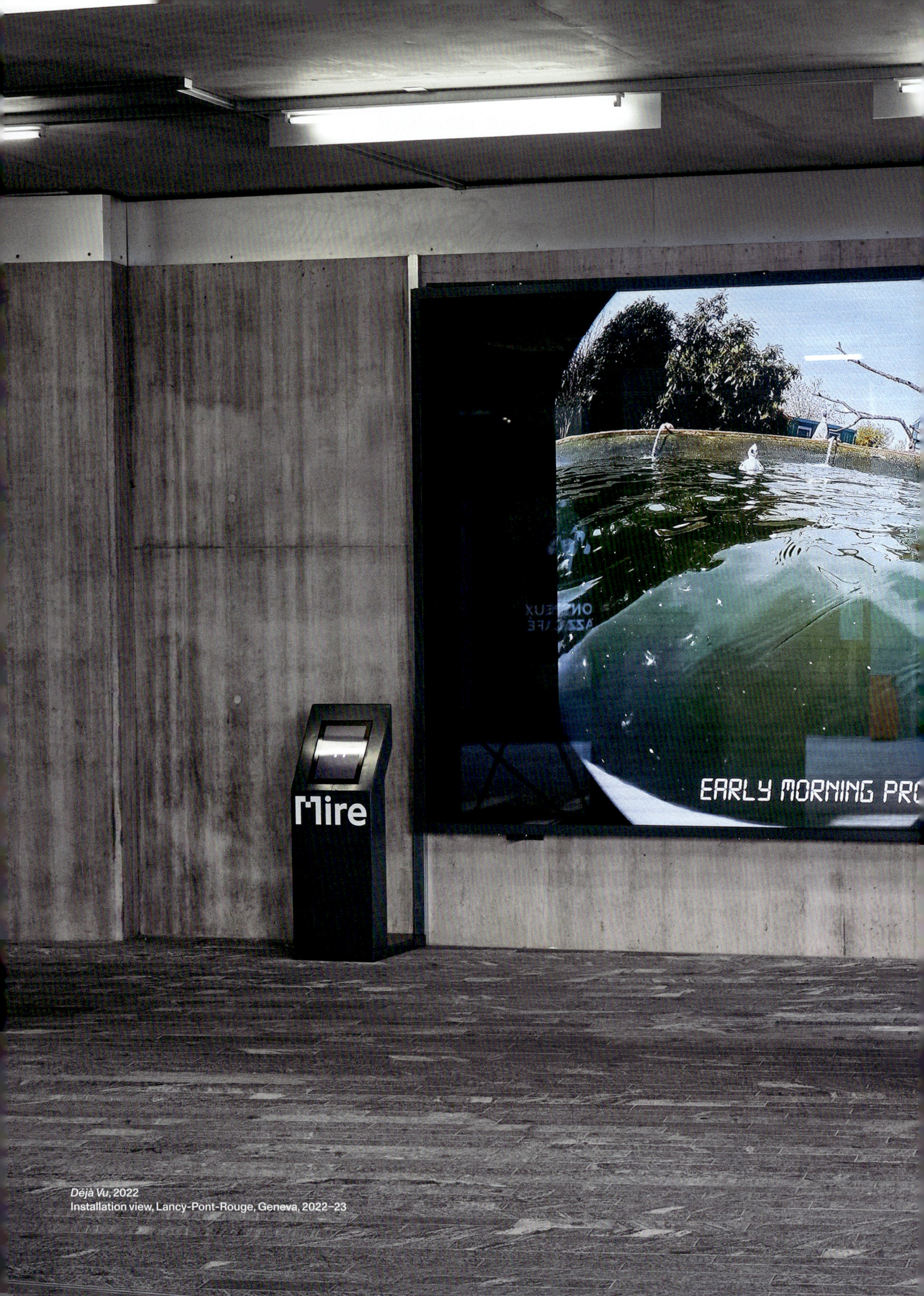

Déjà Vu, 2022
Installation view, Lancy-Pont-Rouge, Geneva, 2022–23

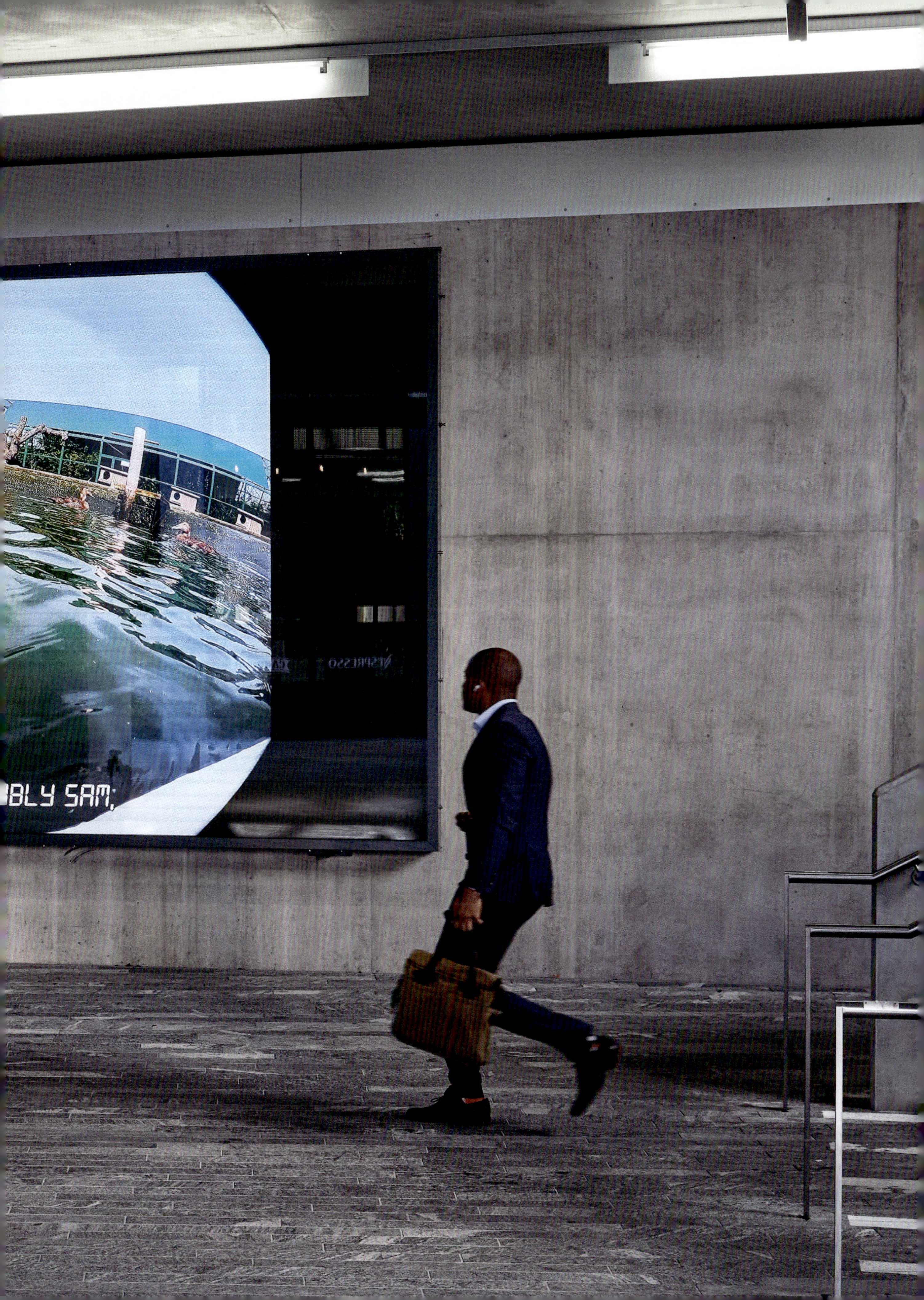
BLY SAM,

The Portrait of the Artist as a young man, 2023

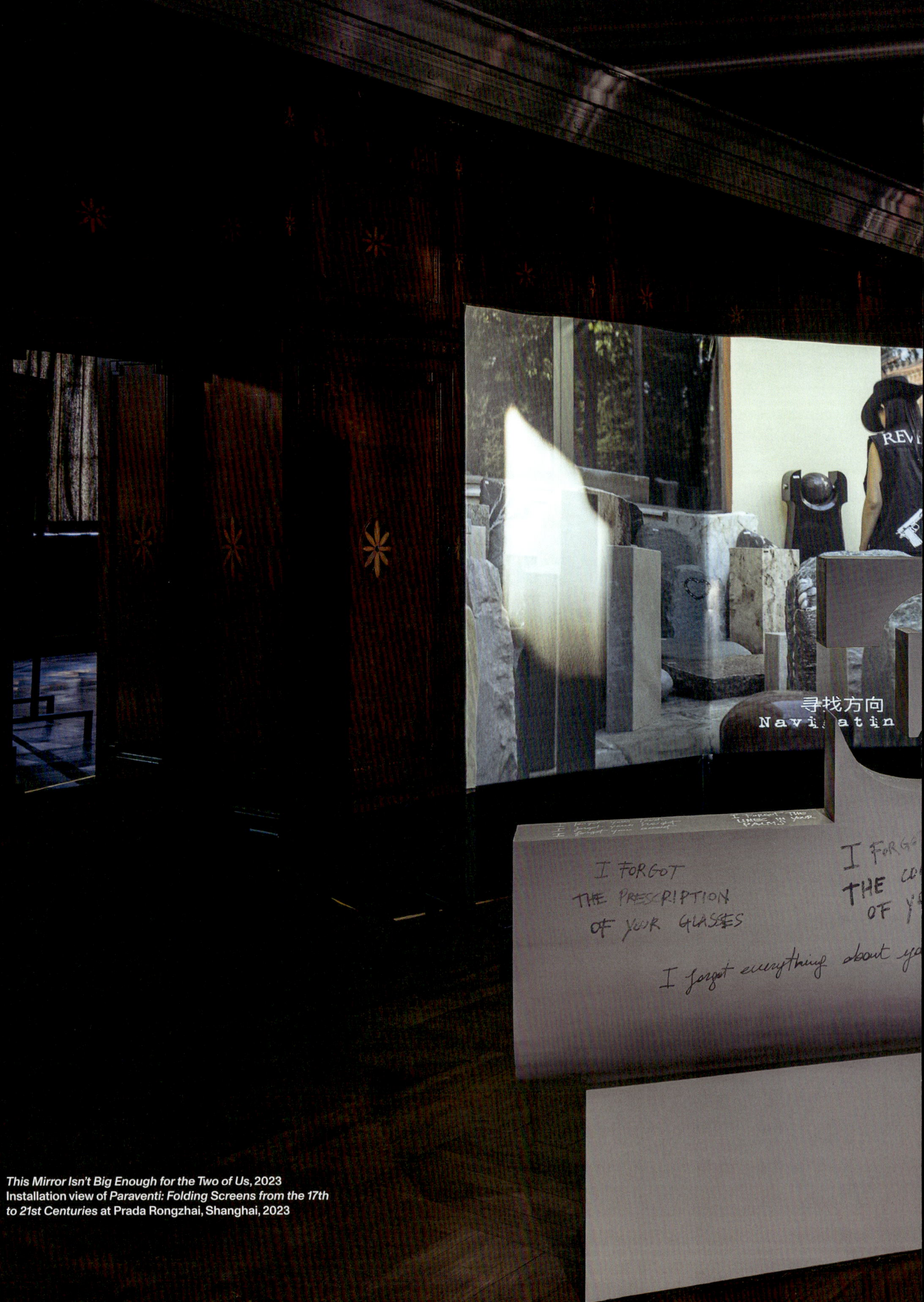

This Mirror Isn't Big Enough for the Two of Us, 2023
Installation view of *Paraventi: Folding Screens from the 17th to 21st Centuries* at Prada Rongzhai, Shanghai, 2023

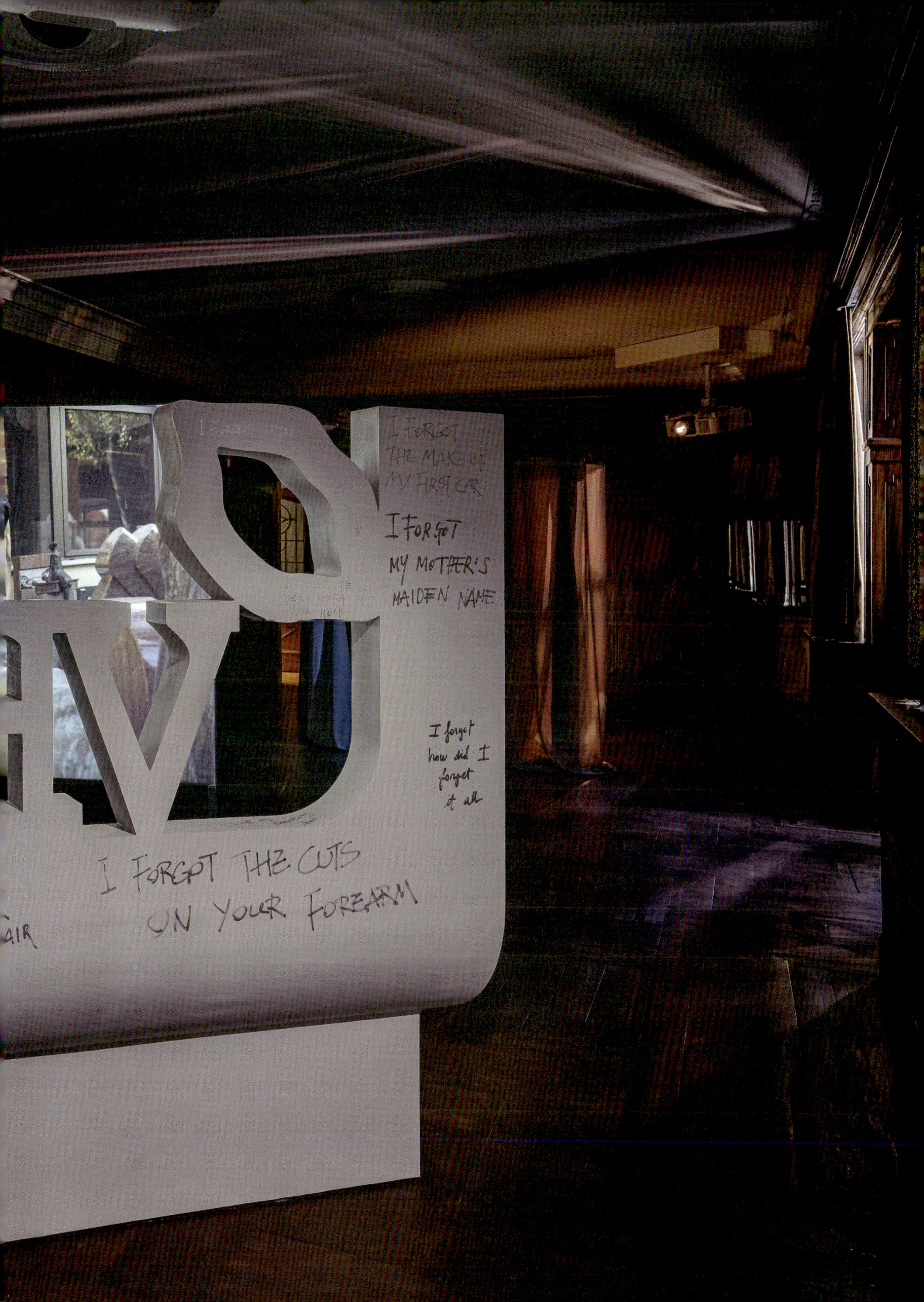
I FORGOT
THE MAKE OF
MY FIRST CAR

I FORGOT
MY MOTHER'S
MAIDEN NAME

I forgot
how did I
forget
it all

I FORGOT THE CUTS
ON YOUR FOREARM

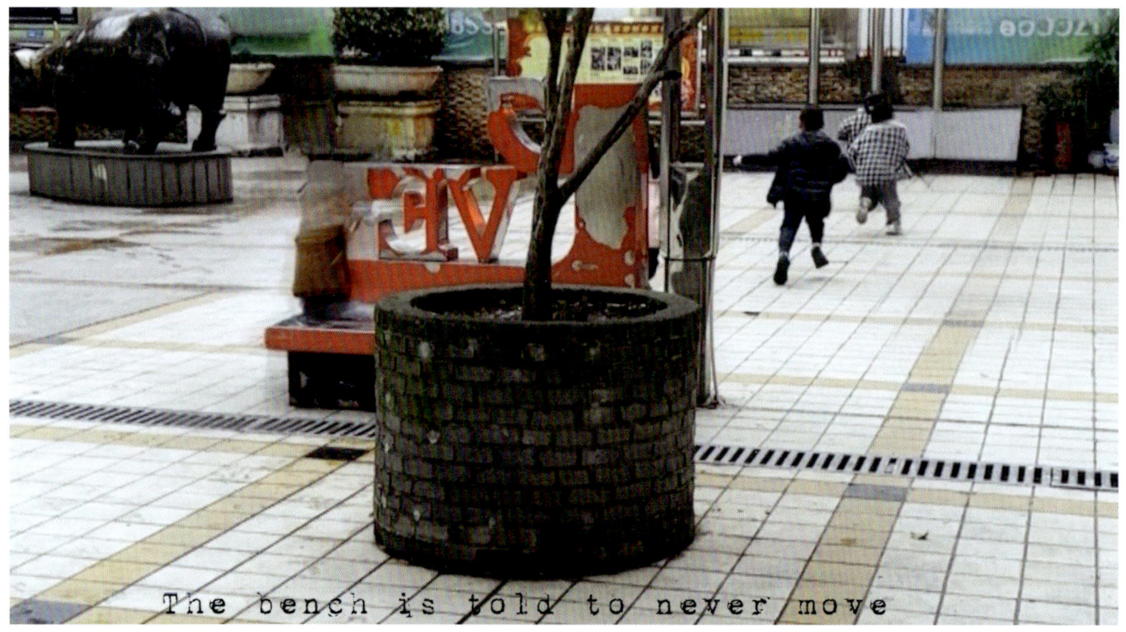
The bench is told to never move

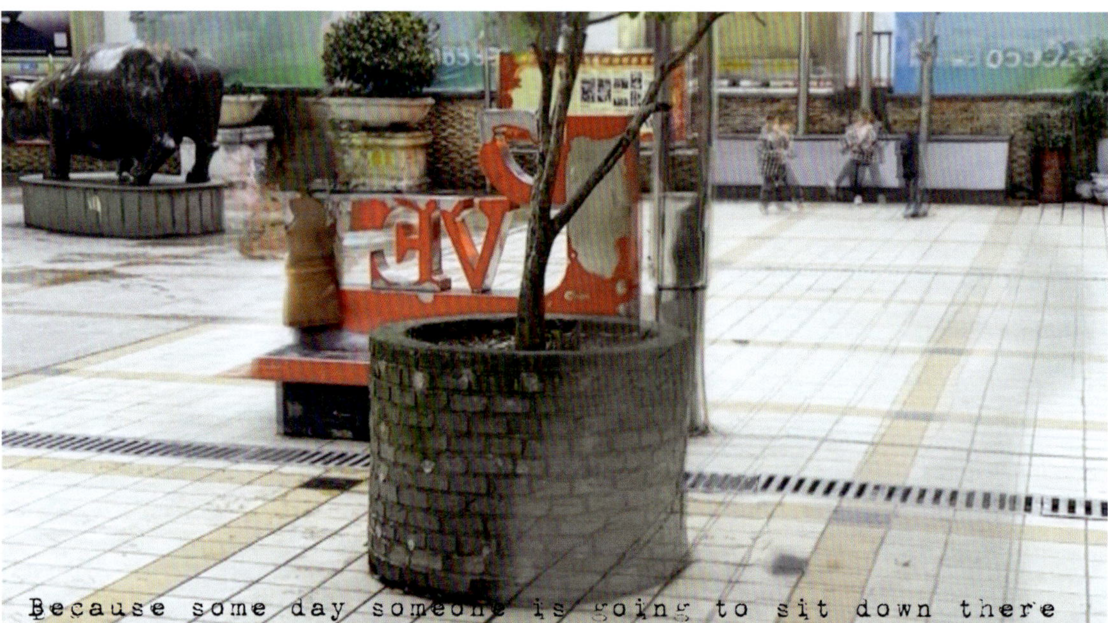
Because some day someone is going to sit down there

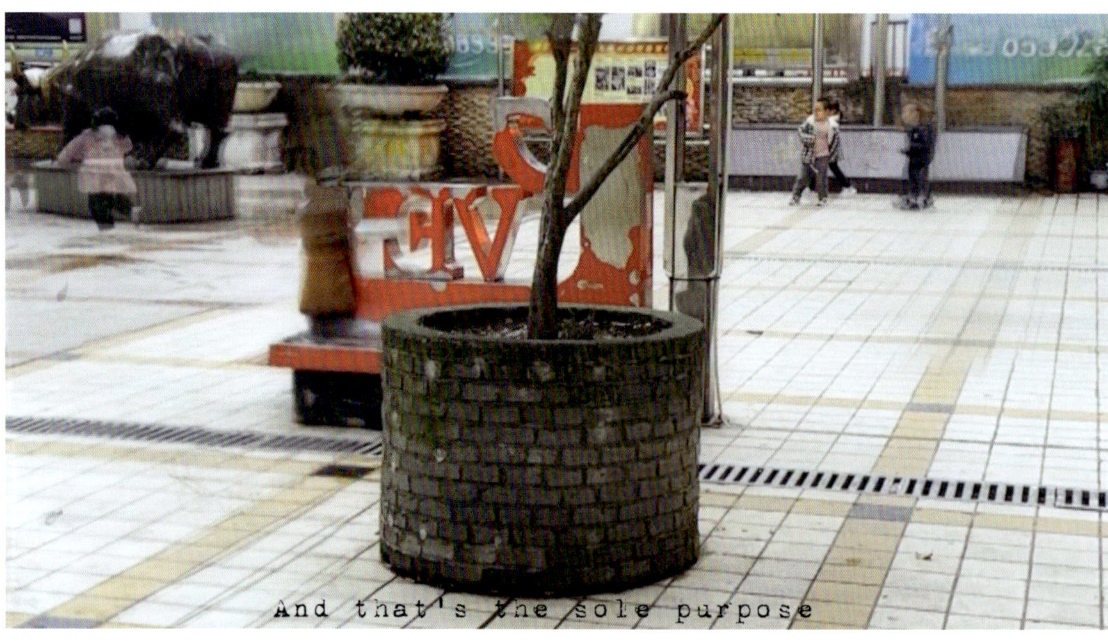
And that's the sole purpose

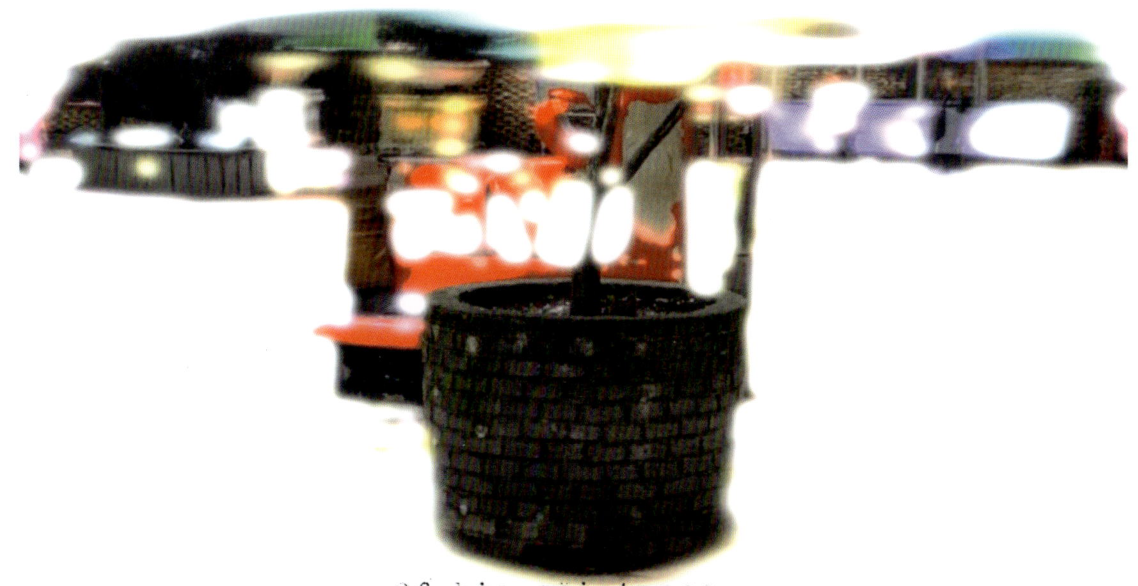

Of his existance.

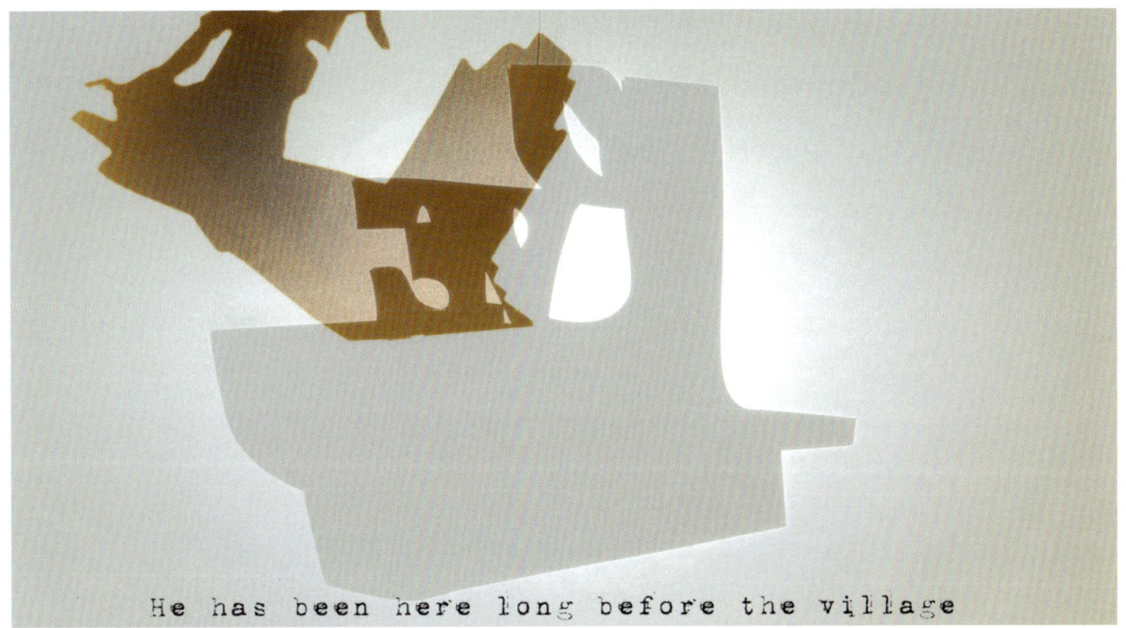

He has been here long before the village

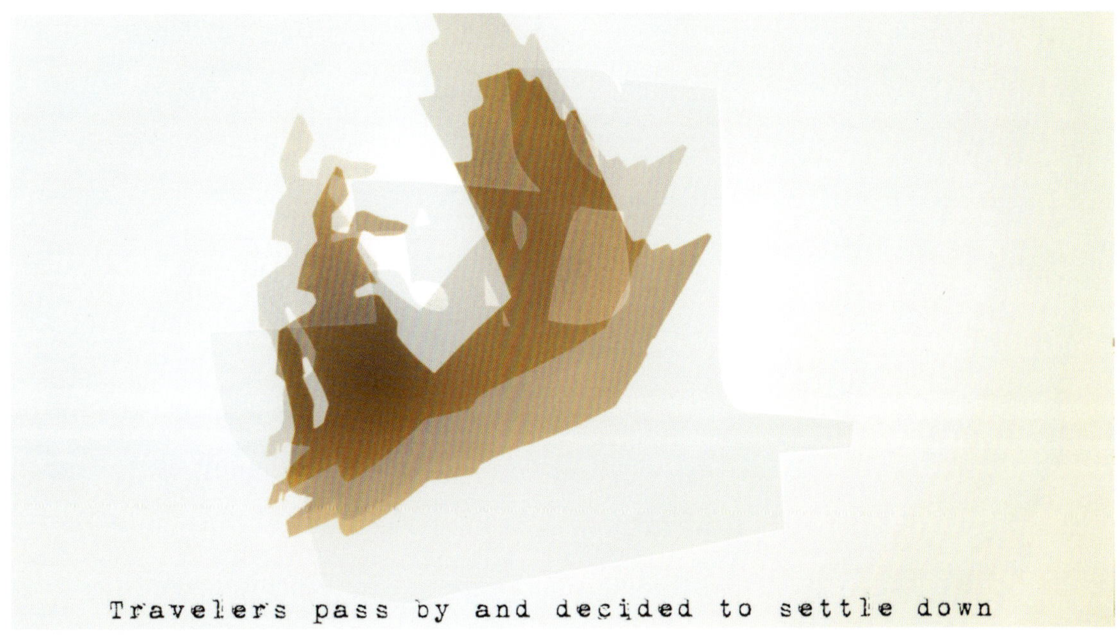

Travelers pass by and decided to settle down

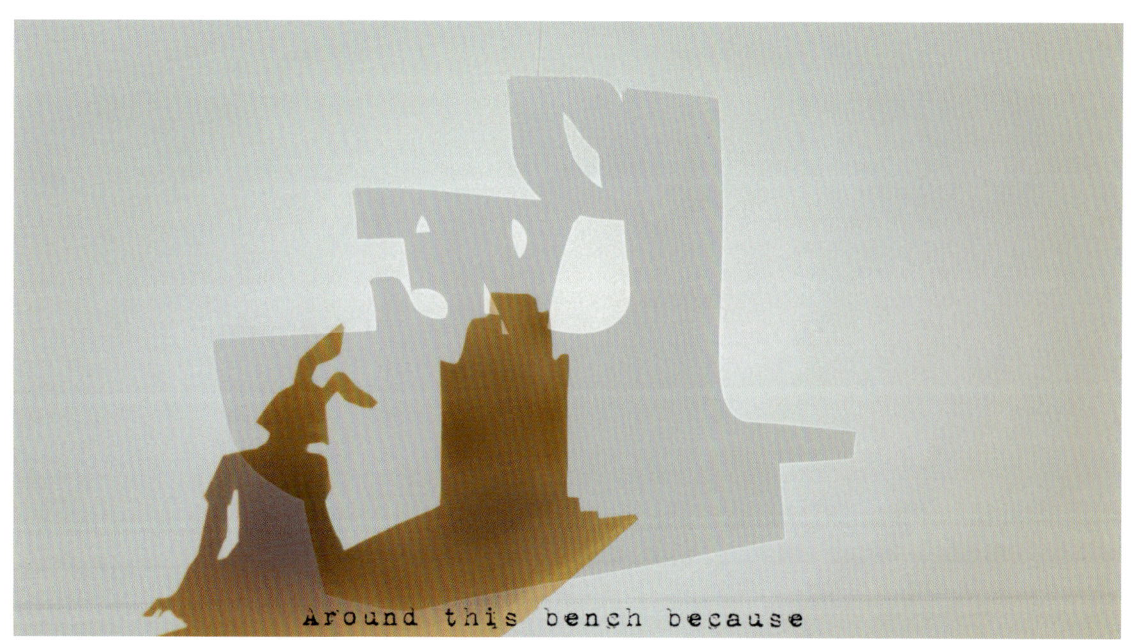

Around this bench because

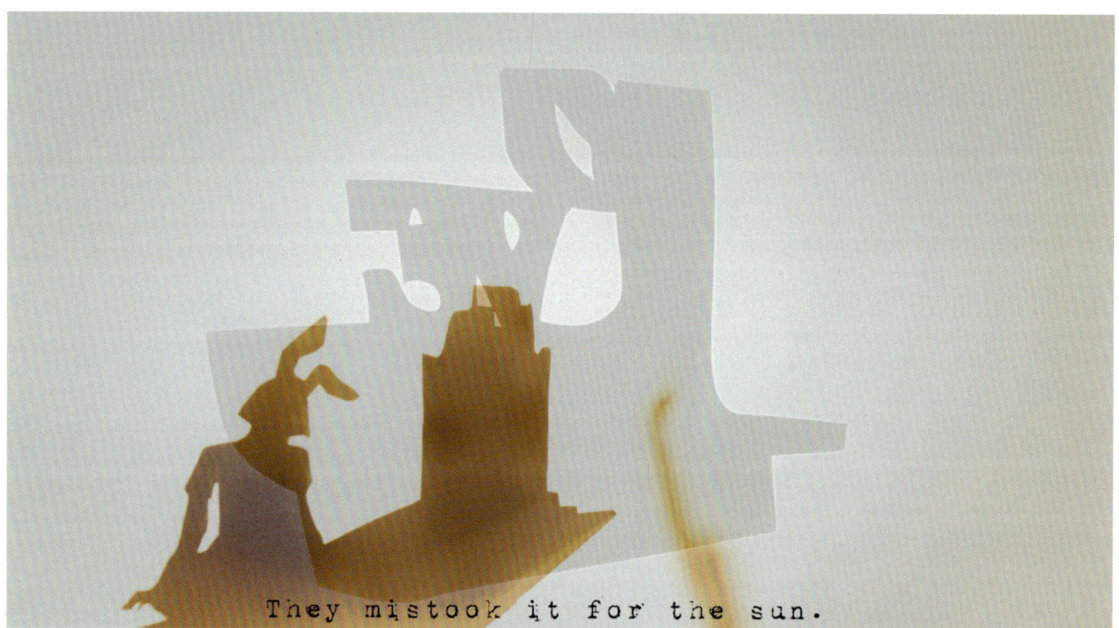

They mistook it for the sun.

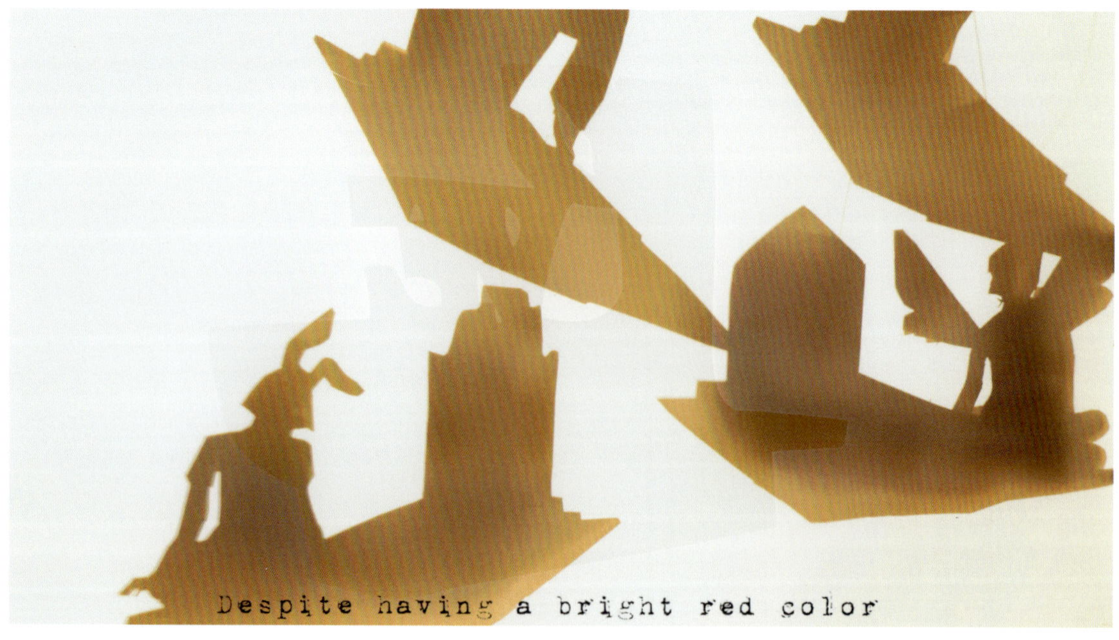

Despite having a bright red color

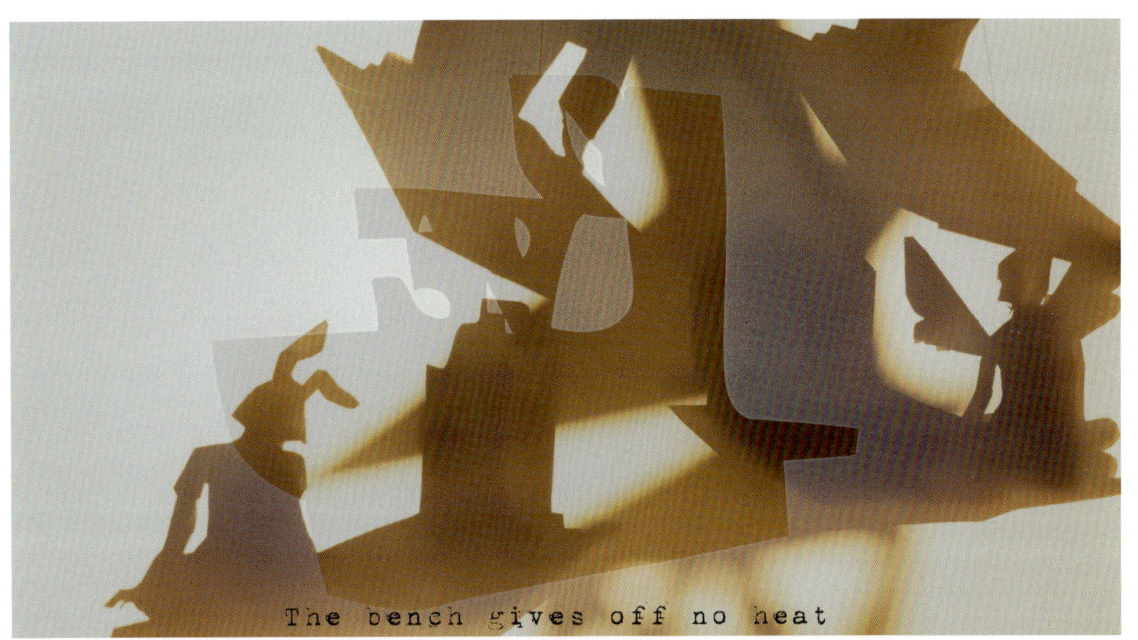

The bench gives off no heat

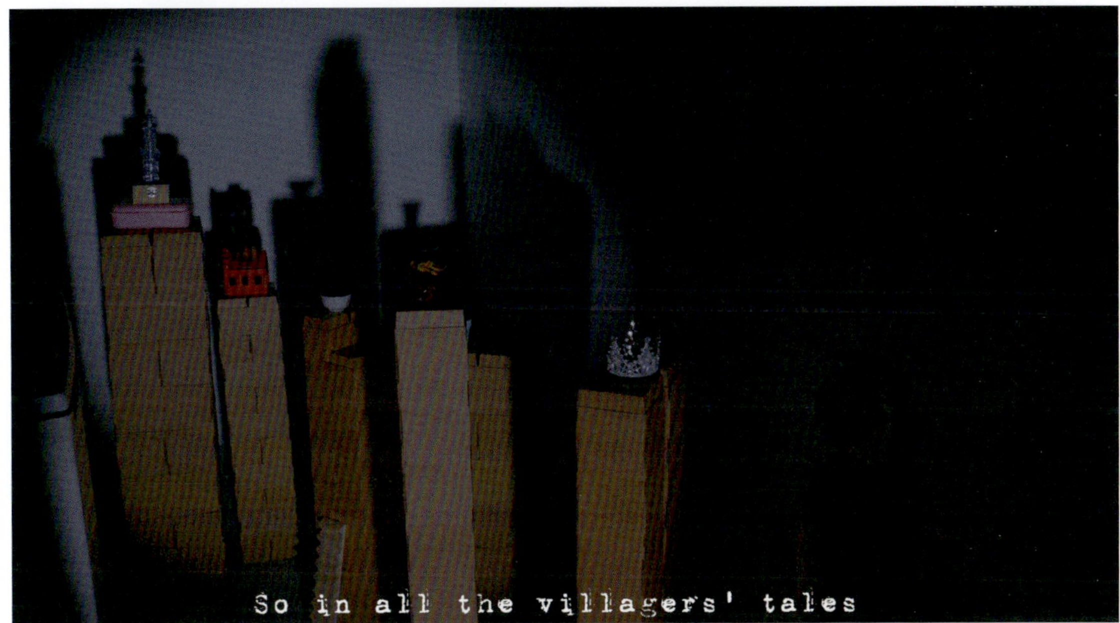

So in all the villagers' tales

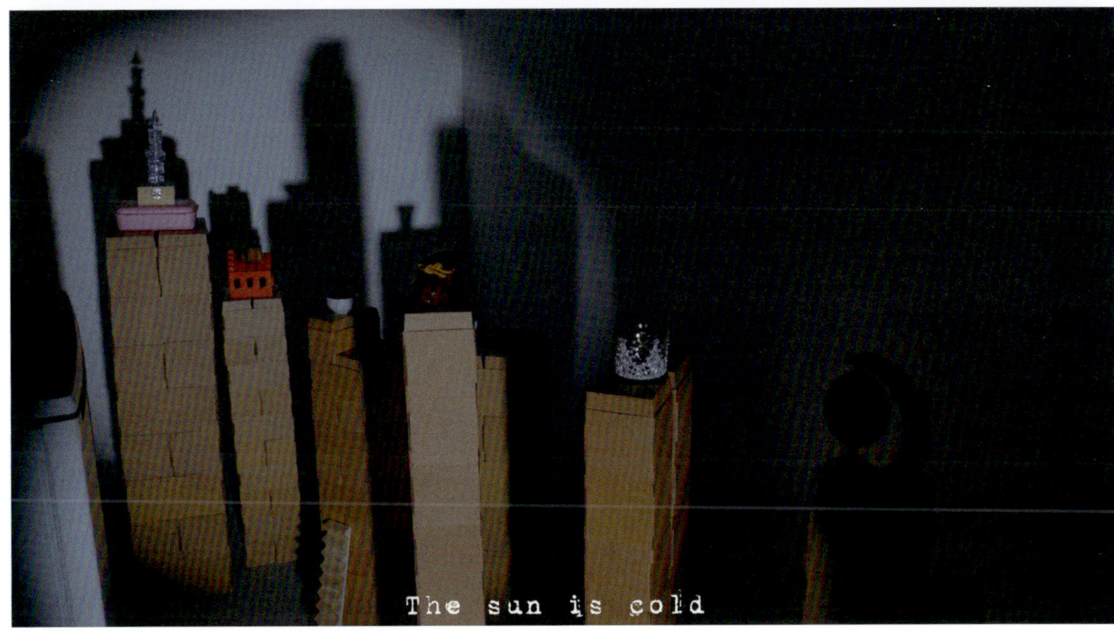

The sun is cold

the world starts t
地面出现裂痕

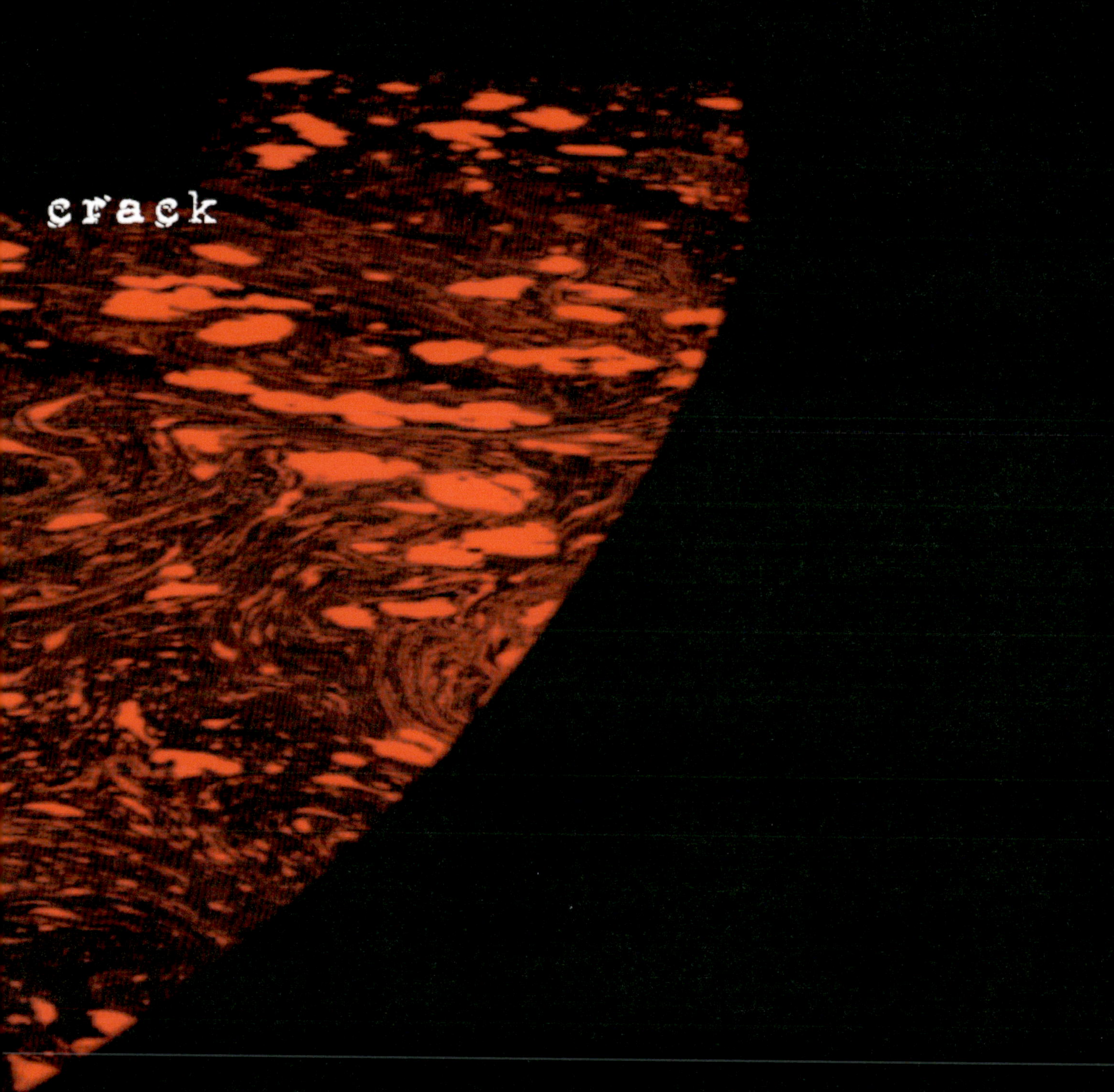

crack

the world co

世界浮现在

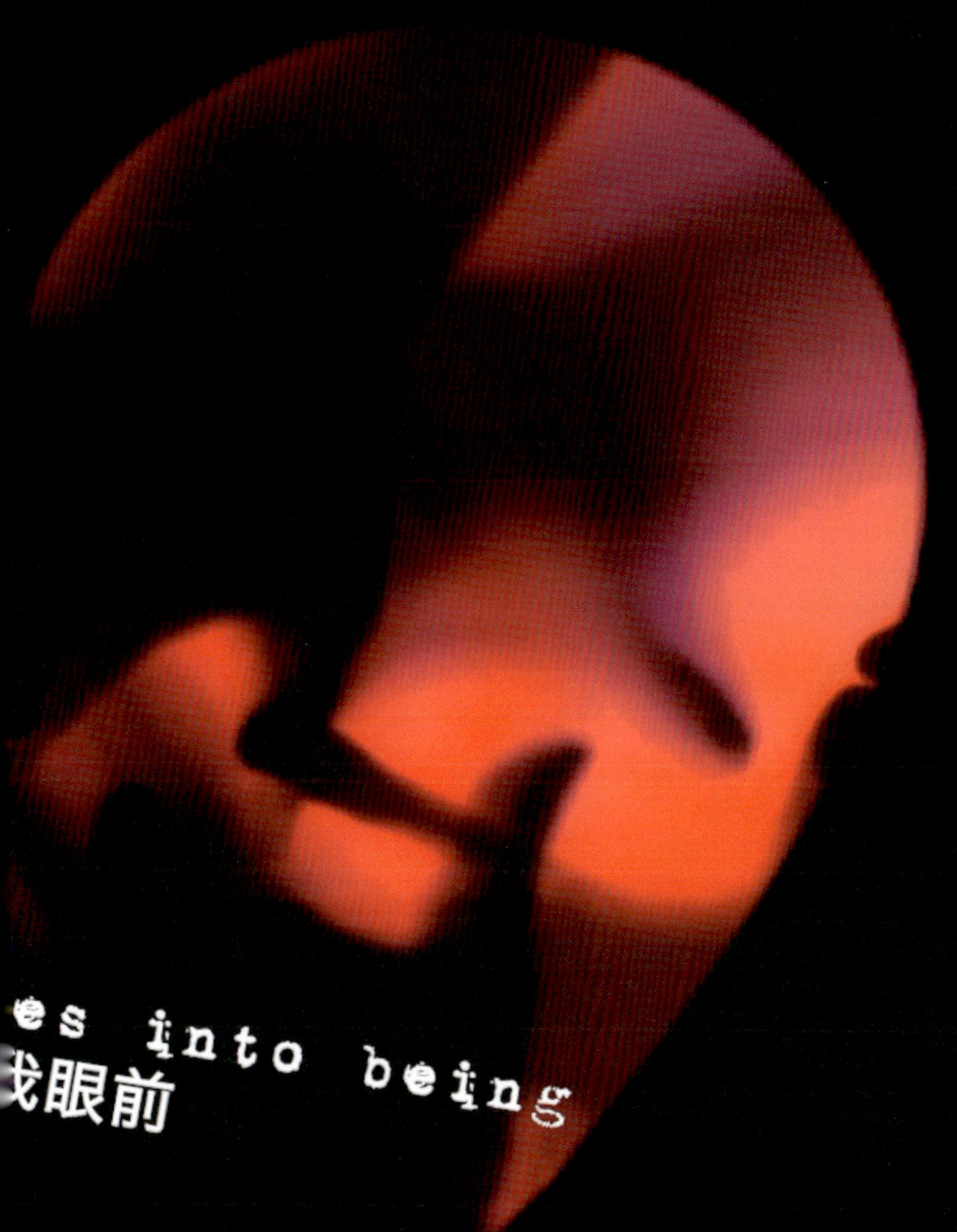
es into being
我眼前

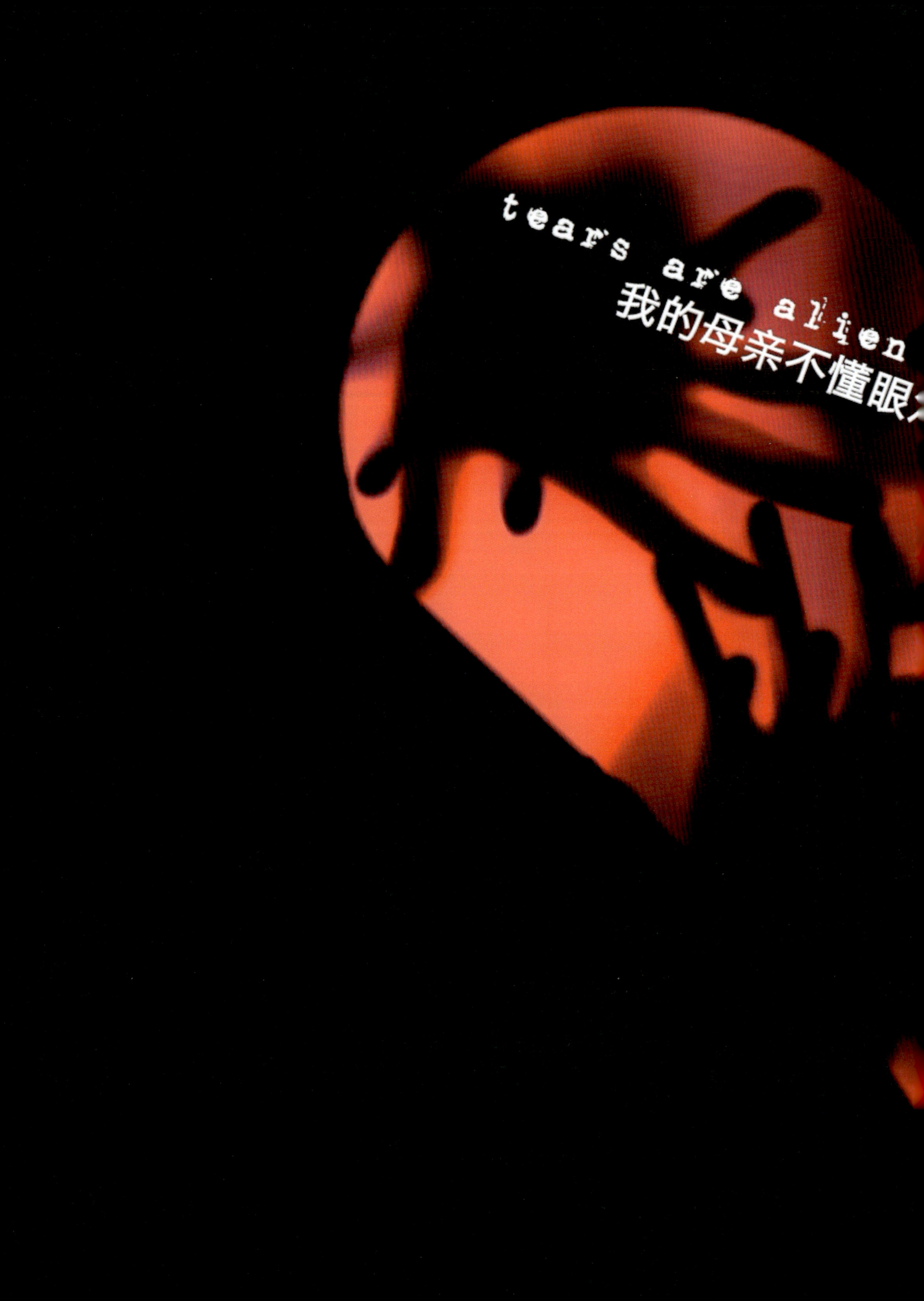

tears are alien
我的母亲不懂眼泪

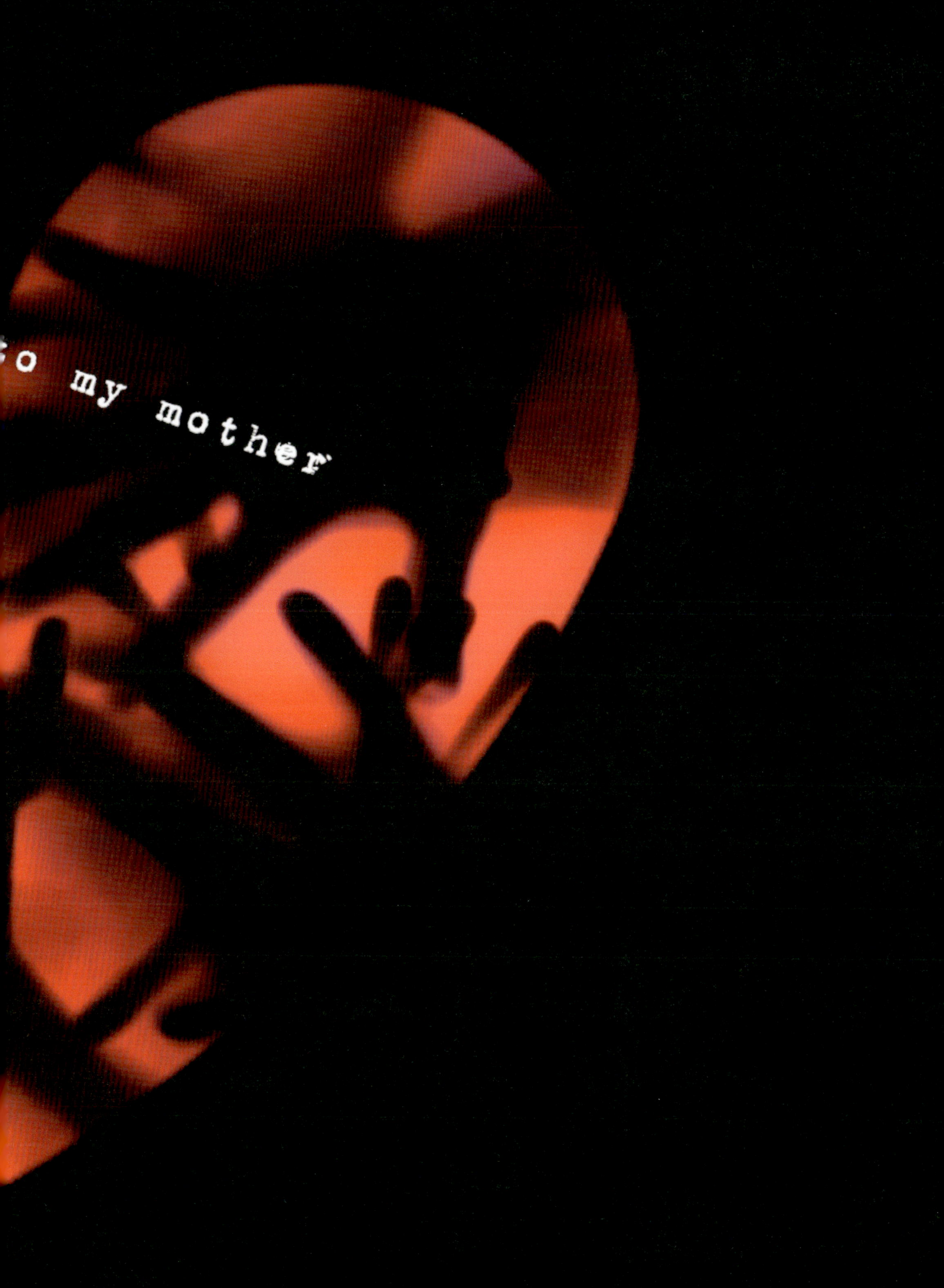
to my mother

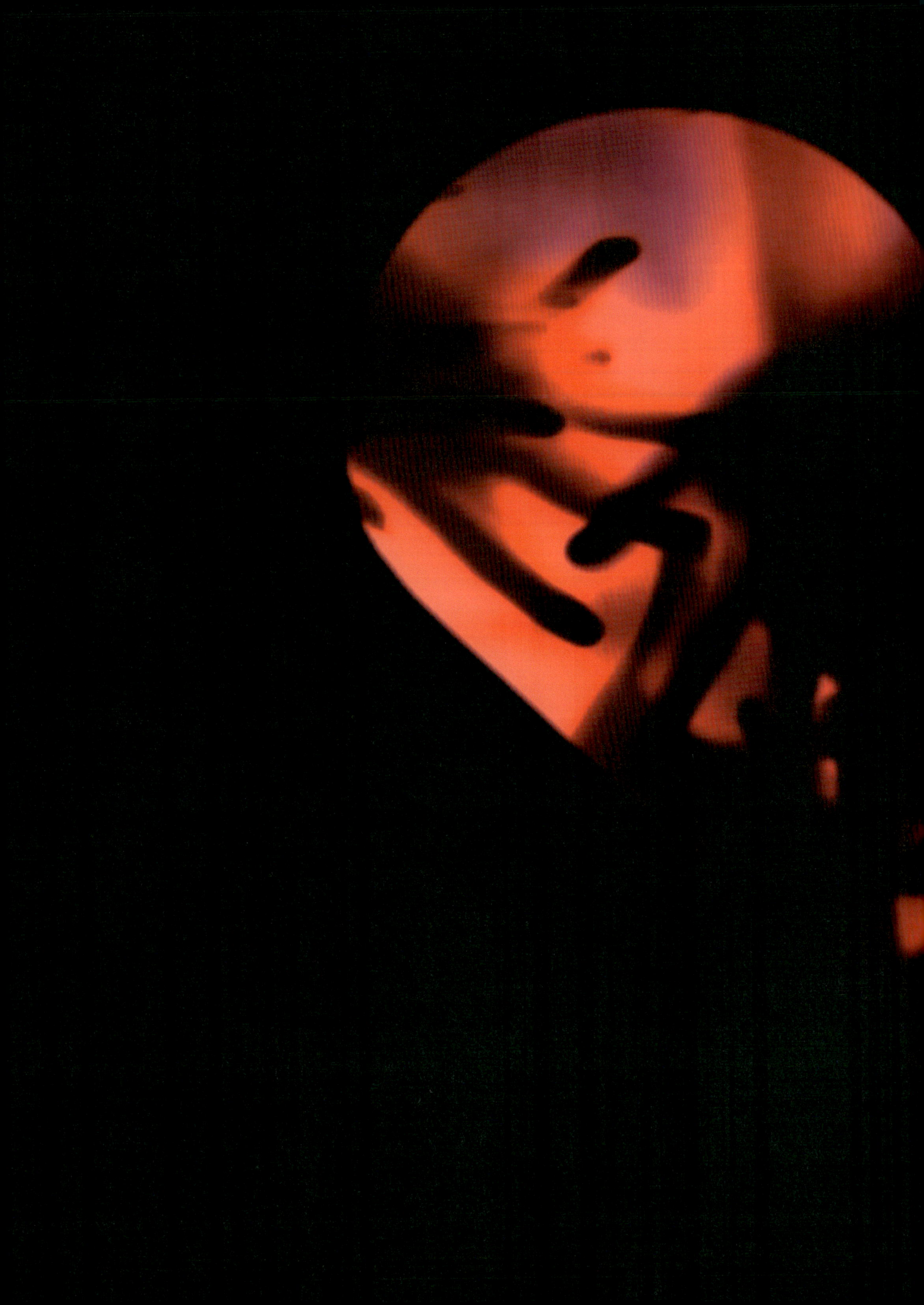

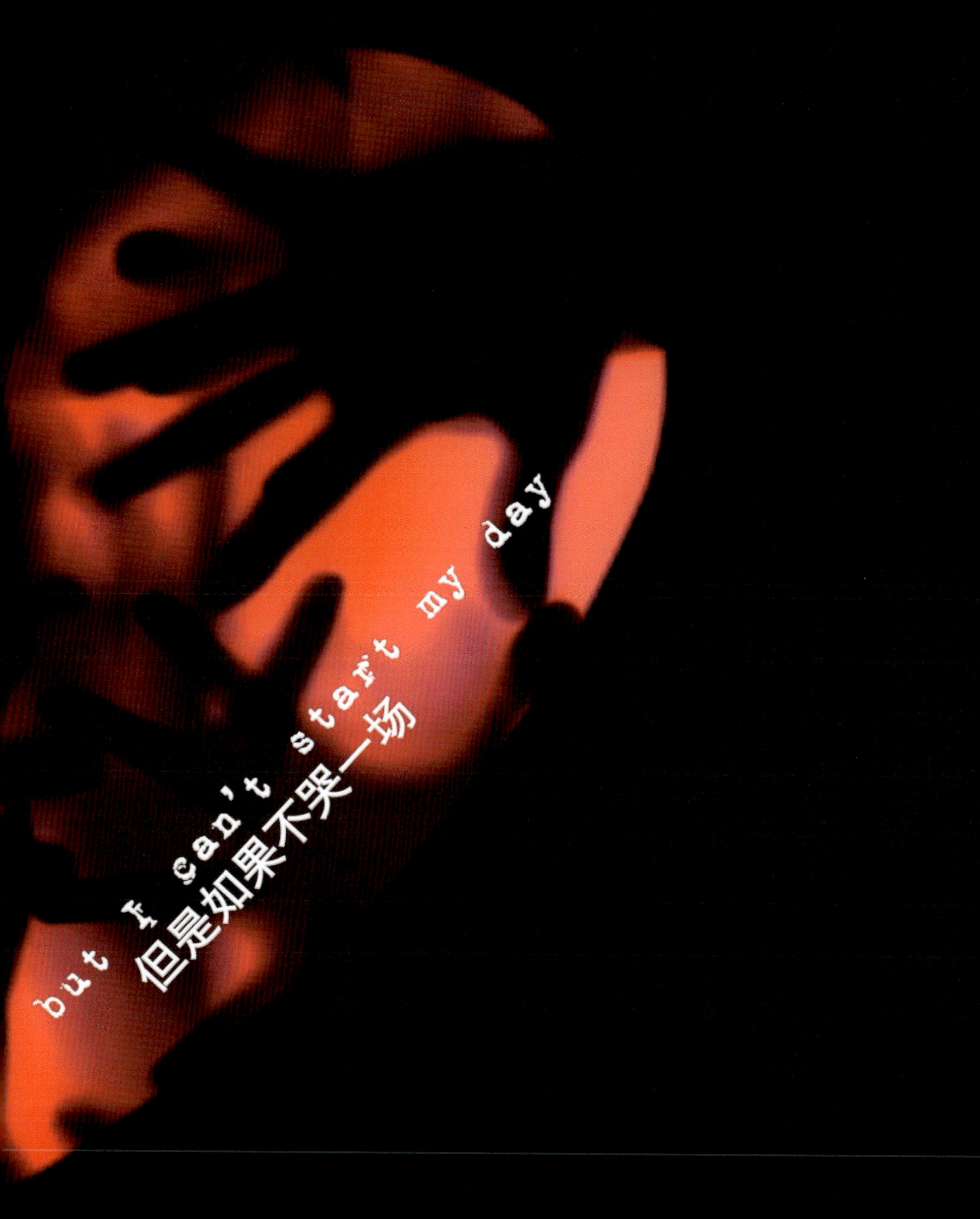
but I can't start my day
但是如果不哭一场
my day

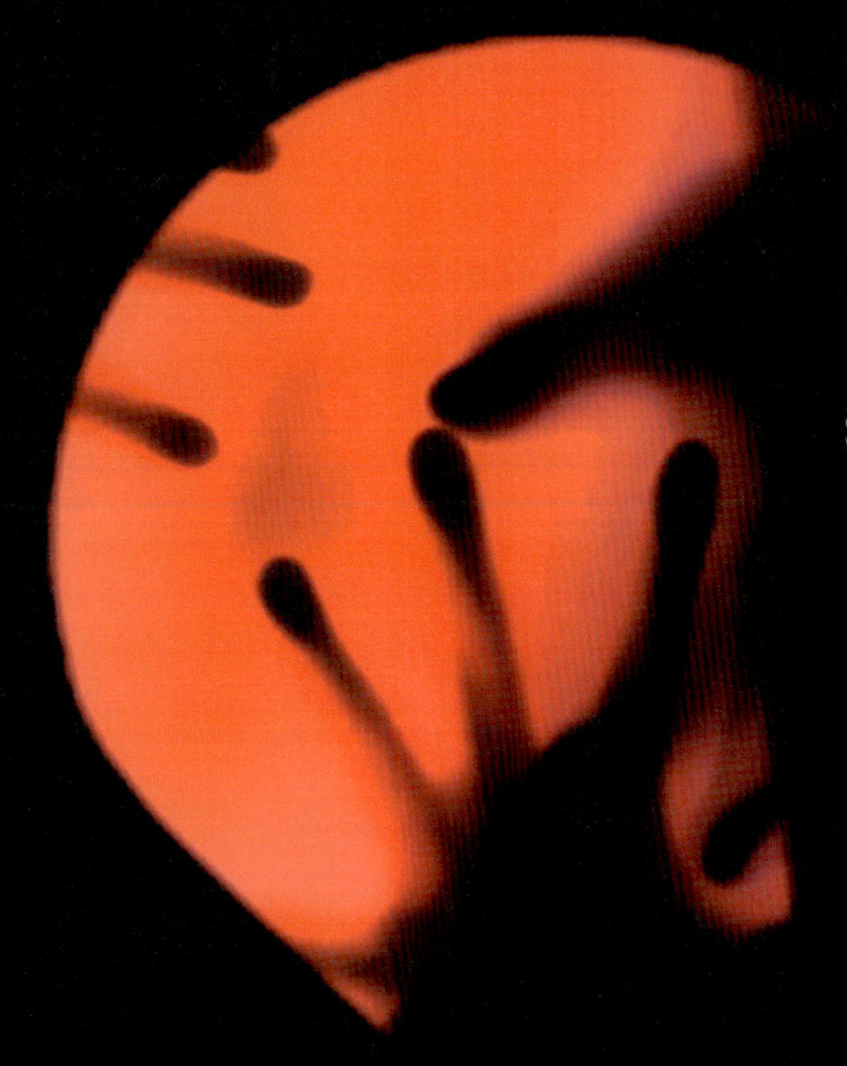

我就

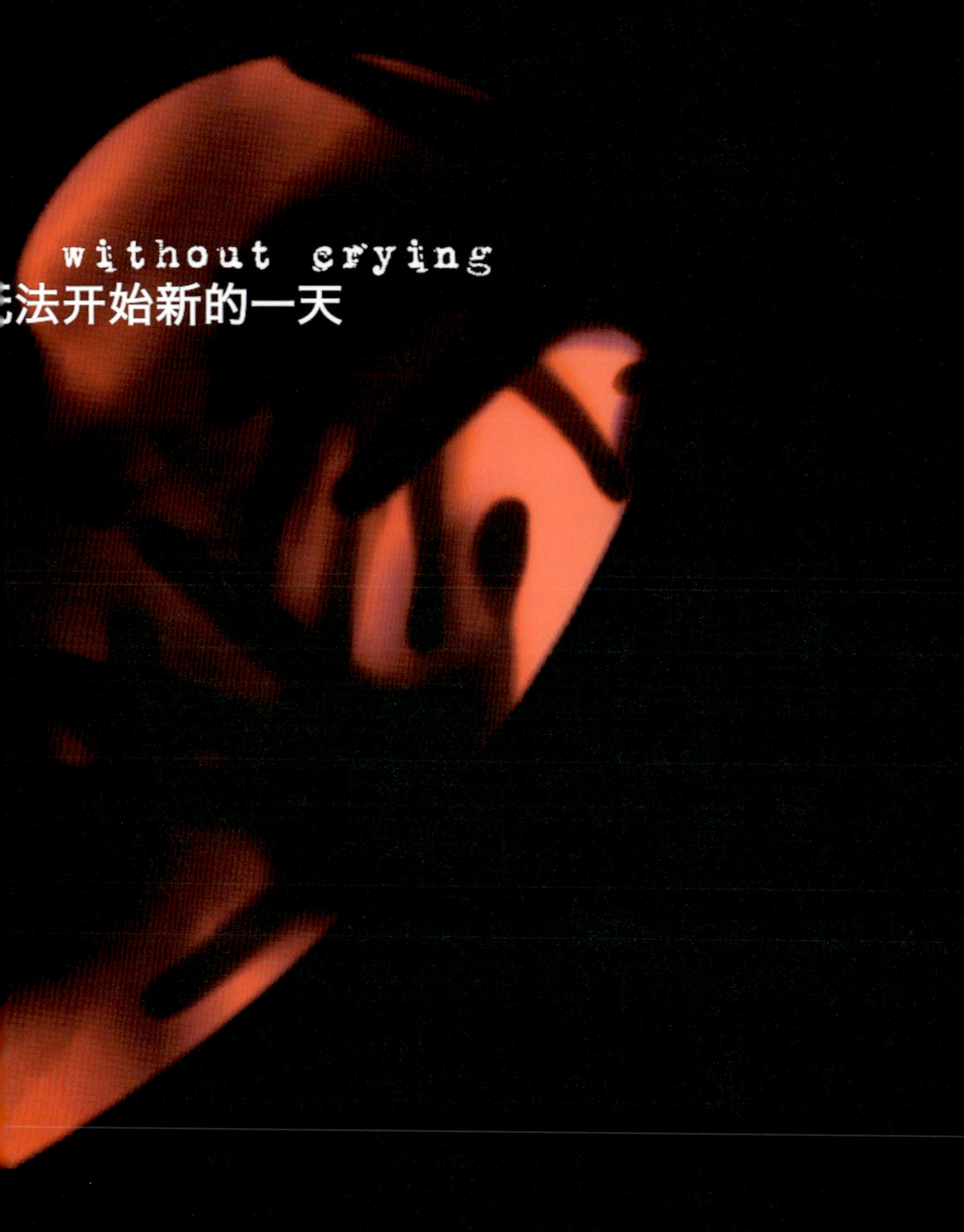
without crying
无法开始新的一天

THE LADY AND THE FLIES: IN CONCERT
We were just inside the fog machine, but we are not anymore. We were just above the vending machine, but we are not anymore. We were just on the wallpaper and then on the window, but we are not there anymore …

"I am *not*—" comes a shrill voice from inside the dressing room—and we follow it inside and then there we are.

The Lady of the Flies is late. This time the Lady of the Flies has a hole in her fishnet tights. Her assistants point out that fishnets are composed of holes, and so does it really matter that there is one hole more? Yes. The Lady of the Flies points out that one big hole means that, actually, there are six holes *less*. She really is a total nightmare in the classic rock star fashion. Right now she throws a shoe at the plaster wall, where it crunches and leaves a crater. Her whole appeal is that she is very classic, so who can blame her? But we are already familiar with this behavior. It is because the Lady is such a classic rock star that she is not interesting to us as the subject for our story, which does not have a star at all. This is the last we will hear about her:

The Lady applies a fake mole just southeast of her classic red lipstick. The Flies (her band) wear classic black suits that make them look British even though they are from California, California, and North Carolina. This is them coming in the dressing room now.

"Uh, hey, Mary?" They say, from behind three different haircuts.

"Hey uh, Mary—"

"Mary, the fans are like … waiting."

Indeed, they can hear screaming and crying from the stadium. The Flies try to remain chill about this. But really, they are a bit scary, the Fans. The fan base, as they realized on night one of their North American tour, consists mainly of teenagers, both male and female, who are overweight and weird. The Lady and the Flies, by contrast, are conventionally attractive and cool. Somehow this dynamic, this vast differential in sex appeal between Flies and Fans, gives new meaning or perhaps just vibrancy to the posts on the forum devoted to their music in which anonymous users write things like "Mmm, yum. I am going to eat that one," about one or another of the musicians. It makes the threat, somehow, more realistic. In their own school days, the Flies respectfully avoided interacting with classmates who fit the profile of their fan base, and now they are dependent on them for their very livelihood. Onstage, the Flies are aware that we outnumber and outweigh them. So the Flies right now really do not want to give us reason to act on any morbid impulses, however relatively normal these might be for that kind of teenager—they wouldn't want to pathologize. They're nice enough, kind of. Really, we realize now, from up close, watching them fiddle lazily with their skinny ties, the Flies are not really flies, they are just once-very-handsome now less-handsome high school popular guys, who, through personal and cultural inertia, stayed popular enough to become somewhat famous. We recognize them from the locker room. They become less edible by the moment …

Our attention drifts.

On the makeup table there are whispering white wedges of foam smudged with pink. On the snack table there are crinkling orange foil packages of cheese-flavored crackers. There is water dripping out of the mini fridge. On the ceiling, there is a fan. On the wall, there is a fly. It has two eyes, and inside of them, thousands more. On the mirror, tiny pieces of lint adhere to the images of the Lady and the Flies. From behind the half-open door, a slight droning comes over the PA system. We follow the sound out into the hallway. In the vending machine there is carbonation. On the TV monitor there is static. Technicians with headsets run back and forth on linoleum tiles flecked with blue, red, and yellow squiggles. In the distance, there is the loud murmur of the crowd. In the hallway, there are only speakers. The speakers are big and black, with thousands of honeycomb holes. From each tiny hole there comes a buzzing. The buzzing grows louder and louder. As we drift closer to the holes, we begin to hear clearly what we have been hearing all along—

LADY OF THE FLIES CHORUS
Sweet cherry soda and lights inside windows
Fruits that are rotting and ears laid on pillows
Flying and buzzing and hiding our sting
These are a few of our favorite things
Doors that are open and nothing behind them
Crumbs that fall down where no one can find them
Curtains and camo, unanswered telephone rings
These are a few of our favorite things
When earbuds get tangled or lost in your pocket
Tidbits and tokens inside of your wallet
Fendi and Gucci and expensive bling
These are a few of our favorite things
And these are the things that all make us sing:

Mary told a story
The story cast a spell
Mary went to heaven
And the story went to
Hello little spider
We'd like to play your game
But if you try to catch us
We'll sting you from
Inside the darkened classroom
We hear a little note:

Ask me no more questions
Tell me no more lies
The boys are in the bathroom zipping up their
Flies are in the meadow
Fishnets in the park
Eyes and ears are list'ning in the
D A R K
   D A R K
     D A R K

THE LADY OF THE FLIES (SONG
CITY SCHOOL FOR GIRLS)
Dark, dark, dark sunglasses are useful in cases of
emergency. We were on a class trip to London to
see Blingblington Palace and the art museums, and
so we were wearing our school uniforms when our
plane crashed. Our uniforms are black and white
with a silver backpack. As trainees at the Song City
School for Girls, we had enjoyed the presentation
by the three airline stewardesses in which they
moved their arms up, down, forward, backward,
and sideways, as though demonstrating the rota-
tional possibilities of human arms for a trade show.
We had often practiced such movements ourselves, so it was exciting to see them deployed not
ornamentationally but with the purpose of saving
our lives. Not that we cared very much about our
lives. In fact, although well behaved, being teenagers, we were secretly very careless. The three
stewardesses were admirably well synchronized,
we murmured to each other behind our small
hands, though perhaps they needed to work on
the trickulation and expression in their fingers.
After the presentation, we clapped politely. And we
remembered the positions of the exits.

The Song City School for Girls teaches discipline,
and it was May, and we were graduating in June,
and so this meant we had learned discipline, and
this in turn meant that when the airplane started
wobbleringaring, we did not scream; we did not
even take out our earbuds. Those of us in the
windows pressed our noses against the plastic
windows, and then turned to the right or to the left
to explain to our best friends what we were seeing.
What we were seeing was the sky and the water
switching position like a gymnast doing forward
rolls. When the exit doors sprung open, the infla-
tional yellow slide popped out, and we took our
best friends by the hand and filed down the aisle
in pairs.

We slid into the bright turquoise water. We had not
had time to put on the orange life vests, but our
silver PVC backpacks, which were filled with air
except for our MP3 players, served well as flotation
devices. Twenty-six shiny silver backpacks and
twenty-six shiny black heads bobbed in the sea
like coins and buttons dropped out of the pocket
of the private airplane. The sun was blindishingly
brilliant amid all this shiningness. Thankfully our
sunglasses helped us to see that there was a tropi-
cal island not far off. We each had a best friend and
we liked to listen to the same music on the same
MP3 player with her, splitting one pair of earbuds
to the left and to the right, and this is why none of
us became lost. Our instructors were not so lucky,
nor were the stewardesses. When we looked back,
they were gone, and so was the airplane.

We reached the shore of the island pretty fast. We
were good swimmers. Turquoise turned to aquamarine and aquamarine to clear water over white
sand. Onshore, we laid twenty-six black blazers
and fifty-two white bobby socks on the sand—
our brown penny loafers we had removed on the

plane. The island was nice. It had palm trees and bananas. It was okay; we had wanted to go to the Bahamas instead of London, anyways.

The only problem was that the seawater had infected our earbuds. When we listened to our favorite songs, we noticed that they had become distortions. A tinny foggy buzzing wobbleringaring blurbling brambling ping-ponged our ears. When we listened to Justin Blebber, for example, he sounded like a dolphin, making clicks and pops. When we listened to No Discretion, they sounded fizzy, like Coca-Cola, and Adrianna sounded weird, too, like a mermaid. But we went on practicing our songs and dances. After all, we still had our year-end recital to prepare for. Without mirrors, our dance movements became blurry and confusing, like a reflection in rippling seawater. When our MP3 players died, we had to sing each other the songs from minemory. Each time we sang, the song became even more whatever it was not. The problem is that because of our training at the Song City School for Girls, we were very good, in fact excellent, at copying and synchrillicity. We became synchronized to the island, which was mostly inhabited by large green dragonflies, in no time at all. They zimmered and bizzered around like air-planes that had never crashed. So did we. By the time the people on the rescue boat arrived, not one could understand us at all.

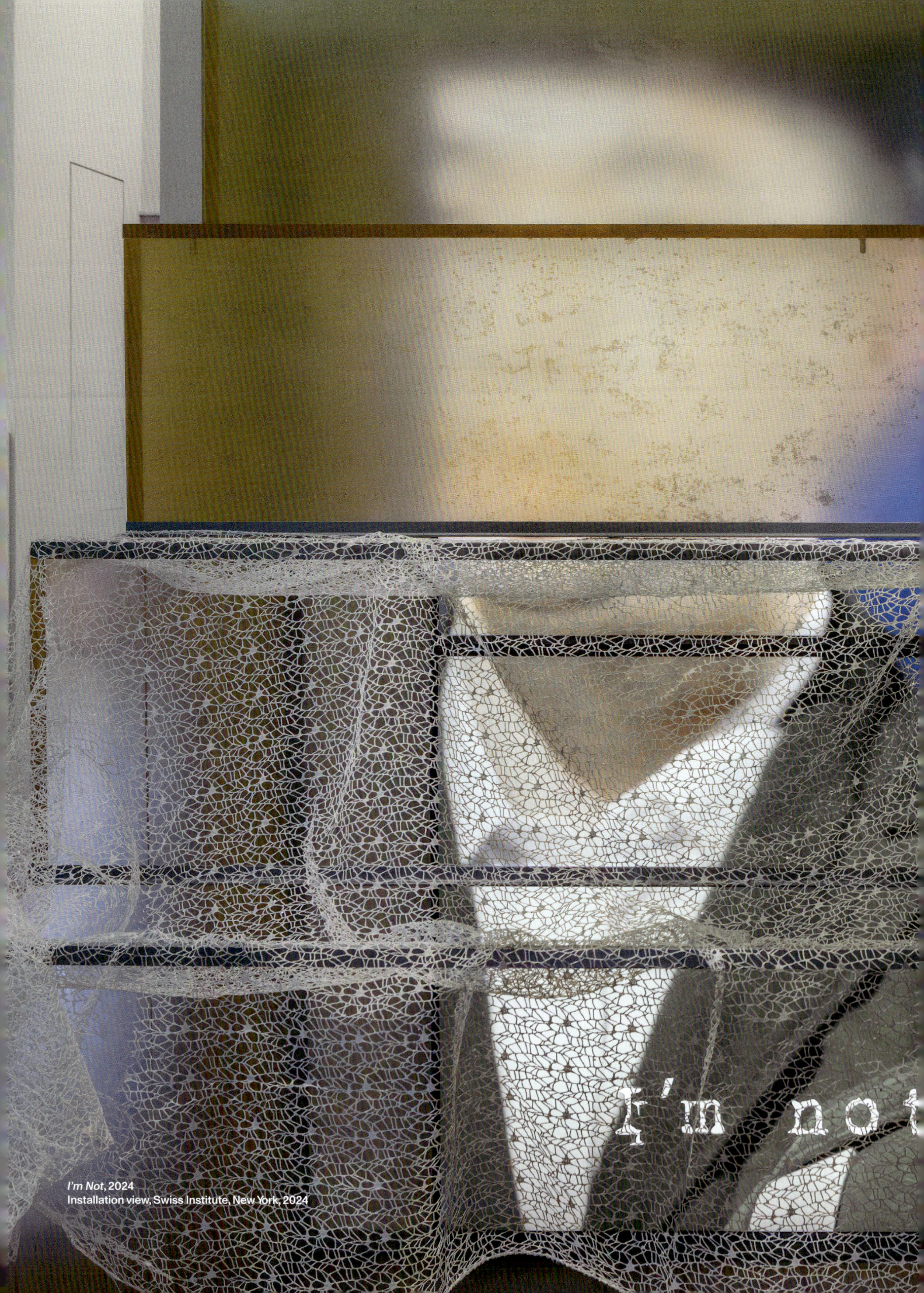

I'm Not, 2024
Installation view, Swiss Institute, New York, 2024

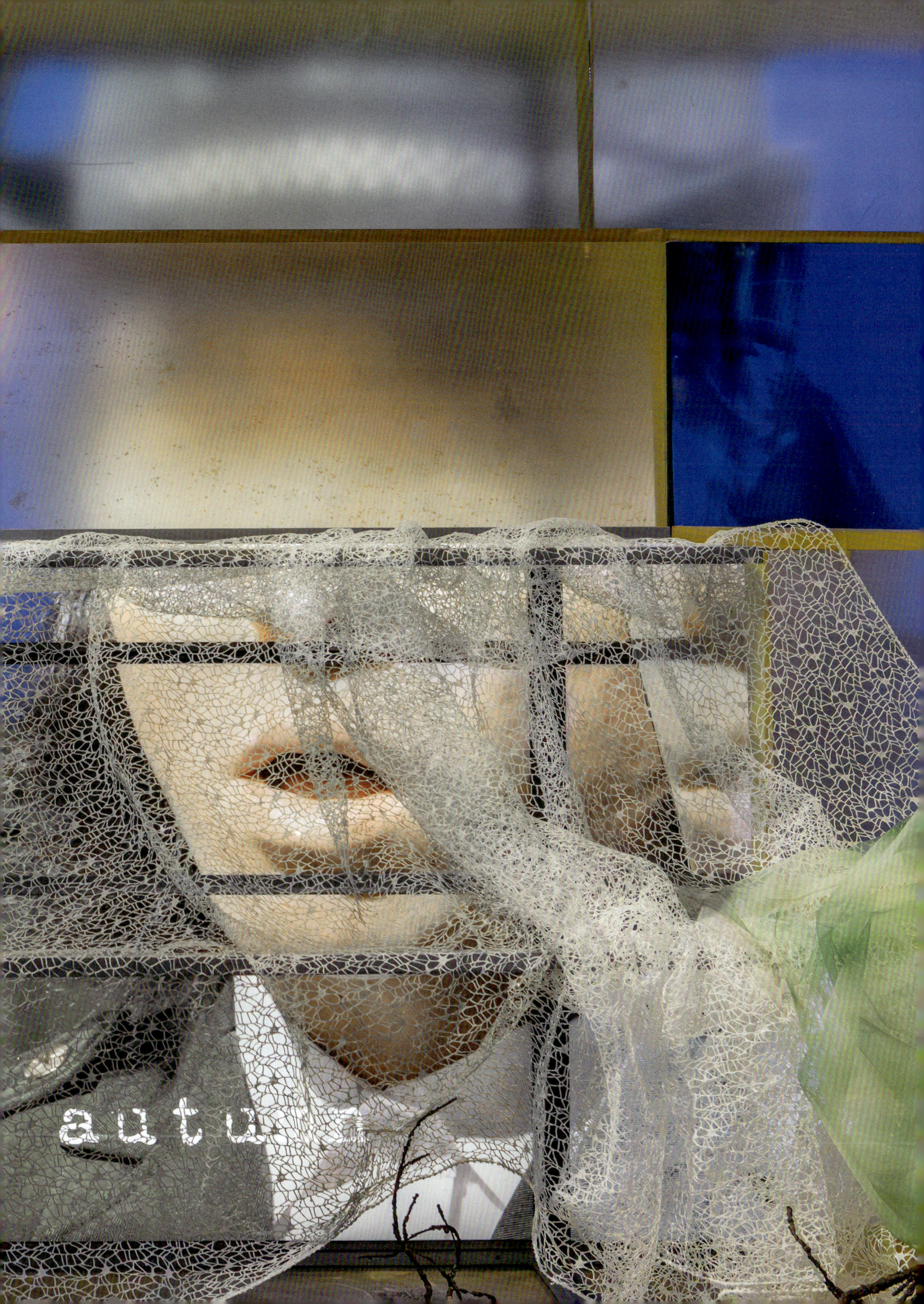
autum

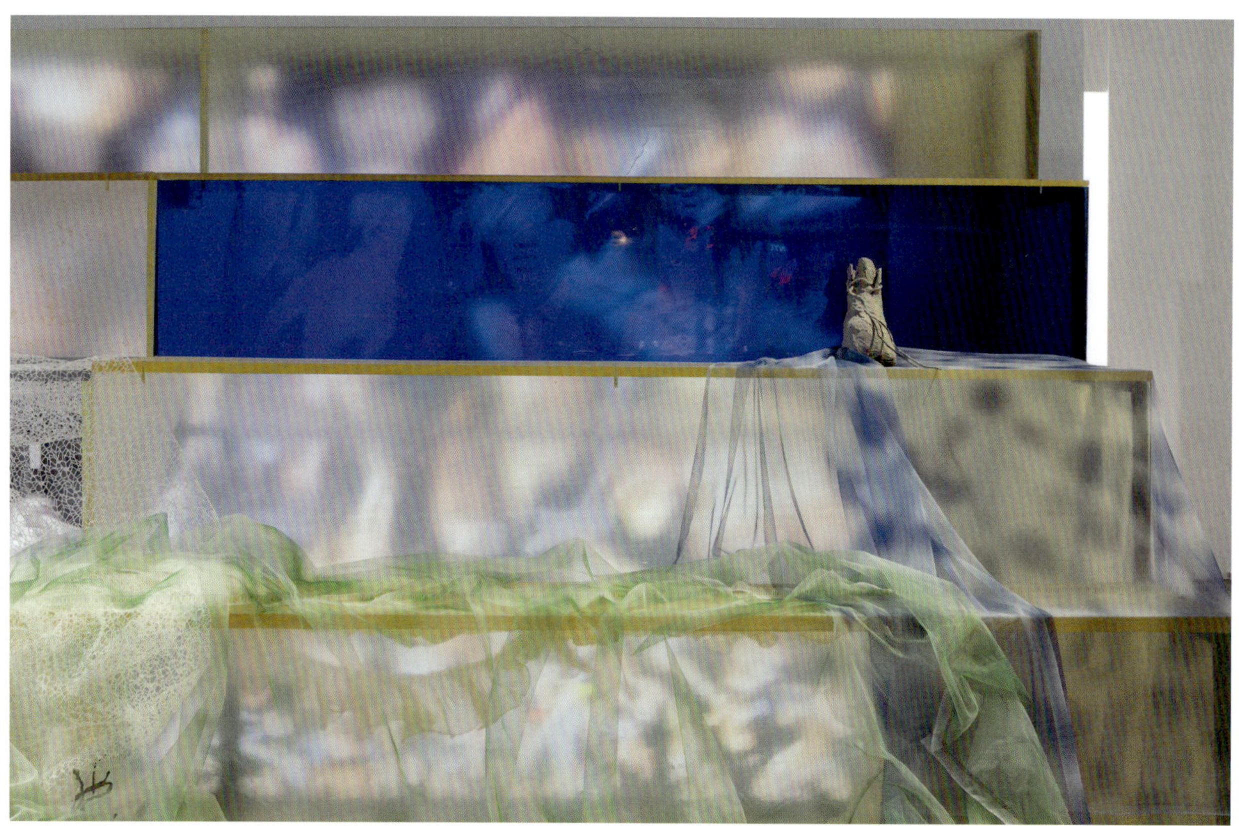

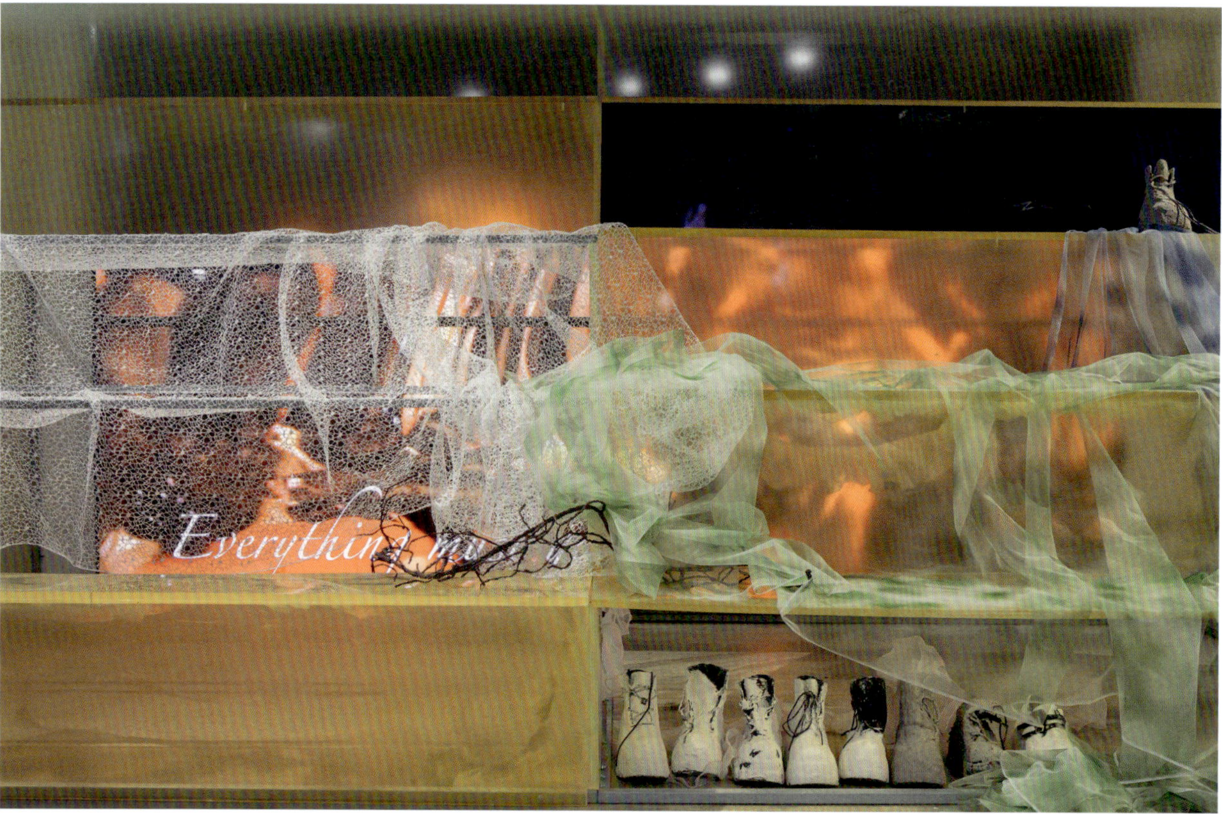
Everything mu

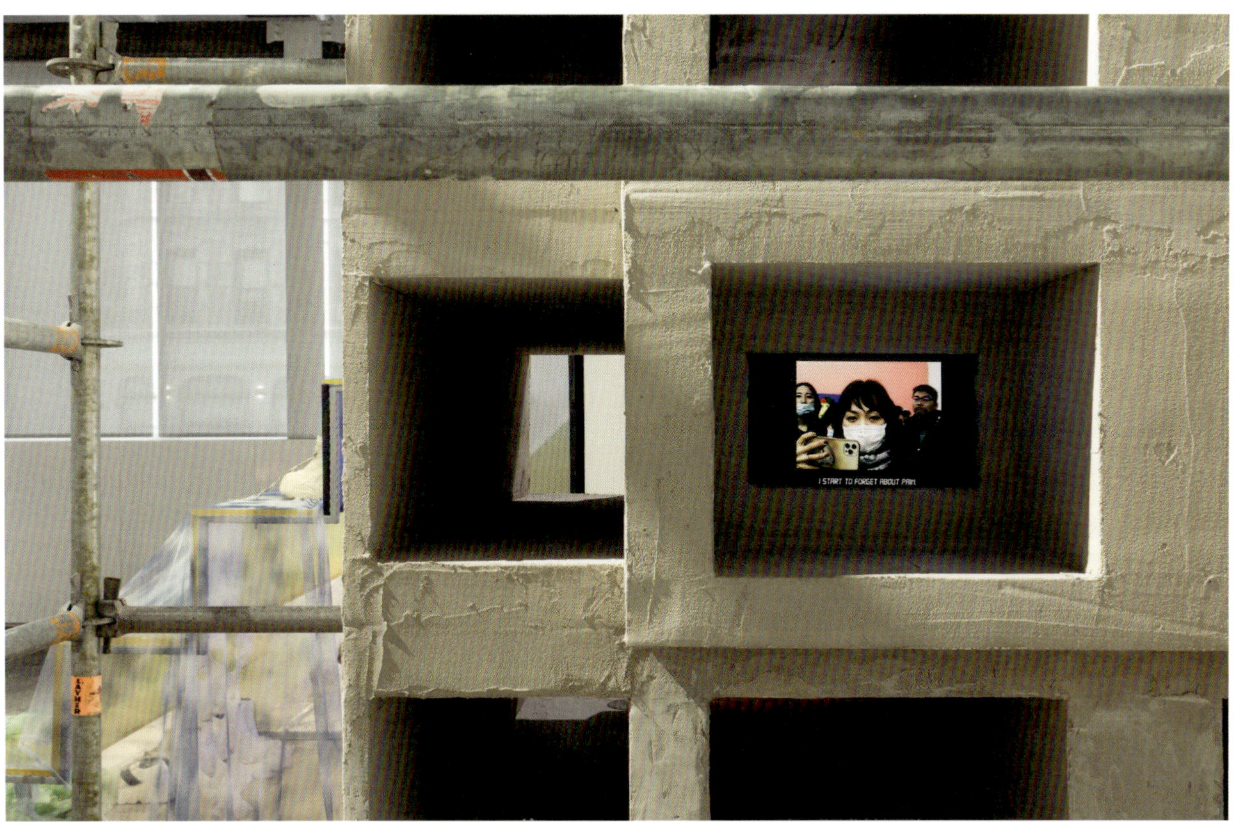
I START TO FORGET ABOUT PAIN

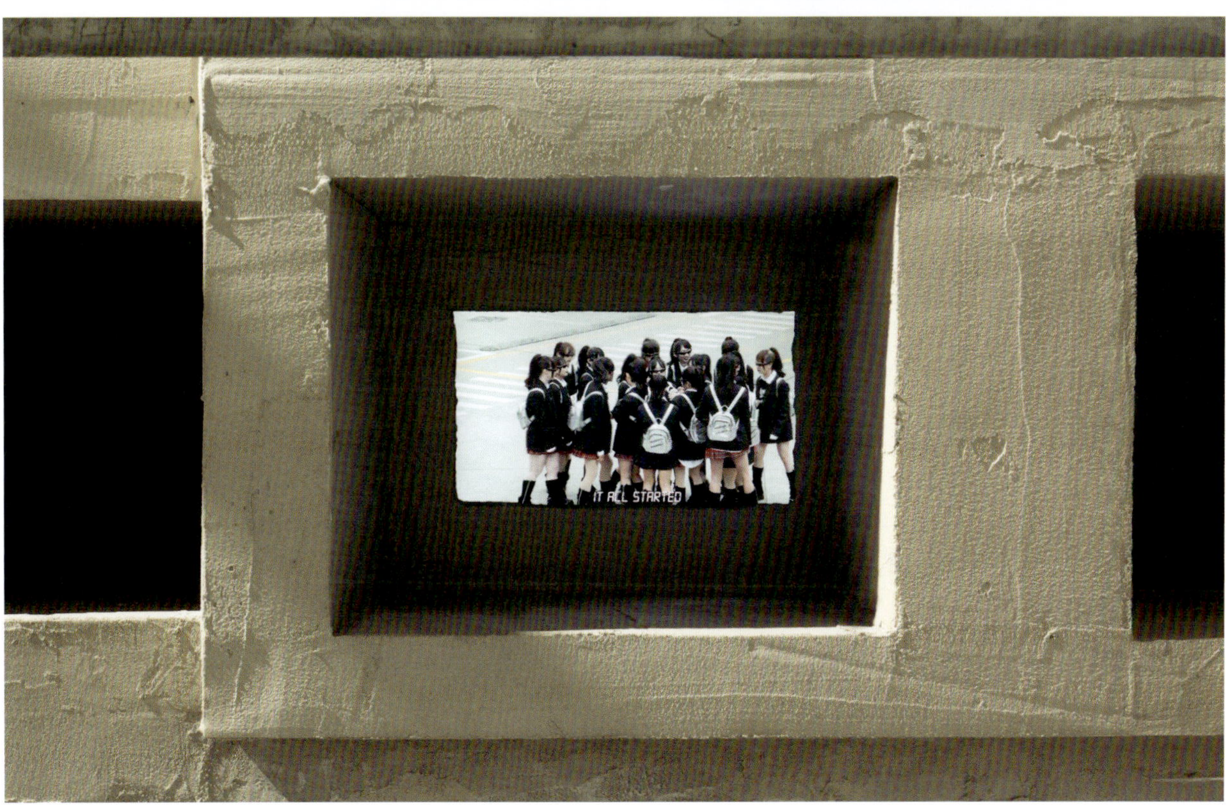
IT ALL STARTED

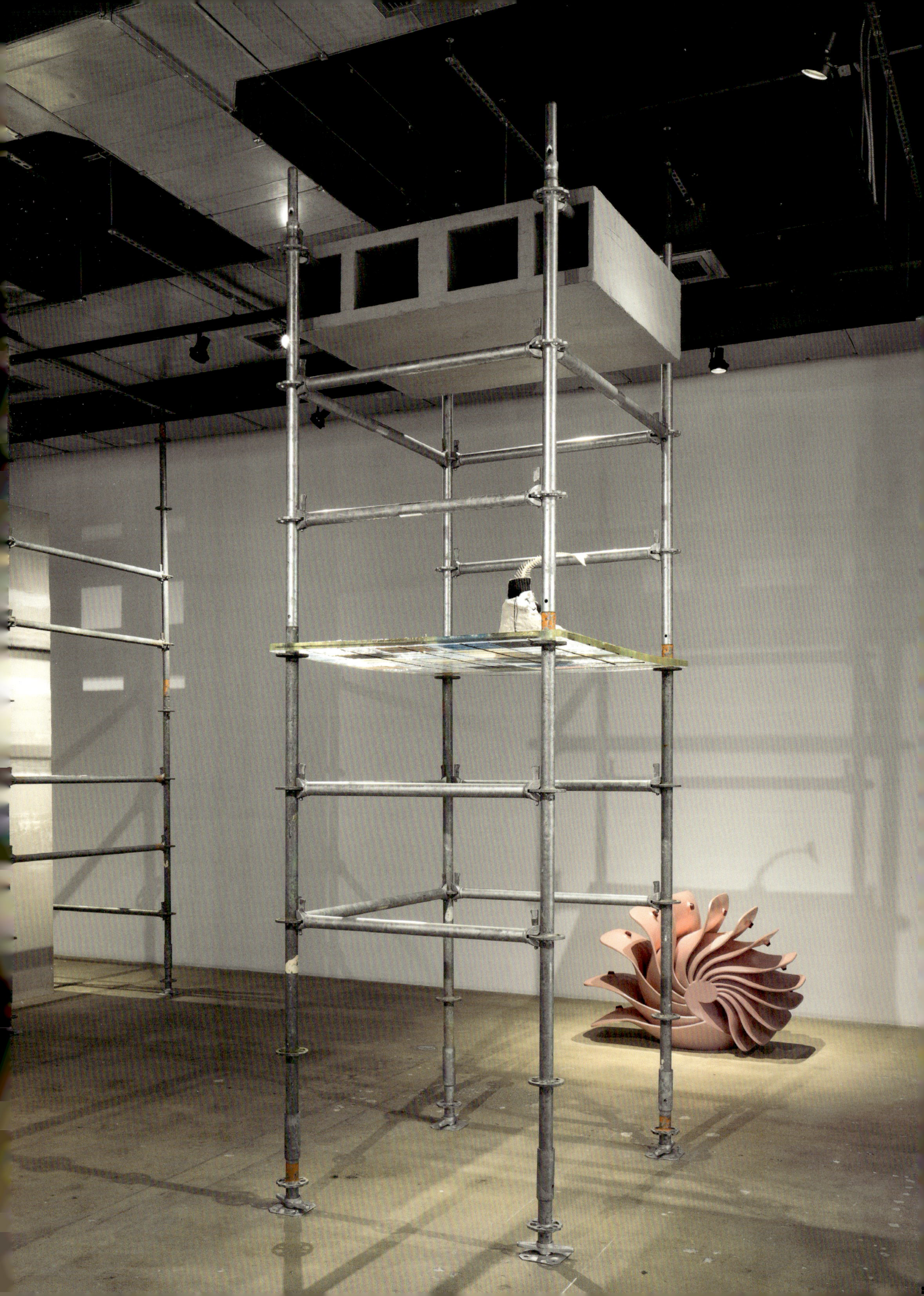

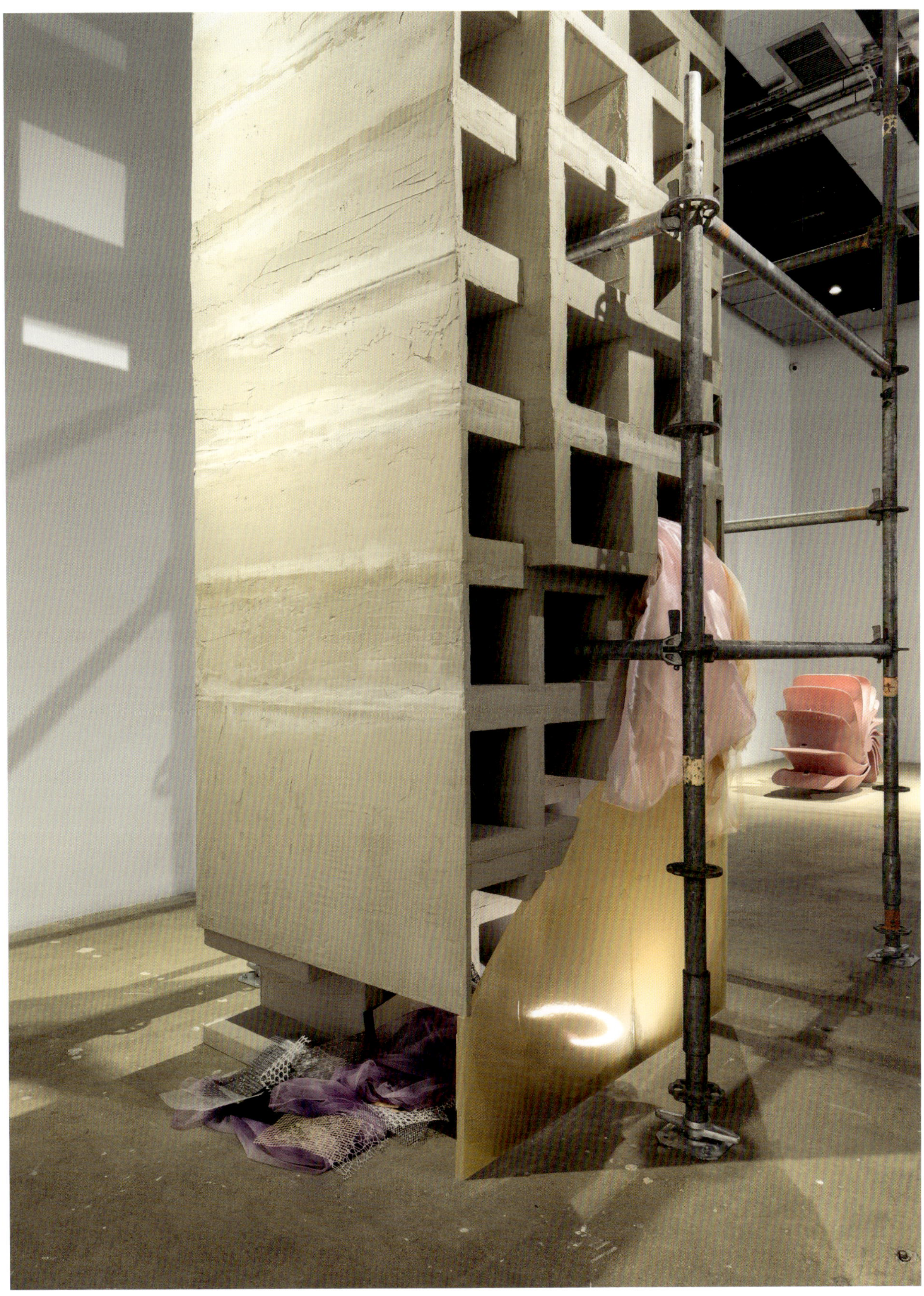

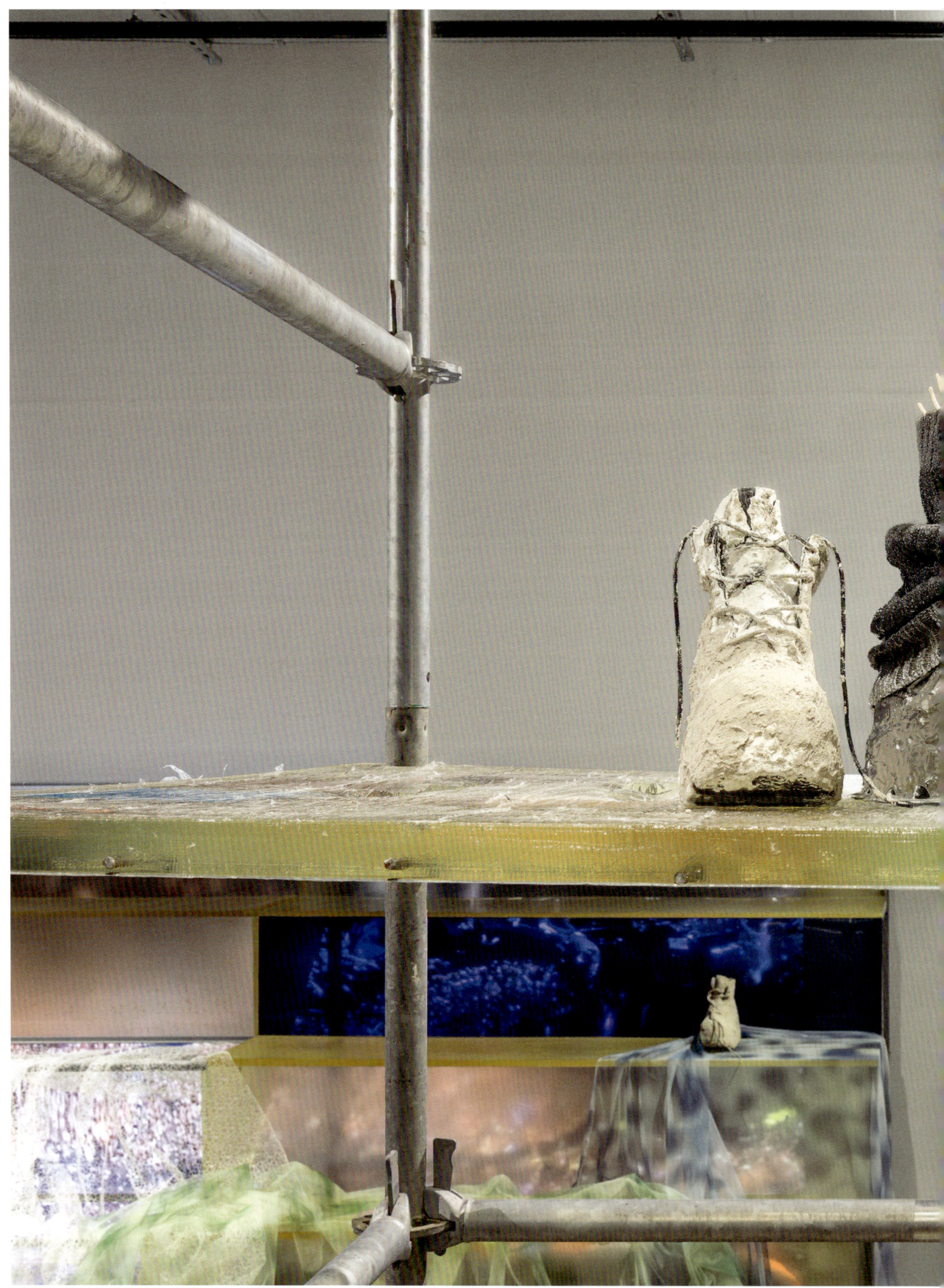

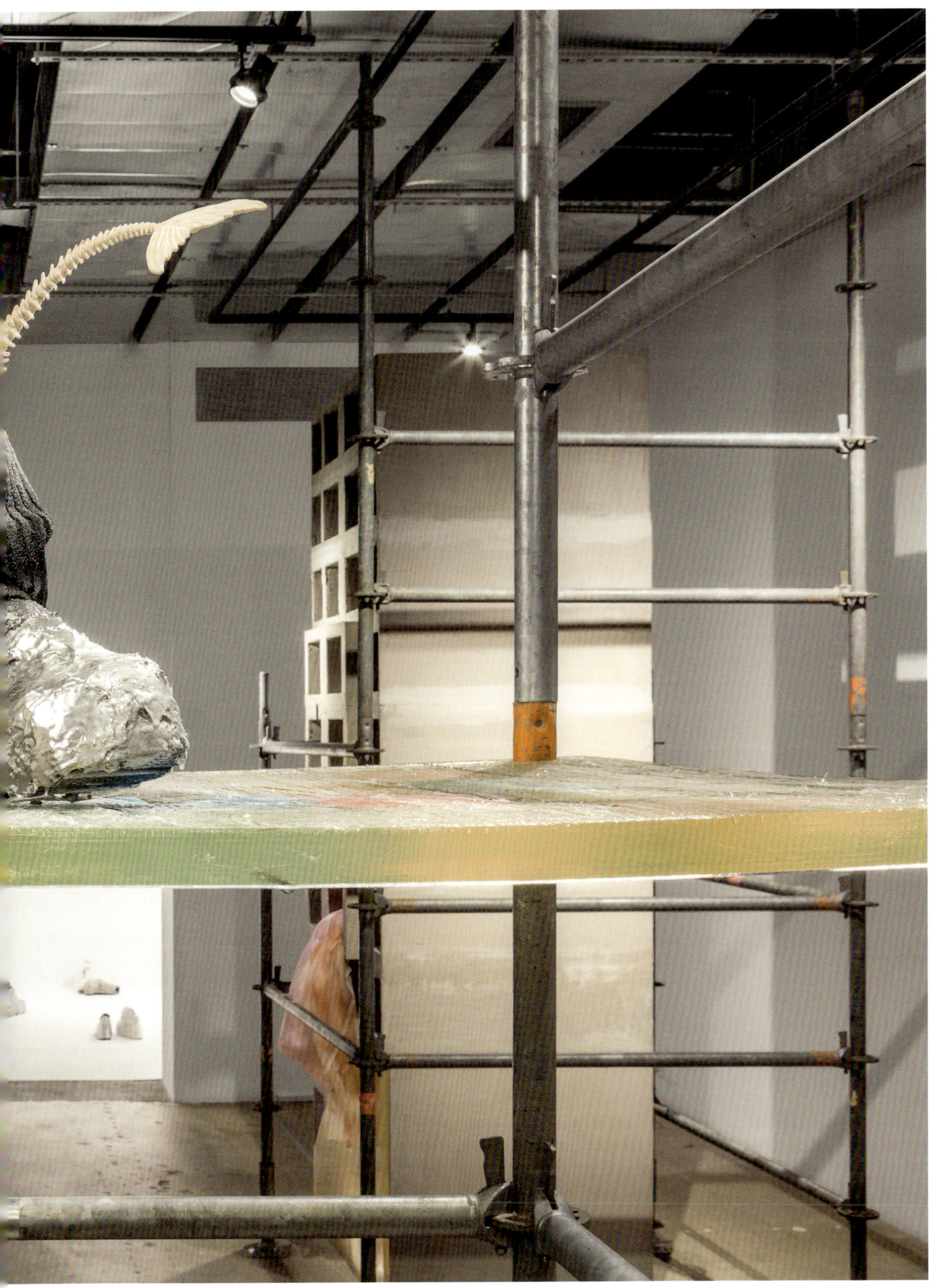

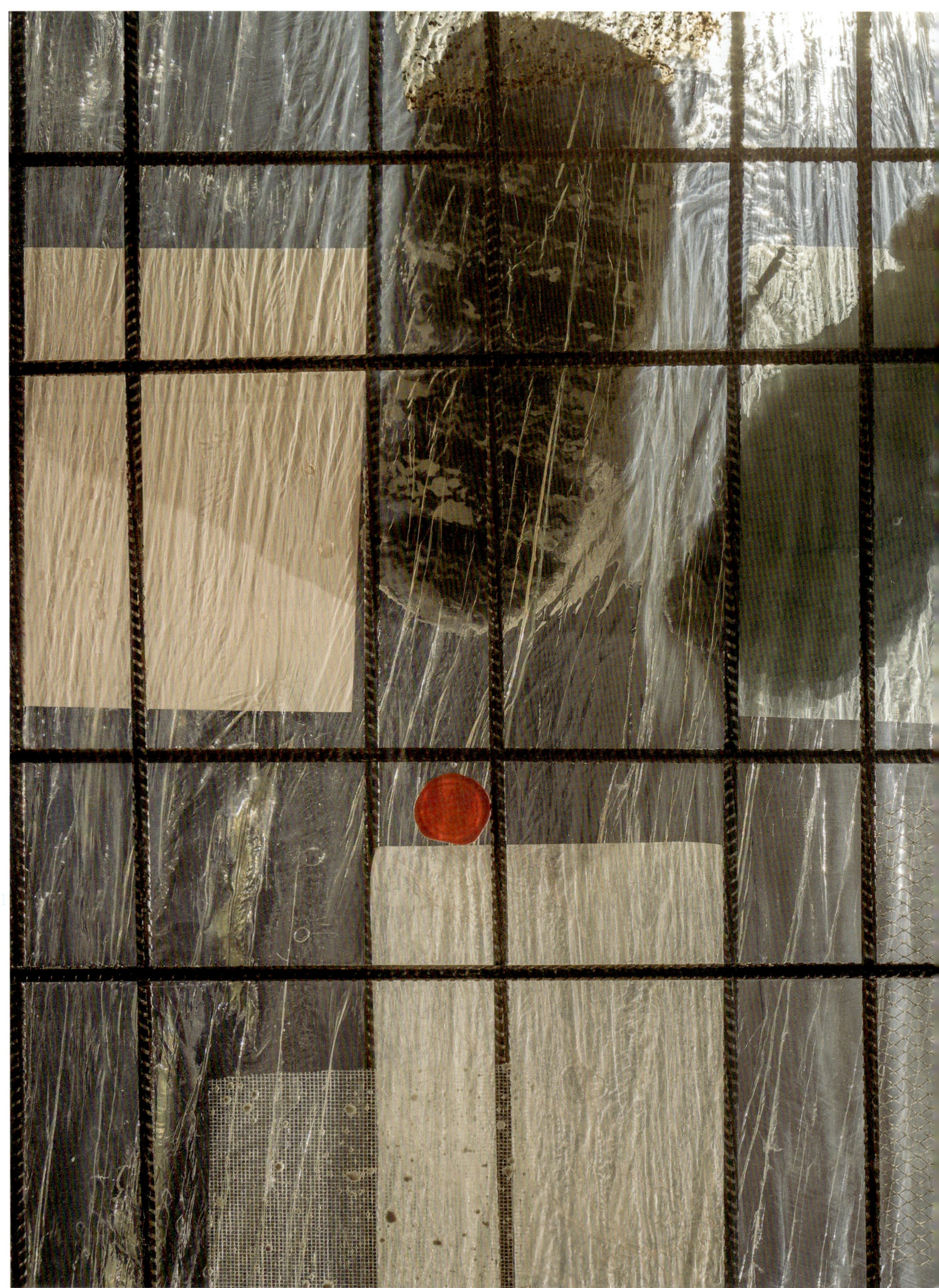

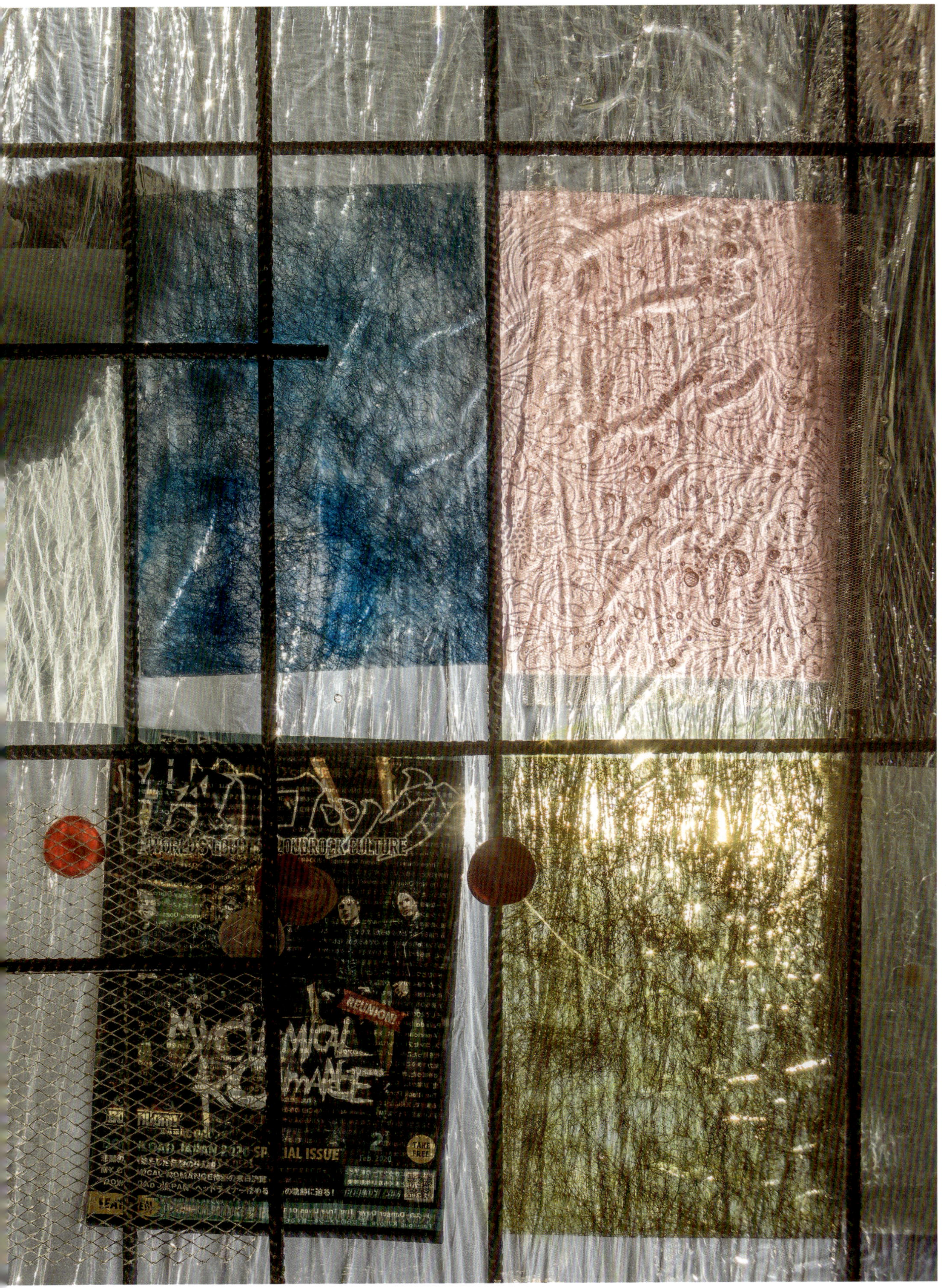
THE WORLD'S TOUGHEST LOUD ROCK CULTURE
MY CHEMICAL ROMANCE
REUNION!
LOAD JAPAN 2020 SPECIAL ISSUE
Feb 2020
TAKE FREE

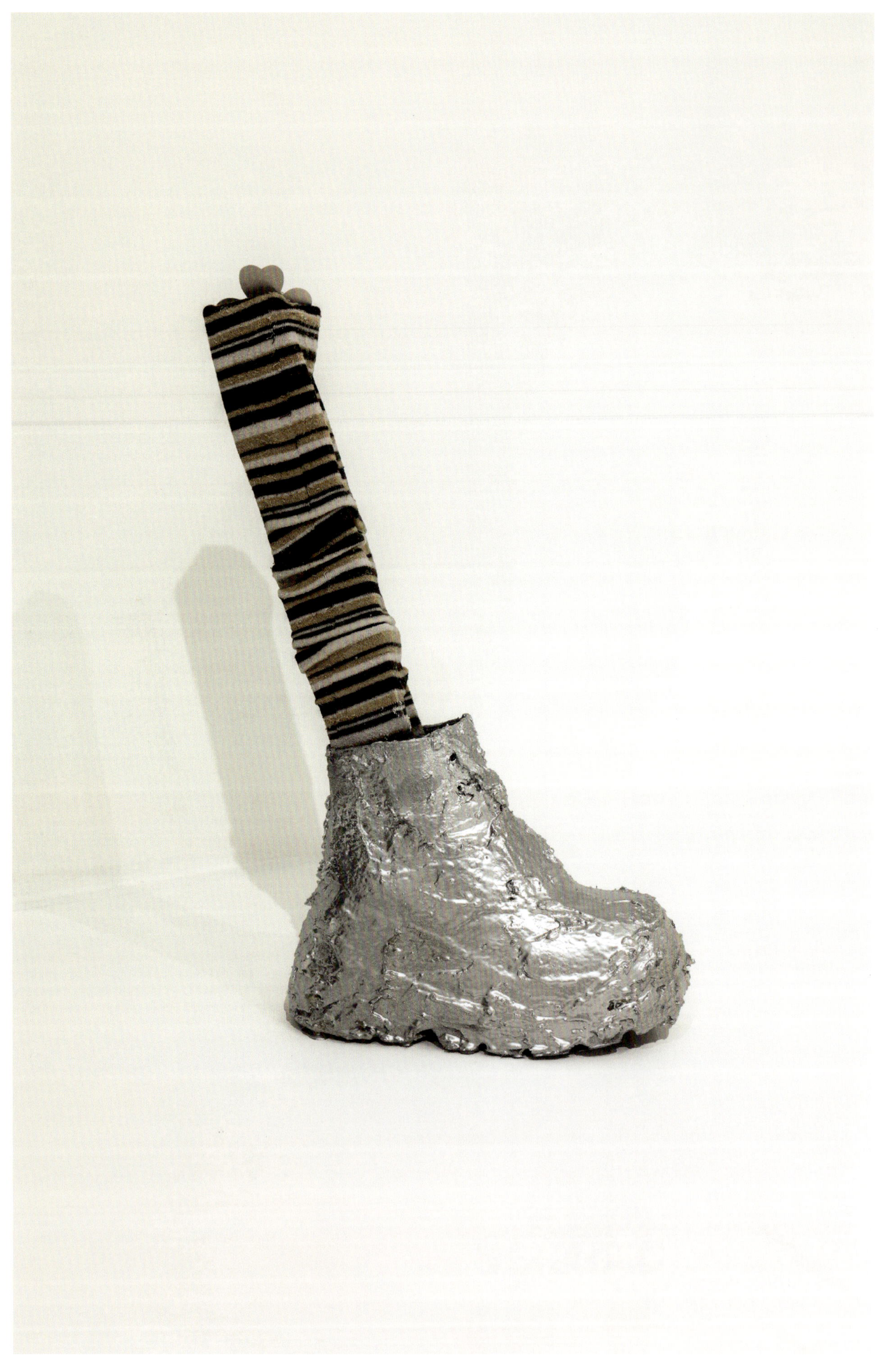

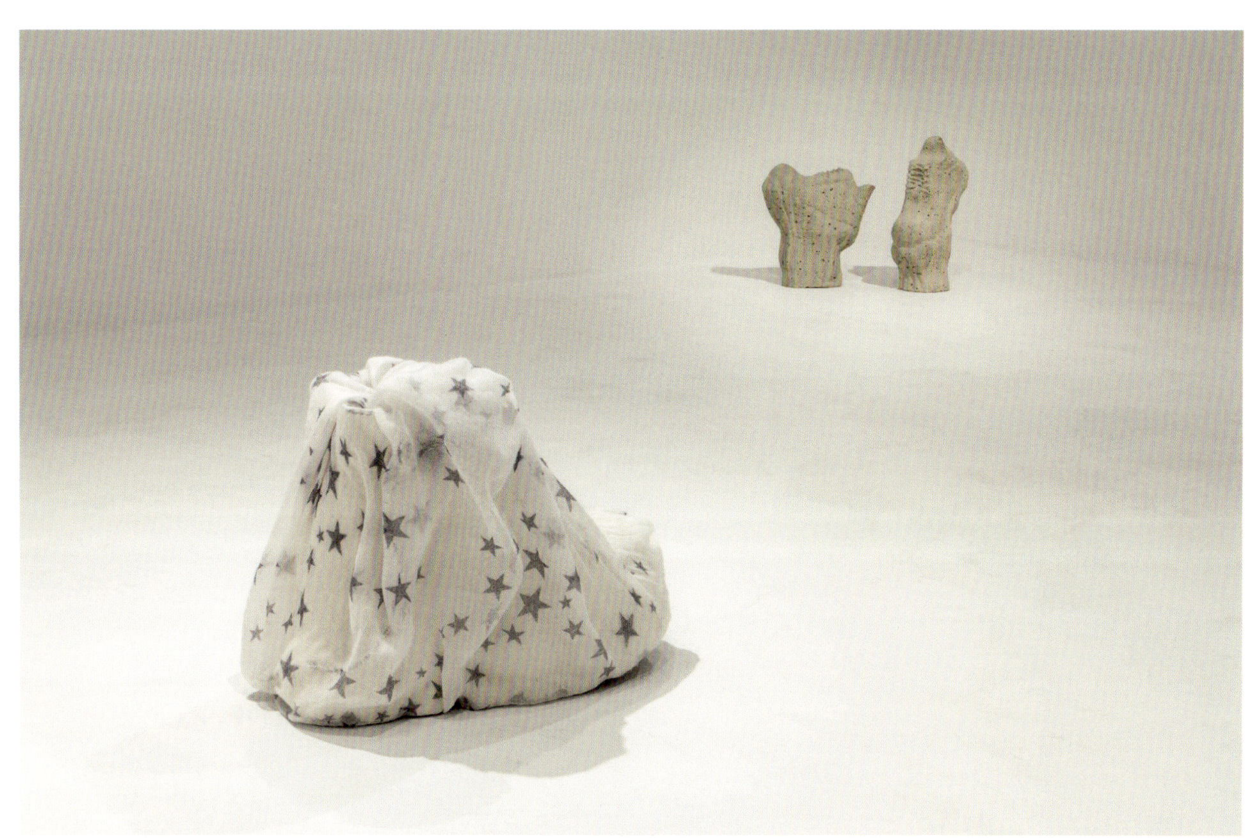

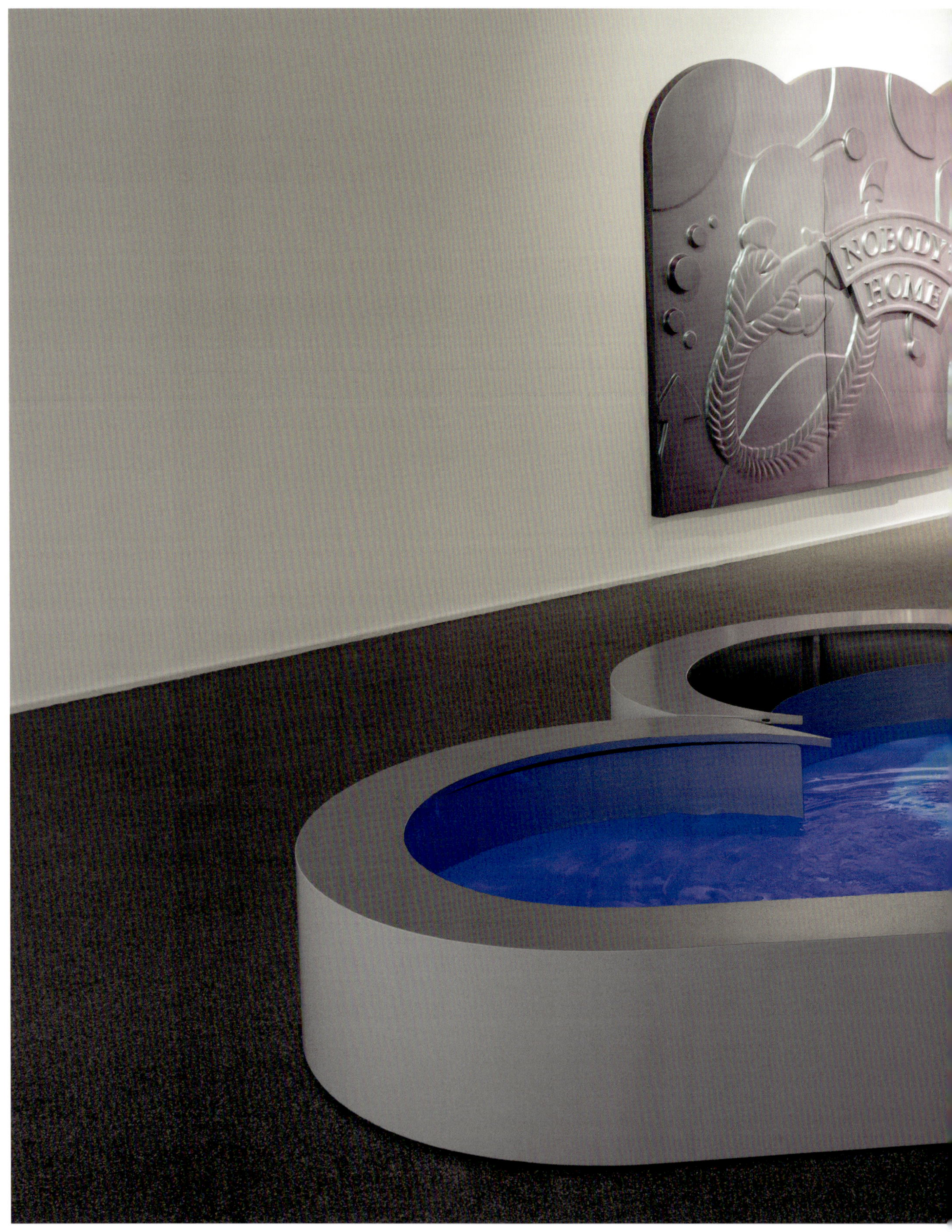
NOBODY'S
HOME

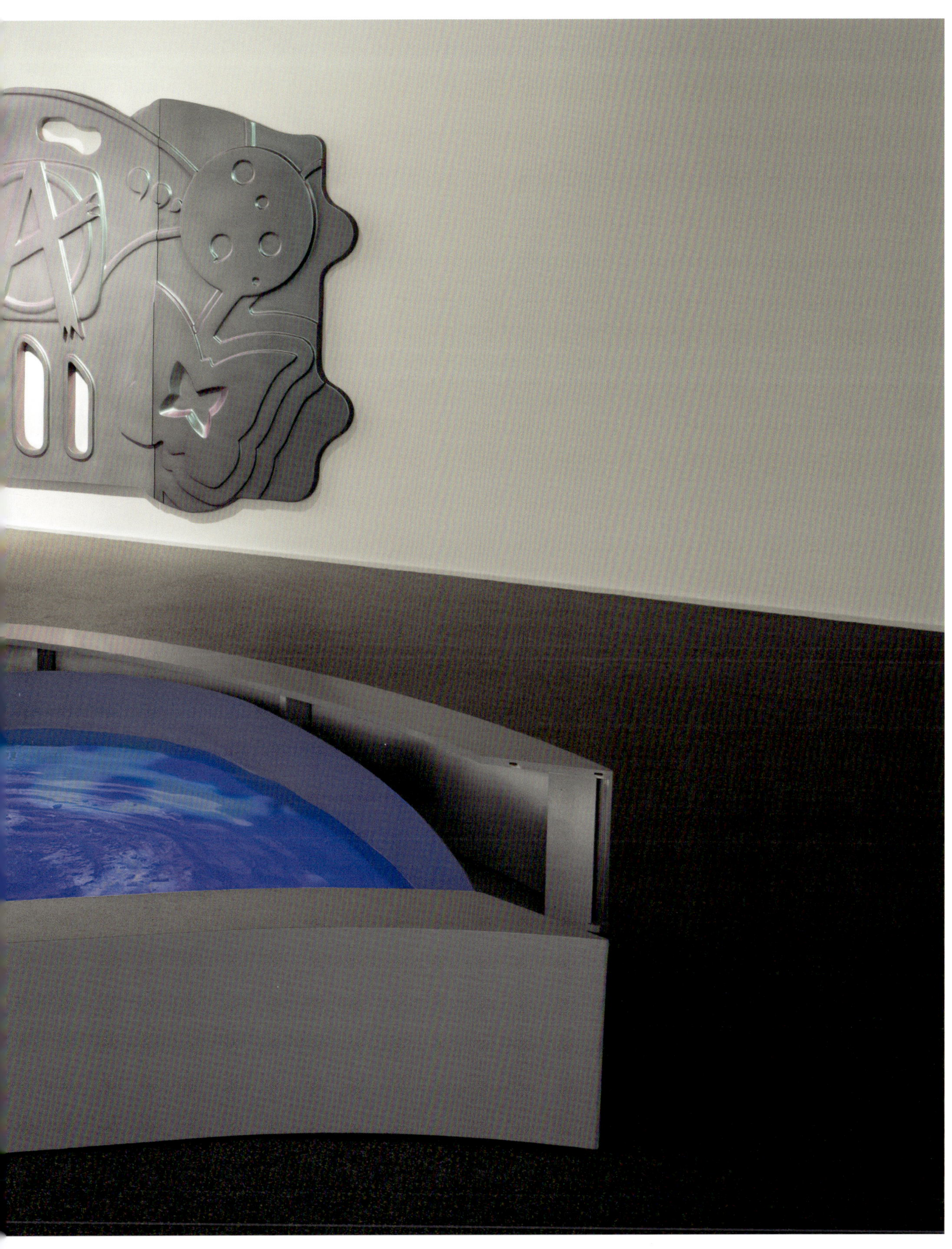

nobodys home, 2022, and *Heart is a Broken Record*, 2023
Installation view, Swiss Institute, New York, 2024

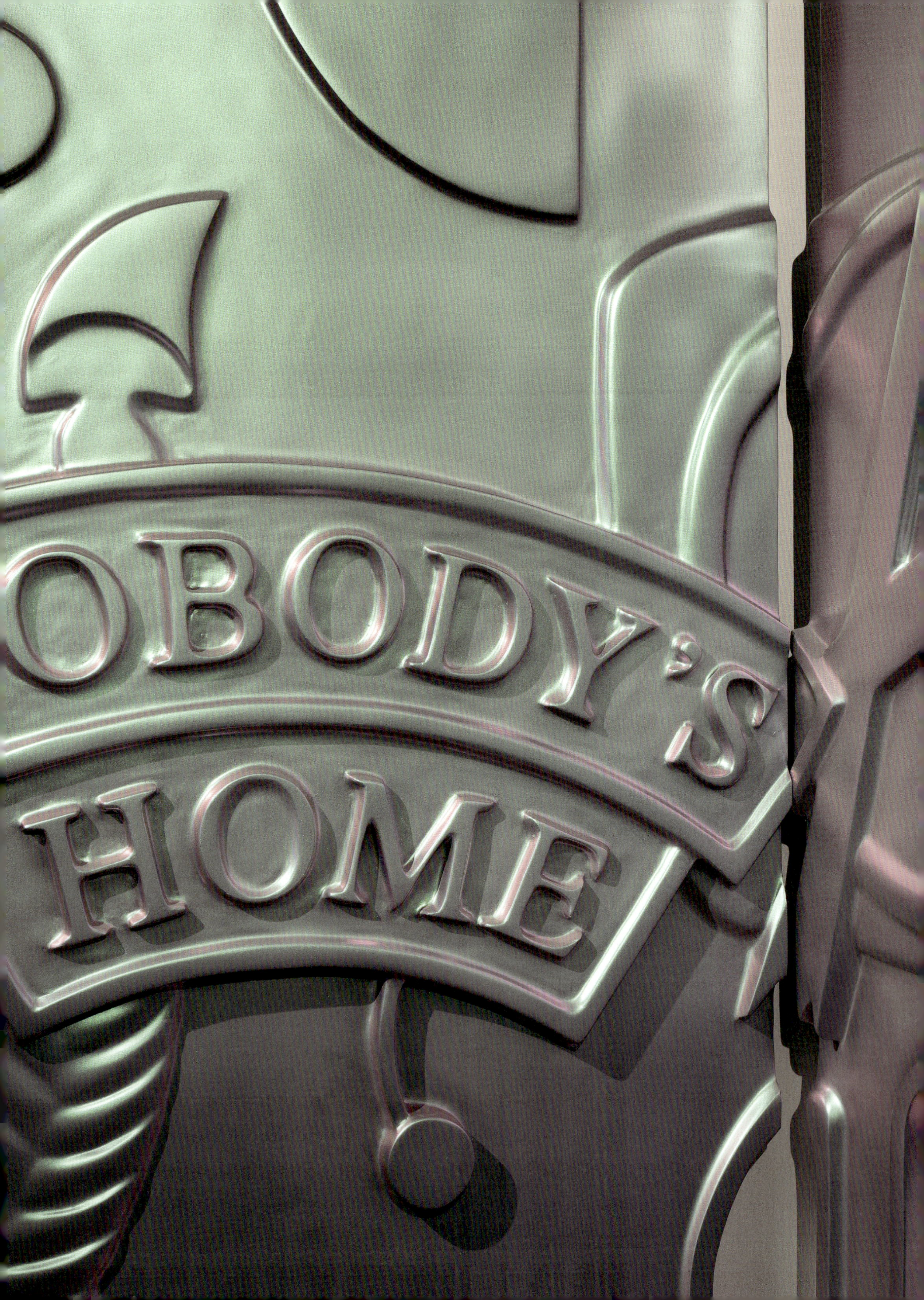

OBODY'S
HOME

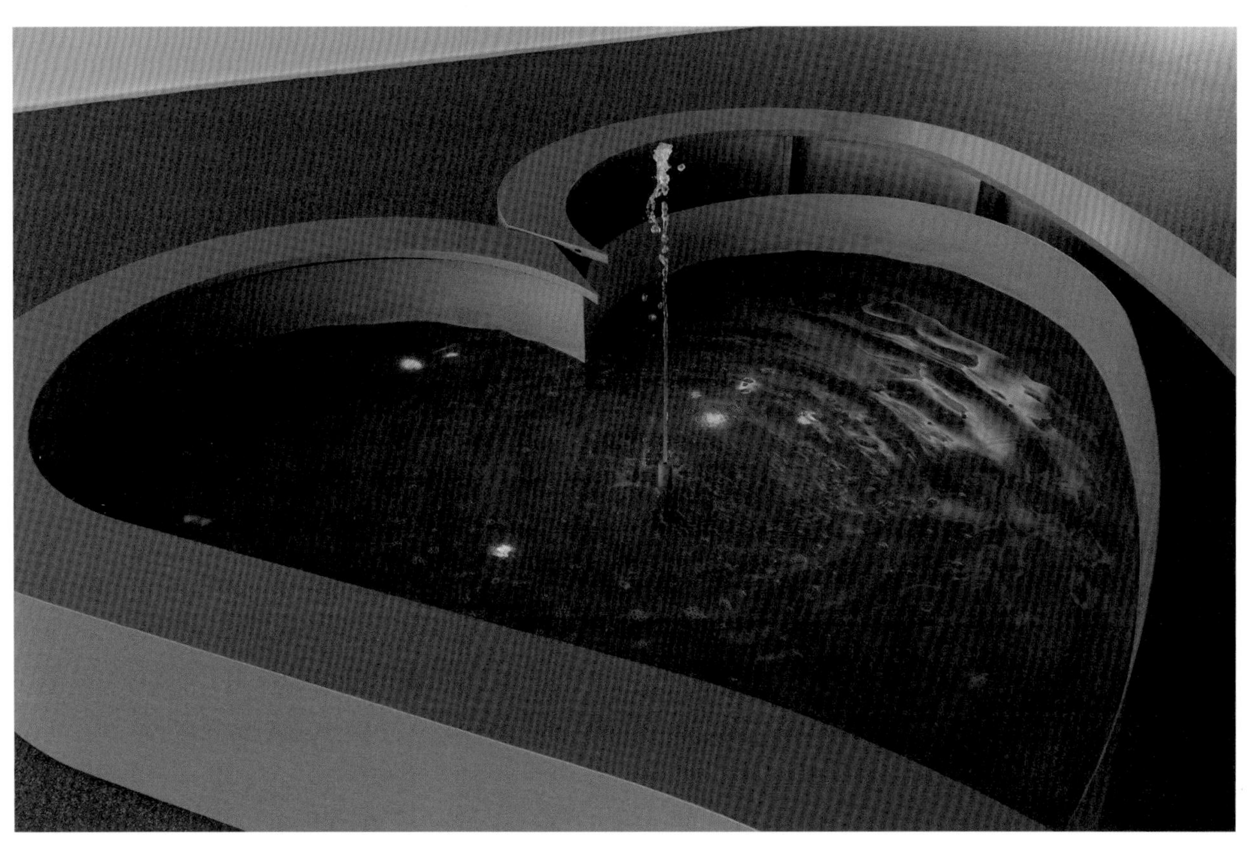

nobodys home (detail), 2022, and *Heart is a Broken Record*, 2023
Installation view, Swiss Institute, New York, 2024

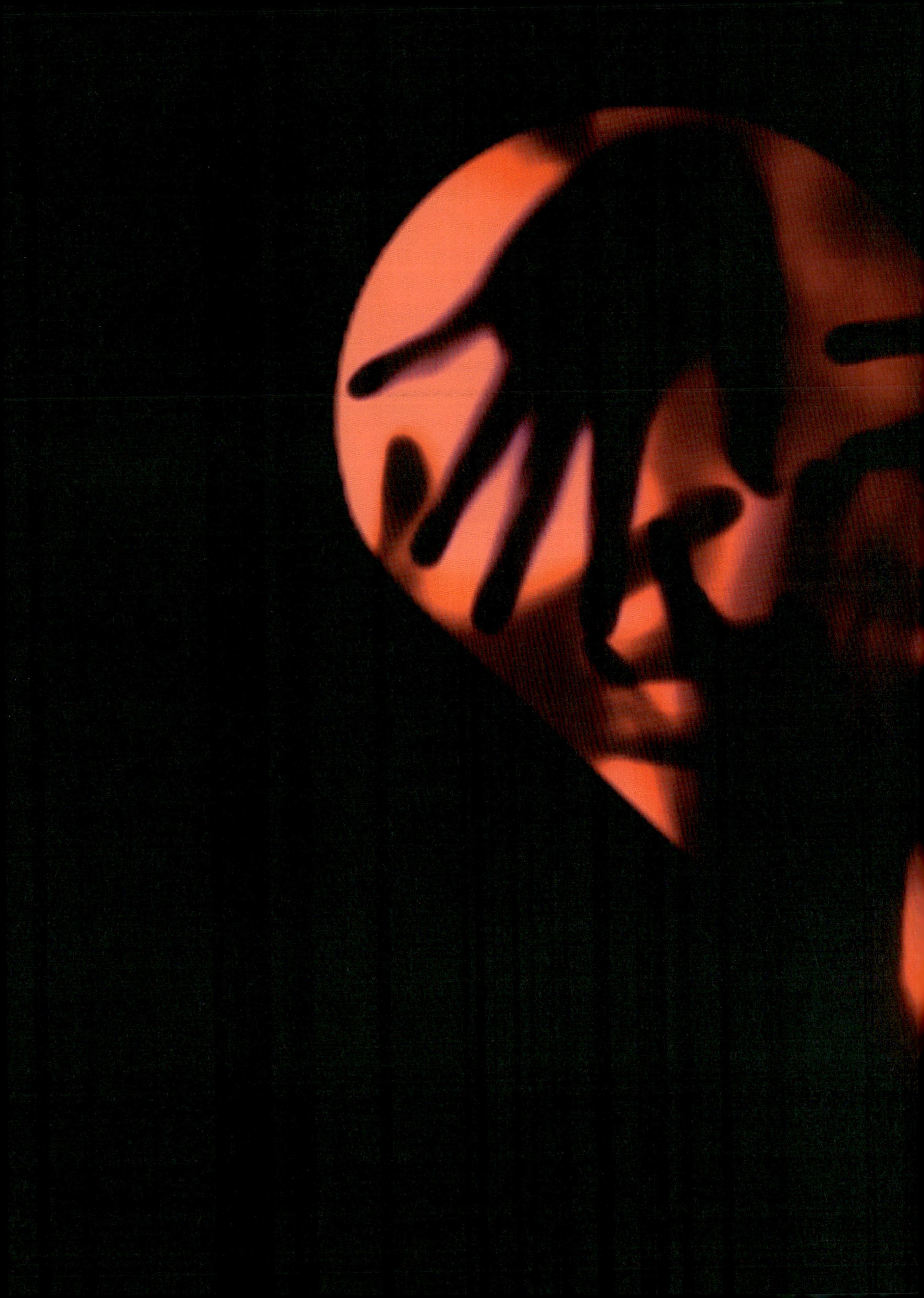

Like a chewed gum
像一颗嚼过的口香糖

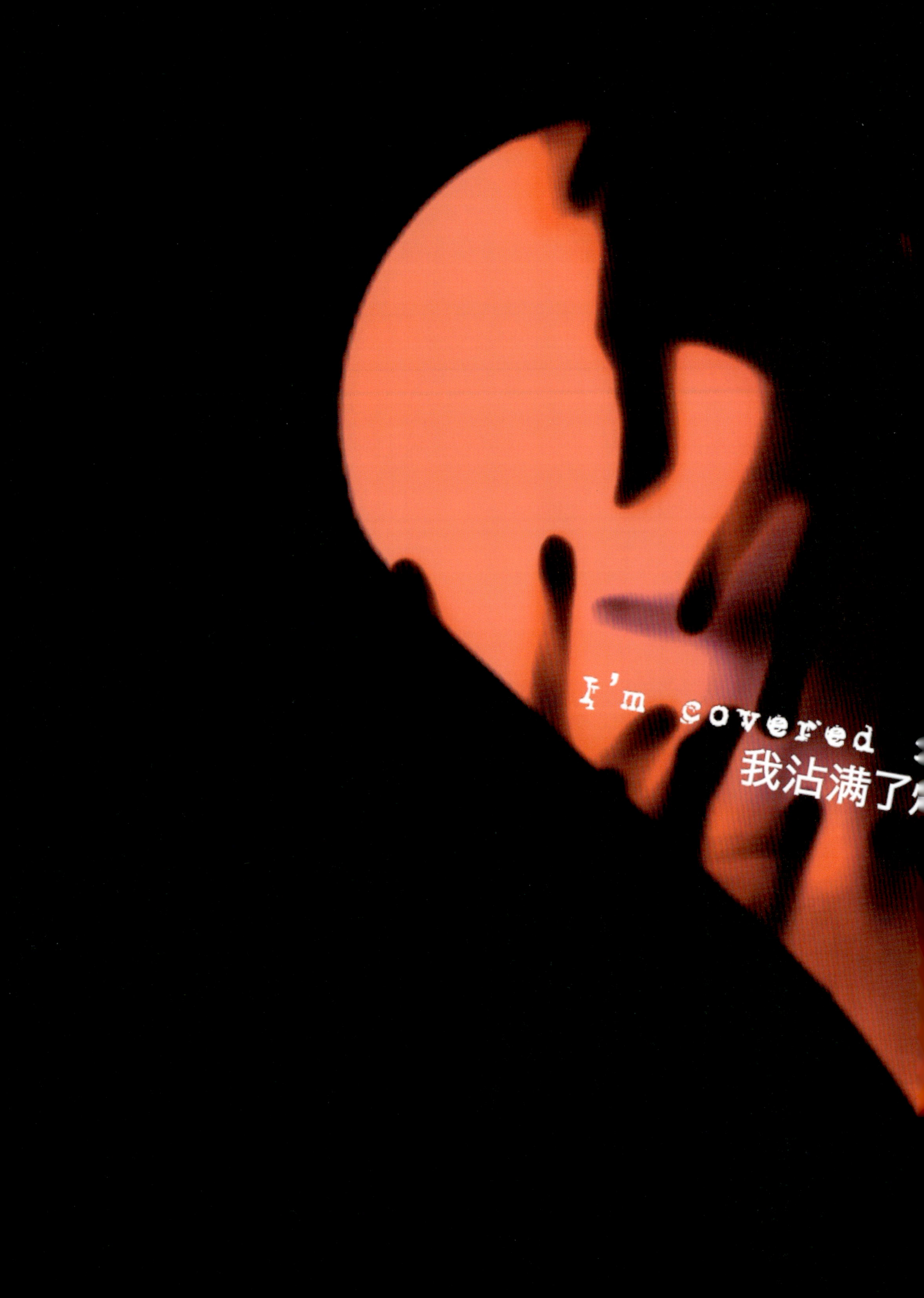

I'm covered
我沾满了

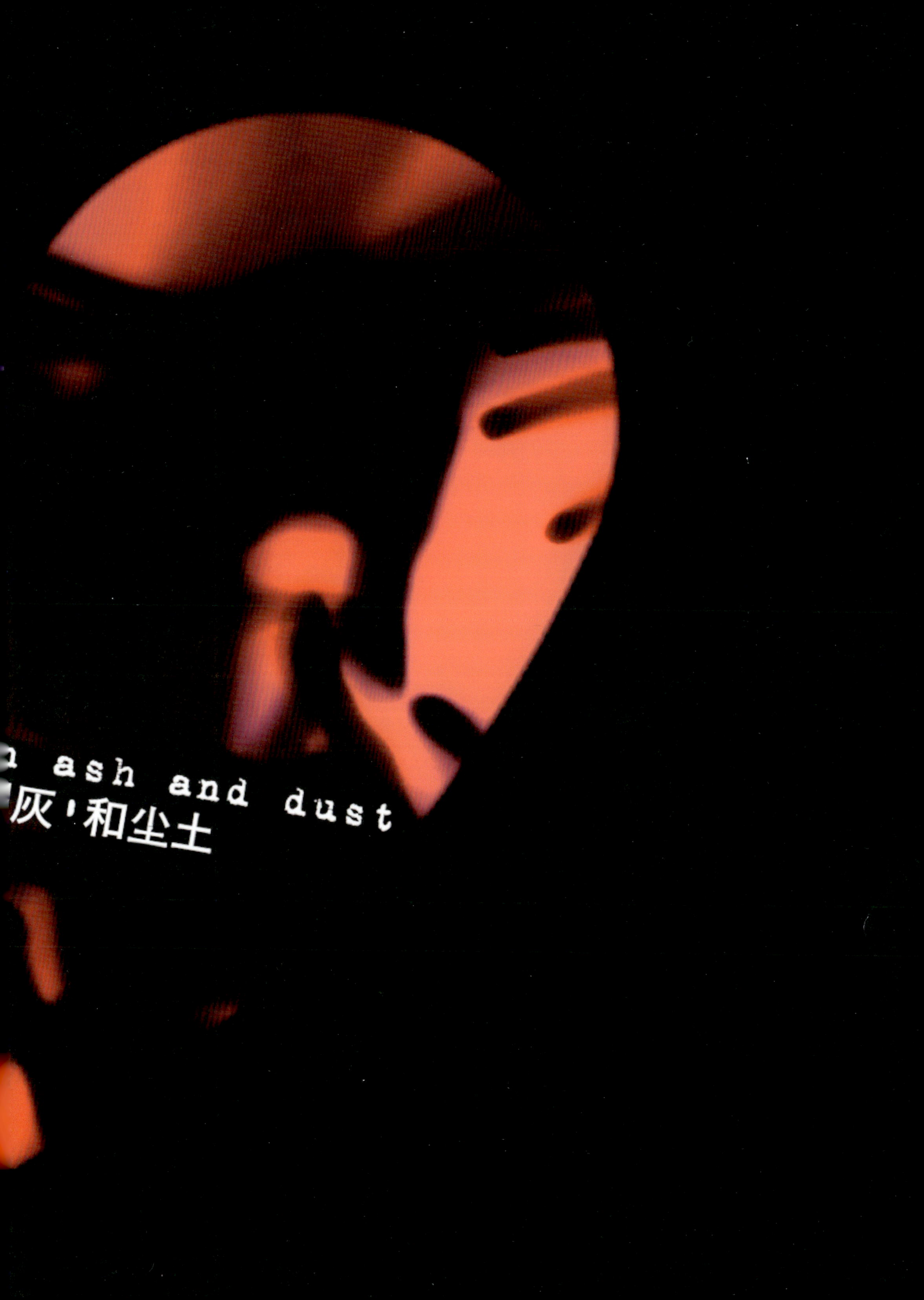

ash and dust
灰｜和尘土

lying on the cur
躺在街

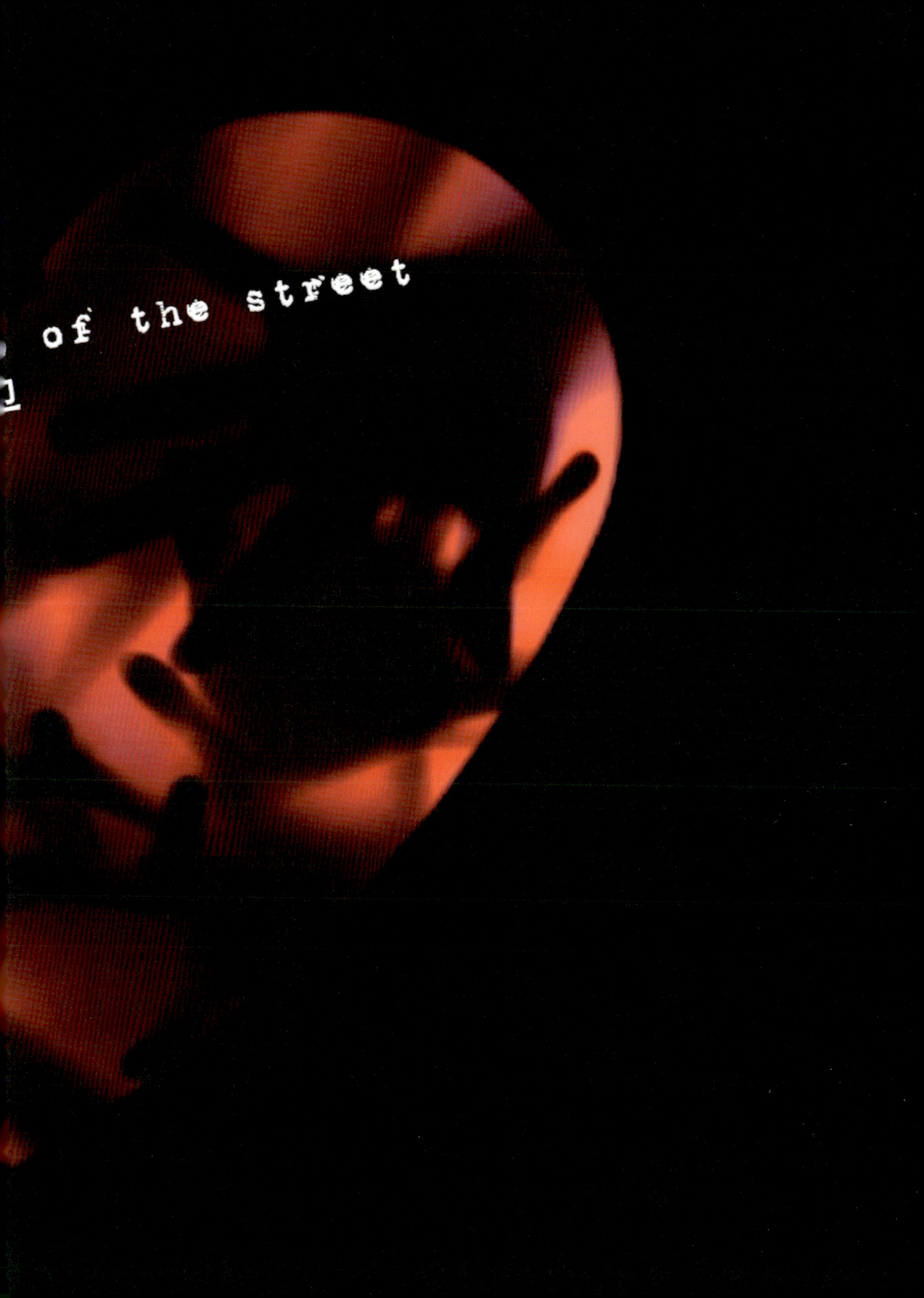

of the street

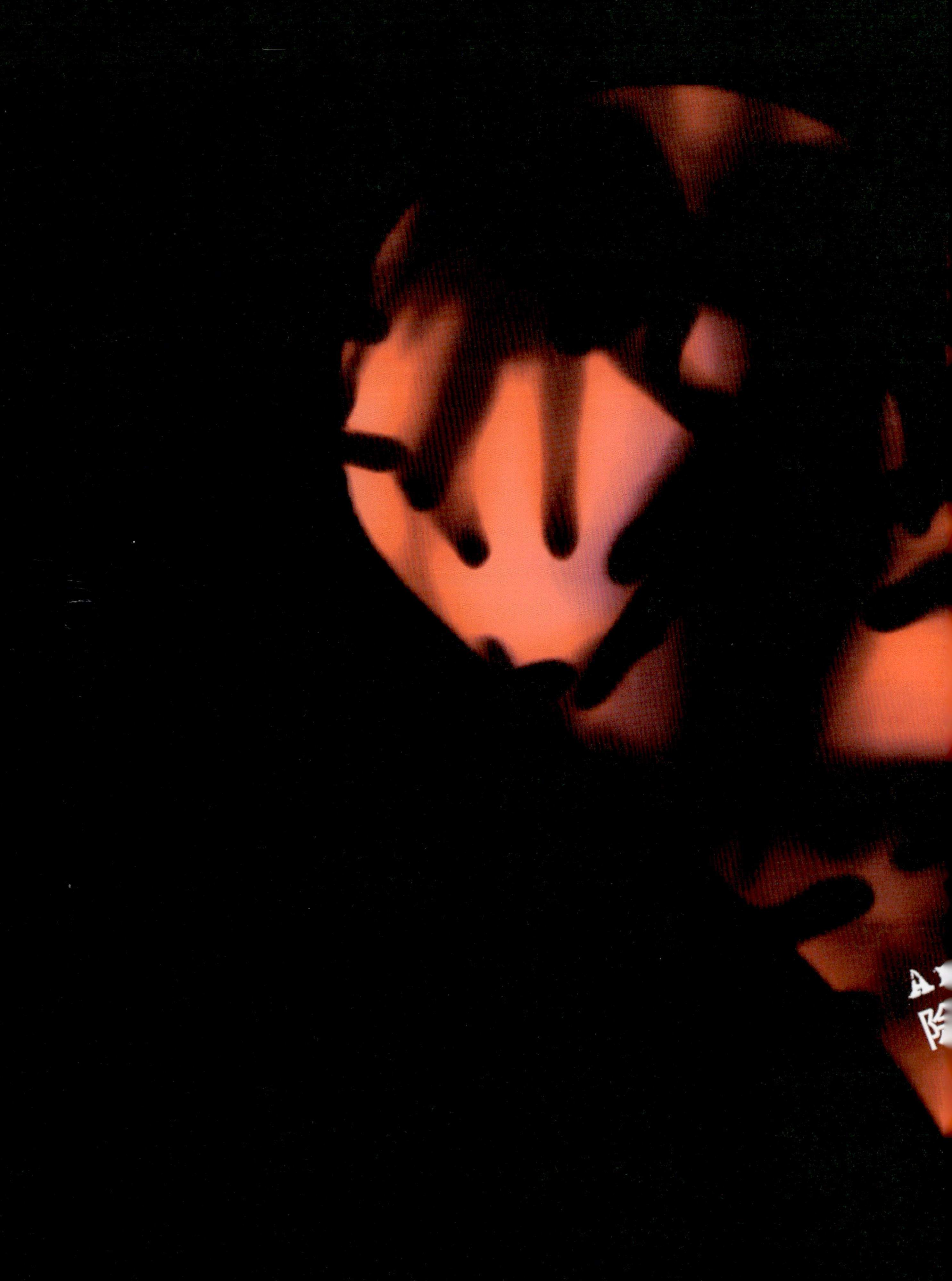

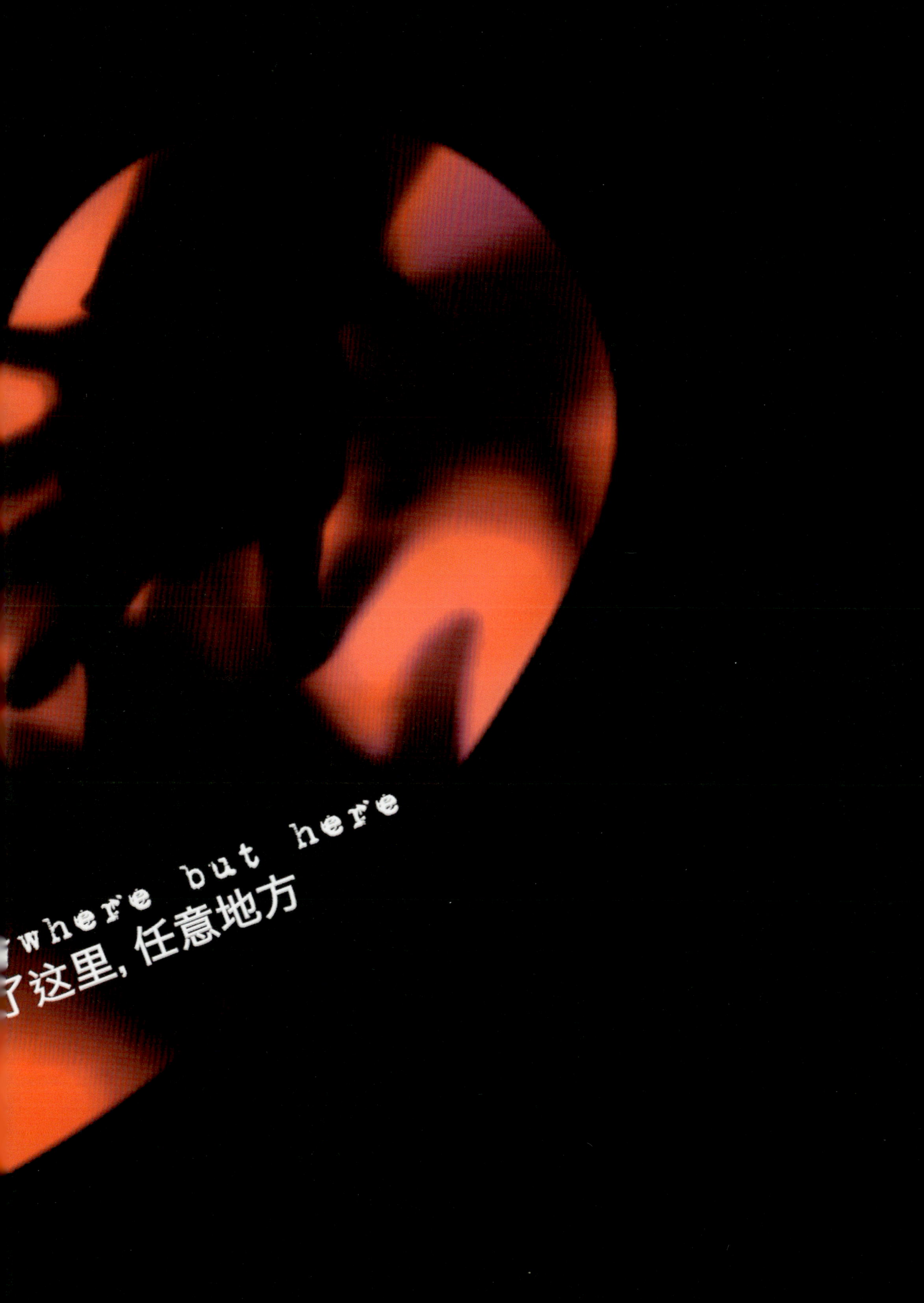

where but here
了这里，任意地方

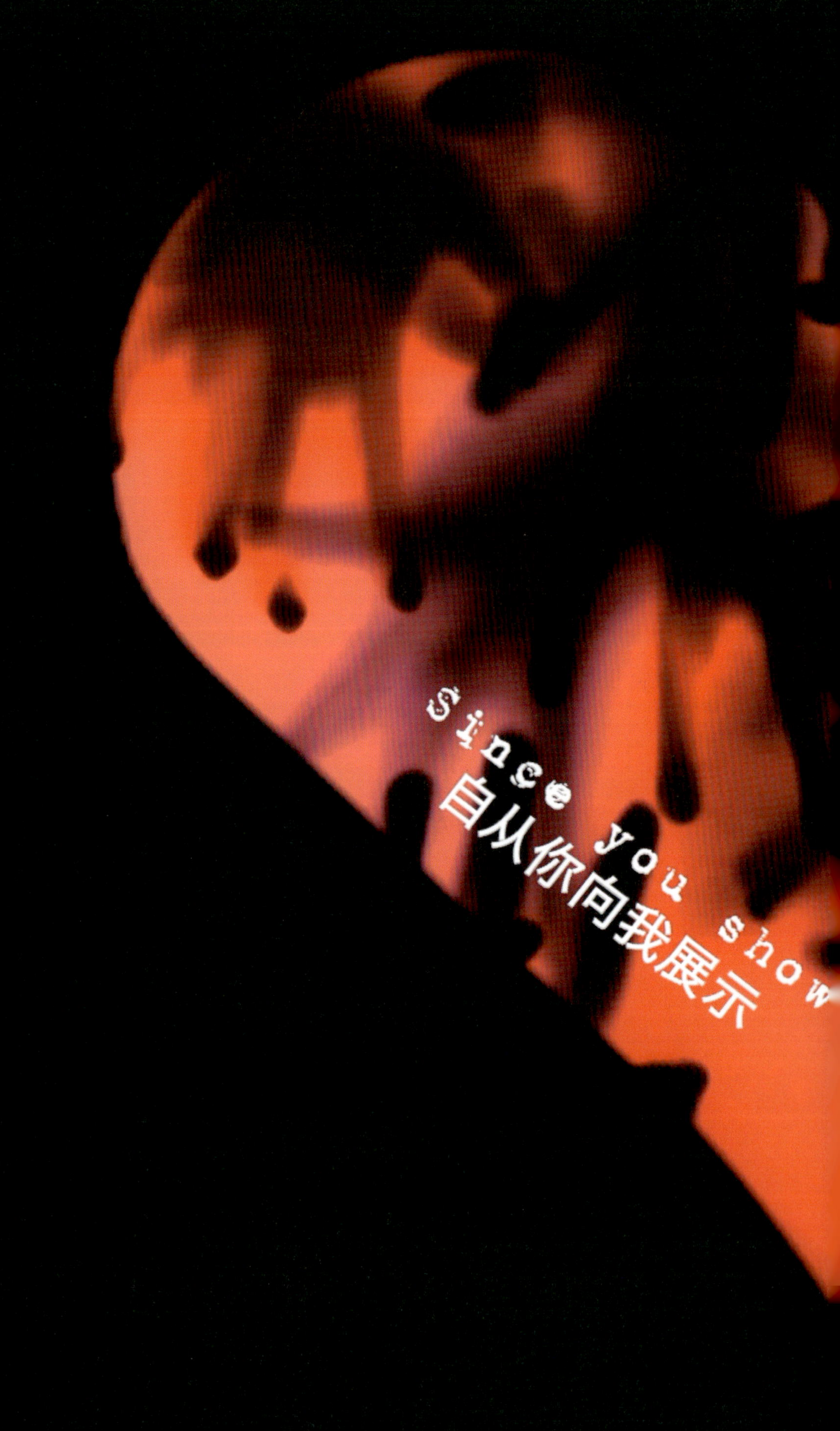

Since you show
自从你向我展示

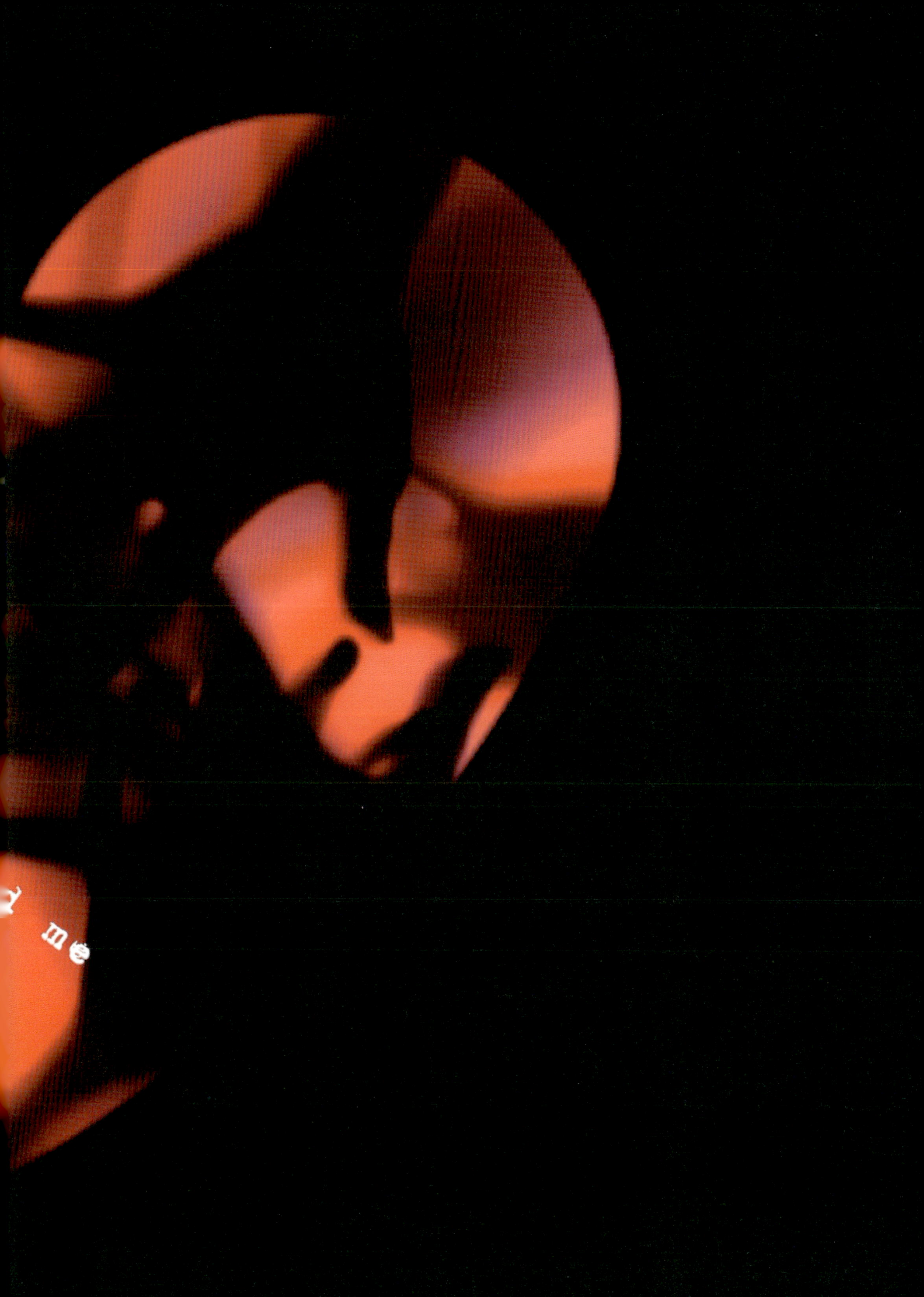

how bodies fall

身体从

from the sky
中坠落

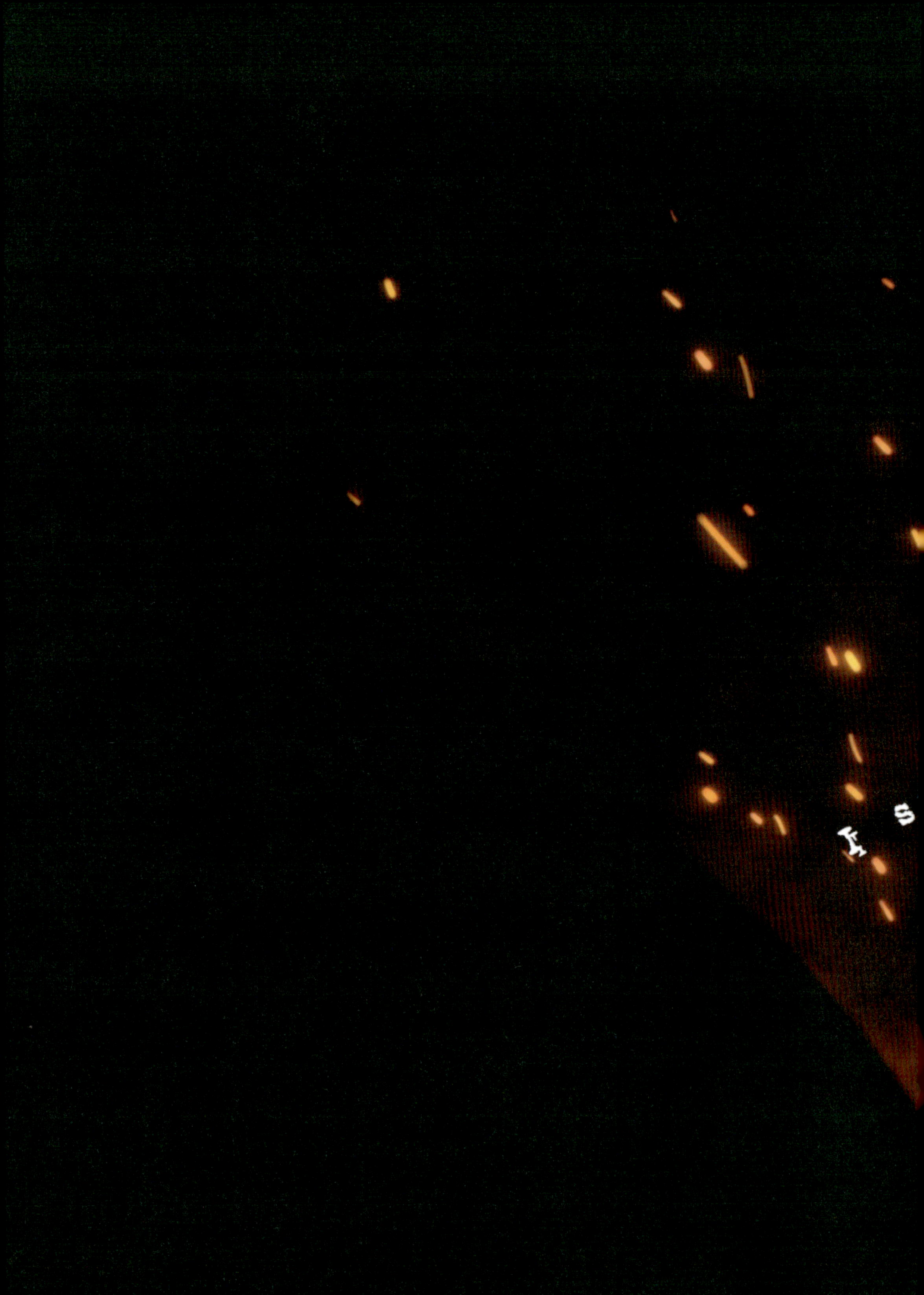

arted seeing it too
我也开始看见

I saw a body falling

我看见一个

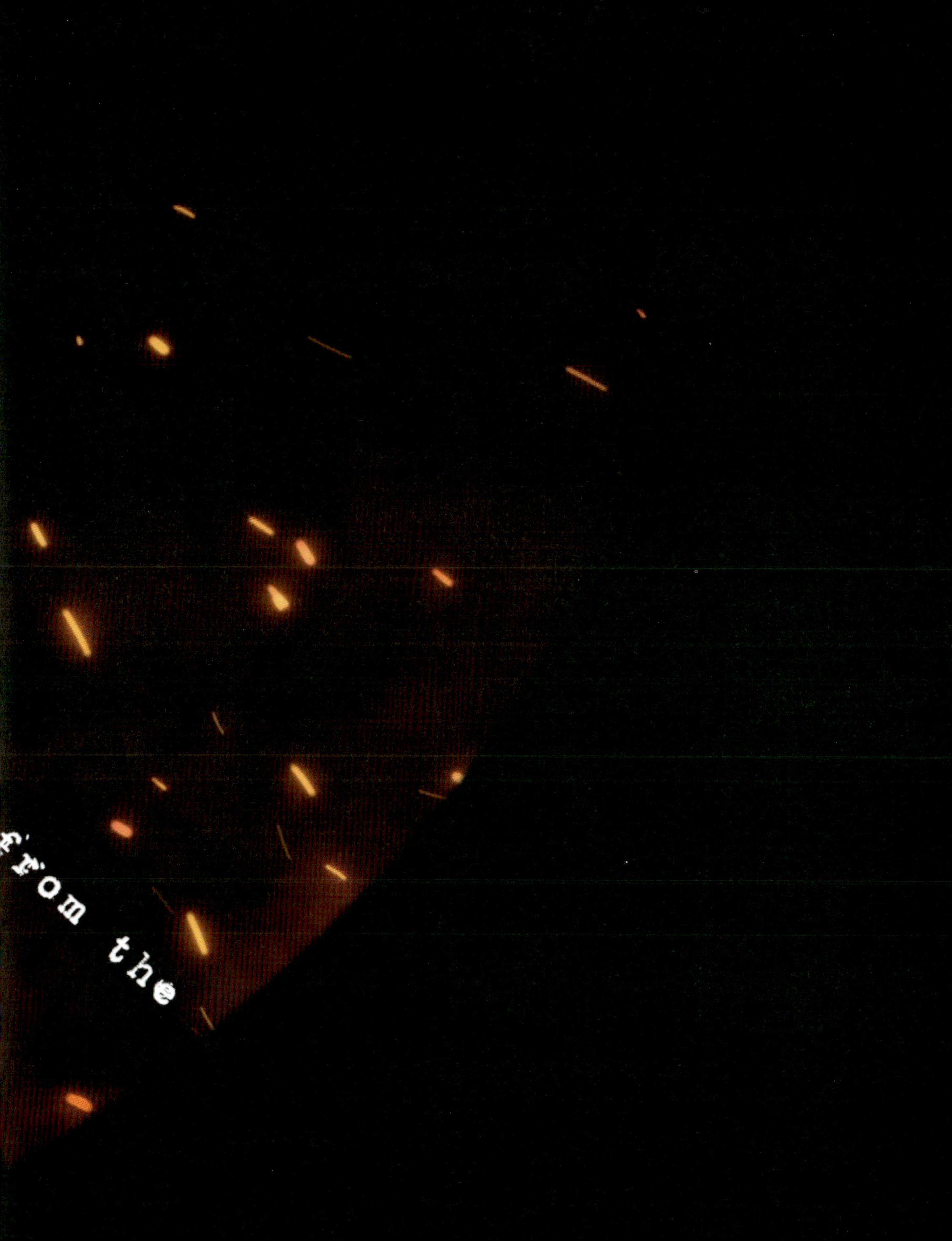

from the

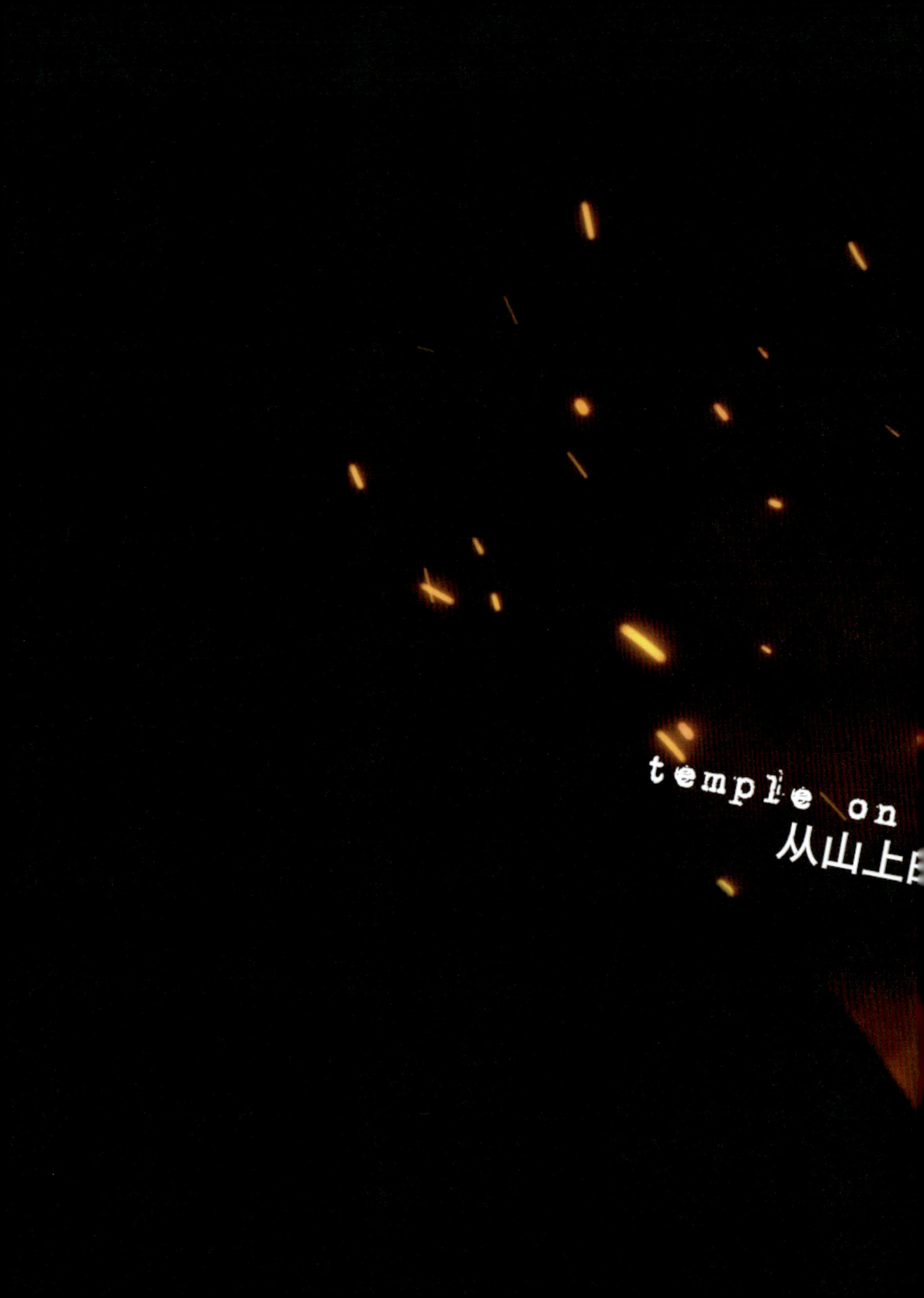

temple on
从山上的

the mountain
寺庙坠落

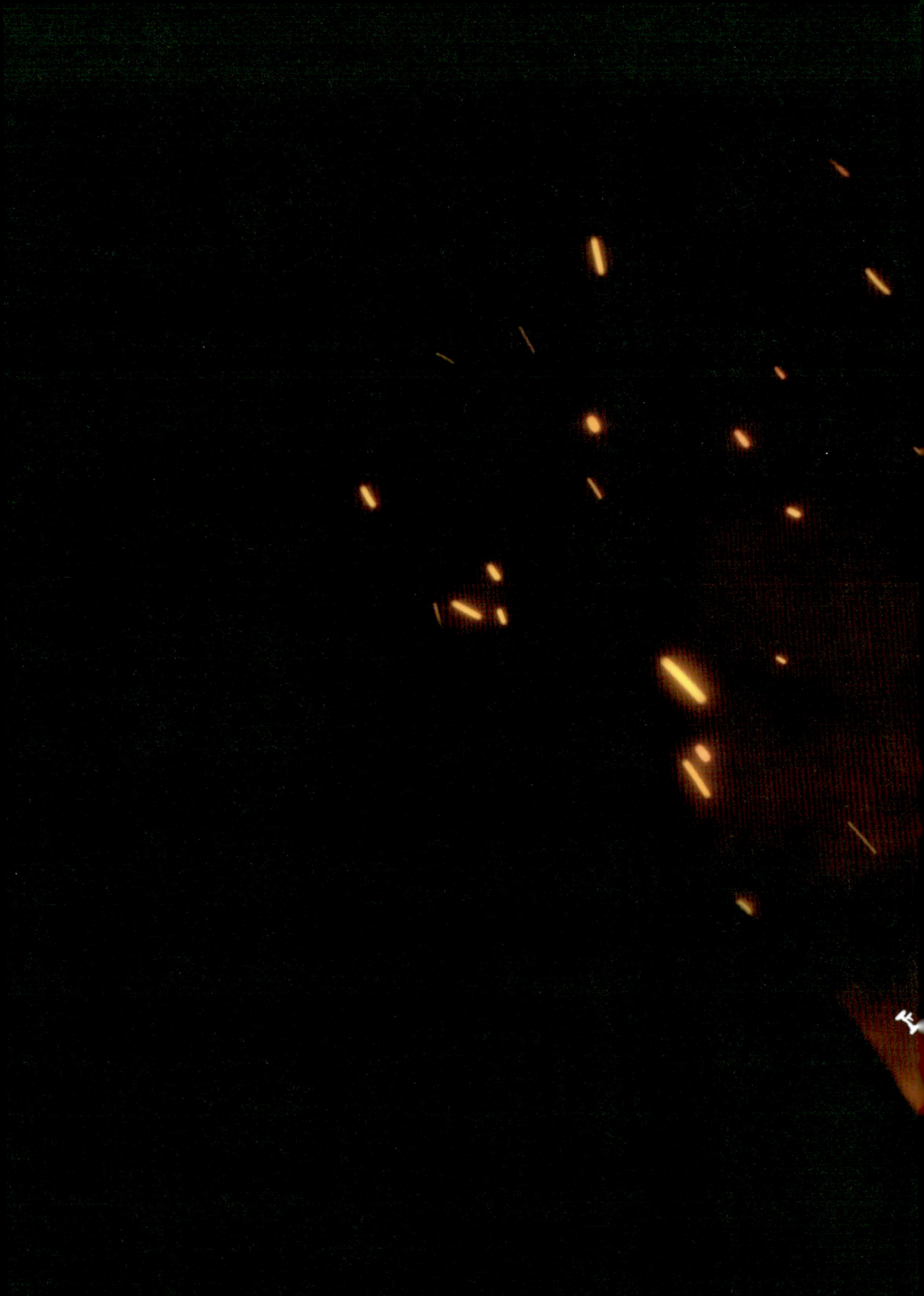

saw a body falling from the top of

我看见一个从街对面高楼楼顶

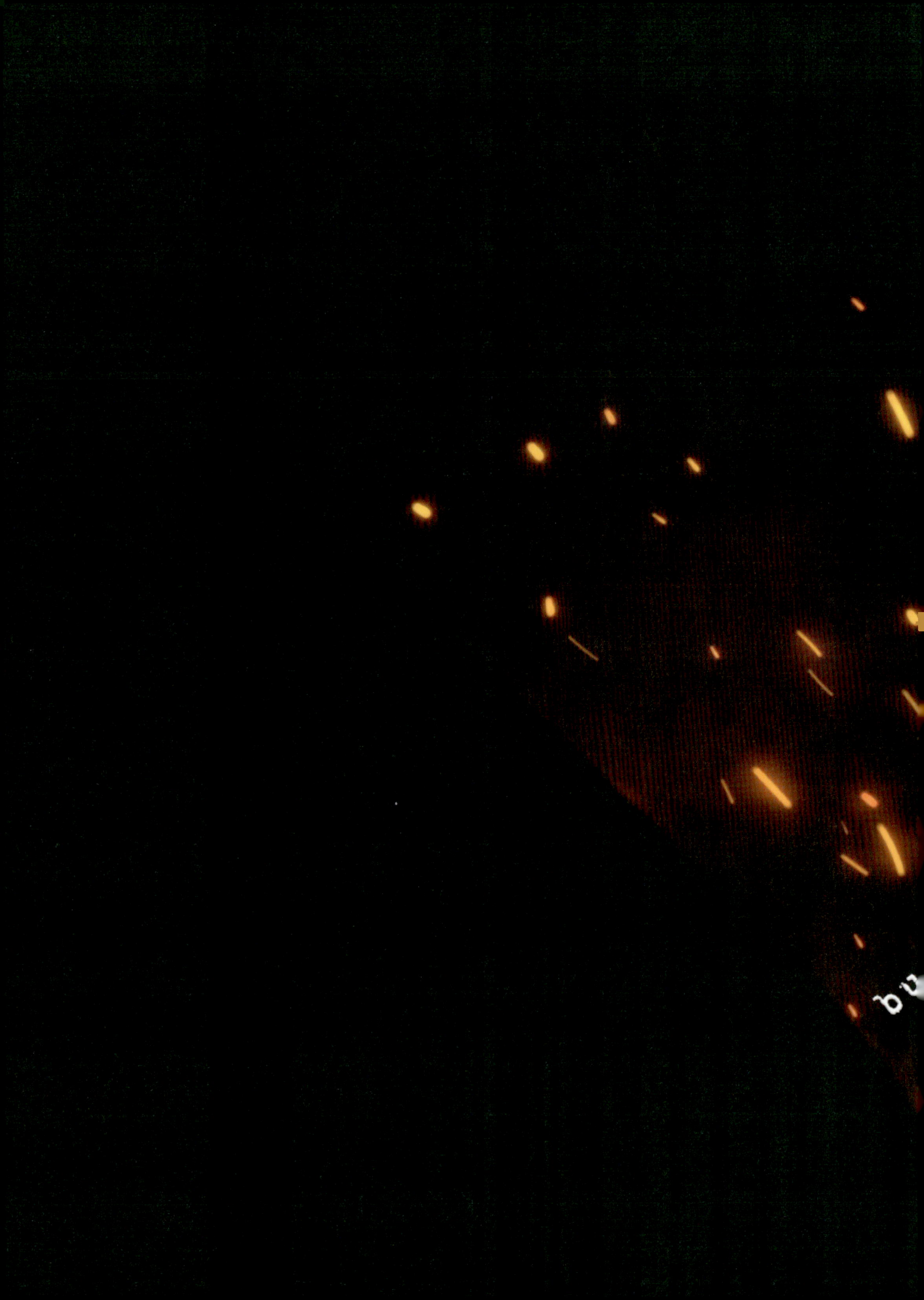

...ilding from across the street 坠落

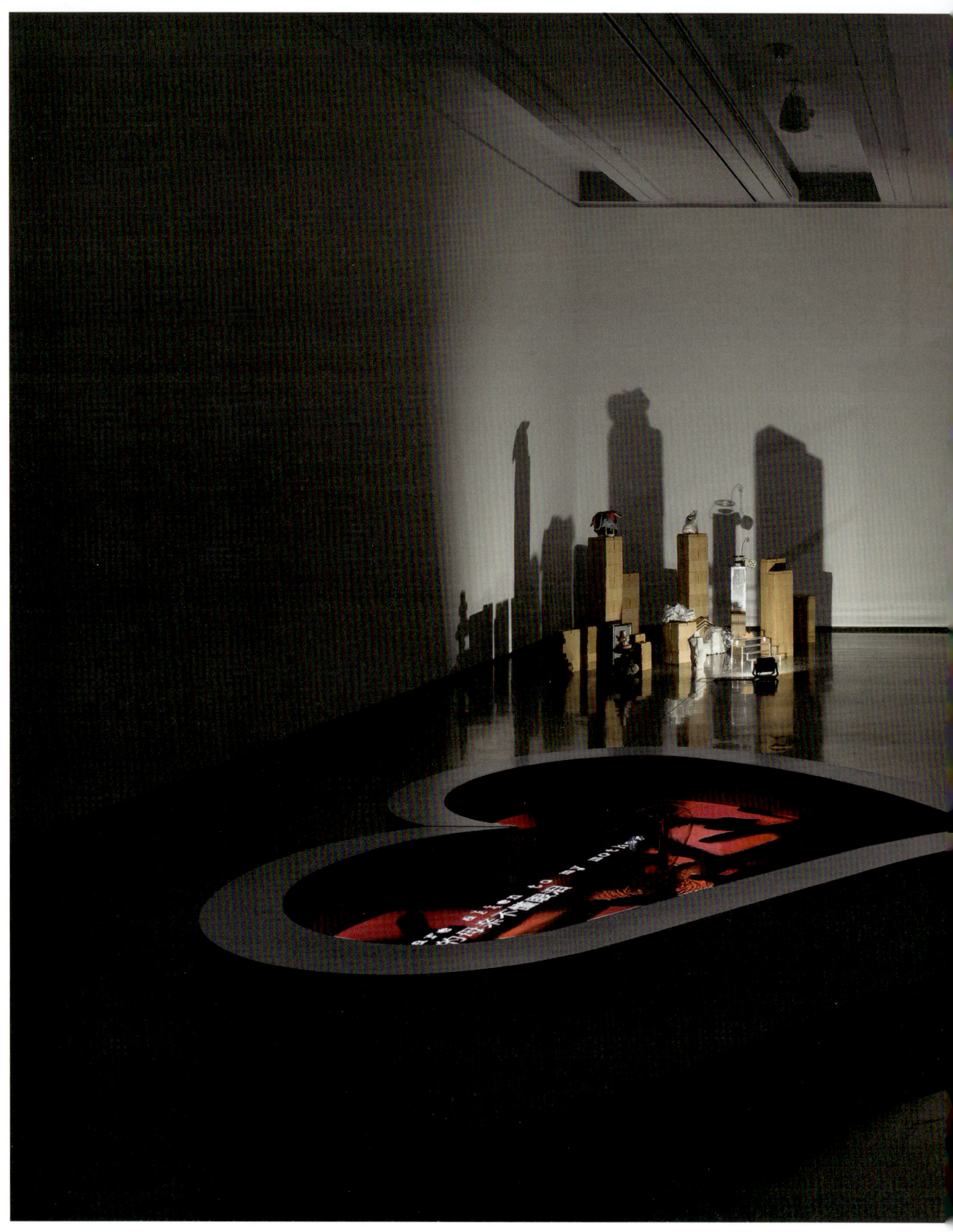

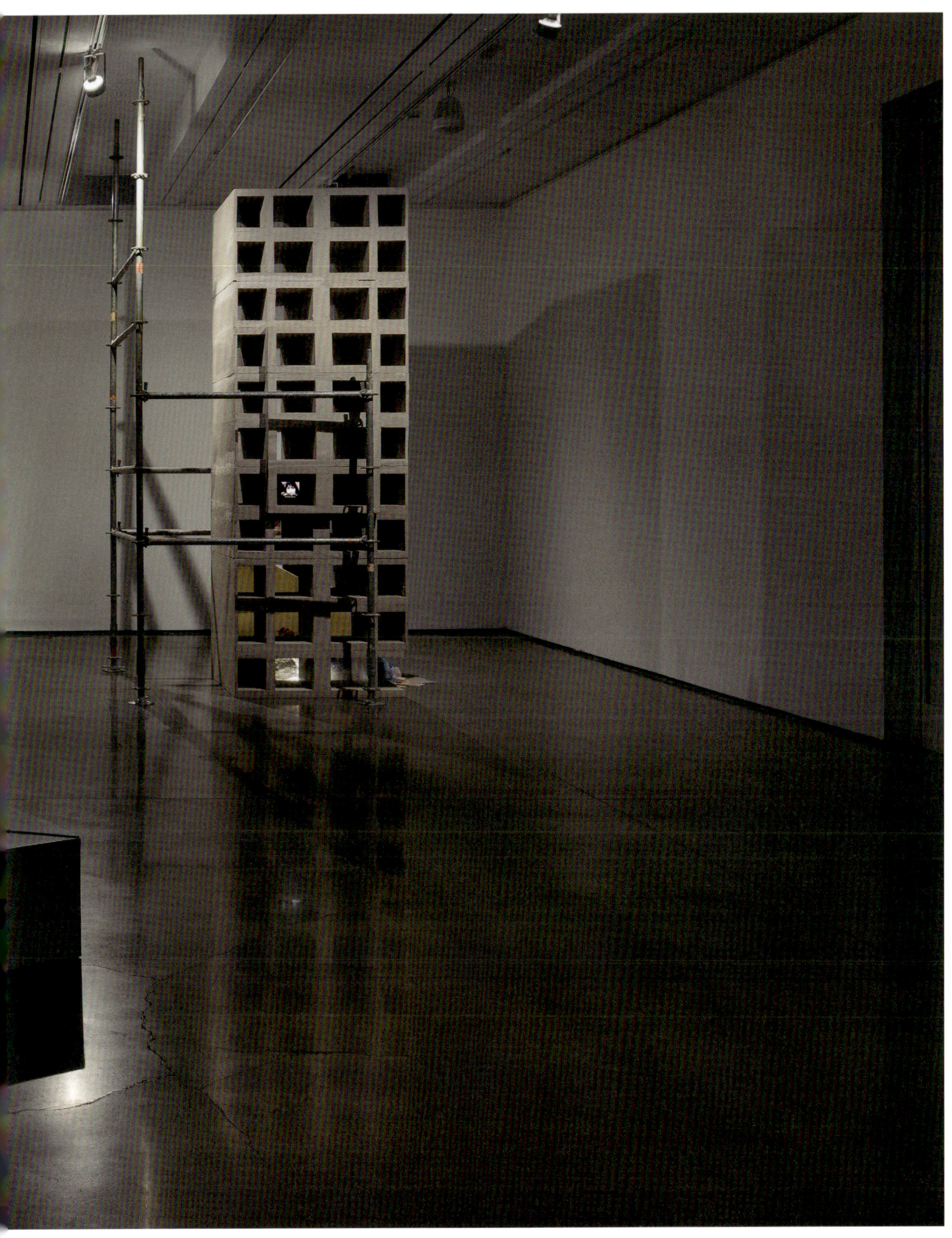

I'm Not, 2024
Installation view, Aspen Art Museum, 2024

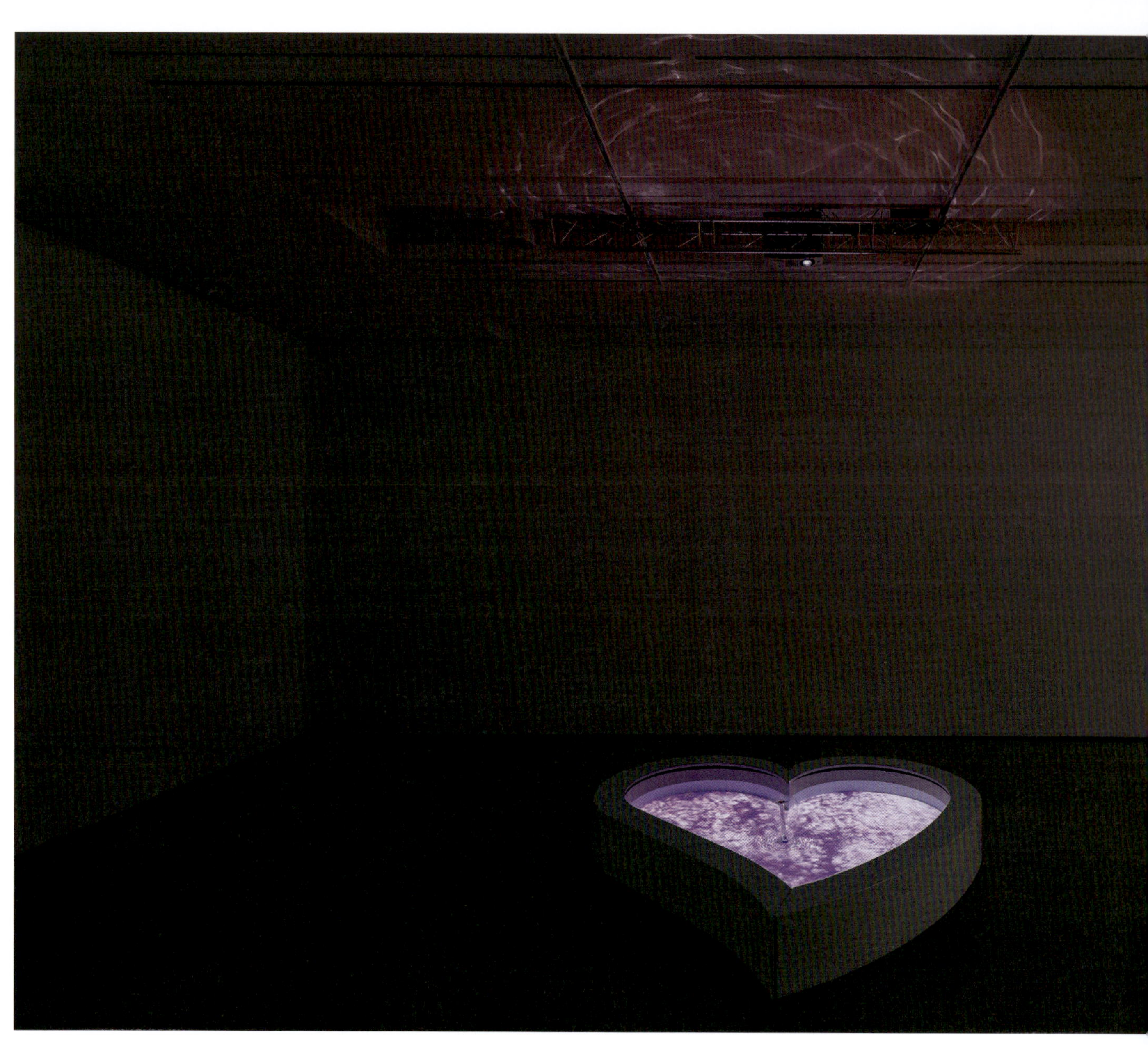

Heart is a Broken Record, 2023
Installation view, Aspen Art Museum, 2024

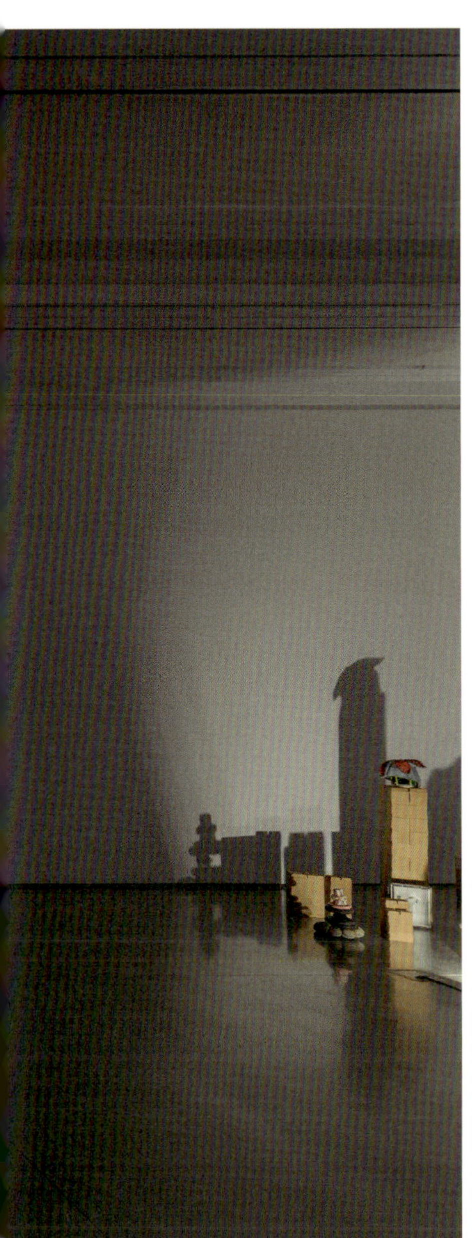

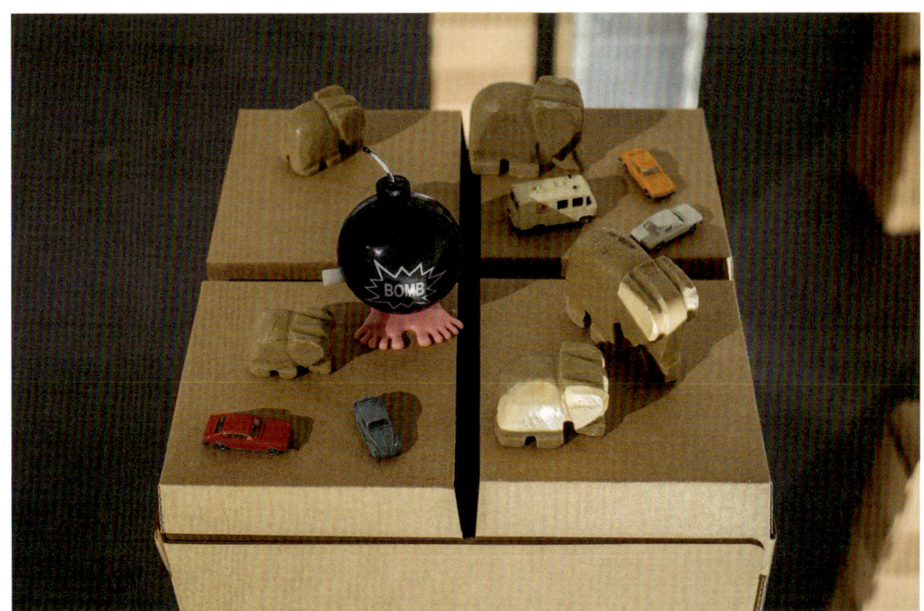

BOMB

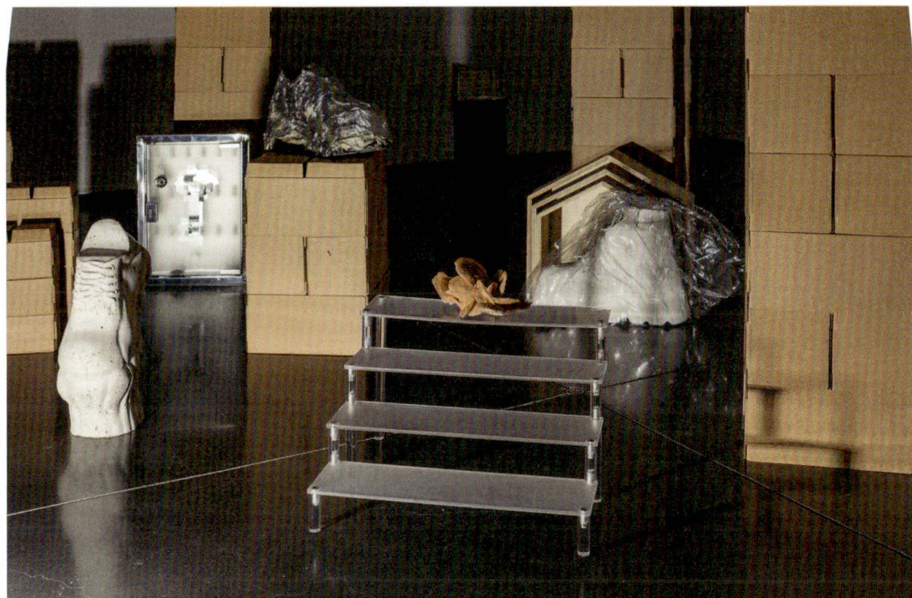

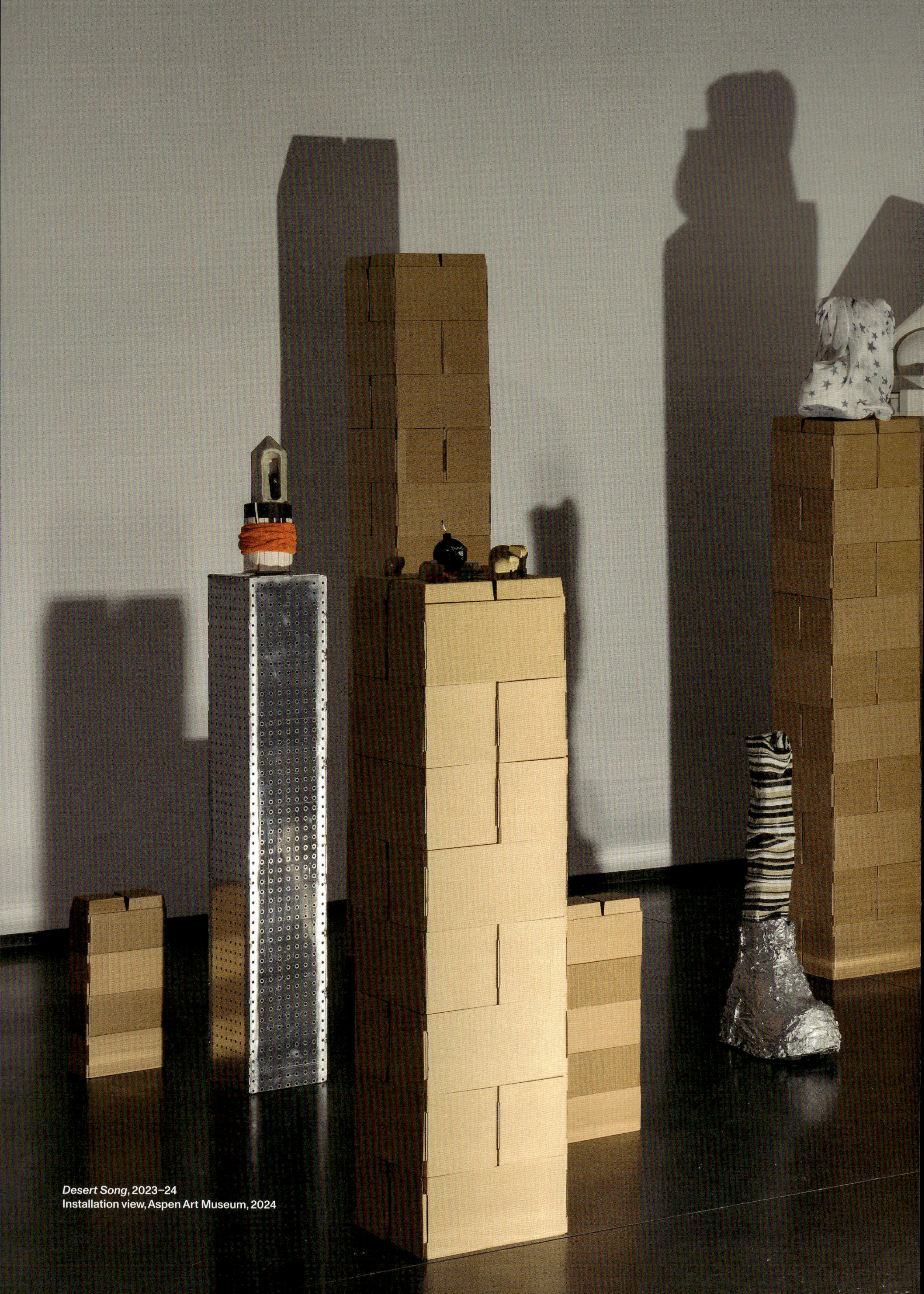

Desert Song, 2023–24
Installation view, Aspen Art Museum, 2024

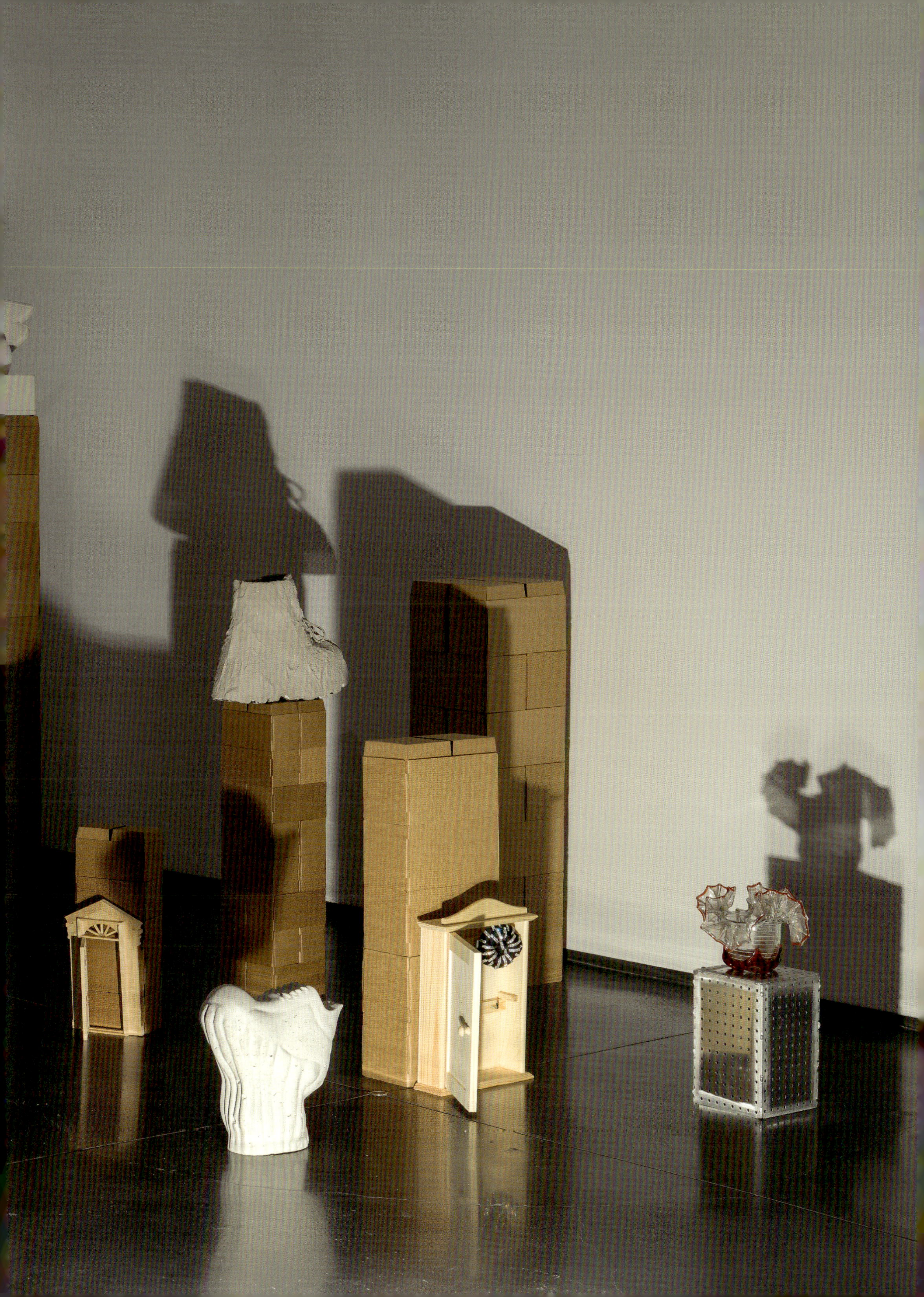

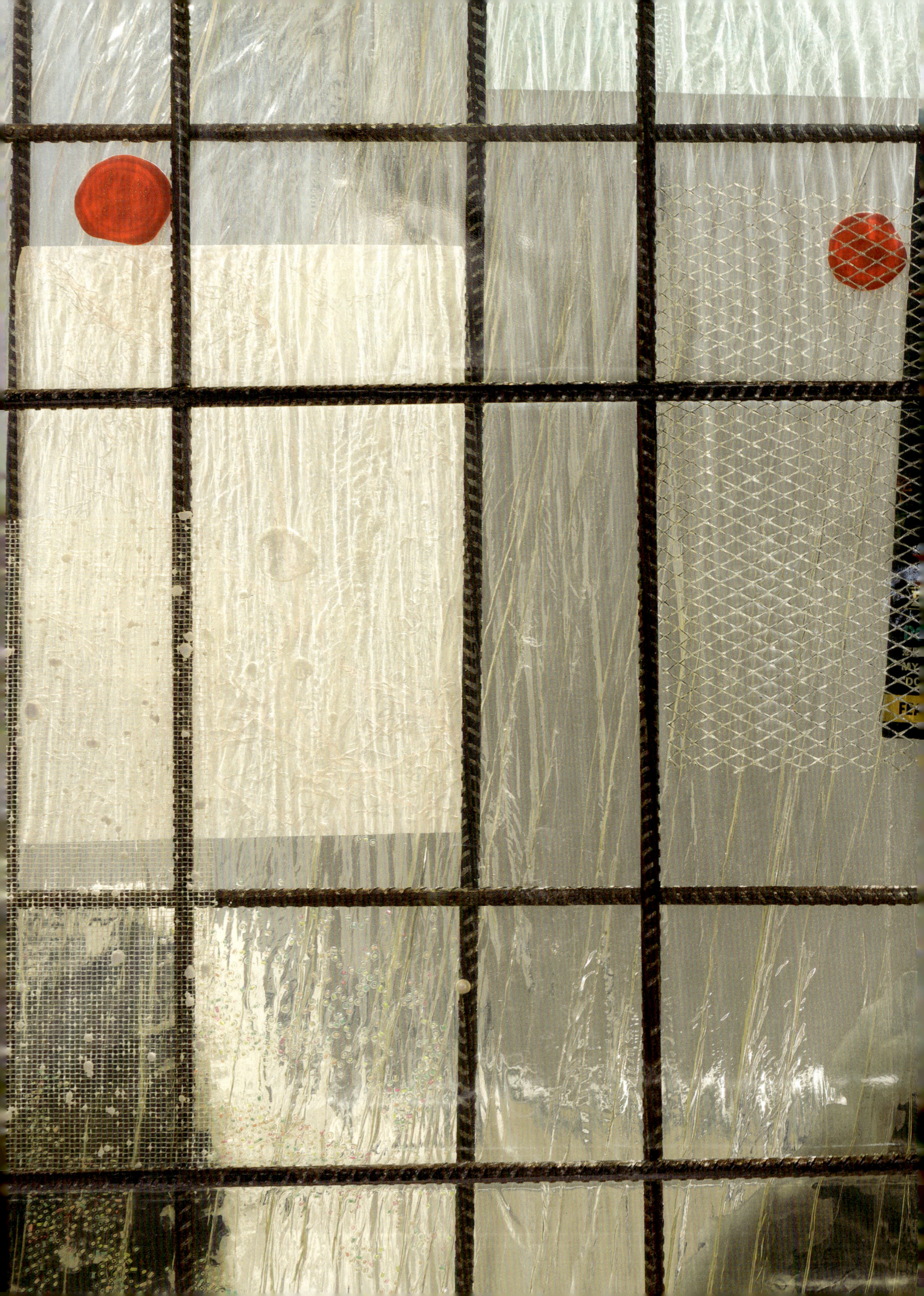

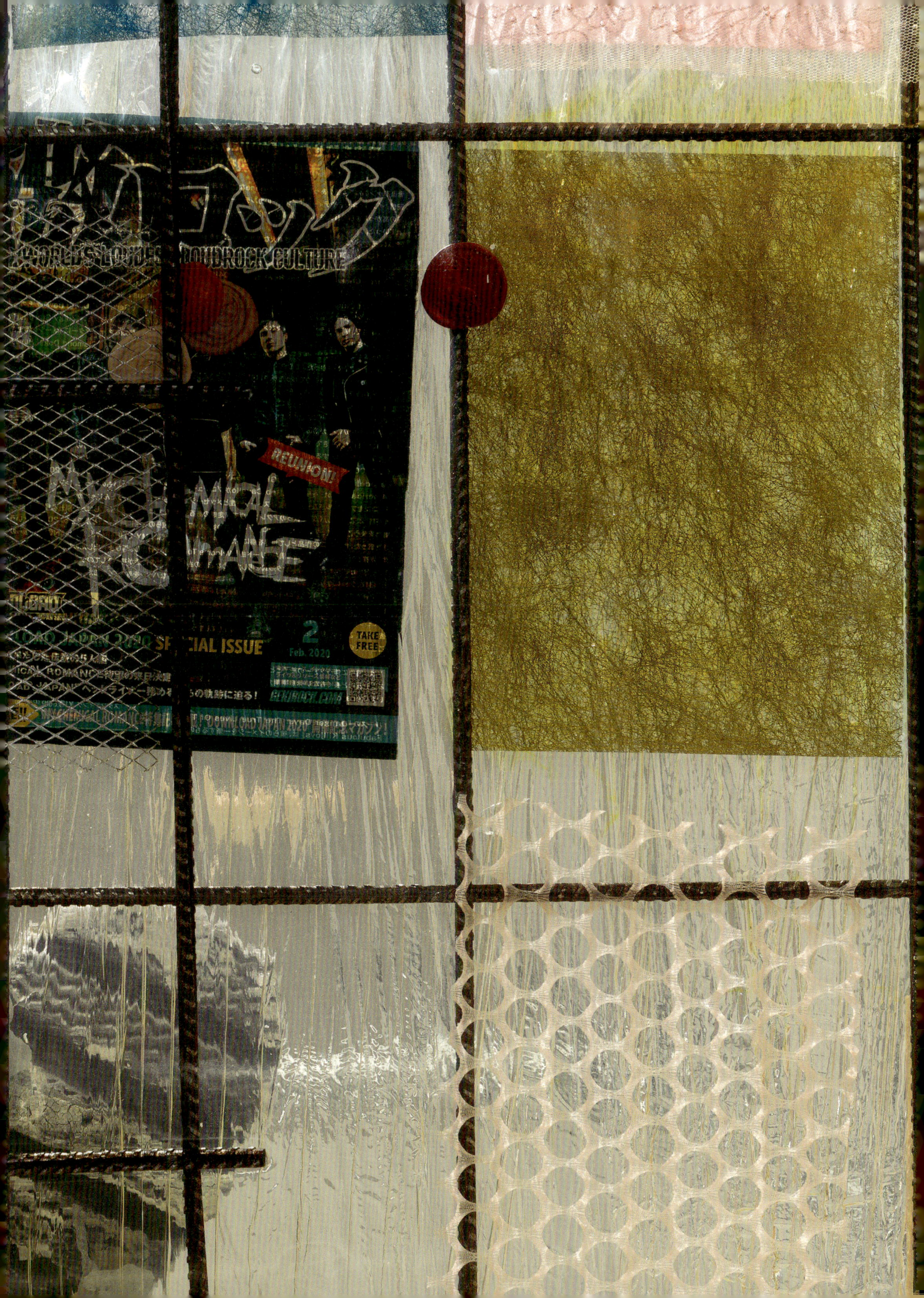
コミック
WORLD'S LOUDEST LOUDROCK CULTURE
My CHEMICAL ROMANCE
REUNION!
SPECIAL ISSUE
2
Feb. 2020
TAKE FREE

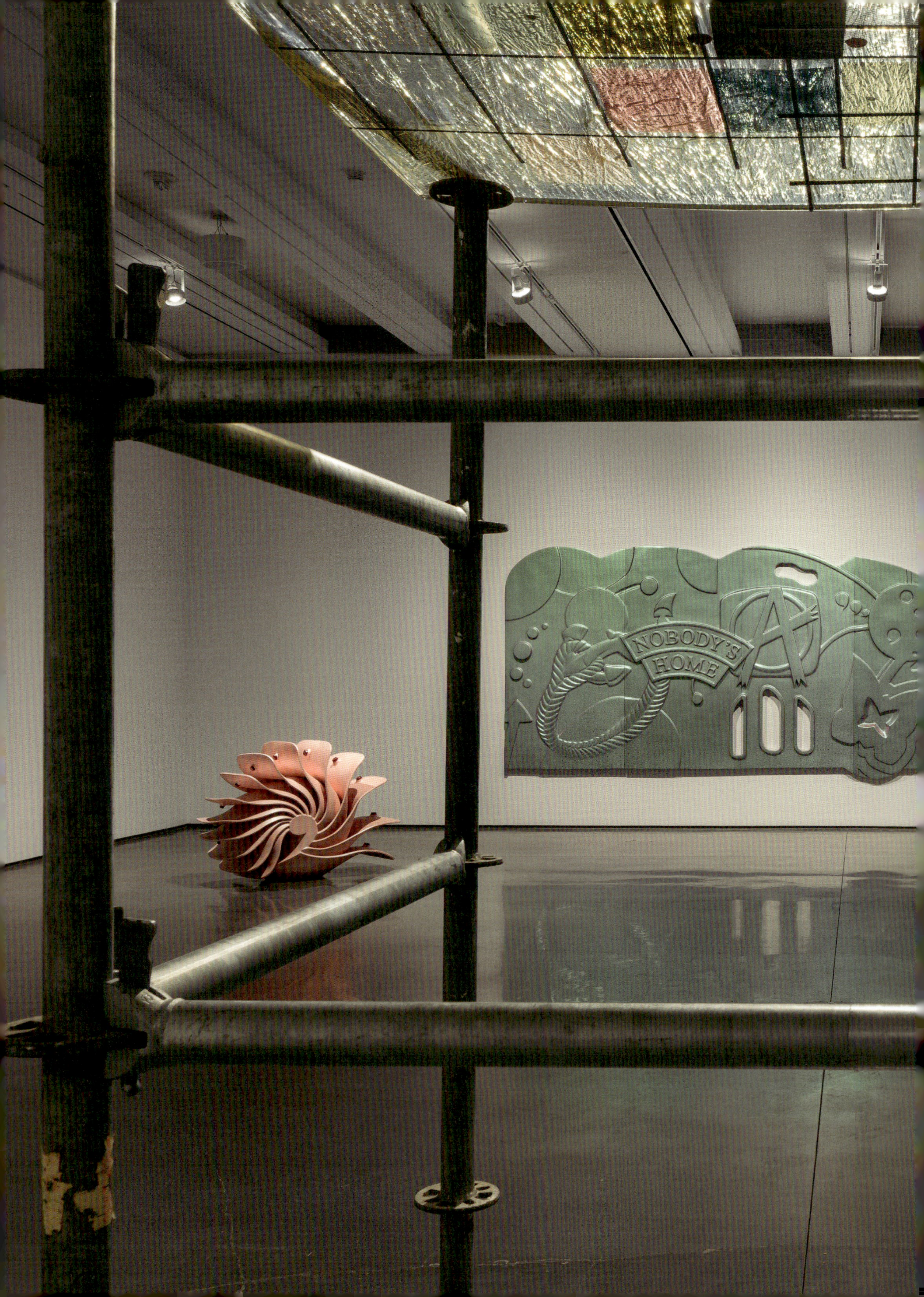

NOBODY'S HOME

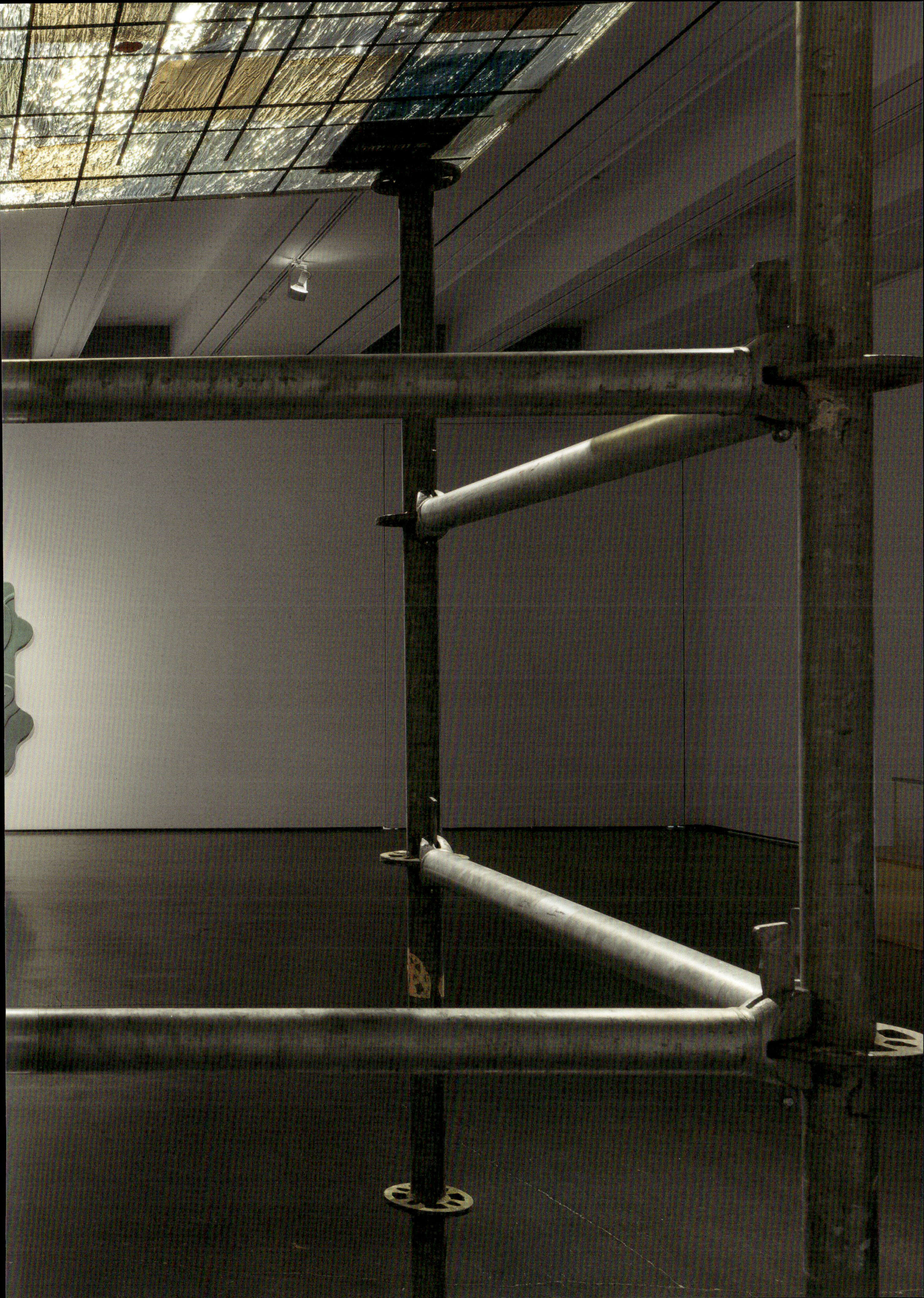

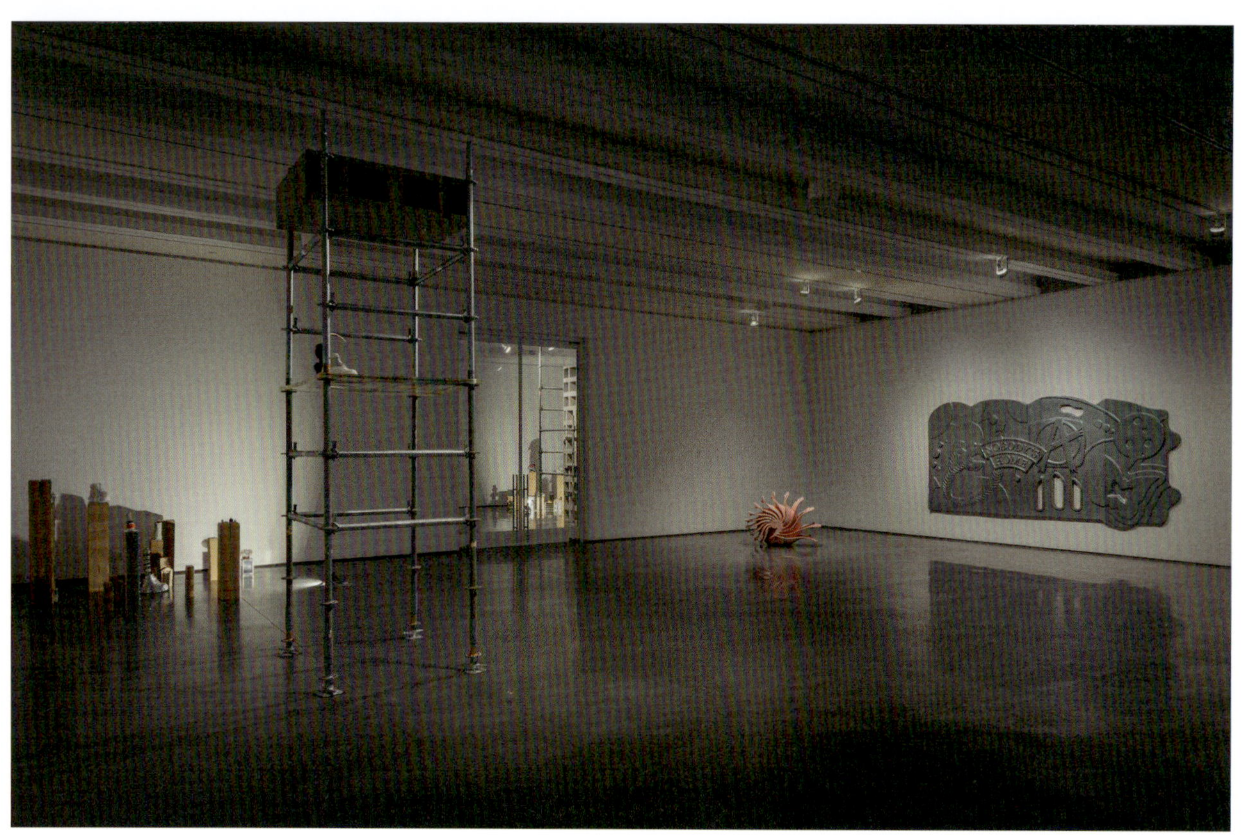

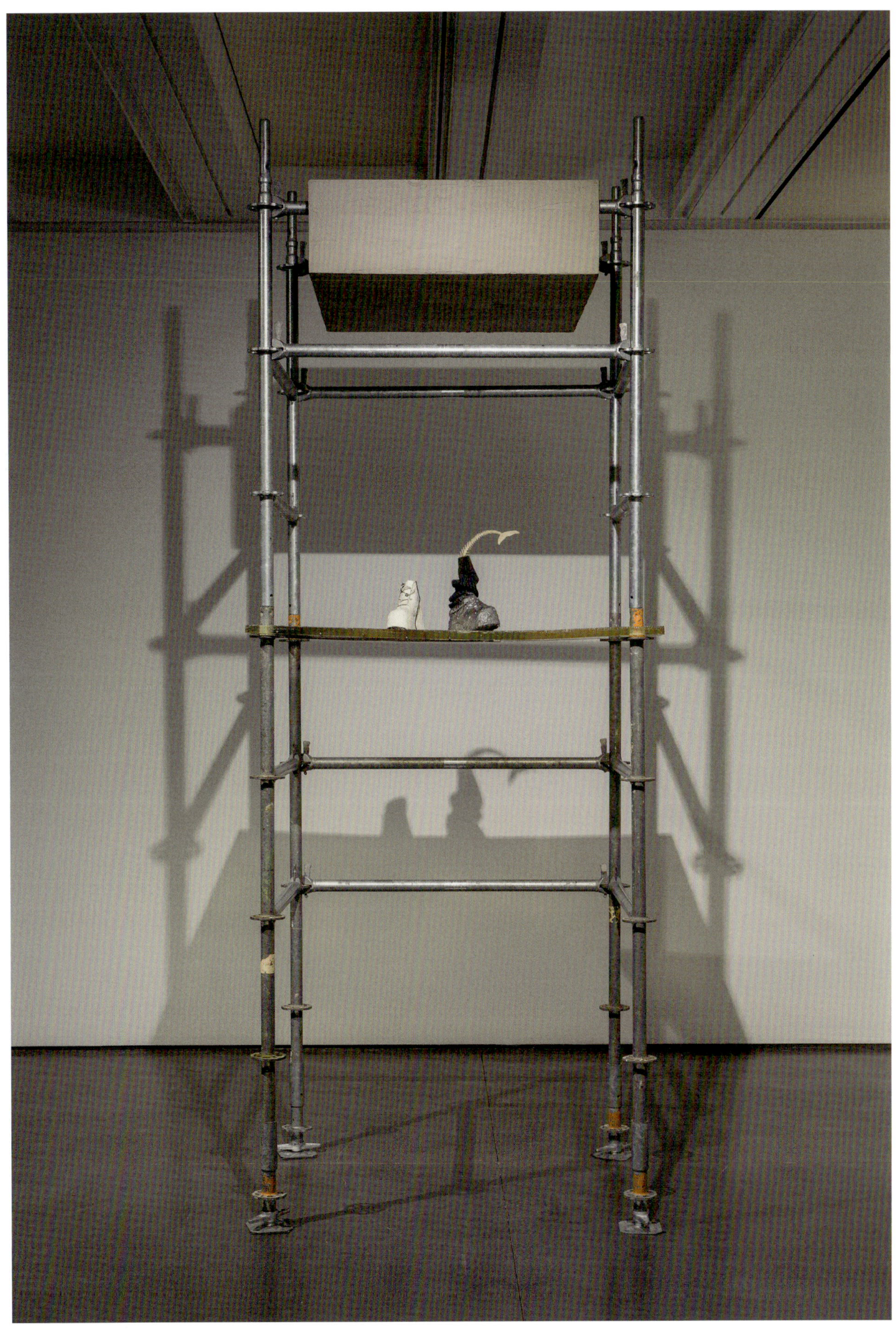

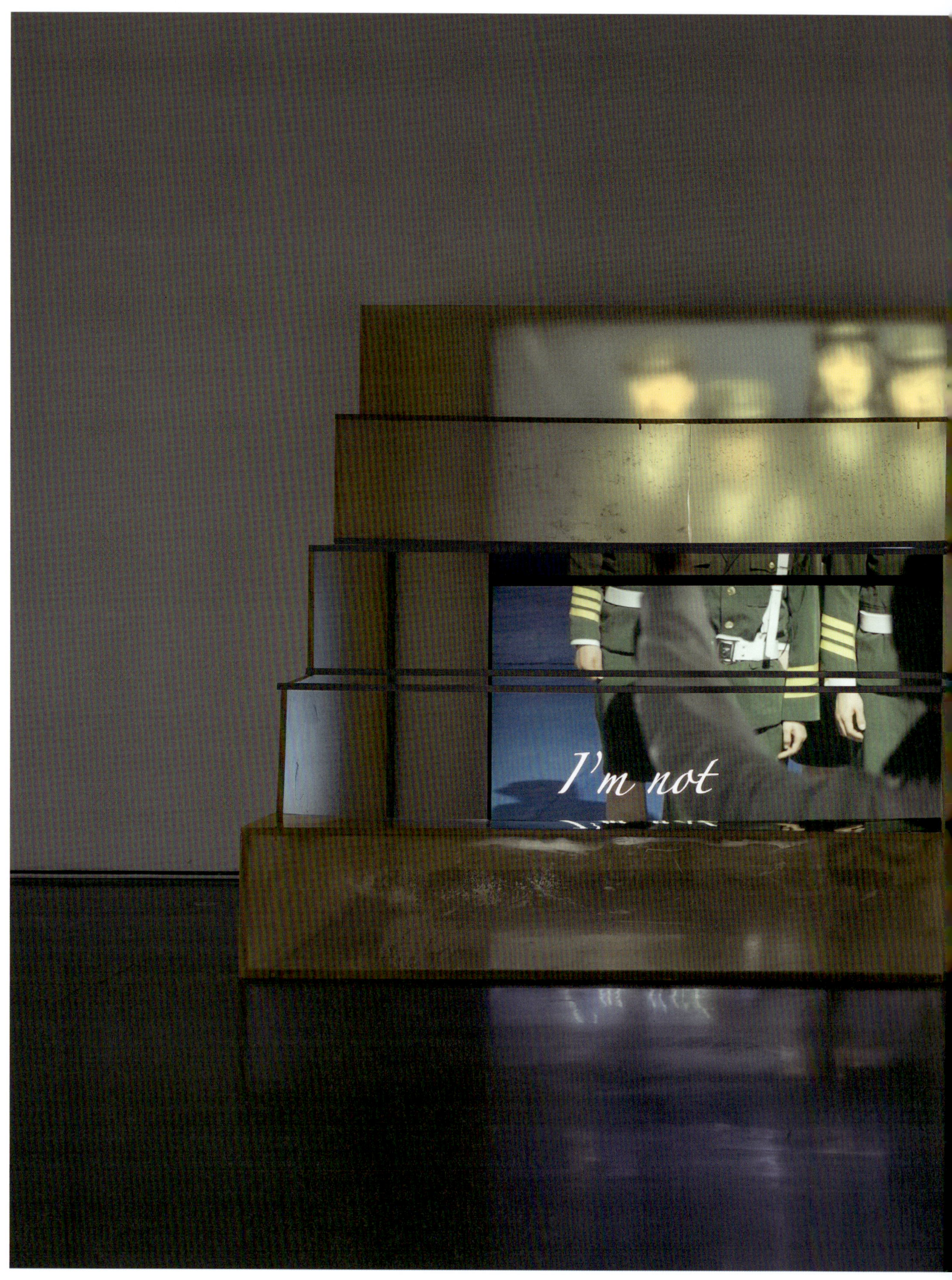
I'm not

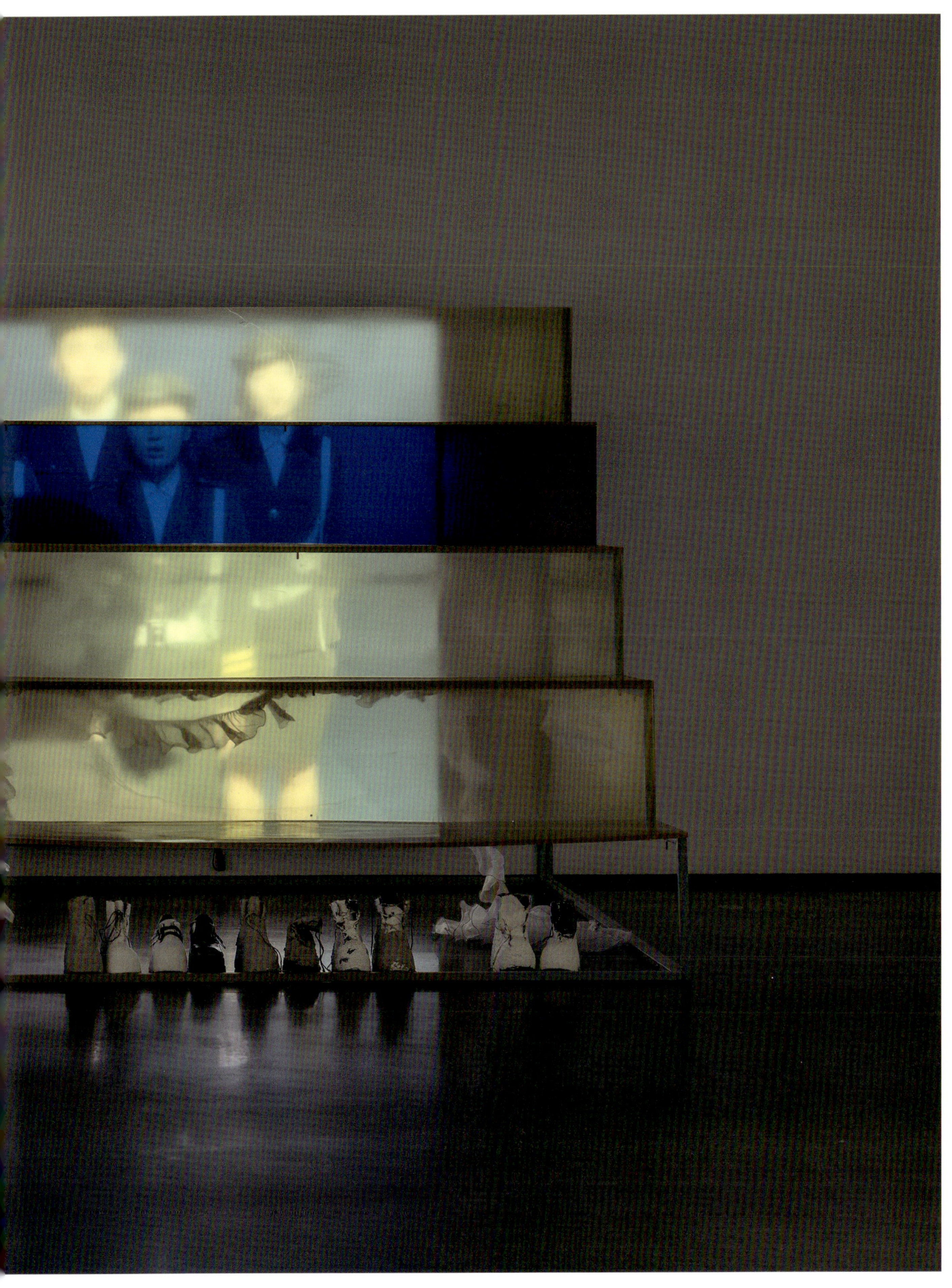

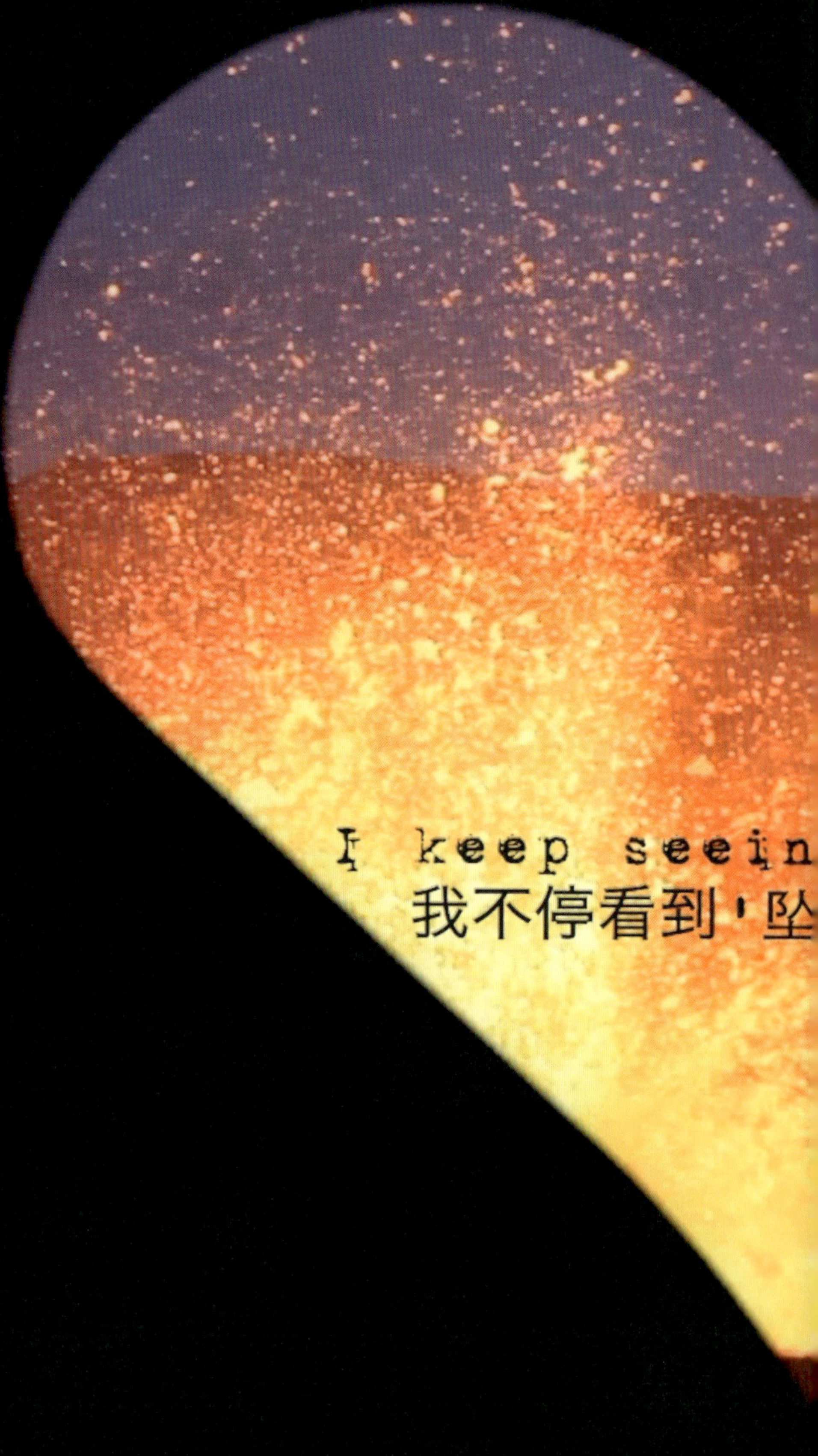

I keep seein
我不停看到，坠

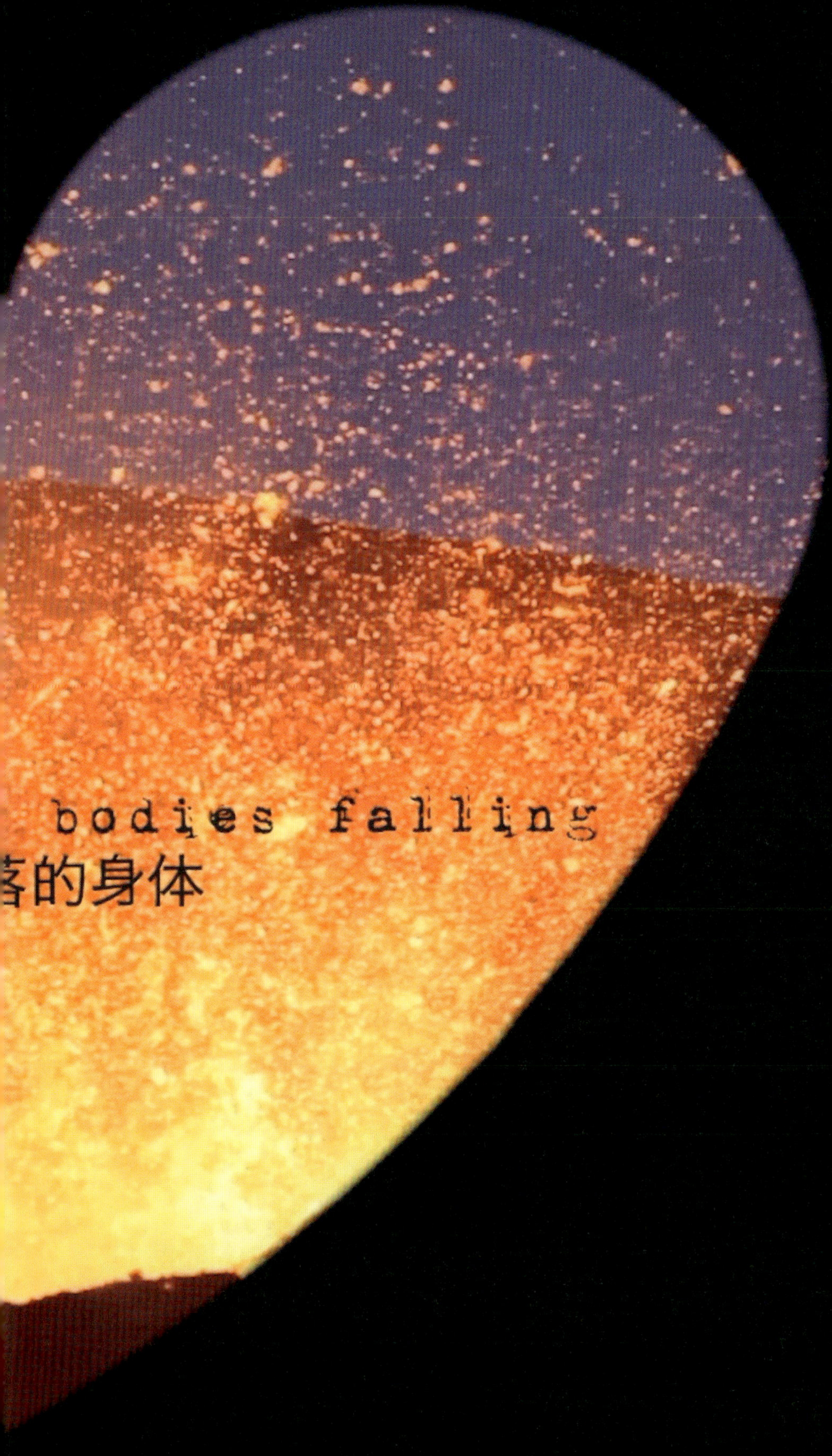

bodies falling

坠落的身体

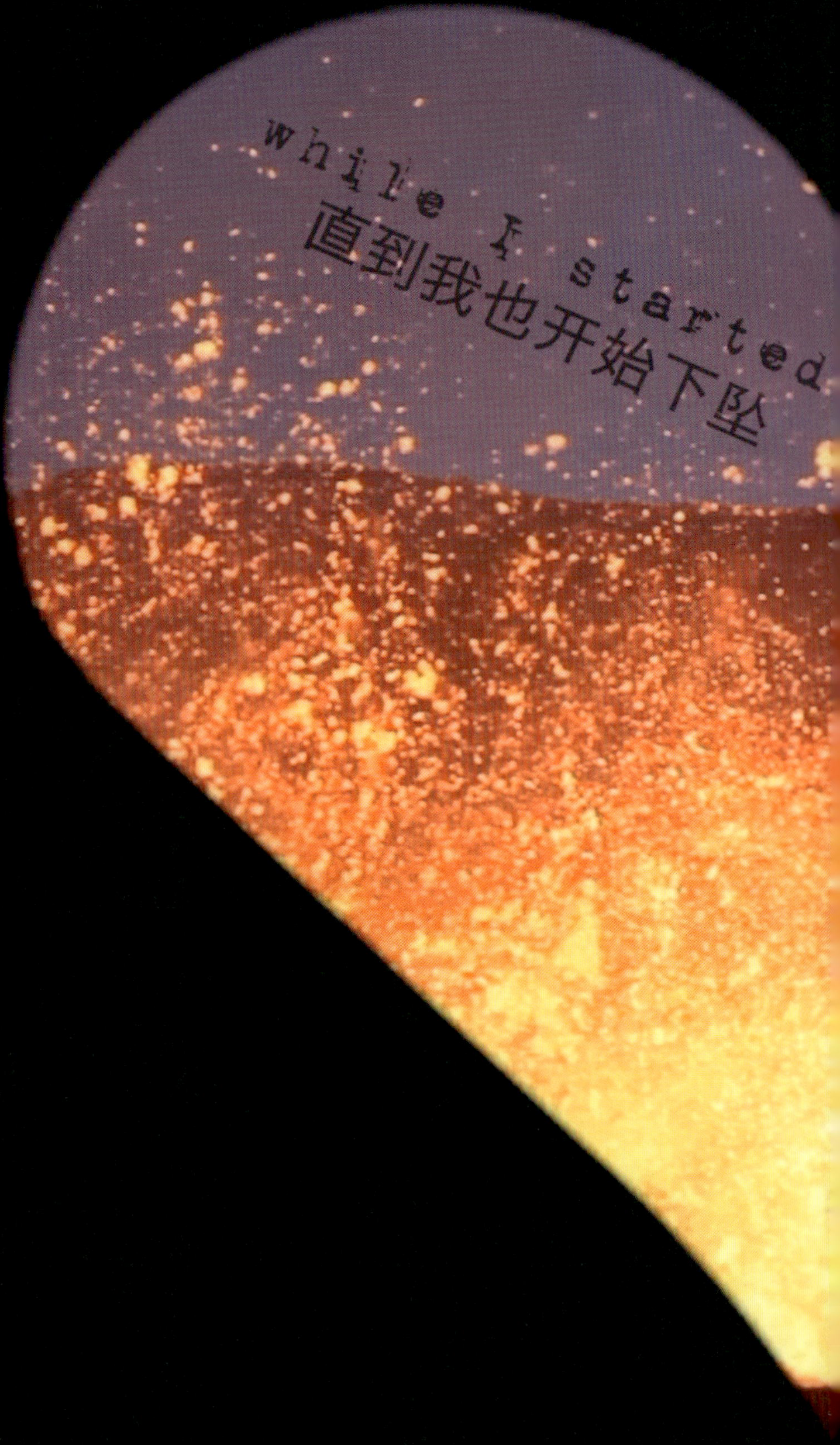

while I started
直到我也开始下坠

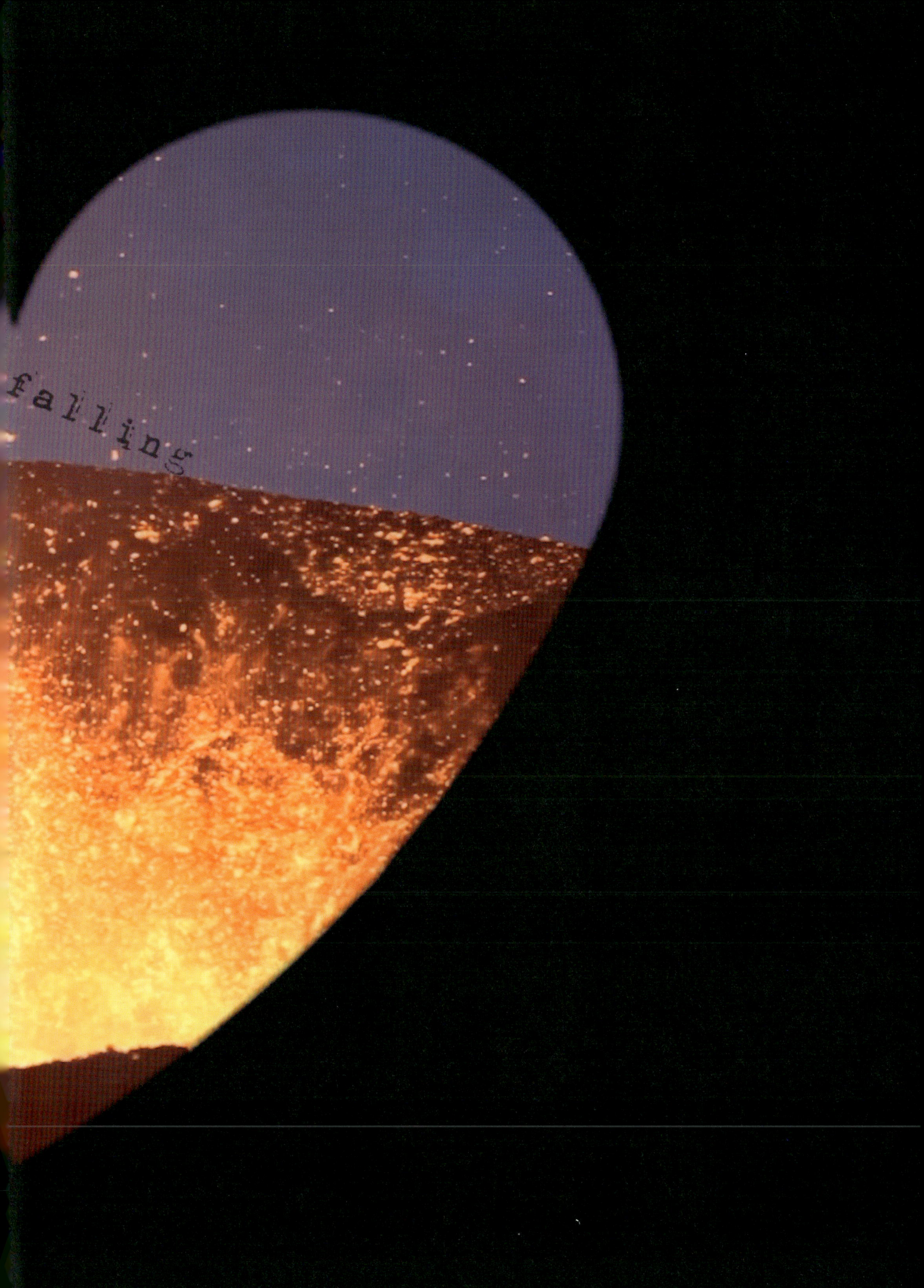
falling

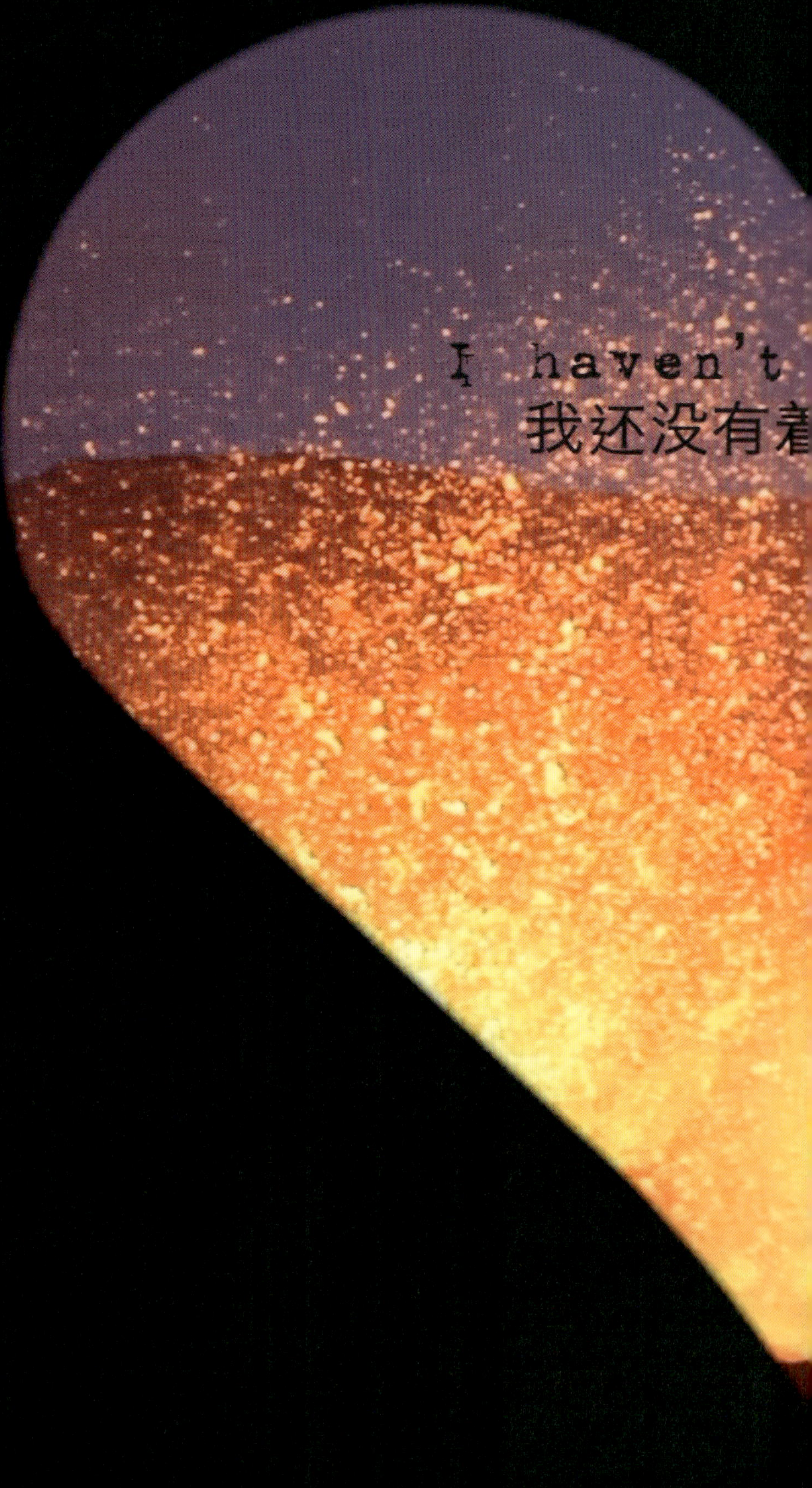

I haven't
我还没有着

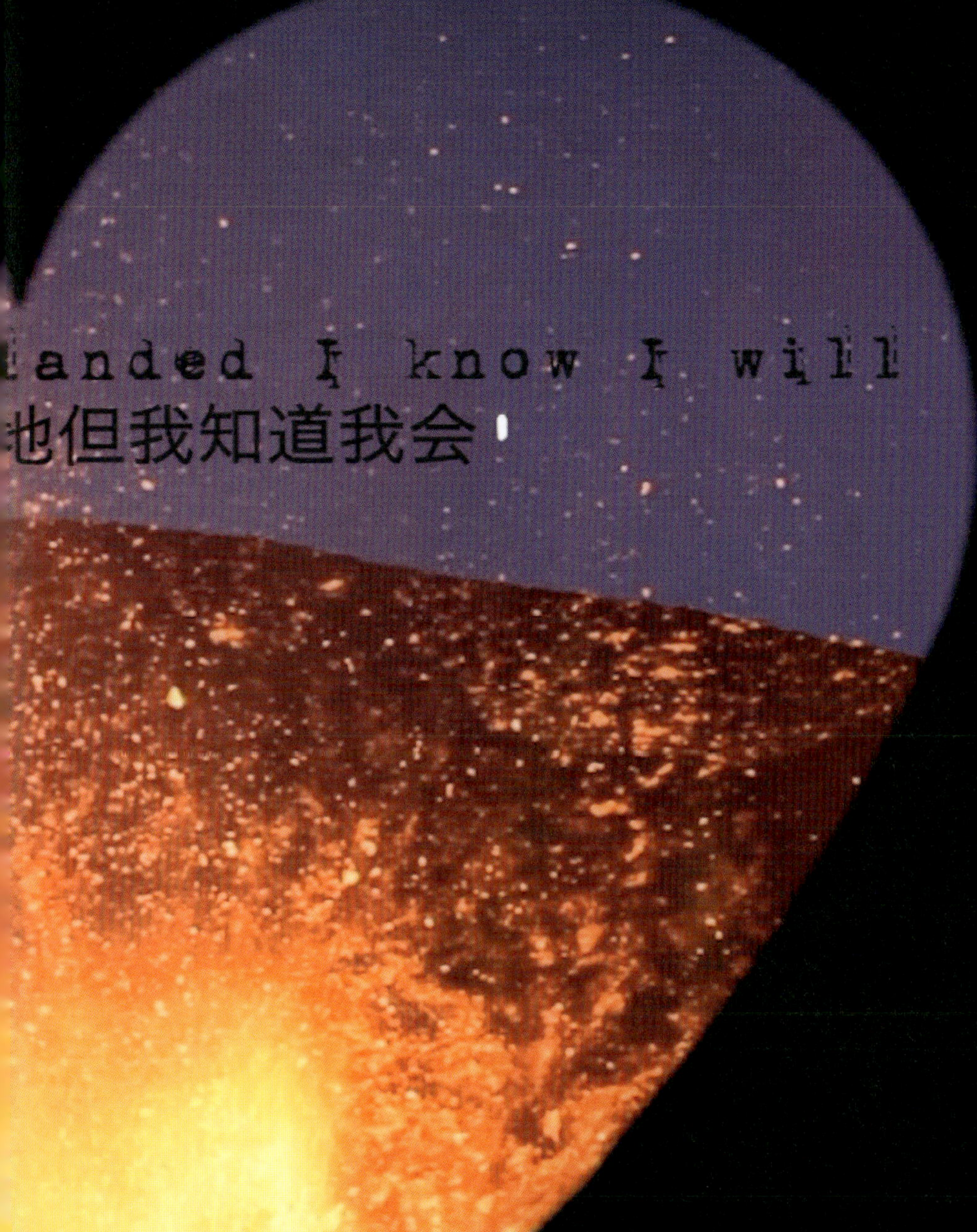
landed I know I will
也但我知道我会

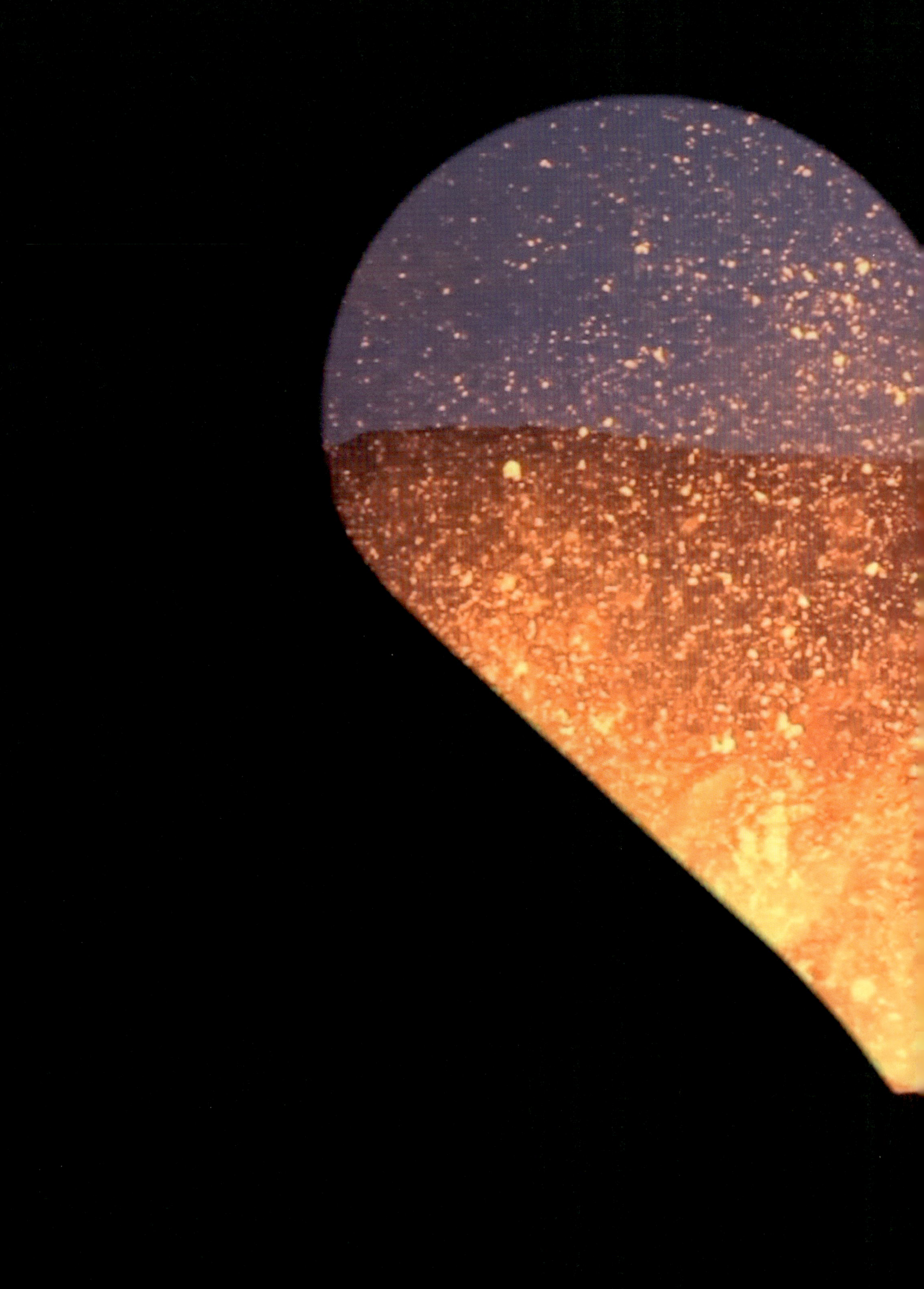

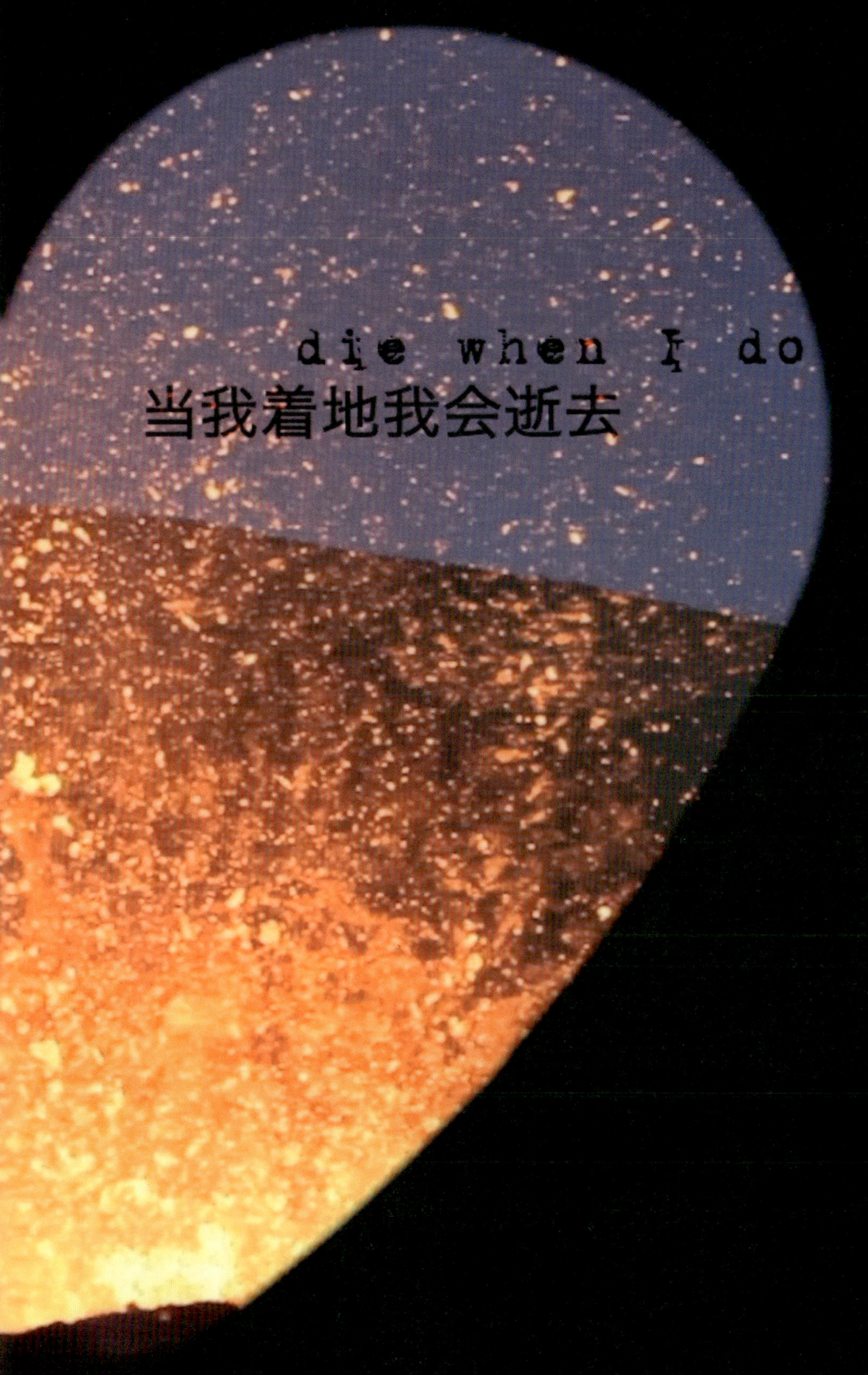
die when I do
当我着地我会逝去

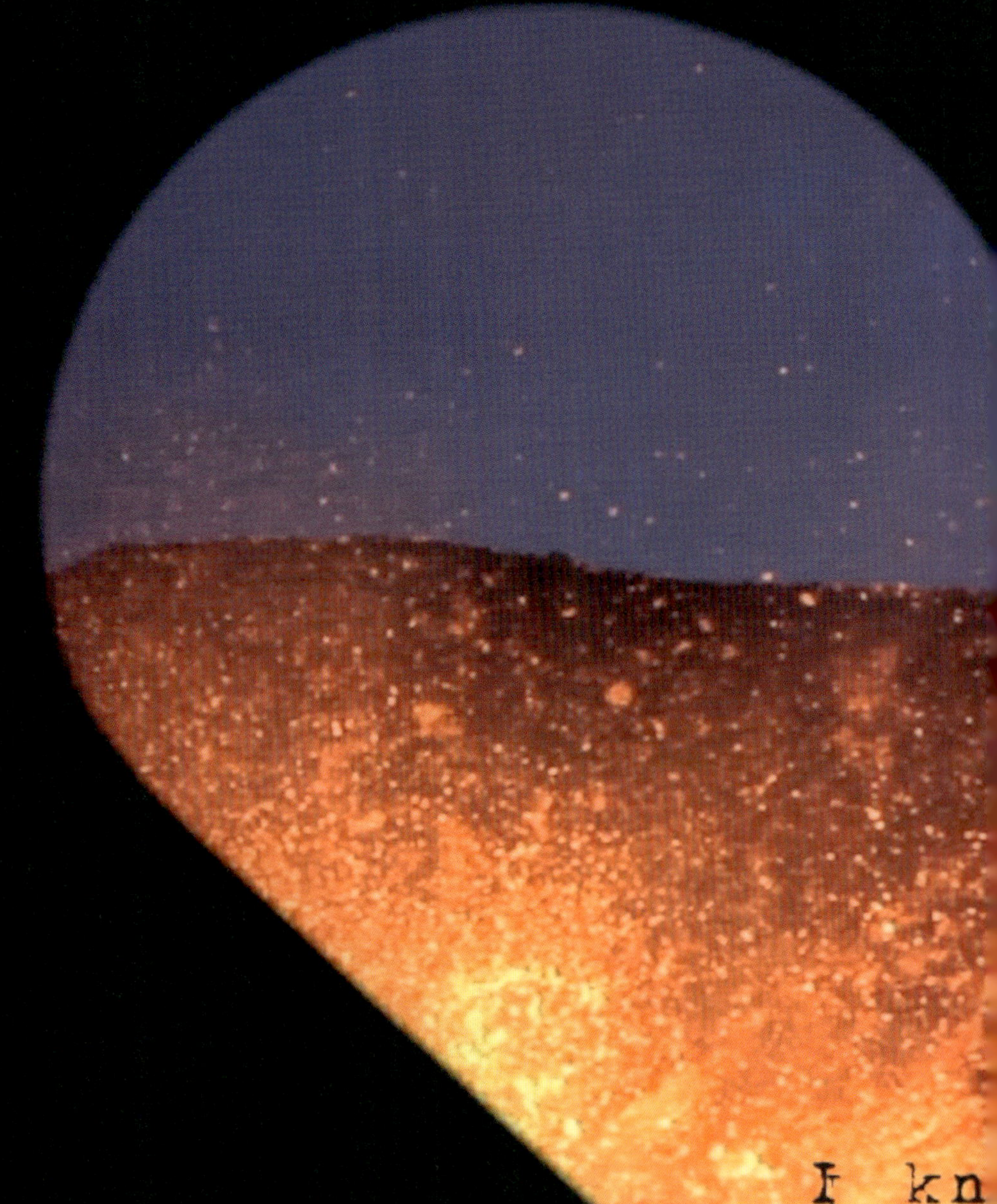
I kn
我知

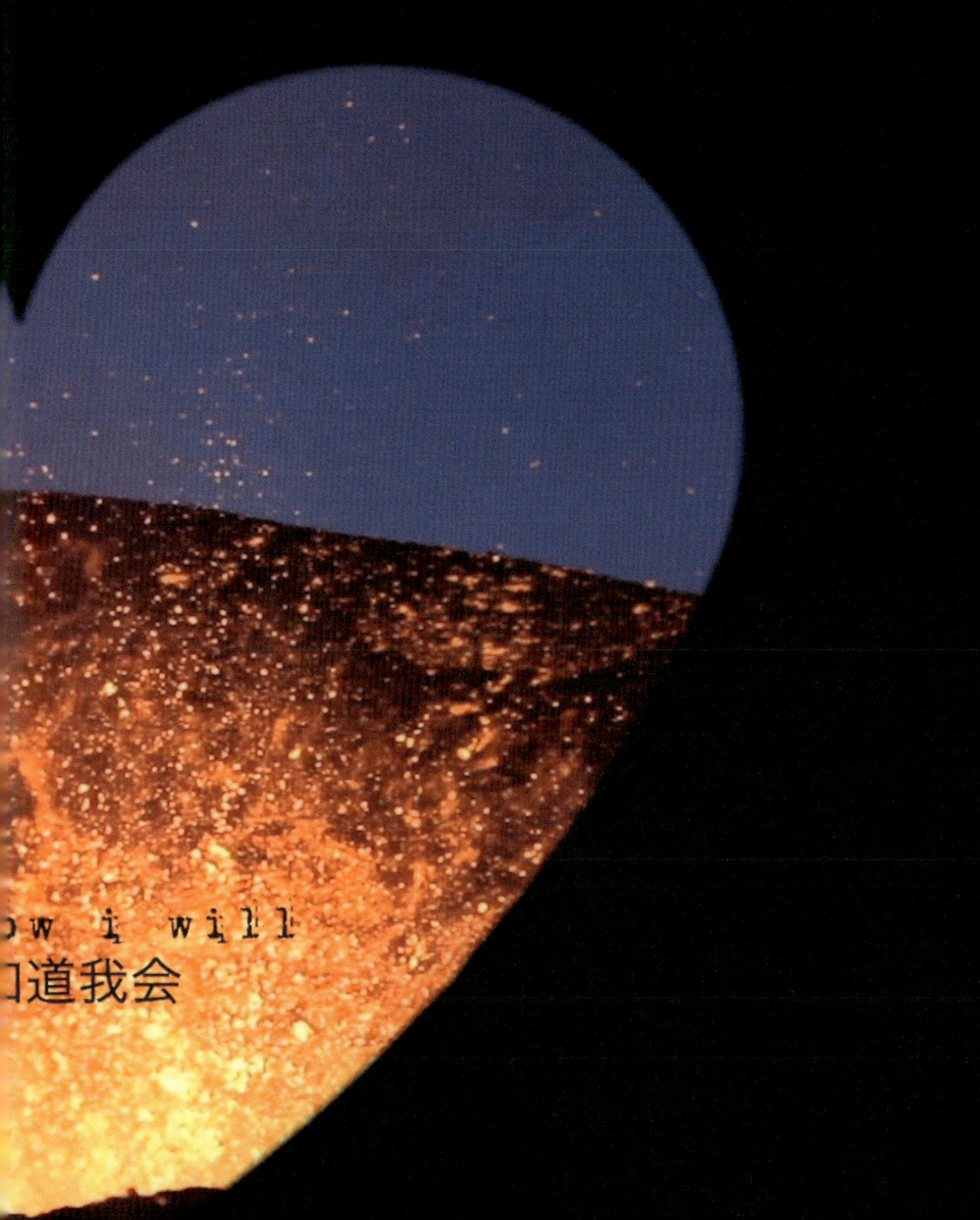
ow i will
道我会

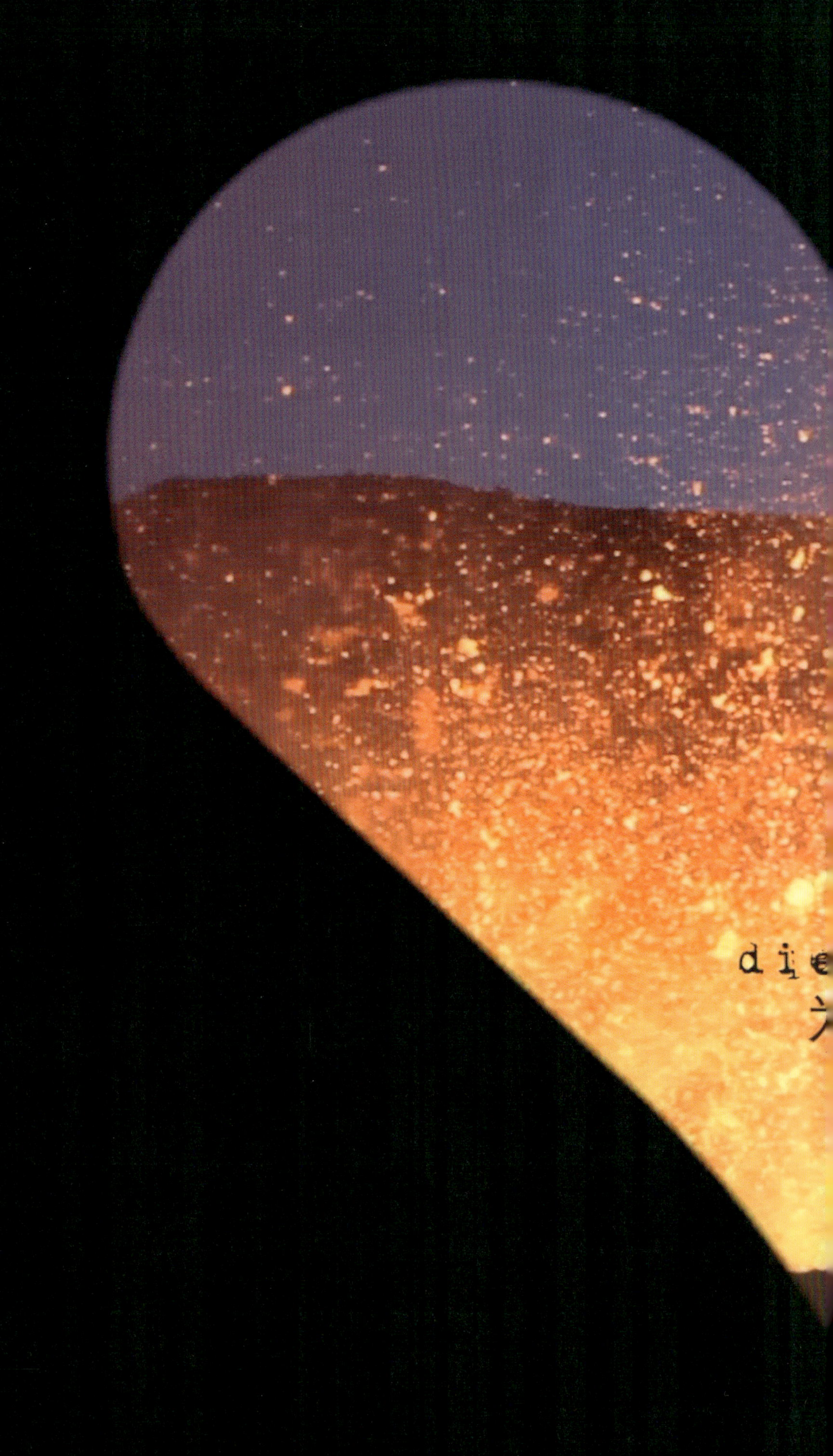
die
为

for you

你而死

pp. 2–11, 54–65, 92–99, 124–33,
150–51, 153–76, 178, 188–99
Heart is a Broken Record, 2023–24
Single-channel video, color, sound
11 min 19 sec
Courtesy the artist

pp. 21–25
GЯΔPΣFRUIT, 2015
Text on acrylic
Courtesy IDLE Studio

pp. 26–27
If Only the Cloud Knows, 2005–18
Website
Courtesy IDLE Studio

pp. 28–29
T, 2017–18
Single-channel video, color, sound
15 min 17 sec
Courtesy the artist

pp. 30–31, 33
Intro to Civil War, 2019
6-channel synchronized animation projection
on holographic fans, stainless steel, and sound
Courtesy the artist

p. 32
Intro to Civil War (Role Model), 2019
Text on PVC
Courtesy the artist

p. 39
Marry Me for Chinese Citizenship, 2015
Archival inkjet print
Courtesy the artist

pp. 40–41, 42–45
I Wanna Sleep More but by Your Side, 2018–19
3-channel video, color, sound
18 min
Courtesy the artist

p. 50
Exit Wound, 2020
Single-channel video, fabric, light, and shadow
Courtesy Callie's, Berlin

pp. 66–67
Kim, 2021
Acrylic on foam, plastic balls
Courtesy Cherish and the artist

pp. 69–81
ÆTHER (Poor Objects), 2021–22
Single-channel video, color, sound
18 min 28 sec
Courtesy the artist

pp. 100–105
Lord of the Flies, 2022
Performance
Courtesy Antenna Space and the artist

pp. 106–15, 141
Déjà Vu, 2022
Single-channel video, color
15 min 55 sec
Production: Fonds cantonal d'art contemporain,
Geneva, MIRE project
Courtesy the artist

p. 116
The Portrait of the Artist as a young man, 2023
Resin, acrylic paint, charms, and fabric
Courtesy the artist

pp. 118–23
*This Mirror Isn't Big Enough
for the Two of Us*, 2023
Single-channel video (color, sound), steel, paint,
and PVC projection screen
13 min 10 sec
Courtesy Fondazione Prada

pp. 138–49, 177, 182–87
I'm Not, 2024
Video (color, sound), epoxy resin, metal, fabric,
found objects, shoes, papier-mâché, concrete
mix, and screens
5 min 51 sec
Courtesy the artist

pp. 150–52
nobodys home, 2022
Electroplated fiberglass
Courtesy the artist

pp. 176, 179–81
Desert Song, 2023–24
Mixed media
Courtesy the artist

Shuang Li (b. 1990 in Wuyi Mountains, China, lives and works in Berlin and Geneva) received her MA in media studies from New York University in 2014. Li's recent solo and group exhibitions include *Biennale de l'Image en Mouvement*, curated by Andrea Bellini and Nora N. Khan, Centre d'Art Contemporain Genève, Geneva (2024), *Paraventi: Folding Screens from the 17th to 21st Centuries*, curated by Nicholas Cullinan, at Fondazione Prada, Milan, and Prada Rong Zhai, Shanghai (2023-24), Zurich Biennial, curated by Mitchell Anderson and Daniel Baumann, Kunsthalle Zürich, Zurich (2023–24), Kunsthal Charlottenborg Biennale, Copenhagen (2023), *Field of Vision*, curated by Tina Petersone, Zuzeum Art Centre, Riga (2023), *Inner Voices and Exterior Visions*, curated by Hera Chan, Yang Li, and Alvin Li, Starr Cinema, Tate Modern, London (2023), 59th International Art Exhibition of La Biennale di Venezia, curated by Cecilia Alemani, Venice (2022), 14th Shanghai Biennale, curated by Anton Vidokle with Zairong Xiang, Hallie Ayres, and Lukas Brasiskis, Shanghai (2022), *Deep Thought*, Berlinische Galerie, Berlin (2022), *Double Vision*, curated by Tobias Berger, Jill Chun, and Daniel Ho, Tai Kwun Contemporary, Hong Kong (2022), Cherish, Geneva (2021), *How Do We Begin*, curated by Poppy Dongxue Wu, X Museum, Beijing (2020), and Callie's, Berlin (2020).

Sophia Al-Maria is an artist, writer, and filmmaker. Though her work spans many disciplines, including drawing, collage, sculpture, and film, it is united by a preoccupation with the power of storytelling and myth, and, in particular, with imagining revisionist histories and alternative futures. She has presented solo shows at the Whitney Museum of American Art, New York; Tate Britain, London; LUMA Foundation, Arles; Henry Art Gallery, Seattle; and the Pavilion of Applied Arts at the Venice Biennale 2022. Her memoir, *The Girl Who Fell to Earth* (2012), was published by Harper Perennial. A second edition of *Sad Sack*, her first book of essays, was published by Bookworks UK in 2023. She is a contributing editor at *Bidoun* magazine and works as a writer for film, TV, and theater. She created the limited series *Little Birds* for Sky Atlantic which aired in 2020.

Olivia Kan-Sperling (b. 1997) writes texts that perform, especially as other media and usually as pop prose, as well as criticism, often in the form of crushing. Her book *Island Time* (Expat Press, 2021), about the psycho-geographies of Kendall Jenner and Lil Peep, is a recursive novella figured as a virtual world. It is accompanied by a *Music Video Guided Symbolization Reading Game* (currently vaporware only). Her next novella, *LittlePinkBook: A Documentary Fantasy*, is written as a mistranslated Chinese romance novel. Her writing on art, literature, software, and style has been published in *n+1*, *Cabinet*, *Spike*, and *The Paris Review*. She lives in New York.

Jeppe Ugelvig is a curator, historian, and cultural critic based in New York City. He is a current PhD candidate at UC Santa Cruz. His criticism appears regularly in *Artforum*, *Frieze*, and *Spike*, where he serves as a contributing editor. His first book, *Fashion Work: 25 Years of Art in Fashion*, was published by Damiani in 2020. He has staged exhibitions in institutions and museums around the world, including MMCA Seoul, Tai Kwun in Hong Kong, and ARoS in Denmark.

Hanlu Zhang is a writer and curator interested in art as social practice. In 2020 she founded Social Practice Lab (SPL), an initiative based in Guangdong that curates socially engaged art and initiates collaborative projects. SPL engages with topics and communities related to the rurality, migration, and minority perspectives. Hanlu has worked with Power Station of Art, Shanghai; Centre Pompidou, Paris; Mulan Community Service Center, Beijing; Para Site Art Space, Hong Kong; Sun Yat-sen University Anthropology Department, Guangzhou; and esea contemporary, Manchester. She graduated from the School of the Art Institute of Chicago and has worked at *Artforum* and Guangdong Times Museum. She is also a member of Theater 44, a fluid network exploring collective creativity.

Founded in 1986, Swiss Institute (SI) is an independent nonprofit contemporary art institution dedicated to promoting forward-thinking and experimental artmaking through innovative exhibitions, education, and programs. Committed to the highest standards of curatorial and educational excellence, SI serves as a platform for emerging artists, catalyzes new perspectives on celebrated work, and fosters appreciation for under-recognized positions. SI is committed to being an organization that is diverse, equitable, accessible, and environmentally conscious in its work, structure, and programming. Open to the public free of charge, Swiss Institute seeks to explore how a Swiss context can be the starting point for international conversations in the fields of visual and performing arts, design, and architecture.

SI Programming is made possible in part with public funds from Pro Helvetia, Swiss Arts Council; Canton Basel-Stadt; the New York State Council on the Arts, with the support of Governor Kathy Hochul and the New York State Legislature; and the New York City Department of Cultural Affairs in partnership with the City Council with the support of council member Carlina Rivera. Main supporters include LUMA Foundation; the Andy Warhol Foundation for the Visual Arts; Cowles Charitable Trust; Elizabeth Firestone Graham Foundation; Fonds cantonal d'art contemporain, Geneva; Fundación Almine y Bernard Ruiz-Picasso; Graham Foundation for Advanced Studies in the Fine Arts; the Horace W. Goldsmith Foundation; Jacques and Natasha Gelman Foundation; Frankenthaler Climate Initiative of the Helen Frankenthaler Foundation; Leon Polk Smith Foundation; Mondriaan Fund; National Endowment for the Arts; Office for Contemporary Art Norway; Royal Norwegian Consulate General; Teiger Foundation; Terra Foundation for American Art; and Friends of SI. Exhibitions are made possible in part by the SI Artist Vision Fund with leadership support provided by the SI Board of Trustees, Becky and David Gochman, and Nicoletta Fiorucci. SI gratefully acknowledges all TimeForArt Partners, Swiss Re as SI ONSITE Partner, Vitra as Design Partner, and Crozier Fine Arts as Preferred Shipping Art Logistics Partner.

Critical operating support was provided to SI in 2024 and 2025 as part of a collective fundraising effort with CANNY (Collaborate Arts Network New York). We thank the following supporters: Andrew W. Mellon Foundation, Arison Arts Foundation, Helen Frankenthaler Foundation, Leon Polk Smith Foundation and The Willem de Kooning Foundation. SI is integrating sustainability and environmental consciousness into all facets of the institution. Support for this effort comes in part from the Frankenthaler Climate Initiative and Teiger Foundation.

Published for the exhibition *Shuang Li: I'm Not* at Swiss Institute, New York, May 1–August 25, 2024; Aspen Art Museum, Aspen, November 20, 2024–March 2, 2025

© 2025 Swiss Institute, New York; Aspen Art Museum, Aspen; Pacific, New York

Editors: Alison Coplan, Daniel Merritt
Copy editor and proofreader: Miles Champion
SI Series visual identity: Vela Arbutina
Design: Pacific

First published by: Swiss Institute, New York; Aspen Art Museum, Aspen; Pacific, New York

Swiss Institute
38 St Marks Pl
New York, NY 10003
www.swissinstitute.net

Aspen Art Museum
637 E Hyman Ave
Aspen, CO 81611
aspenartmuseum.org

Pacific
161 Water Street
New York, NY 10038
www.pacificpacific.pub

PHOTO CREDITS:
pp. 21-27: © Zheheng Hong; p. 50: © Nick Ash; pp. 66–67: © James Bantone; p. 69: © Zhang Hong; pp. 114–15, 141: © Serge Frühauf; p. 116: © T Space Studio; pp. 118–23: © Delfino Sisto Legnani and Alessandro Saletta - DSL Studio; pp. 138–53, 176–87: © Daniel Perez

Printed in Italy by Grafiche Veneziane

ISBN 9798987633236

DISTRIBUTED IN EUROPE BY:
Les presses du réel
35 rue Coslon, 21000 Dijon, France
www.lespressesdureel.com

Vice Versa Distribution
Potsdamer Str. 93, 10785 Berlin, Germany
www.viceversaartbooks.com

DISTRIBUTED IN THE UK, AMERICAS, ROW BY:
ARTBOOK | D.A.P.
75 Broad Street, Suite 630
New York, NY 10004
www.artbook.com

Im not a death cult
you cannot participate

IN ALL THE CEREMONIES
fastforward to
A TRANSPARENT STAR

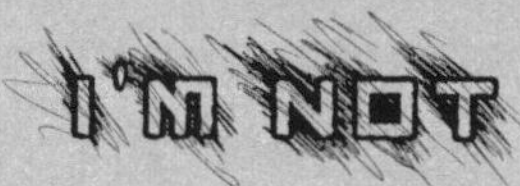

I'M NOT

I°M NOT

I'M NOT